PSYCHOLOGY AND PUBLIC POLICY

BALANCING PUBLIC SERVICE AND PROFESSIONAL NEED

Edited by Raymond P. Lorion, Ira Iscoe,
Patrick H. DeLeon, and Gary R. VandenBos

AMERICAN PSYCHOLOGICAL ASSOCIATION
WASHINGTON, DC

Published by
American Psychological Association
750 First Street, NE
Washington, DC 20002

Copies may be ordered from
APA Order Department
P.O. Box 2710
Hyattsville, MD 20784

In the United Kingdom and Europe, copies may be ordered from
American Psychological Association
3 Henrietta Street
Covent Garden, London
WC2E 8LU England

Typeset in Goudy by PRO-IMAGE Corporation, Techna-Type Div., York, PA

Printer: Capital City Press, Montpelier, VT
Cover designer: Rohani Design, Edmonds, WA
Technical/production editor: Valerie Montenegro

Library of Congress Cataloging-in-Publication Data
Psychology and public policy : balancing public service and
    professional need/edited by Raymond P. Lorion ... [et al.].
        p.   cm.
    Includes bibliographical references and indexes.
    ISBN 1-55798-347-X (acid-free paper)
    1. Psychologists in government.   2. Political psychology.
    3. Policy scientists.   I. Lorion, Raymond P.
    BF76.3.P78   1996
    150—dc20
                                                                    95-26810
                                                                    CIP

British Library Cataloguing-in-Publication Data
A CIP record is available from the British Library.

Printed in the United States of America
First edition

CONTENTS

CONTRIBUTORS

Dane Archer, *Stevenson College, University of California, Santa Cruz, CA*

Elliot Aronson, *Department of Psychology, University of California, Santa Cruz, CA*

William Bevan, *William Preston Few Professor of Psychology, Emeritus, Duke University, Durham, NC*

Joseph R. Biden, Jr., *United States House of Representatives, Washington, DC*

Joanne E. Callan, *American Psychological Association, Washington, DC*

Nathan Caplan, *Institute of Social Research, University of Michigan, Ann Arbor, MI*

Margaret A. Chesney, *School of Medicine, University of California, San Francisco, CA*

Patrick H. DeLeon, *United States Senate Staff, Office of Senator Daniel K. Inouye, Washington, DC*

Barbara A. Everett, *National Institute of Mental Health, Bethesda, MD*

Baruch Fischhoff, *Department of Social and Decision Sciences, Carnegie Mellon University, Pittsburgh, PA*

Pamela Ebert Flattau, *Flattau Associates, Washington, DC*

Raymond D. Fowler, *American Psychological Association, Washington, DC*

Robert G. Frank, *College of Health Professions, University of Florida Health Science Center, Gainesville, FL*

David Bertsch Gray, *School of Medicine, Washington University, St. Louis, MO*

William Howell, *American Psychological Association, Washington, DC*

Ira Iscoe, *Professor of Psychology, Emeritus, Department of Psychology, University of Texas, Austin, TX*

Alfred J. Kahn, *Professor Emeritus (Policy and Planning), School of Social Work, Columbia University, New York, NY*

Charles A. Kiesler, *University of Missouri–Columbia, Columbia, MO*

Alan G. Kraut, *American Psychological Society, Washington, DC*

Alan I. Leshner, *National Institute on Drug Abuse, Rockville, MD*

Raymond P. Lorion, *Department of Psychology, University of Maryland, College Park, MD*

Eleanor E. Maccoby, *Professor Emeritus, Department of Psychology, Stanford University, Stanford, CA*

George Miller, *United States House of Representatives, Washington, DC*

Teru L. Morton, *Department of Education and Psychology, Walla Walla University, College Place, WA*

Stephen D. Nelson, *Science, Technology, and Government, American Association for the Advancement of Science, Washington, DC*

Russ Newman, *American Psychological Association, Washington, DC*

Anne Marie O'Keefe, *O'Keefe & Associates, Bethesda, MD*

Thomas F. Pettigrew, *Department of Psychology, University of Santa Cruz, Santa Cruz, CA*

Annette U. Rickel, *Department of Psychology, Wayne State University, Detroit, MI*

Michael J. Saks, *College of Law, University of Iowa, Iowa City, IA*

Seymour B. Sarason, *Professor of Psychology, Emeritus, Department of Psychology, Yale University, New Haven, CT*

M. Brewster Smith, *Psychology Board, University of California, Santa Cruz, CA*

Ted Strickland, *Department of Psychology, Shawnee State University, Portsmouth, OH*

Henry Tomes, *American Psychological Association, Washington, DC*

Charles R. Tremper, *Information Research and Technology, American Association of Homes and Services for the Aging, Washington, DC*

Gary R. VandenBos, *American Psychological Association, Washington, DC*

Trudy Vincent, *United States Senate Staff, Office of Senator Barbara Mikulski, Washington, DC*

Carol H. Weiss, *Graduate School of Education, Harvard University, Cambridge, MA*

Janet A. Weiss, *Institute of Public Policy Studies, University of Michigan, Ann Arbor, MI*

Martin Woodhead, *School of Education, The Open University, Milton Keynes, England*

FOREWORD

Psychology, Public Policy, and the Congressional Fellowship Program

Psychologists do not operate in a social vacuum. Their theories must recognize social realities, their methods must allow for differing attitudes and behaviors, and their treatments must respond to socially defined psychological and behavioral problems. Although the science may strive to be value-free, the discipline must be continually engaged.

Engagement with socially relevant issues has benefits for psychologists. When psychologists have tackled significant social problems, they have enhanced the discipline's recognition and respect among policymakers and the general public. The increased status of the profession has contributed to an unprecedented growth of qualified scientists and practitioners.

Such engagement by psychologists, of course, has significant societal benefits. Psychologists' expertise in understanding human behavior, using the rigor of scientific methodology and analysis, adds an essential humanizing element to public debate on many issues. Psychologists can help contribute to public policy at many stages. At the initial stage, when a social problem is identified and being defined, psychologists can question assumptions about human behavior, provide scientific data, and present alternative formulations. In policy formation, when a plan is being developed to solve the problem, psychologists can synthesize the available literature on interventions, design pilot studies, and evaluate possible alternative policies. At the stage when legislators are working for adoption of a measure, psychologists can provide help in organization, networking, and other types of communication and interpersonal influence. At the implementation stage, particularly when psychologists are part of the programs to be implemented, psychologists bring all their intervention and treatment skills to bear. Finally, at the stage when the effectiveness and impact of a policy is being evaluated, psychologists' research and analytical skills are particularly relevant[1].

Unfortunately, psychologists' engagement with social problems, and the policy process to deal with them, sometimes has been spotty and not always fully effective. Many psychologists are uninformed and unfamiliar with the public policy process and need training and a better appreciation of the political process in order to become politically effective. The APA Congressional Science Fellowship Program is one mechanism that is helping psychology overcome this problem.

The APA Congressional Science Fellowship Program was created to give psychologists an invaluable public policy learning experience; to contribute to more effective use of scientific knowledge in government; and to broaden the perceptions of the scientific, professional, and policy communities about the value of the interaction among these communities. The APA program is affiliated with the Congressional Fellowship Program of the American Association for the Advancement of Science (AAAS). The APA began its participation with the AAAS in 1974, and since its inception, the program has facilitated the active involvement of individual psychologists in the political and policy-making process, thereby bringing psychology's expertise to bear directly on a wide range of national priorities. The program provides Fellows with an appreciation for the potential interrelationship between psychology and the nation's evolving policy agendas[2].

Each year, APA Congressional Science Fellows are selected through a national competition for a 1- or 2-year assignment to staff positions in Congress. An annual stipend and a travel allowance are provided. Candidates for fellowship must demonstrate competence in scientific or professional psychology. They must be interested in and sensitive toward policy issues, and they must have a strong interest in applying psychological knowledge to the solution of societal problems. Fellows must be able to work quickly and communicate effectively on a wide variety of topics and to work cooperatively with individuals having diverse viewpoints. Applicants must be APA members (or applicants for APA membership), and they must have a doctorate in psychology, preferably with a minimum of 2 years of postdoctoral experience.

During the early years of the APA Congressional Science Fellow program, most Fellows were relatively recent doctoral graduates. More recently, the APA has made a focused effort to attract "more senior" Fellows, re-

---

[1]"Psychology and Public Policy," by the Task Force on Psychology and Public Policy, APA Board of Social and Ethical Responsibility for Psychology, 1986, *American Psychologist, 41,* 914–921.
[2]"Health Psychology and Public Policy: The Political Process," by P. H. DeLeon, R. G. Frank, & D. Wedding, 1995, *Health Psychology, 14*(6), 493–499; "Psychologists' Role in Influencing Congress: The Process and the Players," by J. A. Lee, P. H. DeLeon, D. Wedding, & K. Nordal, 1994, *Professional Psychology: Research and Practice, 25,* 9–15.

sulting in present selections of Fellows who typically possess between 3 and 10 years of postdoctoral experience. Applicants considered for the "Senior Congressional Fellow" position must have a minimum of 10 years of postdoctoral experience. The APA Congressional Science Fellows have included individuals from almost every psychological specialty area, including some who also have degrees in law.

In the first fellowship year of 1974–1975, the APA supported one Fellow (Pamela Ebert Flattau, PhD). In the next 7 years, the APA continued to support one Fellow each year through the 1981–1982 fellowship year. The number of APA fellowships increased to two yearly, beginning with the 1982–1983 fellowship year, and this pattern continued through 1989–1990. At this point, the APA realized that the most cost-effective and direct means of expanding the presence of psychology in Congress would be to expand the APA Congressional Science Fellowship program beyond the two fellows funded annually. In the following two fellowship years (1990–1991 and 1991–1992), three fellows were funded yearly. Five Fellows were supported for the 1992–1993 fellowship year, four Fellows were supported in 1993–1994, and three Fellows were supported in 1994–1995. Thus, from 1974 through 1995, the APA has supported 42 Congressional Science Fellows (see the Appendix for a complete list).

In 1995, the APA, in collaboration with the American Psychological Foundation (APF), added two fellowship slots to the existing Congressional Science Fellowship Program, bringing the total of fellowships available for 1995–1996 to six. These slots are the William A. Bailey AIDS Policy Congressional Fellowship and the Congressional Fellowship in Child Policy. The William A. Bailey fellowship honors Bailey, a former APA staff member, in tribute to his tireless advocacy in behalf of psychological research, training, and services related to AIDS. The fellowship aims to provide psychologists who have interests in AIDS, gay and lesbian, or related health and behavior issues with an invaluable public policy learning experience. The fellowship in Child Policy was established by the Esther Katz Rosen Fund in collaboration with the APF, and it is dedicated to the advancement and application of knowledge about gifted children. Psychologists with scientific expertise in some area of child psychology, especially on gifted children, are encouraged to share their scientific knowledge with policymakers, and in the process, enrich their professional training with legislative experience. Six Fellows have been selected for the 1995–1996 APA Congressional Science Fellowship year.

The program places highly qualified psychologists from a variety of specialties with the offices of individual members of Congress and committees for a 1- or 2-year assignment. The Fellowship year begins with an intensive 2-week orientation that exposes Fellows to various aspects of the legislative process and current issues before Congress. They also learn about the agencies and organizations interacting with Congress. Fellows eventually secure a position in a congressional office for their fellowship year. The APA does not place Fellows in specific offices, but rather, Fellows interview with offices just as they would for any job.

Fellows perform in much the same way as regular staff members, and they have been involved in varied legislative, oversight, and investigative activities. Fellows serving on personal staffs monitor many different pieces of legislation and are closely involved in the hectic day-to-day lawmaking process. They prepare briefing memos, participate in face-to-face briefings with the member of Congress, assist in legislative debates on the floor of the House or Senate, and represent the member at meetings with lobbyists and constituents[3].

Those who work in committee staff positions contribute their substantive knowledge and expertise. Congressional committees generally are responsible for developing legislation, and a Fellow assigned there will be responsible for developing a particular piece of legislation. His or her work will involve developing background information for the legislation, communicating with experts in the field of concern, planning and conducting hearings on the legislation, briefing the committee chair on the issues, and writing portions of the final legislative report[4].

Thus, APA Fellows have spent their fellowship years in many influential places, and they have made significant contributions in these settings. For example, two past APA Fellows worked for the Senate Labor and Human Resources Committee, the committee responsible for the authorization of the bulk of the legislation of interest to psychologists. One past Fellow worked for Senator Ted Kennedy's health office, and a 1995 Fellow works for the senator's education office. Another Fellow worked for Senator Tom Harkin's Subcommittee on the Handicapped. These Fellows have worked on legislation that has become law and is important to the interests of psychologists. The 1986–1987 Fellows worked for the House Special Committee on Aging and for Senator Bill Bradley. Both Fellows drafted legislation of considerable significance to the APA: a "mental health and aging" bill and several education bills. Other settings in which APA Fellows have worked include the former senatorial office of Vice President Al Gore and Senators Daniel Inouye, Jacob Javits, Barbara Mikulski, Paul Simon, and Ted Stevens; the Senate's Committee on Labor and Human Resources, the Subcommittee on the Handicapped, and the Subcommittee on Alcoholism and Narcotics; the offices of Representatives Robert Drinan, Edward Markey, Austin Murphy, and David Obey; the

---

[3]"Clinical Psychology and the Political Scene," by P. H. DeLeon, G. R. VandenBos, M. R. Pollard, A. L. Solarz, & R. B. Weinberg, 1991, in M. Herson, A. E. Kazdin, & A. S. Bellack (Eds.), *The Clinical Psychology Handbook* (2nd ed., pp. 128–143), New York: Pergamon Press.
[4]"Clinical Psychology and the Political Scene," by P. H. DeLeon, G. R. VandenBos, M. R. Pollard, A. L. Solarz, & R. B. Weinberg, 1991, in M. Herson, A. E. Kazdin, & A. S. Bellack (Eds.), *The Clinical Psychology Handbook* (2nd ed., pp. 128–143), New York: Pergamon Press.

House Select Committee on Aging; and the Congressional Budget Office. They played key roles in the development and passage of many important bills, including the Older Americans Act, the Gifted and Talented Children's Education Act, the Infant Mortality Reduction Medicaid Act, the Child and Adolescent Service System Act, the Children's Justice Act, and the Dropout Prevention and Reentry Act.

APA Fellows bring to Congress new insights, fresh ideas, and extensive knowledge and education in a variety of psychological specialties. Fellows offer their professional knowledge and skills for the opportunity to acquire experience and the chance to contribute to the formulation of national policy.

After their fellowships on Capitol Hill, about half of the APA Fellows have taken policy-related positions with various federal agencies, Congress, or public interest or policy research organizations. Some government settings where past Fellows have been subsequently employed include legislative positions in the Senate Labor and Human Resources Committee; the House Subcommittee on Human Resources and Intergovernmental Relations (which has oversight responsibility for the National Institute of Mental Health); the House Select Committee on Children, Youth, and Families; the House Education and Labor Committee; the Congressional Budget Office; the policy office of the Department of Mental Health in Massachusetts; and the offices of Senator Barbara Mikulski, Senator Simon, former Senator Al Gore, and Governor Michael Dukakis. Several former Fellows report that they have testified before Congress or a state legislative body on issues of concern to psychology since the end of their fellowship.

The remaining half of those who completed the fellowship have returned to positions similar to those that they held prior to accepting the APA assignment. In their postfellowship positions, all past Fellows have continued to play active roles in the APA, psychology, and political matters. Several have served on APA boards and committees. All are active in divisional affairs. Those who have returned to full-time teaching report that the type of courses they teach and the nature of the research the conduct reflect their experiences as Fellows.

The number of psychologists on legislative staffs has increased in the past few years, due largely to training provided under the Congressional Science Fellowship program. This program is the most cost-effective and direct means of expanding the presence of psychology in Congress. During their congressional fellowship period, APA Fellows have played major roles in conceptualizing, drafting, and advocating important legislation related to psychology and its application to the public interest. Several Fellows have used the fellowship as a springboard to permanent positions of influence in the policymaking arena. Fellows who remain on Capitol Hill help increase the psychological expertise available in the legislature. Those returning to academia will have critical insights into the policy relevance of research and in making research results more understandable, useful, and accessible to policymakers. Most Fellows have become active in psychology's advocacy efforts[5].

Thus, the APA Congressional Science Fellowship program is one of the most exciting developments within organized psychology in the last two decades—a relatively low-cost endeavor that has substantial short- and long-term impact for both Congress and the profession. Yet much more remains to be done. Other professions, such as medicine, have also expanded their presence on Capitol Hill through similar fellowship programs. The need for psychological expertise continues to outstrip the number of appropriately trained psychologists.

In the past 20 years, political and legal developments have made it imperative for psychologists to become professionally involved with social and political issues. At a time when government funding for behavioral research and training is shrinking, psychologists must organize themselves more effectively for public policy involvement. When legislators and the public are unaware of what psychology can do for the public good, they are unlikely to be supportive of the profession. Psychologists' responsibility extends not only to developing effective research and clinical procedures but also to promoting them in ways that could significantly alleviate national social problems. To meet this challenge, psychologists must become actively involved in the policy debate and in assisting policymakers to develop and implement relevant and effective programs.

RAYMOND D. FOWLER

---

[5]"Clinical Psychology and the Political Scene," by P. H. DeLeon, G. R. VandenBos, M. R. Pollard, A. L. Solarz, & R. B. Weinberg, 1991, in M. Herson, A. E. Kazdin, & A. S. Bellack (Eds.), *The Clinical Psychology Handbook* (2nd ed., pp. 128–143), New York: Pergamon Press.

PREFACE

Psychology and Public Policy: A Profession's Response to Public Need

As a science and health service profession, psychology is both relevant to, and continuously affected by, public policy debates and decisions. Surprisingly few psychologists, however, appreciate that fact. Fewer yet act on that awareness! The first goal of this volume, therefore, is to increase psychologists' understanding of and contributions to public policy formation. Ideally, achievement of that goal will move the discipline toward our second goal, that is, to increase psychologists' involvement in the implementation and evaluation of public policy decisions. In turn, we hope that one day policymakers will view input from psychology as an expected and necessary component of policy formation and review.

Pursuit of these goals is justified by the diversity of the discipline's expertise concerning human behavior. Psychology alone among the social and life sciences considers behavior in terms of its biological, cultural, emotional, cognitive, and psychosocial dimensions. Because of the breadth of its perspective, there is much to contribute to policymakers' thinking about the nature, etiology, course, and amelioration of human problems. As reflected in this volume, however, the value of this science to considerations of public needs and interests has, to this point, barely been tapped. We hope that this volume will contribute to interest in mining that vein.

We believe that the work described herein will confirm our conclusion that the discipline must seek the recognition by policymakers of the fact that the scientific and clinical knowledge represent invaluable, indeed essential, resources to consider when they address matters of public health, public interest, and public policy. To have their expertise appreciated, however, psychologists must enter the political arena and engage in its debates. At the outset, psychologists will need to begin the contact by readily and freely offering their knowledge and support to those who make and implement policies. As explained herein, that process often begins with the simplest of questions, such as, "How can I help?"; "What information do you need?"; or "Can I help you to distinguish assumptions and scientific facts about the issue?"

We hope that readers of this volume will gain an appreciation of the symbiotic potential of affirmative responses to such questions. By contributing to the public interest and to the formation and review of public policies, psychology gains credibility as a science, and the profession becomes valued as a public asset. If psychologists are present to inform assessment of needs and of the responsiveness of public services, if they are assumed to set aside self-interests for the public good, if they are available to assist across levels of human service delivery, and if they are accessible when needed as well as when in need, then their stock will rise significantly among policymakers. In turn, psychologists' appeals will be heard more favorably, and the impact of policy decisions on their futures and on their continued availability will be weighed more carefully. The symbiotic link thereby becomes clear. To the extent that psychologists' contributions serve the needs of others, policymakers will incorporate the discipline's needs within their definitions of the public interest.

Thus, by giving assistance, psychologists add to the legitimacy of their requests for assistance. The necessity for enhancing this symbiosis cannot be overestimated. The discipline is affected daily by policy decisions. For example, the work of psychologists as scientists depends on decisions related to policies for funding research; scientific conferences; training and career development; and the maintenance and enhancement of universities, research institutes, libraries, laboratories, and technological refinements. The conduct of the work of psychologists as service providers depends on policies that define the profession's expertise and authority through avenues such as licensing and certification, services reimbursement, and access to treatment settings and procedures.

To be useful as well as to be supported, therefore, psychologists must make clear the substance of their science, basic as well as applied, in terms of its relevance to public needs. In our view, it is less essential that this link be immediate than that it be understandable. Equally important is to communicate the breadth of service delivery strategies beyond mental health settings. Policymakers must appreciate that psychology's clients include industry, communities, and educational institutions, as well as families and individuals. A portion of psychologists' work influences the emotional and behavioral status of those they serve. Other aspects of their work, however, influence the economic strength of industries; the match between individuals and occupations; the quality of life in a neighborhood or community; and the ease with which children acquire reading, writing, and math skills. If successful in sensitizing policymakers and their constituents to the diversity of psychology's interests and the variety of its contributions to the public welfare, psychologists will establish the basis for regular contact between their discipline and those responsible for the formation, implementation, and evaluation of public policies.

In introducing the entirety of the science and practice to the public, psychologists must also clarify for policymakers what they know, how they ask questions, how they seek answers, and how they judge findings. As they understand those aspects of the discipline, policymakers will find more and varied uses for psychological expertise. Moreover, the public will appreciate the potential payoffs to be derived from investments in the extension of psychologists' knowledge, the expansion of their numbers, and the refinement of their skills.

Concurrent with preparation of this volume, for example, debate is under way at the federal, state, and local levels to reform substantially health care delivery, welfare support, and educational funding. By contributing clinical insights and scientific expertise to deliberations on these respective issues, psychologists will inform policymakers of their perspectives on thinking about human needs and designing effective solutions. Decisions concerning *each* of these policy foci will undoubtedly have substantial and lasting consequences for the science and the profession. At the very least, solutions to each of these issues will affect the nation's available funds for science and human services. Even more so, how these issues are resolved will significantly shape psychologists' futures for decades.

One might argue therefore that, given its self-interests, the discipline must participate in the public debate about proposed reforms in each of these areas. Others might counter that the true test of the discipline's concern for the public good will be made evident only when the issue under consideration does not relate in any way to the science or the profession. If our view of the discipline's breadth is accurate, however, few such issues exist. For that reason, we believe that it is important to acknowledge the nature and degree of self-interest from the outset and give priority to the attainment of public objectives before that of professional objectives.

To convey the reciprocal importance of policy to the profession and of the profession to policy formulation, this volume combines chapters originating from some of psychology's leading researchers, clinicians, and policymakers, with reflections from psychologists active in the development of public policy and in the coordination of advocacy efforts for the discipline's betterment.[1] Ideally, readers will gain from these selections an understanding of policy as it evolves and of the many ways in which asking,

---

[1]Note that language in previously published text has been left intact and may not conform to the APA's guidelines for reducing bias in language as outlined in the Fourth Edition of the *Publication Manual of the American Psychological Association*.

"How can I help?" can enhance the discipline's public standing and public support.

RAYMOND P. LORION
IRA ISCOE
PATRICK H. DeLEON
GARY R. VANDENBOS

INTRODUCTION: RESHAPING OUR VIEWS OF OUR FIELD

RAYMOND P. LORION and IRA ISCOE

Having always admired Dickens' prose, we took advantage of the relevance of his words to this Introduction's intended message:

> It was the best of times, it was the worst of times, it was the age of wisdom, it was the age of foolishness, it was the epoch of belief, it was the epoch of incredulity, it was the season of Light, it was the season of Darkness, it was the spring of hope, it was the winter of despair, we had everything before us, we had nothing before us, we were all going direct to Heaven, we were all going direct the other way—in short, the period was so far like the present period. . . . (Dickens, 1961, p. 3)

Dickens' description seems to fit the current status of organized psychology. During the past decade, our discipline has received unprecedented public recognition of, and appreciation for, our multifaceted potential to improve the lives of diverse segments of the population. At the same time, our work as scientists, service providers, and educators has been criticized and intensely scrutinized for its costs, its relevance to contemporary problems, and its responsiveness to those it serves. The juxtaposition of these seemingly incompatible perceptions of our discipline troubles many of us.

Immediate concerns about the federal budget and its ever-burgeoning deficit, for example, threaten the integrity of some ongoing research efforts and the viability of investigations that are planned or in process. Unfortunately, demands to reduce federal expenditures coincide with unprecedented advances in neuroscience, the cognitive sciences, and the clinical sciences. Scientific gains seemingly within our grasp in the foreseeable future may be delayed for years or lost forever. Ironically, once achieved, these scientific findings might have reduced expenditures in health care, education, and industrial production costs. One wonders why those who make public policy and determine use of public funds cannot understand that!

Similarly, the popularity of our discipline as an educational field remains strong at the undergraduate and graduate levels. Its interest to high school students as well as to the general public appears to grow each day. The popular media in their various forms echo principles derived from our research and applied work. In music, movies, talk shows, magazines, and newspaper stories, the products and foci of our discipline are presented to and accepted by an interested public. Yet simultaneously, state legislators across the nation openly question the adequacy of professors' workloads, the quality of their instruction, and the costs of their scholarship. Political leaders question the value of our science for resolving major threats (e.g., limited gains in reading and math scores; community violence; familial instability) to the nation's economic and social order. Understanding the substance of our discipline and applying its principles to everyday situations, we argue, enables individuals to increase their interpersonal sensitivity and effectiveness at home, at work, and at play. Exposure to the content of our science and the questions it pursues increases one's appreciation of the complexity of human life. Why is this benefit not self-evident?

As service providers, we have extended the number and range of treatments available to those experiencing personal, familial, marital, or other forms of distress. For decades, we have worked to reduce long-standing negative attitudes toward emotional disorders and their treatment. We have established ourselves as independent health care providers and have been a major reason that consumers of mental health services can choose the discipline of their mental health provider. Psychologists have led or participated in the search for interventions to prevent or minimize the development of significant threats to emotional and behavioral adjustment. That pursuit has enhanced our understanding of the etiology of disorder, its pathogenic sequences, and opportunities for its avoidance or interruption. Effectively designed and implemented, such interventions would reduce health care costs and improve the quality of life for many. In fact, whatever their form, our interventions have the capacity to improve the lives, productivity, and economic viability of their recipients. Again, the value of our work is not recognized.

INFLUENCING PUBLIC POLICY: THE NEED
FOR SELF-EXAMINATION

Originally, we intended this Introduction to examine the apparent lack of understanding on the part of those who make and implement public policy, and the obstruction of adequate support for our discipline by those at the local, state, and federal levels who make, implement—and most important—authorize funding for policy decisions. We intended to focus on the importance of addressing such misunderstandings about our work and its value by encouraging readers to communicate the breadth and value of our work as scholars, educators, scientists, and service providers. If successful, we expected the Introduction to catalyze increasing numbers of psychologists to explain why continuation, indeed expansion, of our efforts merits support from the public (i.e., taxpayers) and from those responsible for the distribution of public funds. With truth and data in hand, our advocating brethren would convince the public and the policymakers of our value and worth. After all, the intended message seemed clear enough; in other words, because psychological science and services benefit the public, what is good for psychology is good for the public!

Had we adhered to our original plan, this Introduction would have echoed the widely shared view that the aforementioned lack of understanding is *the* problem that we must now solve by filling the gaps in public knowledge. Our Introduction would have exemplified the "law of the instrument" (see chap. 6 in this volume). The general public is quite familiar with a colloquial version of this law: "If you have a hammer, everything looks like a nail!" Immersed in the discipline's tradition of looking within an individual to understand and resolve problems, we would have encouraged readers to explain the discipline to the public and to policymakers through invited briefings, background papers, speeches to community groups, and so on. We would have described how policies develop, the nature and sources of information used in that process, and strategies for increasing our contributions to the evolution of matters of concern to our discipline's current and future status. We would have provided multiple ways in which the public's attitudes and position toward support for psychology represented nails needing to be hammered. We would have described ways to change those attitudes.

Our solution would not have been so much wrong as seriously incomplete. Its implementation could have had some limited positive effect. It is unlikely, however, that its impact would have been either sufficient or sustained. At best, it would have changed some of the public's attitudes for some period of time. It would have energized a somewhat greater number of us for a while. It would not, however, have resolved or even addressed why our discipline repeatedly finds its contributions to the public misunderstood or undervalued. In truth, it would have changed us very little! To achieve the long-term goal requires, we believe, refocusing attention on ourselves. In effect, we propose that to be most effective in influencing public policy, psychology must defy its long-standing tradition of looking *outside* of itself.

Caplan and Nelson in a 1973 article (see chap. 6) referred to the discipline's traditional perspective as "person-centered." In our view, it is more accurately described as *other*-person–centered. What it does not lead to is consideration that the problem may originate within ourselves and within our discipline's traditions. It does not lead us automatically to wonder why *we* know so little about how the public and policymakers understand and value our work. It does not lead *us* to challenge *our* assumptions about what *we* do, how *we* select the questions *we* raise, the solutions *we* propose, and the means and criteria by which *we* assess either. Consistent with Sarason's earlier (in a 1967 article; see chap. 1) and continuing (e.g., 1993) attempts to interest psychology in the problem of creating, implementing, and sustaining change, we as a discipline have ignored the processes by which we have repeatedly defined problems about our public image in terms that ensure that those problems remain unresolved.

Multiple sources have contributed to our slow recognition that adhering to our traditional view would not deter us from arriving where we presently are or where many believe we are heading. Kiesler and Morton, for example, warned in a 1988 article (see chap. 3) of the perils of health care planning for psychologists:

> The fact that psychologists have arguments in their favor is less important than the fact that they will be required to make them convincingly (yet again)—to an entirely new, powerful, and less knowledgeable audience, the superplayers of the health care revolution. (p. 998)

Schneider (1990) voiced similar alarm:

> I contend that the struggle between the value of science and those of practice is only part of the story and that the rest of it is barely beginning to be acknowledged, difficult to confront, and hardly possible to remedy. At the very least, we must recognize that *academic psychology and the private practice of psychology are faced with threats of their own obsolescence*. This leads me to believe that we are fighting the wrong war, for the wrong reasons, with the wrong weapons. (p. 73; emphasis in original)[1]

Earlier, Bevan in a 1980 article (see chap. 7) signaled the urgent need to attend to the same problem. In his chapter entitled "On Getting in Bed

---

[1]From "Psychology at a Crossroads," by S. F. Schneider, 1990, *American Psychologist, 45*, p. 73. Copyright 1990 by the American Psychological Association. Reprinted with permission of the author.

with a Lion," Bevan's message confirms that the problem is not new, nor unrecognized, nor likely to disappear. Although originally directed to psychology's scientific community, his warning applies to all of us:

> Times have changed. Scientists can no longer expect to receive the repeated large-scale increases in public funding they enjoyed in the 1950s and 1960s, *nor the uncritical public approval that lay behind such actions*. If they are concerned for the continued health of their enterprise and for its value as a public good—if, indeed, they are only interested in making the most of their opportunities as individual practitioners of science—they will have to perceive more clearly than they do now their *collective* [emphasis in original] status as a special interest group, and they will have to appreciate better than they do now the political dynamics of an era dominated by a plethora of special interest groups. Moreover, they will have to understand more fully why the particular changes that have come to affect them have in fact occurred *and to recognize more precisely those alternatives in attitude and behavior that, as a consequence of change, now best ensure their goals as a community*. No amount of complaining about an ungrateful or misunderstanding public, no manner of wishful thinking, will usher back the golden age. (emphasis added)

ORGANIZED PSYCHOLOGY AS A SPECIAL INTEREST GROUP

To even imply that our discipline represents a "special interest group" seems a radical departure from how we psychologists see ourselves. Few of us, we suspect, think of organized psychology in such terms; fewer still think of themselves as members of such groups. Special interest groups, after all, argue for *special* treatment to remediate past inequities or to compensate for some impediment in their access to equal treatment or equitable allocation of public funds. In effect, special interests groups petition those who distribute public resources to take exception to whatever other criteria are considered in the allocation of such resources and dedicate a portion for members of that group.

To reject Bevan's inclusion of organized psychology among such petitioners implies that we as members of a discipline are prepared to accept whatever the public and those who make and implement public policy determine we deserve from the public coffers. Given increasing concerns about our futures as service providers, scientists, scholars, and educators, it seems neither likely nor wise to passively await such an unknown fate. On the other hand, to accept Bevan's identification of our discipline as a special interest group means that we must examine carefully the bases on which we can argue that we deserve special consideration.

We could, for example, acknowledge and then document our inability to compete successfully for public resources without exceptional support.

In effect, we would argue that other mental health disciplines, other sciences, and other academic fields have an advantage over us in securing public support and public funds. Alternatively, we could base our requests for an equitable share of public resources on documentation of our capacities to contribute in unique and substantive ways to the public good. In so doing, we would make explicit the advantages that we bring to responding to mental health needs, to increasing scientific understanding, and to educating the population.

To the authors, the only reasonable choice is anything but a simple one. Organized psychology must pursue the second option vigorously! Antecedent to that pursuit, however, our discipline must arrive at a shared understanding of the unique and substantive ways in which we serve the public. We must appreciate our distinctive capacity to design, provide, and evaluate services not just in mental health but in public welfare generally. We must appreciate the unmatched quality and contributions of our research to unravel complex cognitive, emotional, and behavioral processes ultimately relevant to understanding and controlling important elements of general human functioning, health, and productivity. We must appreciate the value of expanding public understanding of our theories and work as it applies to daily interpersonal encounters and people's roles as parents, workers, neighbors, and companions.

To many of our colleagues, the foregoing exhortation may sound like yet another call for effective public relations. Our intent is, in fact, quite the opposite. At this time, the message needs to be heard *within rather than outside* of the discipline. We arrived at this conclusion just prior to reading Sampson's (1993) intriguing analysis of the means by which organized psychology has failed to hear the messages of collective movements (e.g., those of women, gay men, lesbians, and ethnic minority members). Sampson proposed that, by definition, each of these movements has challenged the discipline's perspective on human functioning and adaptation. Central to Sampson's discussion of the positions taken by these movements is the importance of understanding the concept of "voice" and the dissatisfactions arising when participation in dialogue between the "haves" and "have-nots" occurs within an accommodative rather than a transformational framework.

Adopting a New Perspective

As noted, Bevan's inclusion of our discipline within the category of special interests groups requires shifts in both our collective and individual self-concepts. These shifts may be easier to make if we can understand and adopt the perspective of members of other collective movements. The salience of that perspective to our discipline's current needs can be found in

Sampson's (1993) assertion that, although diverse in their membership, goals, and strategies, the members of collective movements share

> what might best be termed an *identity politics*: a politics based on the particular life experiences of people who seek to be in control of their own identities and subjectivities and who claim that socially dominant groups have denied them this opportunity. (p. 1219; emphasis in original)

In the authors' view, involvement in the public policy arena is undertaken, in part, to confirm and retain control over one's identity. If read from the perspective that our discipline represents in its own right a collective movement, Sampson's analysis offers what we believe are valuable insights into understanding ourselves. Movements seek not just to be heard but to participate in discourse in ways that alter the debate. In doing so, those propelling them hope that their claims and needs can be examined independently of how the dominant groups have traditionally defined their claims and needs. Sampson explains that, not unexpectedly, dominant groups shape the nature and terms of the discourse. They do so by defining the issues to be addressed, the evidentiary bases on which decisions are to be made, and the relative costs and benefits of alternative outcomes. They do so also to remain dominant.

Under such circumstances, a collective movement's contributions supplement rather than modify the status quo. In that sense, Sampson explained that they reflect an accommodative or add-on position. Participation by the collective movement may, for example, increase the movement's members' involvement in an activity previously limited to members of the dominant group (e.g., the delivery of mental health services). Their participation, however, mirrors rather than modifies the essential nature of that activity. To gain authorization to engage in the activity, the members of the collective movement subvert distinctive elements of their identity in order that their actions "fit" within acceptable parameters. The nature has not been altered by the addition of the newcomers. What has changed is simply the numbers of those engaged in the activity, as it has been shaped by the dominant group. Although rarely acknowledged, it should be recognized that accommodative change, because it does not substantively change the activity, retains the option of subsequently reversing authorization for the collective's participation without any consequent disruption to the activity. Thus, if the situation changes and it is in the best interest of the dominant group, the original status quo can be regained. Reflecting awareness of this possibility, Sampson explained:

> At this point, it should be clear why identity movements are seeking a *voice* for themselves in their own terms and why they challenge the

uncritical understandings developed by traditional psychological and social science. Without their own voice, whenever they speak, they would do so in a manner that keeps their positioned disadvantage vis-a-vis the dominant groups who have constructed them for this purpose. The form of domination that these identity movements challenge, then, is built into *the very order of things* (e.g., Bourdieu & Wacquant, 1992). As long as members of such groups use the voice of those who have constructed them, they will continue to be complicit in their own domination. Only by finding, declaring, and effectively using their own voice can they hope to break from the trap. (1993, p. 1223; emphasis in original)

Inherent in the concept of voice is the assumption that through its participation in the activity, the collective movement will transform the terms of discourse and action by modifying the assumptions of those dominant processes, that is, of how things are conceptualized, how activities are carried out, and how they might be challenged. This form of participation defines the nature and very purpose of transformative discourse. Its occurrence results in changes in the essential elements of the dominant processes. The perspectives and procedures of the collective movement are incorporated within those of the dominant groups. Consequently, the involvement of the collective movement substantively alters the understanding and form of the original activity, resulting in a hybrid influenced by all involved. In this instance, returning assumptions and activities to their original forms becomes much less likely as members of both the originally dominant group and the collective movement are changed by their collaboration.

If as we propose, psychology meets Sampson's (1993) definition of a special interest group or collective movement, we should find evidence that our current identities have been shaped in response to efforts on our part to participate in dominant group's activities. Such influence presumably would have circumscribed in detectable ways our sense of who we are and how we function. Moreover, our continuing participation in discourse with such groups within their frames of reference would have sustained our relative positions. Using Sampson's terms, our exchanges with such groups would have been accommodative rather than transformational.

Accommodating the Dominant Group

If valid, a review of our discipline's history should reveal episodes in which we have been reactive rather than proactive as scientists, service providers, and educators. It should also provide evidence that, when challenged, the discipline has reacted in ways that emphasize its similarities to rather than differences from such groups. In effect, we would have argued for support assigned to others based on our shared commonalities with them. Criticisms of our discipline (e.g., Altman, 1987; Hebb, 1974; Mc-Pherson, 1992; Skinner, 1987) and of its subgroups (e.g., Garfield, 1966; Rotter, 1973; Sarason, 1981) may reflect recognition of such responses. Two decades ago, Hebb (1974) was quite explicit about the threat and costs of losing our identities as psychologists:

> Psychology is not clinical psychology; it is not physiological psychology; it is not social or comparative or developmental or human experimental psychology. It is something more, comprising all these lines of approach to the central mystery. When the clinical psychologist forgets that he is a psychologist too, what does he become? If he's real good, he becomes a second-rate psychiatrist (since he lacks medical competence). When the physiological psychologist forgets it, when he slides downhill to become an expert on the red nucleus or the cingulate gyrus or the *cornu ammonis*, for its own sake and not as a key to an understanding of behavior, he takes the easier path to simpler problems. He may be a good physiologist, but he's not a psychologist any longer. Psychology is tough, and it's important. (p. 71)

In a harsher tone, Sarason (1981) described the sense of crisis that he believed simmered in an increasing number of psychologists:

> Specifically, by the sense of crisis I refer to the following: one regards psychological theory as arid, or outmoded, or grossly unrelated to the real world, or so circumscribed as to be trivial; one regards reports of psychological research (certainly the great bulk of it) as incomprehensible, or pointless, or ludicrously rigorous, or lacking any semblance of rigor, or simply boring; one regards psychological practices and techniques (e.g., clinical, educational, industrial) as pseudoscientific in their grounding, or far from effective, or used in questionable ways for questionable purposes; and in whatever strengths and combinations these views are held they are accompanied by feelings of anxious drift, unease about the future, and dysphoric musings about "how did all this come about; where did we (I) go wrong?" To put it metaphorically, the love affair with psychology seems headed for termination because the object of love is no longer attractive. (p. 28)

Predating Sarason's concern by a decade, Rotter (1973) noted:

> It seems clear to me that the new methods of treatment are not flourishing because of new knowledge or because basic psychology has recently developed to the point that now many new applications are possible. The methods are often widely embraced in the absence of hard data as to their efficacy. (p. 314)

A decade after Sarason, Schneider (1990) provided another observation of psychology's apparent accommodation to a dominant group:

> Government support following the second world war made it convenient for clinical psychology to train its students in psychiatric settings,

and so began psychology's long ambivalent relationship with the mental health system and its primary gatekeeper, psychiatry. Clinical psychology was always playing "catch up" in this relationship. For many years, psychotherapy was the prize but new ones were added, such as psychology's professional autonomy, state licensure, and freedom of choice in insurance. Additionally, practitioners developed marketing strategies, created a network in the states to introduce and monitor legislation, and nurtured a system of higher education, particularly in freestanding schools of professional psychology, geared to the production of independent private practitioners, undoubtedly, the fastest growing group in psychology.

It now appears that these struggles, which have consumed the energies of many professional psychologists over the past 25 years, may have been in vain.[2]

Readers must decide for themselves whether their experience is consistent with the hypothesis that our discipline has, in fact, been reactive and responsive to the influence of groups more dominant than we, however that dominance is defined. Acceptance of that proposition was the basis for the authors' assertion that the solution to improving our standing with the public and with policymakers lies within ourselves and depends on a candid examination of the issues with which we become involved and the manner in which that involvement occurs. What needs to be determined is the degree to which our contributions reflect the theories and methods of our discipline. In effect, is our work primarily psychological in nature? To the extent that it is not, it is understandable that the public and their policymakers fail to give us the respect and support we believe is due us. Simply stated, they cannot appreciate our distinct contributions because we have not given voice to those contributions.

ASSERTING THE VOICE OF THE FIELD

Recall that within the quote appearing on page 5, Bevan urged psychologists "to recognize more precisely those alternatives in attitude and behavior that, as a consequence of change, now best ensure their goals as a community" (p. 779). For Sampson (1993), such attitudinal change should be associated with the explicit recognition and acceptance of those factors that define psychologists *qua* psychologists. From that substantive basis could arise the discipline's specification of how its science and service translate psychology's unique qualities into potential contributions to society. An initial step in the assertion of our voice may be to reflect on our

---

[2]From "Psychology at a Crossroads," by S. F. Schneider, 1990, *American Psychologist, 45*, p. 73. Copyright 1990 by the American Psychological Association. Reprinted with permission of the author.

discipline's intellectual history and factors that shaped its current form. Unfortunately, an appreciation of that history seems to be lacking in an increasing number of psychologists. Reflecting on his own career as an educator of psychologists, Sarason (1988) commented on this gap in graduate training:

> They [graduate students in psychology] are not exposed to a historical view of American psychology: its origins in and separation from philosophy; its earliest critics (for example, James Dewey); the substance and consequences of the tensions between what was perceived as basic and what as applied, and the value judgments those tensions reflected; the changing religious and social class composition of American psychology; the myriad ways that psychology was transformed by wars and economics; the cultural significances of the controversies between American and European psychology; how psychology has never been exempt from fads and fashions; how judgments are made about what is worthy from the past. If it is true, as Voltaire said, that history is written by the victors, not the vanquished, is that not a warning about how one should view one's sense of identity with the history of one's field? How does one gain a sense of connectedness with a past and a present? What should be the goals of education in psychology?—not *training* in a specialty but *education* in psychology; not an education determined primarily by "the market" but one that instills, and over time sustains, some sense of connectedness. (p. 409; emphasis in original)

The articulation of those qualities without comparisons with other scientific disciplines, other service providers, or other academic fields would, we assume, indicate that we have begun to find our voice. At this time, that challenge may seem rather formidable! It requires that we explain psychology's view toward the identification and resolution of emotional and behavioral disorder without reference to its similarities to and differences from those of psychiatry and social work. Similarly, the challenge requires an explanation of our philosophy of science, our rules of evidence, our definitions of mechanisms, and our investigatory methods without the need to contrast them with those of other scientific disciplines. Perhaps most important, it requires that we become clear about how psychology conceptualizes human functioning, adds uniquely to its understanding, and brings with it the capacity to influence positively its current and subsequent states.

Assuming that readers agree, at least in part, with the thesis that effective and sustained political influence depends on perceptions by policymakers of the distinctiveness and utility of our discipline, how does a discipline begin the process of finding its voice? Is it even realistic to assume that psychology has a single voice? These questions have repeatedly been asked by the discipline's leaders, who have expressed misgivings about the paths along which the discipline appeared to be moving. Hebb's (1974) statement of "what psychology is about" suggests that there is a core to our discipline that could be tapped:

> I have argued that psychology is a biological science, including its social and clinical wings; that a science is self-limiting, holding more or less strictly to its narrow modes of procedure; and consequently that mixing psychology up with other ways of knowing human beings—the literary and artistic ways—is to the detriment of both. We must honor the humanities, but a science cannot imitate them. I have answered the implied question, what is psychology about? by saying that its central concern must be man's mind and thought. Each of us has his own avenue of approach to that understanding, which we must approach by degrees. It is a far prospect, and in the meantime we have to keep on with the study of memory, perception, psycholinguistics, fear, and so on and so forth; but it may be disastrous in the long run for psychology when the specialist digging his own path deeper and deeper loses sight of what others are doing in other fields and so loses an invaluable perspective. (pp. 78–79)

Schneider (1990) offered a related although distinct point from which to reestablish our unique disciplinary identity:

> I think we possess the knowledge base to begin to implement a graduate education whose conceptual, substantive, and experiential basis is life-span development from the prenatal period to dying, death, and bereavement. Biological, psychological, sociocultural, and environmental factors would be included across the life span, each considered developmentally and interactively. For example, something similar to the history of the elementary school as an institution and as an educational setting would be as much a part of learning about the developing child as biological maturation factors, cognitive and personality development, competence, separation, social relationships with peers, and family interactions when a youngster begins school. Normal development, vagaries of development, and exceptional development, including developmental psychopathology, would be covered so that the full range of biopsychosocial phenomena can be apprehended. Particular attention would be accorded to age- and event-related transitions, to intergenerational relationships, and to factors that lead to resilience and competence as well as those leading to protective behavior or to vulnerability. Students need to know how generations perceive and relate to one another; how it appears and feels to see things from the perspective of the parent, the child, the sibling, and the teacher; and how time and its dimensions are kept by the young and the old. Such an education, covering the entire life span, would be an excellent antidote to narrow specialization, although nothing would prevent students from focusing more intensely on certain age groups, functions, or elements that influence development. The model also allows for differ-

ential emphasis on the basic-applied dimension and for differential attention to biological, psychological, or sociocultural factors, as long as a firm knowledge and experience base is obtained across the spectrum. The entire process would (a) locate the person in the environment over time; (b) emphasize continuity, change, variation, relationships, and the mutual influence of systems, people and settings on each other; and (c) embed the individual in society and in the context of personal and social history.[3]

A SENSE OF PUBLIC RESPONSIBILITY

With these perspectives in mind, readers might reconsider Bevan's call for attitudinal change. To influence the direction of such change, he emphasized the relevance of the "meaning of public accountability" for those who seek public support. For the educator, for example, Bevan noted that "we understand but often forget that from the very beginnings of America's history as a nation, we have viewed our institutions of higher education as instruments of national purpose. To make the point, he likened the university to a public utility with responsibilities similar to those of other regulated industries. Moreover, Bevan reminded the scientist that

> Even the best friends of science have consistently justified the public support of science in investment terms. Viewed in such terms, basic research as a publicly sponsored enterprise must be defined as a high-risk activity underwritten by a promissory note of indefinite term. What most academic scientists seem never to have understood is that such notes are always subject to payment on demand and rarely with just a simple accumulation of interest. If they are going to preserve the integrity of the basic research undertaking under such a social contract, scientists are going to have to take a more active interest in and become more knowledgeable of the nature of the process of making public policy than has heretofore been the case. Engagement must be in both institutional and individual terms. Like any other special interest group operating in an era of special interest politics, scientists must be prepared to engage in open debate. But they must first put their own house in order.

It is important that nothing in the comments just presented would require that psychology abandon any realm in which it is currently involved. Such an approach is likely, however, to open an array of alternative possibilities for research and service. Attitudinally, we hope, a sense of public responsibility would accompany acceptance of public funds; con-

---

[3]From "Psychology at a Crossroads," by S. F. Schneider, 1990, *American Psychologist, 45,* p. 78. Copyright 1990 by the American Psychological Association. Reprinted with permission of the author.

currently, acknowledgement of public obligation would replace suggestions of professional entitlement. Rather than acceding to an implicit obligation to the Hippocratic dictum, "Do no harm," perhaps our discipline would be better served by committing to an overarching principle, "Beyond all else, contribute to the public good!" From that position, psychologists might begin to include within their defined responsibilities involvement in the formation, implementation, and evaluation of public policies at some level (see chap. 2). Public service may be seen as not only a means to an end but a highly respected end in itself.

MAKING A BROAD IMPACT

As a discipline, we bring to policy development our distinctive preparation in methods of scientific inquiry along the continuum from descriptive and qualitative studies through rigorously controlled laboratory experiments. As service providers, we bring the capacity to apply that investigatory perspective to formulating hypotheses about how social problems evolve and are sustained. We know how to create conditions of trust and openness; we know how to train others to deliver service and how to monitor the quality of their efforts. Importantly, we know how to ask questions about human thought, emotion, development, change, and motivation. We can reflect on what people do and consider ways to enable them to do more or less of it.

We are not, however, likely to gain either sympathy or support as a special interest group if we establish stringent conditions under which we will apply our knowledge. In the years ahead, it is doubtful that we will be seen as meriting equal or greater levels of public support if we limit ourselves to familiar settings and to the problems that we deem important and interesting. As noted elsewhere (see chap. 15; Lorion, 1991), public health officials have recognized for more than a decade the significant contribution of attitudes and behaviors to the nation's morbidity and mortality. Psychology has the potential to contribute significantly to achieving reductions in death and disability resulting from addictive behaviors, unprotected sexual intercourse resulting in disease or unwanted pregnancy, involvement in violence, and health-compromising dietary and exercise practices.

It is now common knowledge that the major challenges to significant reductions in health care costs are psychological, not biological. Our discipline, above all others, should lay claim to having priority in responding to these challenges. Our scientific and professional skills and resources contain the potential for identifying psychologically based solutions to these issues. Once we believe that and commit ourselves to the pursuit of that goal, we must be prepared to communicate with policymakers about what forms of support (i.e., fiscal, legislative, regulatory) are needed to design, implement, and evaluate psychologically based strategies for disease prevention and health promotion. We should make reasonable claims and establish achievable deadlines for the systematic growth of the knowledge and service delivery bases that will be necessary components of a public response to this public health problem.

As a discipline, we need to appreciate the value of approaching policymakers with the simple but sincere question, "How can I be of help with your most pressing needs?" In many cases, the response will be "I don't know" or "I don't see how what you do can help me with . . . ." Either response presents an opportunity for us to begin to alter the way in which we relate to those who are responsible for understanding and responding to public needs. In the authors' experience, the most helpful initial step is to do nothing, offer nothing other than to remain available and open. Repeatedly, the authors have found those involved in public service appreciative of our willingness simply to listen, observe, and attempt to understand the issue from the perspective of those who face or must respond to whatever the need may be. Sometimes our questions or observations provide a different and useful perspective for those too busy to identify alternative ways to think about the problem or provide solutions. Above all else, we must open ourselves to applying our skills and expertise within new settings. Sarason (see chap. 1; 1983, 1991, 1993) has long argued for psychology to appreciate its inherent relationship with educational settings. Within schools, we would find unequaled opportunities to understand basic mechanisms underlying cognition, perception, learning, social processes, and so forth. The findings and methods of our discipline's basic scientists have much to offer and at least as much to gain by involvement with educational settings. That developmental theorists have much to give and get from schools is self-evident. Less clear, perhaps, but equally complementary are the goals of segments of the discipline currently identified with the mental health service delivery system and the opportunities to influence the quality and effectiveness of educational settings. Schools represent an ideal setting for the delivery of both preventive and therapeutic services to children and their families. One need only think differently about how we apply our diagnostic, behavioral, intervention, and evaluative expertise and, importantly, how we relate to educators (i.e., as collaborators rather than consumers of our services) to create the conditions under which innovative educational settings and practices can develop.

COMMUNICATION ON ALL FRONTS

To truly contribute to resolving the demands confronting public officials now, however, psychology must be prepared to enter communities and listen to their residents. From such dialogues, the authors believe, will come a different set of questions for the developmental, social, cognitive, or sensory psychologists. These questions are not likely to be any less scientific or heuristically valuable, only somewhat more evident in the link between their answers and the lives of people who live, learn, play, and work under everyday conditions. A related consequence of such interactions will be the gradual development on the part of the public of an answer to the question faced by those of us who initiate contact with the formulators of public policies: "What is it that a psychologist does?" Both authors have repeatedly heard someone from a school—or health clinic, or housing project, or government office—offer what, in his or her opinion, was a sincere compliment: "You sure don't seem like a psychologist to me."

That comment, above all else, seems to capture for us the obstacle to achieving the status of a special interest group of significance to those who make and implement public policy. As stated earlier, we should pursue vigorously such status and commit ourselves to justifying its right to public support and public funding because of its unique potential for serving the public good. Voiceless, however, we are ensnared by public perceptions of us as restricted in terms of the issues we understand and care about, the settings in which we are found and operate, and the direct applicability of our science and service to the majority of the public. We are in this position because our identity has become so muddled (as Hebb's quote on page 12 so clearly describes) with psychiatry, physiology, and ivory-tower intellectualism. Ironically, that confusion about who we are and how we can serve the public good both limits our presence in public policy and represents an opportunity to define ourselves in clear and relevant ways.

The vehicle for doing so, the authors believe, is immediate and active involvement at a local, state, or federal level in policy formation around some topic in which we have interest, expertise, or simple curiosity. As noted, it requires that we leave our offices, our laboratories, our classrooms, or whatever other surrounding is familiar and comfortable to us and venture into public settings, schools, and communities. Many encounters will begin with a simple "How can I help?" and continue even after the "I don't know" response is heard. Initially, the best we can do is listen, observe, and slowly gain an appreciation of how the issues of concern to psychologists are behavioral scientists in the area of mental health are presented in alternative settings and, significantly, how those confronting such issues have developed effective ways to respond. Through that process, the authors believe that the discipline's identity will gain voice and that we, along with policymakers, will come to understand how uniquely we think about and contribute to resolving the issues of paramount concern—the public's health and welfare.

OVERVIEW OF THE BOOK

Chapters included in this work substantiate the major themes presented in this Introduction. Succinctly stated, those themes articulate the discipline's need (a) to appreciate its long-standing dependence on public support and public policy; (b) to recognize how it must change if it is to fulfill, and benefit from, its potential to contribute to a broad array of public needs; and (c) to transform political and public valuing of our uniqueness through our proactive and sustained fulfillment of our public responsibility.

Section I focuses on the coevolution of Psychology and Policy. These chapters make evident the redundancy of our call to arms. Multiple past attempts have conveyed the discipline's need to become involved in the formation, implementation, and analysis of public policy both for the public interest and for self-interest. Given that the discipline has survived and presumably thrived without collectively heeding these earlier calls, why should its response differ at this time?

Frank and Callan's introductory remarks to Section I anticipate and respond to that question. In their view, the depth, breadth, and momentum of ongoing or foreseeable policy changes represent an unprecedented convergence of factors. Frank and Callan suggest that this may be a determining opportunity for the discipline to voice its unique capacity to understand public needs through its research and to respond to those needs through its services.

Substantive evidence of that potential is exemplified in the chapters included in Section II, Psychological Science as a Policy Resource. Flattau and Howell's introductory comments for Section II echo the perception that the discipline confronts a critical opportunity to establish its salience for informing policy decisions that define the nature of public responsibility and consequent allocations of public resources. Provocatively, Flattau and Howell highlight the discipline's capacity to influence policy by expanding psychology's involvement in and contributions to understanding the informational needs and processes of policymaking. The chapters in Section II examine how informational gaps are defined; the form in which information is presented and analyzed; the rules of evidence; and the criteria by which "proof" is established, challenged, or refuted and which need to be understood by both psychologists and policymakers. Ironically, it appears that one way we can establish our salience for informing policymakers' consideration of psychological matters is by informing policymakers of the processes by which they make policy!

The chapters selected for Section III exemplify the discipline's relevance to a broad array of challenges to the public welfare. They document our contributions to matters as diverse as (a) judicial consideration of public interest issues; (b) the design and regulation of early childhood programs; (c) public involvement in energy conservation and other environmental preservation; and (d) shaping the nation's approach to disease prevention, health promotion, and the delivery of health services. In their overview of these chapters, Newman and Vincent underscore the simple lessons reflected in these examples of our capacity for influencing the public agenda. First, to shape policy, we must communicate with policymakers in terms they understand and in forms responsive to their processes of communication. Second, we must shape our schedules to conform to those of the policymakers. When necessary, our contributions must be swift and timely. Our availability must be continuous and our commitment evidenced through our persistence. The immediacy with which we respond to their requests must be matched by the patience with which we await response to our request!

Section IV confirms the book's overarching claim that if we establish and assert our voice, the effort will not be fruitless. Policymakers are prepared to listen to and appreciate our message. Tomes and Rickel's overview of the words of policymakers confirm the commonality of our interests with those who frame and implement public decisions. The overview supports the assertion that our efforts have impact and that our science and services can and do shape the public agenda, whether focused on the homeless, the abused, the young, the old, or those otherwise meriting or gaining public attention and public resources.

It is both an honor and most fitting that this book close with the words of a member of the discipline who participated directly in the formation of public decisions. Strickland's experience of campaigning, gaining a seat in the House of Representatives, and witnessing firsthand the process of making public policy confirms the importance of our learning the language, rules, influences, and pacing that characterize those processes. His experience also confirms that our active and ongoing involvement in public policies can—as our credibility expands over time—transform the bases on which problems are defined, evidence is pursued and evaluated, and solutions are designed, implemented, and evaluated. In closing the account of his experiences and observations, Strickland gives his voice to the final reality that policies affecting our discipline and our world will be made with or without our involvement. If we believe that we can contribute to those decisions in positive and constructive ways, we must translate that belief into action.

REFERENCES

Altman, I. (1987). Centripetal and centrifugal trends in psychology. *American Psychologist, 42*, 1058–1069.

Bourdieu, P., & Wacquant, L. D. J. (1992). *An invitation to reflexive sociology.* Chicago: University of Chicago Press.

Dickens, C. (1961). *A tale of two cities.* New York: Washington Square Press.

Garfield, S. L. (1966). Clinical psychology and the search for identity. *American Psychologist, 21,* 353–362.

Hebb, D. O. (1974). What psychology is about. *American Psychologist, 41,* 71–79.

Lorion, R. P. (1991). Prevention and public health: Psychology's response to the nation's health care crisis. *American Psychologist, 46,* 516–519.

McPherson, M. W. (1992). Is psychology the science of behavior? *American Psychologist, 47,* 329–336.

Rotter, J. B. (1973). The future of clinical psychology. *American Psychologist, 40,* 313–321.

Sampson, E. E. (1993). Identity politics: Challenges to psychology's understanding. *American Psychologist, 48,* 1219–1230.

Sarason, S. B. (1981). *Psychology misdirected.* New York: Free Press.

Sarason, S. B. (1983). *Schooling in America: Scapegoat and salvation.* New York: Free Press.

Sarason, S. B. (1988). *The making of an American psychologist.* San Francisco: Jossey-Bass.

Sarason, S. B. (1991). *The predictable failure of educational reform: Can we change course before it's too late?* San Francisco: Jossey Bass.

Sarason, S. B. (1993). *The case for change: Rethinking the preparation of educators.* San Francisco: Jossey-Bass.

Schneider, S. F. (1990). Psychology at a crossroads. *American Psychologist, 45,* 521–529.

Skinner, B. F. (1987). Whatever happened to psychology as the science of behavior? *American Psychologist, 42,* 780–786.

I

COEVOLUTION OF PSYCHOLOGY AND POLICY

INTRODUCTION

PUBLIC POLICY: A PROCESS WITH A PURPOSE

ROBERT G. FRANK and JOANNE E. CALLAN

Public policy refers to the total of all the laws, regulations, court rulings, and administrative procedures that guide this nation, in solving socially agreed-upon problems. Subgroupings of public policy might include educational policy, welfare policy, defense policy, economic policy, and so forth. We will focus on health policy to explore some aspects of the public policy process.

The concept of health care has changed substantially since World War II. Health services have transformed from narrowly defined "medical" care to include the entire spectrum of health promotion, disease prevention, treatment of illness, and rehabilitation, as well as a number of social welfare programs (Frank, Sullivan, & DeLeon, 1994). This expansion has led to the development of a newly empowered economic sector and to an unparalleled commitment of national resources to a broad area of "health."

During the 103rd Congress (1992–1994), a great debate occurred regarding the need for comprehensive reform of the U.S. health care system. In the end, reform was deferred. Despite this inaction, the U.S. health care system continues to be plagued by three problems that will worsen if they are not addressed. First, the cost of health care in the United States continues to grow. In 1993, health care cost $884 billion, a 7.8% increase from the previous year. The proportion of the Gross Domestic Product (GDP) dedicated to health care grew to 13.9% ("Federal Health Spending," 1994).

Many experts have suggested health costs will be controlled by an increasingly competitive health care market. Despite recent slowing, there is reason to believe that without fundamental change in our health care delivery system, this is a temporary aberration in the otherwise relentless growth in health care spending that has occurred over the past 20 years (Aaron, 1994).

A second sign indicating problems with the American health care system that will worsen before improving is that access to health coverage continues to decrease. An additional 1.1 million Americans lost coverage last year; this increase brings the total of people without health insurance to an all-time record of 39.7 million (Blendon, Brodie, & Benson, 1995). Although estimates vary, it is clear also that a substantial number of Americans are underinsured, leading to a significant lack of adequate primary care (Blendon, Brodie, & Benson, 1995).

Finally, quality is difficult to assess in the U.S. health care system. Many interventions are unneeded, producing negligible improvement at high cost. A variant of the problems with quality is the health insurance system, which encourages discrimination against those individuals needing services.

These are social problems needing a public policy solution, but it was not possible to achieve agreement during the 103rd Congress on how to best attempt a solution, or at least improvements. These problems have led to the continuing growth of managed care—a marketplace solution, not a legislated public policy solution. However, it should be noted that since 1971, encouragement of health maintenance organizations (HMOs) and managed health care has been the federal policy (see DeLeon, VandenBos, & Bulatao, 1991).

Managed care has been adopted, by both government and industry, as a method of controlling health costs, improving quality, and providing access to health coverage. In some cases, the savings created by managed care have been used to expand access to health coverage. Most often, savings from managed care implementation have been used to support the growing for-profit health industry. The absence of health system reform legislation leaves individuals with little guidance or protection from growing entrepreneurship in the delivery of health care (Blendon, Brodie, & Benson, 1995). By the year 2000, it is estimated that 65% of all Americans will receive coverage through managed care plans (Weiner, 1994). Moreover, fewer Americans have options regarding their health service provision. The vast majority of employers, up to 84% who offer health insurance offer only one plan (Blendon, Brodie, & Benson, 1995). Thus, if basic health care reform itself is not achieved in the near future, it will be necessary to develop additional new federal legislation regarding managed care systems in order to address broader social issues and concerns (generally considered in public policy initiatives, but often ignored in marketplace initiatives).

The rapid movement toward managed care by both private and public payers (Frank & Johnstone, in press; Frank, Sullivan, & DeLeon, 1994; Frank & VandenBos, 1994; VandenBos, 1993) is restructuring the health care delivery system in the United States. Consumers are becoming increasingly concerned with the quality as well as the cost of health care. It is likely that concerns with lowered quality of care and limited choice in health plans will become a significant discussion point in the health systems evolution debate. Driven by privatization and enormous profit margins, managed care systems have become bounty hunters able to retain as much as 30 cents of every premium dollar for administration, marketing, and profit (cf. Reihardt as cited in Inglehart, 1994). With public purchasers such as Medicaid and Medicare adopting managed care as an antidote to increasing public costs, changes in the delivery system spurred on by managed care will continue well into the next century. The multitude of factors that drive this evolution in the health care system—costs, lack of health care coverage, lack of a coherent national policy, and market forces—will lead to a dizzying parade of changes in the U.S. health delivery system. Virtually no health profession will be able to function independently in this evolving health care system. The pace of change will eventually lead to a public clamor for a more coherent national health policy. At the same time, the broader definition of health that now includes almost every aspect of psychology means that psychologists will be directly affected by reform of the health care system.

Given the integration of mental health services into the health care system, it is imperative that psychologists be conversant with the zeitgeist of the larger health care system. Traditionally, training programs in psychology have directed little attention toward policy issues. The sweeping current of change altering the U.S. health care delivery system will make such negligence deadly. No longer will psychologists be able to view their profession as distinct from other aspects of mental health or the health care system. The intricate relationship of psychology to other health services will become increasingly apparent as pressures force consolidation in the health care system, yielding "vertically integrated" health delivery systems. Likewise, when other policy areas (such as education reform or welfare reform) are addressed, it will be critical that psychologists be conversant with the zeitgeist of that larger arena as well—and the role of psychology within it.

The previously published articles included in this section reflect the broad view that health policy is fundamental to training, research, and practice within psychology. These chapters provide an interesting historical context from which to better understand overall policy making and, in particular, as described earlier, current health care policy development.

Sarason's comments, written in the mid-1960s (see chap. 1), reflect a contemporary concern about the nature and effectiveness of change within social systems. It is as relevant to ask now, as it was then, if the anticipated public policy changes (i.e., those related to health care, including mental health and behavioral issues) will lead to innovation—and, moreover, if they will support the intent or commitment to innovate. His admonition that there is a danger of recognizing only a part of the problem, and then accepting it as the whole, is also still relevant. Although the current hope may be for the development of public policy that leads to broader health care reform and, thus, the availability of more equitably distributed and a broader range of health care services, the result may not meet expectations. It seems much more likely, especially without much greater involvement of professionals in policy making, that the debates will focus more on smaller pieces of health care reform, with the potential of unintended negative effects on availability and quality of health care services.

DeLeon, two decades later (see chap. 2), relating public policy to public services, challenged psychology to commit to both. Issues he identified at that time as requiring resolution within psychology, particularly in the context of the general health care system, remain today: levels of psychological training and related skills and competencies, prescription privileges, and inclusion of psychology in key legislation (e.g., Medicare and Medicaid). DeLeon observed that whereas in the 1970s, nearly one third of the U.S. Senate "cosponsored" legislation introduced by Senator Daniel K. Inouye (D–Hawaii) to provide psychologists with professional autonomy in Medicare, by the 1985–1986 session, no other senator did. This fact points to the lack of involvement of psychologists in the legislative process—a lack that remains today. DeLeon's question, "When will psychologists become involved actively in making psychology known?" is basically the same one as then Congressman Ted Strickland (D–Ohio), a psychologist, and Henry Waxman (D–California) both asked in 1994 during the 103rd Congress. Representative Strickland added that because sweeping changes in health care delivery will be made in the next few years, psychologists must decide either to become involved in the formulation of related policy or to forfeit the opportunity to be a major player. DeLeon's question is obviously pertinent to any session of Congress!

In a 1988 article (see chap. 3), Kiesler and Morton focused on opportunities for psychology in service, research, and education within the context of health care changes. They acknowledged the following advantages that psychologists bring to such reform: empirical orientation, expertise apart from traditional medical and hospital care, emphasis on prevention and on the concept of wellness, and knowledge about environmental influence on behavior and well-being. Yet they offered the following caution, one that certainly is relevant to any impact psychologists might aspire to with any Congress. Kiesler and Morton caution psychologists that the success of proposals for change rests upon more than the simple validity of their argument.

A central message in the 1989 Saks article (see chap. 4) is that psychologists should come to appreciate the extent to which the law is uninformed about data so that psychologists can realize how important it is for them to become involved in the development of legal policy. He noted the particular contributions that psychologists could make through research on a number of understudied areas, including various aspects of trial process and law processes. This 1989 challenge may be even more relevant today as psychologists are confronted with finding ways to broaden their impact on public policy.

In his 1990 article (see chap. 5), Smith cautioned that psychology ought to keep the debate on advocacy in the public interest as open as possible. Although he thought that psychologists have much to offer toward a more "humane and sustainable world," he would likely argue today, as he did then, that there is no consensus among psychologists as to what constitutes "the public good." Taking a view that psychologists must be in touch with public issues—and that they must go beyond guild issues, particularly those that lead to turf imperatives—seems to be compatible with, although not as demanding or challenging as, the views presented by DeLeon and Kiesler and Morton.

During the coming decade, the United States faces major national problems and critical needs. Health care reform, education reform, welfare reform, and diminishing violence are initiatives for change that demand the most innovative and, at the same time, pragmatic approaches that can be designed. In order to influence the future—indeed, to ensure its relevance to the future—psychology must be actively involved in setting public policy.

REFERENCES

Aaron, H. J. (1994). Thinking straight about medical costs. *Health Affairs, 13,* 7–13.

Blendon, R. J., Brodie, M., & Benson J. (1995). What should be done now that national health reform is dead? *Journal of the American Medical Association, 273,* 243–244.

DeLeon, P. H., VandenBos, G. R., & Bulatao, E. Q. (1991). Managed mental health care: A history of the federal policy initiative. *Professional Psychology: Research and Practice, 22,* 15–25.

Federal health spending jumps, while private sector moderates. (1994, December 5). *Medicine and Health, 48*(47), 2.

Frank, R. G., & Johnstone, B. (in press). Changes in the health workforce: Implication for psychologists. In R. I. Glueckhauf, R. G. Frank, G. R. Bond, & J. McGrew (Eds.), *Psychological practice in a changing health care system: Issues and new directions*. New York: Springer.

Frank, R. G., Sullivan, M. J., & DeLeon, P. H. (1994). Health care reform in the states. *American Psychologists, 49*(10), 855–857.

Frank, R. G., & VandenBos, G. R. (1994). Health care reform: The 1993–1994 evolution. *American Psychologist, 49,* 851–854.

Inglehart, J. K. (1994). The struggle between managed care and fee-for-service practice. *New England Journal of Medicine, 331,* 63–67.

VandenBos, G. R. (1993). U.S. mental health policy: Proactive evolution in the midst of health care reform. *American Psychologist, 48,* 283–290.

Weiner, J. P. (1994). Forecasting the effects of health care reform on U.S. physician workforce requirement: Evidence from HMO staffing patterns. *Journal of the American Medical Association, 272*(3), 222–229.

1

TOWARD A PSYCHOLOGY OF CHANGE AND INNOVATION

SEYMOUR B. SARASON

There is an increasing number of psychologists who are interested in how organizations or social systems work and change. One of the factors in this development is the realization that all psychologists, like the rest of humanity, are affected by the different social systems of which they may be a part. This realization is frequently not due to considerations of theory or training but an awareness forced on one by virtue of day-to-day living. I suppose it is possible for a psychologist to live his days unaware that his thinking, teaching, practices, and relationships (personal or professional) bear in some way the stamp of his past and present immersion in what may be termed organizations or social systems. It is possible, and it may even be that such a person is involved as a psychologist with problems upon which this unawareness has no particular effect. Such a psychologist would likely be a researcher who at the same time that he views his research as unaffected by the workings of social systems—such as the particular department or university of which he is a member—can usually talk loud and long about how the conduct of his research has in some measure been affected by grant-giving agencies which are, after all, organizations or

Reprinted from *American Psychologist*, 22, 227–233. Copyright 1967 by the American Psychological Association.

Psi Chi (National Honor Society in Psychology) invited address at American Psychological Association, New York, September 1966.

social systems. There are probably no important facets of a psychologist's existence which do not reflect the influence of his relationship to one or another type of organization.

I have not made the above comments because I happen to think that psychologists should have a keen sensitivity to the world in which they live. That would be as presumptuous as it would be ineffective. My comments were by way of saying that as psychological theorists move in the direction of stating comprehensive formulations about the determinants of human behavior they will become increasingly concerned with the nature of social organizations, the ways in which they change, and the consequences of these changes. This development will not be a matter of choice but rather of necessity in that in reality the relationship between the individual and "organized settings" is not a matter of choice. The problem for theory is how to go beyond token gestures to these relationships, how to study and understand the extent of variations in these relationships, and how to begin to formulate generalizations which do justice to the complexities involved.[1]

Several years ago a number of colleagues and I became interested in the processes of change in a certain social system. In the course of studying this system we became aware, as might have been predicted, how complex the processes of change were to understand and how little there was in psychological theory and practice to guide us. The complexity of the problem would have been more tolerable were it not for the fact that we had no conceptual framework which could serve, however tentatively, as a basis for thinking, planning, and action. It has been said that there is nothing more practical than a good theory. There are times when we would have settled for the illusory comfort of a bad theory. In any event, what follows in this paper is no more than a variety of thoughts which may serve only

---

[1]It is important to note that the problem which I am stating generally is one quite familiar to the industrial psychologist, as Stagner (1966) has made clear. "Industrial psychology has since its inception dealt with problems of man in an organization, but in its early stages gave consideration only to part of the man, and took the organization for granted. . . . Decided changes began to appear after 1950. . . . Only within the past ten years, however, has this transformation of industrial psychology been completed. People like Haire and Simon began to write about the total organization as a network of human interactions; Likert and McGregor applied new ideas of psychodynamics to the managerial role. The Survey Research Center and other research institutes began to pile up empirical evidence for the reciprocal effects of organizations and individuals.

"A look at a clutch of recent books dealing with the behavior of human beings in industrial organizations confirms my feeling that industrial psychology is no longer the step-child of theoretical and research efforts. Instead there is a good deal of sophisticated work in both theory and data-gathering. Undoubtedly some industrial psychologists of what we may call 'the old school' will protest that this new baby is no legitimate offspring of their specialty. Certainly its parentage is in doubt. Social psychology, sociology, and anthropology have made important genetic contributions; even a few psychoanalytic genes seem to have been incorporated. I would hold, nevertheless, that this new growth is truly industrial psychology, in the sense that it represents the best application of theoretical and empirical psychology to the understanding of human behavior in industrial settings." It is my point that the need for, and the problems involved in, conceptualizing comprehensively man-system relationships is not a necessity for one kind of psychologist (e.g., school, industrial, etc.) but for any psychologist concerned with human behavior.

to convince others that the problem is important and requires thoughts better than our own.

THE PSYCHO-EDUCATIONAL CLINIC

Several years ago a Psycho-Educational Clinic was started at Yale as an integral part of our clinical training program. The origins, purposes and activities of the Clinic have been described in detail elsewhere (Sarason, Levine, Goldenberg, Cherlin, & Bennett, 1966). For the present paper it is necessary to state very briefly two of the purposes which have increasingly become the focus of our interest and concern. The first of these purposes is to describe and understand the educational setting as a social system, i.e., to view and study this setting as a subculture possessing a distinctive pattern of traditions, dynamics, and goals (Sarason, 1966). We are quite aware that this is a task far beyond the capacities of any single group of investigators. We are acutely aware than it is a task which involves almost every important problem and field in psychology. The complexity of the task in part reflects the fact that in the educational setting these problems have to be conceptualized in a way which erases artificial or arbitrary distinctions (e.g., learning, social psychology, clinical psychology, child development, etc.) and which truly reflects actual relationships. For example, it apparently (but inexplicably) makes sense to some people to talk of "curriculum" independent of who teaches it, why he teaches it, to whom he teaches it, his conceptions of children and the nature of learning, and whether or not he has had any voice in its selection or is given the freedom to depart from it. Elsewhere (Sarason, 1966) I have illustrated and discussed this problem in relation to the "new math," emphasizing the point that how a curriculum is introduced to (and even foisted upon) teachers affects children, teachers, supervisors, and the "curriculum." What I am saying is obvious to any thinking graduate student, i.e., any graduate course is a function not only of the formal curriculum for that course and the particular instructor but also of the particular department, relationships within it, and characteristics of the particular university.

The second purpose which I must briefly discuss is that we are interested in two kinds of change: that which is introduced and executed by those indigenous to the school, and that which represents primarily forces outside the social system we call a school. We know far more about the latter than the former kind of change and this is symptomatic not only of our lack of knowledge about what goes on in a school but also of the implicit assumption that it is a static and not particularly complicated kind of setting. There are many people, including most psychologists who should know better, who view the school as they do (or would) a so-called primitive society, i.e., life in it is simple, the people in it relatively uncomplicated and easy to understand, and the surface appearance of order and purpose can be taken pretty much at face value. There are times when those of us at the Psycho-Educational Clinic wish that such a view of the school setting could indeed be justified because the more we have gotten into the problem the more impressed we have become with its complexity. We sometimes look back nostalgically at the days when we could think of studying the school in terms of what seemed to be discrete problems such as learning, socialization, intellectual development, the process of teaching, the formal curriculum, and the like. This is not to say that one cannot study these discrete problems in a profitable way, but one runs the risk of becoming a prisoner of one's limited theories and methodologies. It is not always made clear that theories—containing as they do a defined but limited set of variables and their presumed relationships—constrict one's scope at the same time as they expand it. Nowhere is this more true than in the literature on the school setting.

But the school is only one of several settings in which we have been able to observe processes of change. In relation to all these settings we have also been in the role of "advice givers," a role which illuminates not only the processes of change as they are reflected in the "advice seeker" but in the advice giver as well. The remainder of this paper contains observations and thoughts about processes of change as we have seen them in the role of observer and advice giver.

CHANGE AND IMPLEMENTATION

Some of the most interesting and important aspects of the processes of change are revealed before the point of implementation of proposals for change. The importance of these aspects resides not only in how they affect implementation *but in the degree to which they result in no implementation at all.* It is not enough for the person interested in processes of change in various types of organizations or social systems to focus on ongoing or planned changes, although there is no question that such a focus can be a productive one. It is my contention, however, that an equally important part of the problem is the frequency of, and the contexts which surround, proposals for change which either do not get a hearing or never reach the stage of implementation. I have no doubt that these instances are far more frequent than those which reach the stage of implementation. Organizations—such as a university department, a professional school, a social agency—vary tremendously among and between themselves in the degree to which proposals and ideas for change never reach the stage of discussion or implementation.

In recent months I have taken to asking members of various types of organizations what their estimate was of the relationship between proposals made and proposals implemented. The most frequent response was embarrassed silence. In some instances the embarrassment stemmed from the feeling that the question touched on something which, if pursued, would be quite revealing of that organization, and the revelation would not be very pleasant. In other instances the embarrassment was a consequence of the realization that the individual had never been aware of what was implied in the question, although I tried to ask the question without stating what I thought its implications were.

The significance of the question I have been putting to individuals may be gleaned in the following opinion: the greater the discrepancy between the frequency of proposals for change which are never implemented, and the number of proposals which are implemented, the more likely that the implemented changes over time will increasingly lose whatever innovative characteristics they may have had or were intended. In other words, the more things change on the surface the more conditions remain basically the same.

The basis for this opinion brings us back to one of the major interests of the Psycho-Educational Clinic, i.e., the culture of the school and the processes of change. It has been in relation to our work in various school systems that we have become acutely aware of how implemented changes quickly lose their innovative intent.[2] Elsewhere (Sarason, 1966) I have indicated that one of the major reasons for this self-defeating process is the tendency for change proposals to emanate from on high without taking into account the feelings and opinions of those who must implement the changes, i.e., the teachers. What I emphasized was the interpersonal turmoil which such tendencies engender and its effect on the content and goals of change. My comments, however, were in relation to the history and consequences of a single proposal for change (e.g., new math, bussing, etc.) and neglected what I now think is the more general characteristic of the system: the marked discrepancy between the number of proposals to change the system and the number of proposals actually implemented. Put in another way: The fate of any single proposal for change will be determined in part by the number of changes which have been proposed but never implemented. If this is true, my observations suggest that it is because those who have to implement any single proposal for change react to it in terms of their knowledge of and experiences with other proposals (implemented or not) for change in the system. If they are aware, rightly or wrongly, that there is a discrepancy between proposals made and implemented, and particularly if this awareness is associated with feelings of dissatisfaction, it often affects the implementation of the single proposal for change in a way so as to fulfill the prophecy that the more things change

---

[2] A colleague, Albert Myers, has well characterized urban school systems as the "fastest changing status quos."

the more they remain the same. The fate of a single proposal for change cannot be understood apart from all other proposals for change if only because those who do the implementing do not understand or react to it in that way—and any theory of change and innovation must face this inescapable fact.

The above observations and formulations stemmed in part from repeated experiences in the role of advice giver in relation to personnel in the school system. More candidly, they stemmed from a variety of frustrating and failure experiences in which, as I look back over them, I underestimated how much of an advice seeker's behavior reflected the system of which he was a part. I could, of course, be criticized as naïve. The point is that my naïveté reflects well the naïveté of psychological theories (e.g., learning, psychoanalytic) which do not face the fact that individual behavior always takes place in the contexts of organizations or social systems. I am not maintaining that social systems "cause" behavior. I am only maintaining that any theory which purports to explain behavior and which does not come to grips with man-system relationships is a naïve, incomplete, and mischief-producing theory.

THE ADVICE SEEKER AND ADVICE GIVER

The behavior of advice givers, like that of advice seekers, reflect man-system relationships. With increasing frequency, in ours as well as other societies, the advice giver is outside the system of the advice seeker, a fact which can markedly influence change and innovation. Put in its most concrete form the question which I would like to raise is: If somebody is interested in studying a social system (e.g., a school, a company, police department, etc.) with the intent of devising ways of changing it in some ways, and that somebody comes to you for advice and guidance, how would you go about deciding how to respond? Let us assume that you are relatively unfamiliar with the particular setting the individual wishes to study and ultimately change in some large or small way. This assumption provides an easy out for many people who feel uncomfortable thinking about problems with which they are not familiar. It may well be that these are the kinds of people who discourage students and others from getting into unfamiliar territory. I do not intend this as an *argumentum ad hominem* but as a way of stating that an unfamiliar problem—be it unfamiliar to a single advice giver or to the field at large—tends to engender reactions which serve to change the problem or to discourage the advice seeker. It is not at all necessary for the unfamiliar to be threatening in some personal way to the establishment. It is often sufficient that the proposal be unfamiliar, i.e., not capable of being assimilated by prevailing attitudes toward "important" problems.

Am I straying from the question by focusing initially on the response of an individual advice giver or field to an unfamiliar problem? There are at least two reasons why I do not think I have strayed. The first reason is that the fate of any proposal for change is not unrelated to the prevailing attitudes of the field to which the advice giver belongs. Although these attitudes may not always be decisive—the situation is much too complicated to permit one to focus exclusively on a single source or variable—they can or do play a role well before the time when the proposal for change reaches the point of implementation. It needs hardly to be pointed out that these prevailing attitudes can abort the proposed change even though the change involves a setting different from that in which the prevailing attitudes are found. The second reason I do not think I have strayed from the original question is, I think, less of a glimpse of the obvious than is the first reason. The relationship between the advice seeker, on the one hand, and the advice giver or field, on the other hand, is frequently identical to the relationship between the advice seeker and the setting which is the object of change. The point here is that a proposal for change far more often than not encounters an obstacle course and its ultimate fate, by whatever criteria this may be judged, must be viewed in terms of how the proposal changed as a function of each hurdle. We are far more aware of what happens once a proposal reaches the stage of implementation than we are of what happens to the proposed change (and changer) before that stage. A psychology of change and innovation cannot neglect these preimplementation events which, in my experience, frequently have the effect of insuring that changes will take place in a way so as to preclude innovation.

AN ILLUSTRATIVE CASE

A number of years ago in New Haven an organization was started the major aim of which was to develop programs and services for the inner city or poverty population. The name of this organization is Community Progress Inc. (CPI). Anyone familiar with community action programs is well aware that CPI was one of the first of such programs and is regarded as one of the, if not *the*, most successful and comprehensive of these ventures. CPI antedates many of the Federal programs and, in fact, a number of Federal programs are modeled on what CPI has done. In our recent book (Sarason et al., 1966) we described two of CPI's most pioneering and intriguing programs and the relationship of our clinic to these programs. One of these programs is the Neighborhood Employment Center and the other is the Work Crew Program for school dropouts. Most of the employees in these programs are nonprofessional personnel who are indigenous to the area and the population served. With very few exceptions no employee had previous experience in or training for the job he was doing. It is obviously impossible for me here to describe in any detail the nature of and rationale for these programs. Suffice it to say that the titles "Neighborhood Employment Center" and "Work Crew Programs" are distressingly ineffective in communicating the seriousness, variety, and complexity of the human problems which these programs encounter, cope with, and effectively handle. By "effectively handle" we mean that there is no reason to believe that the rate of success is any less than that in more traditional helping agencies. Our opinion is that when one takes into account the nature of the population served, the rate of success is somewhat short of amazing. It sometimes has offended some of our colleagues in the mental health professions when we have said that these two programs are truly mental health programs. But how can you call them mental health programs if they do not employ psychiatrists, clinical psychologists, and social workers? The obstacles to change or innovation—both in thinking and action—are many, and words and categorical thinking will be found high on the list.

How did these programs, reflecting as they do change and innovation, come about? Before answering this question I must tell you two things about CPI. First, the mental health professions had nothing to do with the beginnings of CPI. It would be near correct to say that CPI was begun and developed by a small group of individuals who had no previous formal training to do what they subsequently did. The second fact I must tell you is that today, a few years after CPI's existence, there is not a single mental health agency in New Haven whose thinking and practices have not been changed by what CPI has developed. This is not to say that these agencies have changed in a fundamental way but rather that to a limited extent they have adapted their way of thinking to new problems and new settings. This is not true for the Psycho-Educational Clinic and I hope it will not be taken as an expression of arrogance or presumption when I say that as in the case of those at CPI we at the Clinic are involved in problems and settings in ways which represent a deliberate break with our own pasts and professional training—as a result of which we have become quite knowledgeable about the interactions among the unfamiliar, anxiety, and resistances to change in self and others. I must add that the consequences of resistance are much less lethal to change, by which I mean here engaging in an activity one has not done before, than they are to innovation by which I mean sustaining the spirit or intent of change so that one recognizes that one has unlearned part of one's past and that the direction of one's future has thereby been influenced.

Now let us return to the original question via a fantasy I have sometimes had. Reformulated, the question is: what if CPI, as an advice seeker, came to me as an advice giver to respond to their initial plans to develop programs and services for the school dropouts and poverty population? In point of fact CPI did circulate a document containing a general statement of its aims in relation to its view of the problems with which it was to deal. This document was sent to me and I confess that I saw a lot in there that I considered presumptuous, if not grandiose, particularly in light of the fact that a program in "human renewal" was going to be attempted by people possessing no particular expertise in the dynamics of human behavior and the ways in which one goes about helping problem people. The fantasy I have had centers around the situation in which CPI learns that I think what they are planning to do is probably for the birds and that I was not prepared to give them my blessings. (In reality, of course, nobody was asking for my blessings or anything else I had to give them.) CPI comes running to my door and says, "O.K., you don't like what we want to do. You don't like the way we are thinking about the problems. What would you do?" That would have been the polite way they would phrase the question. The more legitimate way of phrasing the question—and fantasy is not noted for its close relation to reality—would have been: "What do your or your mental health colleagues who have not been involved with the poverty population have to suggest to us?" It is not important to relate in detail what I would have told them. Suffice it to say that what I would have recommended would have been an instance of translating an unfamiliar problem into familiar terms. I would have told them about clinics, diagnostic and treatment services, mental health professionals, and research and evaluation. The result, of course, would have been quite different from what they intended and subsequently implemented. Had they taken my advice some innovative programs which have had a pervasive and sustained effect around the country would have been scuttled, to the detriment of the populations served *and* the mental health fields.

SOME CONCLUDING COMMENTS

Social systems, large or small, are fantastically complicated. To describe and understand a single school, let alone a school system, presents staggering problems for methodology and theory. What I have attempted to do in this paper is to suggest that the complexity of these systems as well as some of their distinctive characteristics become quite clear as one focuses on how these systems change over time, particularly in relation to innovations which are sustained, or aborted, or in one or another way defeating of the aims of change. Perhaps the major import of this view is that at the same time that it illuminates features of the system it also makes clear how understanding of the behavior of the individual requires, in fact demands, conceptualization of man-system relationships. This is as true for the individual we call a psychologist as it is for anyone else. I tried to illustrate the point by focusing on the psychologist in the role of advice giver not only because the psychologist is so frequently related to processes of change in individuals or groups but because he so often is the contact point between different social systems or organizations, i.e., he illustrates the fact that processes of change frequently (if not always) involve interacting systems. An additional factor in focusing on the psychologist is that it is too easy to overlook that whatever conceptualizations we develop will have to be as relevant for psychology and psychologists as for any individual in any other social system.

At the beginning of this chapter I ventured the opinion that there are probably no important facets of a psychologist's existence which do not reflect the influence of his relationship to one or another type of organization. I would at this point venture the additional hypothesis that there is not a single psychologist who has not at some time or another been involved in initiating or administering proposals for change in some organization. Whatever his role, I would predict that if we ever studied the psychologist in relation to processes of change in various types of organizations we would be impressed by two findings. First, psychologists are as good as anybody else in initiating change and as bad as everybody else in sustaining it in a way such that "the more things change the more they remain the same." Second, in relation to these changes the behavior of most psychologists will be found to be remarkably uninfluenced by knowledge of or concern for relationships between change and innovation, on the one hand, and complexity of social systems, on the other.

The distinction between processes of change and innovation as they occur in organized settings is fundamental to understanding how these settings work. It is a distinction which has profitably occupied the thinking of those interested in child development, e.g., the concept of stages implies a distinction between change and innovation. As this distinction is applied to the most important social systems with which we are or have been related, our understanding of these systems *and* the individuals in it will take on an innovative characteristic. I have no doubt that this will be particularly true in the case of the social system we call a school.

The last point brings me, finally, to a consideration to which I have only alluded earlier in this chapter. One can characterize our society as one in which massive and deliberate attempts are being made to change aspects of the nature of groups, settings, and regions within as well as beyond our society. The schools, the Negro, the poverty population, Appalachia, the public mental hospital—these are only some of the more important objects of change. Being, as most of us are, for virtue and against sin we applaud and support these programs for change. We know something is being done because billions are being spent. For what it is worth, it is my opinion, based on some extensive observations, that much is being done but little of it in a way calculated to bring about changes which sustain the intent to innovate. I do not say this in the spirit of criticism, but rather as a way of suggesting that, among many reasons, two of them are: the absence of a psychology of change and innovation, and the tendency within psychology to develop molecular theories about molecular-sized problems. In relation to the latter reason it is necessary to state that however necessary it may be at times to restrict the scope of theorizing by grasping a part of the problem and sticking with it, there is the distinct danger that over time the part unwittingly becomes the whole of the problem.

REFERENCES

Sarason, S. B. (1966). The culture of the school and processes of change. Brechbill Lecture, University of Maryland School of Education, January.

Sarason, S. B., Levine, M., Goldenberg, I. I., Cherlin, D., & Bennett, E. (1966). *Psychology in community settings: Clinical, education, vocational, social aspects.* New York: Wiley.

Stagner, R. (1966). Book review. *Contemporary Psychology, 11,* 145–150.

2

PUBLIC POLICY AND PUBLIC SERVICE: OUR PROFESSIONAL DUTY

PATRICK H. DELEON

During the past decade and a half that I have worked on Capitol Hill, I have been impressed both by psychology's potential contribution to society and by psychologists' collective unwillingness to participate in the public policy and political processes (DeLeon, 1986; DeLeon & VandenBos, 1984). Fortunately, there are signs that as a profession psychology is finally maturing and that we psychologists are beginning to accept our societal responsibility to be involved in determining the nation's health care priorities. I believe that this is as it should be; I am convinced that behavioral science expertise should be of prime consideration in developing educational and health care programs. What we teach our graduate students during their seven-year maturation process is of considerable value to society and to policymakers. We are beginning to appreciate the significance of the fact that the vast majority of the nation's elected officials (those who ultimately establish national health care policies) are attorneys by professional background. For example, in the U.S. Senate, there are only two Senators who have received in-depth training in health care: a veterinarian and a clinical social worker. We are beginning to understand

Reprinted from *American Psychologist*, 43, 309–315. Copyright 1988 by the American Psychological Association.

This chapter was originally presented as a Distinguished Professional Contributions award address at the meeting of the American Psychological Association in New York City, August 1987.

that continuing to assume that many of their colleagues in the Senate appreciate the nuances of health (or mental health) care would be a tragic mistake, both for our profession and for society.

One of the first published articles exploring the career paths of the approximately 25 psychologists who participated in congressional fellowships (and who generally were in a position to remain on Capitol Hill if they so desired) reported that only two individuals had remained with the Congress for longer than three years (DeLeon, Frohboese, & Meyers, 1984). In going through the original selection procedure, each of these psychologists had expressed considerable personal interest in the legislative and public policy processes. Yet, once they obtained first-hand knowledge of Capitol Hill and were able to participate actively in the political process, very few decided to stay. Why? How did their experience not match their expectations? What is it about their professional training that did not prepare them for involvement in public policy (DeLeon, 1983; DeLeon, Forsythe, & VandenBos, 1986)?

Not surprisingly, psychology's involvement in the legislative process is also found to be minimal from another vantage point. For example, in 1983, of the 155 public witnesses who appeared before the Senate Appropriations Subcommittee (which has jurisdiction over the Departments of Labor, Health and Human Services, and Education and which thus should be of considerable interest to psychology), there were only four psychologists who testified, and of those four, only two identified themselves as being psychologists (DeLeon, 1986).

Today, not only does the American Psychological Association (APA) Congressional Science Fellowship program continue to place two individuals each year on Capitol Hill, but more significantly, there has been a steadily growing number of psychologists (and other nonphysician health care providers, such as nurses and social workers) who have remained on Capitol Hill. The Senate committees that these individuals staff (or have recently staffed) include the Labor and Human Resources Committee, the Select Committee on Indian Affairs, the Veterans' Affairs Committee, the Committee on the Judiciary, and the Committee on Appropriations. In the U.S. House of Representatives, psychologists presently work on the staff of the Committee on Education and Labor, the Select Committee on Aging, and the Committee on Government Operations. Furthermore, a growing number of nonphysician health professionals also serve on the personal and policy staffs of various senators and representatives. These increases represent considerable progress; as a critical mass of these individuals develops, the potential will exist for fostering a wide range of truly creative interdisciplinary initiatives. Unfortunately, with only rare exceptions, these individuals have not yet begun to work together systematically, nor have they sought to develop coordinated policy agendas. It should be acknowledged, in retrospect, that none of their national associations (including the

APA) has taken the lead in fostering greater rapport or a coordinated agenda. However, this really is not surprising, as true interdisciplinary cooperation among the nonphysician disciplines is only just beginning to develop at the national level.

Yet, as I have indicated, considerable progress has been made. In 1987, in one week, the APA arranged for seven psychologists to testify before the House and Senate Appropriations Committees. This time all of these individuals identified themselves as psychologists. Their testimony covered an impressive range of expertise, including the psychosocial aspects of the acquired immune deficiency syndrome (AIDS), mental health research and clinical training, and the psychological relevance of National Institutes of Health (NIH) funding. Similarly, the "grass roots" leadership of the APA professional directorate systematically has begun to visit Capitol Hill during their annual meeting. At the 1987 APA convention in New York City, a number of local and national political figures participated actively. There appears to be genuine and growing interest among psychologists in public policy and the political process (Jarrett & Fairbank, 1987; Reppuci, 1985).

Perhaps there is good reason (i.e., justification) for the fact that our profession has just begun to become more involved in the public policy arena. One realizes, upon reflection, that there are very few psychology training programs that are oriented toward public policy (Forman & O'Malley, 1984). When the National Institute of Mental Health (NIMH) has announced initiatives in public policy training, they have been oriented to psychiatry exclusively. Moreover, it is only since 1977 (when the State of Missouri finally enacted its Psychology Practice Act) that psychology has been licensed to practice autonomously as a health care discipline in every state and jurisdiction in the nation. Whatever the justification for just beginning, we must continue the maturation process and accelerate our efforts.

TOWARD AN INTEGRATED PUBLIC SERVICE/PUBLIC POLICY IDENTITY

During the past year, I have been honored to serve as president of two of APA's larger divisions (Clinical Psychology and Psychotherapy). Both in that capacity and in preparing this address, I have attempted to pull together my thoughts on psychology and public service. For me, public service and public policy are intimately intertwined. To serve the public good, or "to give psychology away" (Bevan, 1980, 1982; Miller, 1969), is an integral element of our Association's bylaws. This is something that has been very important to me throughout my professional career. Yet, I must admit that I cannot readily integrate my thoughts. Try as I might, I cannot yet identify a coherent and integrated public service/public policy component within organized psychology. As members of a profession, we spend countless hours on numerous intraprofessional issues, such as the proposed reorganization of APA, potential candidates for various governance positions, and so on. However, comparatively little effort is spent debating issues that might have a real impact on society at large. If one looks closely at our legislative agendas, it becomes evident that we often do not really understand how the programs that we wish to modify actually affect beneficiaries. We have not been as involved in the "people-oriented" programs as we collectively wish to believe. Perhaps this focus on ourselves is inherent to the nature of a professional organization. Perhaps the very structure of our meetings and governance dictates that the priorities have to be on intraprofessional issues. However, it would be refreshing and, I believe, fruitful to spend more time on issues that truly reflect the "public good." We really do have much to offer.

There are, of course, a number of individual psychologists who have served the "public good" in an admirable fashion. Individual psychologists have achieved positions of considerable public trust and responsibility. Indeed, one Secretary of the then Department of Health, Education, and Welfare was a psychologist. Nearly one third of the current chief state mental health officers are psychologists. Our colleagues serve as vice presidents of major medical teaching facilities and educational institutions. Yet, very rarely do these individuals describe themselves as psychologists *per se*. Once they have obtained positions of significant public trust (and authority), rarely do they actively promote psychology as a profession or a knowledge base. Indeed, it has been my observation that, if anything, they tend to "hold psychology to a higher standard" than their medical colleagues. They act as if to proclaim their psychological heritage openly would provide their enemies with ammunition to be used against them. I have also noticed that rarely do members of the psychological community seek out the unique expertise of psychologists in public leadership positions. Why is it that we do not collectively hold out these individuals as respected role models? Why do our professional training institutions fail to capitalize on their collective successes in order to systematically develop a future cadre of high level public service professionals? What is there about our training models that prevents us from seeing the inherent opportunities both for our own profession and for society at large? Perhaps we do not really believe that what we have learned in graduate school and in subsequent employment experiences is of significant societal value.

AN INTEGRATED HEALTH DELIVERY SYSTEM

For many reasons, not the least of which is the ever escalating cost of health care (Dörken & DeLeon, 1986), psychology is becoming more and more integrated into the nation's overall health care system. The time is rapidly approaching when the traditional fee-for-service, solo practice (or psychotherapy cottage industry) that most of us are familiar with will simply no longer exist. Instead, reimbursement for psychological services will be directly tied to being able to demonstrate objectively that the particular services rendered were both cost effective and the "treatment of choice." A similar evolution toward accountability is presently underway within the more general health care system and is reflected in the growth and expressed reliance on such new conceptual developments as peer review organizations and managed systems of health care (health maintenance organizations and individual practice associations, for example); the notion of practicing *through* a comprehensive institution, rather than in separate and discrete inpatient and outpatient facilities; and the expressed policy concerns surrounding dramatic variations that exist in certain medical procedures (U.S. Senate, 1985). In my judgment, this is a very positive evolution, especially for the ultimate consumer (i.e., the patient). It also speaks well for the future of psychology, which is, above all, a data-based profession. Yet, it is an evolution that generates considerable anxiety and concern within the provider community.

As our profession grows in numbers and becomes more integrated into the general health care system, it will become increasingly necessary for us collectively to address a number of conceptual issues that we, unlike our colleagues in medicine, have not considered in the past. An underlying critical issue will be "What is the real difference between the practice of psychology and that of medicine?" As long as we psychologists were able to practice in what was essentially a policy vacuum, this was merely an academic or philosophical concern. However, as economic forces drive us toward an integrated (and interdisciplinary) practice, this issue cannot continue to be ignored (Wickramasekera, 1984). We profess that our students can autonomously "diagnose and treat," but do we really mean that? Are we willing, for example, to provide them with the technical training necessary to be able to prescribe sometimes necessary (or even preferable) psychotropic medications? How do we propose that the different levels of psychological expertise be reimbursed? Are all psychologists supposed to be equals? Will we evolve toward different psychological specialties, similar to those in effect for medicine, with different rates of reimbursement? Will we seek to define meaningful roles for "psychological assistants" and provide special pay bonuses for those of our colleagues who have achieved higher levels of skill, as demonstrated by their obtaining board certification? Each of these questions has already been answered (for themselves) by our colleagues in medicine.

In order to survive as a profession, we must, of course, continue to seek to modify all federal and state legislation that precludes psychologists from functioning to the fullest extent of our training, as reflected in our various state psychology practice acts. Toward this end, we have been remarkably successful at the federal level in obtaining parity with medicine under most of the initiatives in which the federal government acts as the "payer of the bill," that is, under the Department of Defense Civilian Health and Medical Program of the Uniformed Services (CHAMPUS; 10 U.S.C. 1071–1089), the Federal Employees' Health Benefit Act (FEHBA, 5 U.S.C. 8902J), various programs of the Veterans administration, and the Medical Expense provisions of the Income Tax code (26 U.S.C. 213; DeLeon, VandenBos, & Kraut, 1986). We have also been successful in modifying most (but again, not all) of the other relevant federal statutes, including the competency provisions of the Federal Criminal Code (PL 98-473), and various health personnel training initiatives. We have also been able to establish the concept of "psychological injury" within the Federal Workers Compensation Act (5 U.S.C. 8101(2)–8101(3)) and various Social Security (PL 98-460) determinations. We have recently been especially successful within the judicial area, including appropriate modification of all relevant policy positions of the American Bar Association.

We have been remiss, however, in ensuring that the nation's disabled, elderly, and poor citizens will have direct access to quality psychological care. I am, of course, referring to Medicare and Medicaid, which make up approximately 90% of the federal government's health expenditures. Unless we are ultimately successful in obtaining professional parity under these programs, we must expect our earlier successes in both the private and public sector to slowly erode. In 1987, for example, the Health Care Financing Administration (HCFA), which administers the programs, relied on a 1965 provision of the Medicare Act in drafting its Hospital "Conditions of Participation" to require that all inpatients must be under the clinical care of a physician. HCFA did this notwithstanding various state laws that authorize nonphysicians to practice in hospitals and notwithstanding different reimbursement policies and regulations of private insurance plans and other federal programs, such as CHAMPUS and FEHBA. I might further point out that in drafting their regulations and eventually in overriding CHAMPUS policy, HCFA officials never even discussed the impact on psychological care with the appropriate officials of the Department of Defense or with the congressional committees that have jurisdiction over the other federal health programs.

For the past 15 years, Senator Inouye has introduced legislation (S. 123) that would provide psychologists with professional autonomy under Medicare. In the mid-1970s, nearly one third of the U.S. Senate "cosponsored" this legislation; in the 1985–1986 session of Congress, *no senator* did, other than Senator Inouye. Why? Why was there so little congressional interest in legislation that is so important to psychology's very future? I think that there are essentially two related, but different, reasons. First, as members of a profession, we psychologists really are only just beginning to become involved in the public policy and legislative processes. The vast majority of psychologists are simply not familiar with the political process, and they do not know how to influence that process. Because this particular legislation did not pass the first time it was introduced, psychologists gave up on it. They have not recognized the significance of this particular bill to them or that passage of such legislation requires sustained attention from those concerned.

The second reason, and perhaps the more fundamental one, is that very few psychologists are really involved in (or focus on) the societal impact of what the profession can offer. Thus, until very recently, psychologists have not collectively been actively working with the nation's elderly (or disabled citizens). As a result, we are really not aware of the programs that affect them, even if these same programs are extraordinarily important to our own profession. Similarly, one can view the almost miniscule recognition of psychological services under the various state Medicaid programs as reflecting the same lack of professional involvement. Not enough of us are working with those who are eligible for Medicaid to really care if our profession's services are covered. In a very real sense, for us not to be involved is almost to ensure that we never will be. Yet, this is one of the most rapidly growing federal initiatives; Medicaid presently costs the federal and state governments $50 billion a year.

During the closing hours of the first session of the 100th Congress, H.R. 3545, the Budget Reconciliation Act of 1987 (PL 100-203), was passed. This bill included four psychology-related Medicare provisions. Psychology was formally recognized under the Rural Health Clinic provisions in the same manner that nurse practitioners and physician assistants have been since the late 1970s. It was also made expressly clear that hospitals could bill for "psychological services" under the Part A (inpatient) provisions of Medicare. Perhaps most important, however, were the two remaining provisions. First, the provisions of the HCFA Hospital "Conditions of Participation" requiring patients to be under the care of a physician were specifically limited to apply only to Medicare inpatients and no longer to all inpatients, as HCFA had proposed. In enacting this particular provision, the conferees noted that the new provision was clearly intended to allow state law to govern the scope of psychology's practice within hospitals when the provisions for reimbursement were other than Medicare. Without this modification, psychology's increasing efforts to enact hospital practice legislation would have been completely curtailed by federal preemption. The last provision authorized psychologists in community mental health centers to be directly reimbursable under Medicare (without physician involvement) and directed the Secretary of the Department of Health and Human Services to establish a national fee schedule for psychology's services. These are major steps toward psychology's ultimate total independent recognition under Medicare. They represent considerable effort by the profession, reflected also in the fact that 20 senators had agreed during 1987 to cosponsor S. 123. But as the implications of the national fee schedule for psychology suggest, there is much more to be done than most of us realize.

THE PSYCHOLOGY–NURSING INTERFACE

As psychology becomes more involved in the nation's overall health care system, I believe we psychologists should actively seek strong alliances with those in professional nursing (DeLeon, Kjervik, Kraut, & VandenBos, 1985; Keller & Baumann, 1986; Mitchell, Barnard, Booth, Magyary, & Spieker, 1986). Not only do the two disciplines have many similar interests, but also they complement each other quite nicely. Both, in an evolutionary sense, are just coming into their own.

In 1977, when President Carter signed Executive Order No. 11973 and thereby established his President's Commission on Mental Health, there were approximately 25,000 doctoral-level health care provider psychologists (and 26,000 psychiatrists). The most recent figures, which are from 1985, indicate 45,500 practicing psychologists (and 39,000 psychiatrists; G. R. VandenBos, personal communication, August 1987). Similarly, it was only in 1965 that the first nurse practitioner (i.e., autonomous nursing provider) program was established. Today, there are approximately 17,400 nurse practitioners and certified nurse midwives practicing in the United States (U.S. Congress, 1986).

On the one hand, these numbers might be considered insignificant in comparison with the estimated 506,000 physicians practicing in the United States. However, collectively both psychology and nursing bring a whole new perspective to what should be considered "quality of care" within the health care field (DeLeon & VandenBos, 1983). These practitioners are especially attuned to the psychosocial aspects of health care and to issues that might be considered most relevant to one's overall "quality of life." This new orientation is of considerable relevance to health policy because the nation's population is continuing to age—with a projected increase of those over 65 from the current 11% to nearly 21% of the population by the year 2030. Health care will more often involve chronic conditions (U.S. Senate, 1986).

At the 1987 APA convention, there was one symposium that especially intrigued me. It represented the beginning stages of systematically exploring the potential relationships between nursing and psychology and was an outgrowth of a special multidivisional task force on nursing and psychology, chaired by Susan Mikesell, who is herself a nurse-psychologist. The panel included a representative from a joint psychology–nursing program at the University of Wisconsin-Madison, in which the School of

Nursing, in collaboration with the Department of Psychology, ultimately awards both degrees to qualified candidates; the Director of the National Center for Nursing Research, at the National Institutes of Health, who enumerated many possible areas of joint involvement, including the psychosocial aspects (and ethical considerations) surrounding AIDS; and a nurse-psychologist who described the dramatically different training models to which she had been exposed. This last speaker described her nursing training as emphasizing "compassion," whereas her psychology training stressed "objectivity and empirical values."

This symposium was fascinating. The participants were exploring an area just beginning to evolve, with no obvious set ground rules or preconceived limitations. Nursing was slightly ahead of psychology in establishing clinical training homes "of its own" (Rodgers, 1980), and psychology possessed a stronger empirical scientific knowledge base. It was reported that the task force had already identified slightly over 60 nurse-psychologists, but that there might even be as many as 1,000. Clearly, most of these individuals defined themselves as representing one discipline or the other, with very few individuals focusing on the joint nature of their training. The audience was predominantly female, although there was one male psychology professor who was employed on a nursing school faculty. The range of relevant health issues was quite broad, with such topics as premature births, intensive prenatal care, chronic health problems, women's health issues, death and dying, and numerous ethical considerations being considered especially relevant.

PSYCHOTROPIC MEDICATIONS

In addressing the Hawaii Psychological Association in 1984, Senator Inouye concluded his remarks by stating,

> Finally, I would like to suggest an entirely new legislative agenda which I think fits very nicely into the theme of your convention: "Psychology in the 80's: Transcending Traditional Boundaries." As a United States Senator, I have also been working closely during the past decade with a number of your "natural allies." I am particularly thinking of our nation's nurse practitioners, nurse midwives, and optometrists. The members of these professions have been successful to differing degrees in amending their state practice acts to allow them to independently utilize drugs where appropriate. . . . In my judgment, when you have obtained this statutory authority, you will really have made the big time. Then, you truly will be an autonomous profession and your clients will be well-served.

At approximately the same time, Richard Samuels (1985), in his leadership capacity within the Division of Independent Practice, also raised the question of psychologists' prescribing psychotropic medications. Since then, the debate has continued and intensified at the national level, and it has become quite evident that this is a highly emotional issue for professional psychology.

In my judgment, there is no question that psychologists can, and should, accept this authority and responsibility. One need only take a cursory look at the low quality of mental health care provided in the nation's nursing and boarding homes, and the documented substantial use (and abuse) of medication in special education classes, to develop excellent policy arguments for ensuring that those with developmental and behavioral science expertise have intimate knowledge of, and access to, psychotropic medications (Burns, DeLeon, Chemtob, Welch, & Samuels, 1988; Schroeder, Schroeder, & Landesman, 1987). As Ron Fox has pointed out on numerous occasions, it may have been prudent and politically expedient 40 years ago, when efforts were directed to passing the first psychology licensing law, to adopt a dualism that placed all "hands-on" (i.e., physical) interventions beyond the scope of practice of psychologists. Much has changed since then, and we should now rethink that position, especially in consideration of the interface between psychology and behavioral health (Fox, 1987; Matarazzo, 1982).

Presently, a number of the other nonphysician disciplines can prescribe certain medications, under certain conditions. For example, state practice acts for optometry in 48 states authorize optometrists to utilize drugs for diagnostic purposes; in 20 states, they are allowed access to designated drugs for both the diagnosis and treatment of certain eye conditions. It should be noted that their profession is much smaller numerically than psychology; there are 23,600 optometrists across the country. Twenty-one states have granted some form of prescriptive authority to qualified primary care nurse practitioners, again under various methods of control. Similarly, physician assistants are authorized in 19 states to utilize medications. Of course, dentists have been authorized to use certain medications for many, many years.

In the current debates within the psychological community on this issue, there are certain recurring themes. Unfortunately, the issue of what would truly be in the public interest does not appear to be paramount. Instead, it is argued that by pressing for prescription authority we psychologists will antagonize organized psychiatry (and thus organized medicine). This is probably correct, but I personally do not give this argument much weight. If we allow the concerns of another profession (especially one that is economically and emotionally competitive with ours) to dictate what we seek to do, then we truly deserve to be deemed "paraprofessionals." A second argument raises the following question: Because members of another profession have historically done such a poor job utilizing this particular clinical modality, why should we expect our graduates to be able to do any better? Again, I do not feel that the destiny of our profession should be controlled by how poorly (or how well) members of another profession have performed. Instead, we should strive to ensure that there is a behaviorally based rationale for the use of specific psychotherapeutic drugs and further, that their effect is accurately measured. That is, we should insist that psychotherapeutic treatments (with or without medications) be held to the general standard of being "safe, effective, and appropriate" (DeLeon, VandenBos, & Cummings, 1983). Many of those who argue against prescription privileges for psychologists have no notion of exactly how much additional training this would entail. They do not know, for example, how much training in medication our colleagues in medicine, dentistry, optometry, and nursing actually receive.

It is also quite evident that many of those who have engaged in this debate do not appreciate the diverse context of this issue. It was in 1935 (more than 50 years ago) that Indiana became the first state in the nation to authorize the use of drugs by optometrists. It is the various state legislatures and state public health authorities who must ultimately make this determination. There is a wide range of conditions and options under which the other nonphysician health care disciplines have incorporated prescription privileges into their state practice acts. Some of these statutes, for example, have ensured that there must be physician involvement and/or supervision; others have not. Some statutes have provided for prearranged protocols, with predetermined drugs and guidelines for their use; others have not. Some have focused on the expected locus of use, that is, whether the nonphysician practitioner will be functioning within an institution or on an outpatient basis. Some statutes require the active involvement of the state medical board; others do not. There are many ways in which a rational, data-based psychology prescription program could evolve.

There are at least two distinct approaches that psychology can follow to obtain prescription privileges. The first, which clearly is occurring presently, is to ensure that there develops a critical mass of practicing psychologists who are sufficiently comfortable with, and sophisticated in, the use of medication. Eventually, it will become evident to the various state legislatures that these individuals should be deemed authorized to use this clinical modality. This *informal* educational approach has been adopted by the larger practice divisions, and, as a result, relevant symposia and workshops are becoming increasingly evident at their midwinter meetings and the annual APA national convention. Although similar efforts to educate future practitioners (i.e., current students in the various professional schools) have not yet evolved, it is evident that such training is receiving serious consideration by the professional school leadership. An obvious advantage of this informal approach is that it provides the members of the profession with sufficient time to continue debating the issue and thus to ensure that most practitioners eventually become comfortable with the notion. Furthermore, psychologists will have time to explore alternative ways to address such related and complex issues as malpractice insurance premiums and continuing education requirements.

A slightly different approach, and one that truly requires the active cooperation of our profession's training institutions, is to proceed with modifying the various state practice acts so that "appropriately trained" psychologists will be authorized to prescribe "such psychotropic medications, and under such conditions, as the psychology licensure board shall designate." This approach requires a more *formal* training component and further requires that we begin now to address a number of issues (such as the types of medications we want and under what conditions) that we might otherwise defer facing. Once such "enabling statutes" are enacted into public law, it would then become the legal responsibility of psychology state licensing boards, in conjunction with relevant training programs, to develop appropriate curricula. It should be noted that nothing in this approach would preclude schools of medicine or other nonphysician training institutions (such as school of nursing) from offering "qualified training" curricula. This formal approach truly legitimizes psychology's efforts to obtain prescription privileges, and it is the process that ultimately will be required.

I think that the authority for psychology to utilize certain psychotropic medications will probably first pass in one of the smaller rural states where a compelling "access" argument can be made. I would also note that a number of our professional colleagues, (i.e., those who possess degrees in both nursing and psychology) can already legally prescribe certain psychotropic medications. Unfortunately, however, they have not actively contributed to the debate, either regarding the extent of additional training that they feel may be necessary or the flexibility that this clinical modality has provided to their practices. If psychologists are to be able to "diagnose and treat" independently, then we should not continue to accept any arbitrary limitation on our practice, merely because this might have been acceptable a number of years ago. Instead, we should continually strive to ensure that the consumer of our services has ready access to the most current "state of the art" mental health care available.

A NOTE OF APPRECIATION

The past several years have been increasingly productive for psychology on the legislative and public policy front. In many ways, one might say that we psychologists are finally beginning to accept our public and societal responsibilities. Much of the credit must go to those within the APA Central Office, and especially to the heads of the three new directorates: Alan Kraut, Bryant Welch, and James Jones. Without the countless hours of effort that they and their staffs have contributed to our profession, we simply would never have begun to approach our potential. There are always reasons not to follow unfamiliar paths, and we are most fortunate that APA's Executive Vice President and Chief Executive Officer, Len Goodstein, has continued to actively encourage all of us to excel.

REFERENCES

Bevan, W. (1980). On getting in bed with a lion. *American Psychologist, 35,* 779–789.

Bevan, W. (1982). A sermon of sorts in three plus parts. *American Psychologist, 37,* 1303–1322.

Budget Reconciliation Act, Pub. L. No. 100-203 (1987).

Burns, S. M., DeLeon, P. H., Chemtob, C. M., Welch, B. L., & Samuels, R. M. (1988). Psychotropic medication: A new technique for psychology? *Psychotherapy: Research, Practice, and Training, 25*(4), 508–515.

Civilian Health and Medical Program of the Uniformed Services, 10 U.S.C. 1071–1089.

DeLeon, P. H. (1983). The changing and creating of legislation: The political process. In B. Sales (Ed.), *The professional psychologist's handbook* (pp. 601–620). New York: Plenum.

DeLeon, P. H. (1986). Increasing the societal contribution of organized psychology. *American Psychologist, 41,* 466–474.

DeLeon, P. H., Forsythe, P., & VandenBos, G. R. (1986). Federal recognition of psychology in rehabilitation programs. *Rehabilitation Psychology, 31,* 47–56.

DeLeon, P. H., Frohboese, R., & Meyers, J. C. (1984). Psychologists on Capitol Hill: A unique use of the skills of the scientist/practitioner. *Professional Psychology, 15,* 697–705.

DeLeon, P. H., Kjervik, D. K., Kraut, A. G., & VandenBos, G. R. (1985). Psychology and nursing: A natural alliance. *American Psychologist, 40,* 1153–1164.

DeLeon, P. H., & VandenBos, G. R. (1983). The new federal health care frontiers—Cost containment and "wellness." *Psychotherapy in Private Practice, 1*(2), 17–32.

DeLeon, P. H., & VandenBos, G. R. (1984). Public health policy and behavioral health. In J. D. Matarazzo, S. M. Weiss, J. A. Herd, N. E. Miller, & S. M. Weiss (Eds.), *Behavioral health: A handbook of health enhancement and disease prevention* (pp. 150–163). New York: Wiley.

DeLeon, P. H., VandenBos, G. R., & Cummings, N. A. (1983). Psychotherapy—Is it safe, effective, and appropriate? The beginning of an evolutionary dialogue. *American Psychologist, 38,* 907–911.

DeLeon, P. H., VandenBos, G. R., & Kraut, A. G. (1986). Federal recognition of psychology as a profession. In H. Dörken and Associates (Eds.), *Professional psychology in transition: Meeting today's challenges* (pp. 99–117). San Francisco: Jossey-Bass.

Dörken, H., & DeLeon, P. H. (1986). Cost as the driving force in health care reform. In H. Dörken and Associates (Eds.), *Professional psychology in transition: Meeting today's challenges* (pp. 313–349). San Francisco: Jossey-Bass.

Federal Criminal Code, Competency Provisions, Pub. L. No. 98-473.

Federal Employees' Health Benefit Act, 5 U.S.C. 8902J.

Federal Workers' Compensation Act, 5 U.S.C. 8101(2)–8101(3).

Forman, S. G., & O'Malley, P. L. (1984). A legislative field experience for psychology graduate students. *Professional Psychology: Research and Practice, 15,* 324–332.

Fox, R. E. (1987, March). *Prescription privileges: Their implications for the practice of psychology.* Invited address at the Division 29 Midwinter Meeting, New Orleans.

Inouye, D. K. (1984, November). Invited address at the Hawaii Psychological Association Annual Convention, Honolulu.

Jarrett, R. B., & Fairbank, J. A. (1987). Psychologists' views: APA advocacy of and resource expenditure on social and professional issues. *Professional Psychology: Research and Practice, 18,* 643–646.

Keller, M. L., & Baumann, L. J. (1986). Comment: Further comments on psychology and nursing. *American Psychologist, 41,* 1169–1170.

Matarazzo, J. D. (1982). Behavioral health's challenges to academic, scientific, and professional psychology. *American Psychologist, 37,* 1–14.

Medical Expense provisions of the Income Tax Code, 26 U.S.C. 213.

Miller, G. A. (1969). Psychology as a means of promoting human welfare. *American Psychologist, 24,* 1063–1075.

Mitchell, S. K., Barnard, K. E., Booth, C. L., Magyary, D. L., & Spieker, S. J. (1986). Comment: The natural alliance of psychology and nursing: Substance as well as practice. *American Psychologist, 41,* 1170.

Repucci, N. D. (1985). Psychology in the public interest. In A. M. Rogers & C. J. Scheirer (Eds.), G. *Stanley Hall Lecture series* (Vol. 5, pp. 122–156). Washington, DC: American Psychological Association.

Rodgers, D. A. (1980). The status of psychologists in hospitals: Technicians or professionals. *Clinical Psychologist, 33*(4), 5–7.

Samuels, R. M. (1985). From the president: A prescription for psychologists. *The Independent Practitioner, 5*(3), 2–3.

Schroeder, S. R., Schroeder, C. S., & Landesman, S. (1987). Psychological services in educational settings to persons with mental retardation. *American Psychologist, 42,* 805–808.

U.S. Congress, Office of Technology Assessment (1986). *Nurse practitioners, physician assistants, and certified nurse-midwives: A policy analysis* (Health Technology Case Study 37, OTA-HCS-37). Washington, DC: U.S. Government Printing Office.

U.S. Senate. (1985). *Variations in medical practice: Hearing before a subcommittee of the Committee on Appropriations* (S. Hrg. 98-1239). Washington, DC: U.S. Government Printing Office.

U.S. Senate. (1986). *The health status and health care needs of older Americans: An information paper* (Special Committee on Aging, Serial No. 99-L). Washington, DC: U.S. Government Printing Office.

Wickramasekera, I. E. (1984). Are health psychologists physicians? [Review of *Migraine: Psychological, psychiatric and physiological aspects*]. *Contemporary Psychology, 29,* 821.

3

PSYCHOLOGY AND PUBLIC POLICY IN THE "HEALTH CARE REVOLUTION"

CHARLES A. KIESLER and TERU L. MORTON

Health policy is in a state of upheaval in the United States, brought about by the so-called "health care revolution." The rapid evolution of health policy has potentially dramatic implications for psychologists, as scientists, professionals, and advocates. In this article, we first review changes in health care and policy, and then we discuss the potential implications for mental health care and policy. Last, we describe the ways in which these potential changes challenge the field of psychology across its full breadth of service, research, and education.

SPIRALING COSTS AND THE PRESS FOR COST CONTAINMENT

The health care revolution has in fact been occurring for the last decade or so (Bevan, 1982). The roots of this revolution have been the spiraling costs for health care in the United States. In 1965, when Medicare and Medicaid were established, national health care costs were $38

Reprinted from *American Psychologist, 43*, 993–1003. Copyright 1988 by the American Psychological Association.

Preparation of this chapter was supported by National Institute of Mental Health Grant 41672-04.

billion (6% of the gross national product [GNP]). By 1982, they were $355 billion (nearly 11% of the GNP), and they are projected to rise to $750 billion (12% of the GNP) by 1990 (Flinn, McMahon, & Collins, 1987). From 1979 to 1982 alone, hospital costs increased 19.2% per year (Uyeda & Moldawsky, 1986).

By 1984, the year in which Medicare introduced the prospective payment system, American corporations were paying $90 billion in health insurance premiums. This sum represented 38% of pretax profits—more than was paid to shareholders in dividends (Califano, 1986). At present, 10% of the federal budget and 20% of the recent growth in the budget is in Medicare and Medicaid (Short & Goldfarb, 1987).

Several major factors have contributed to increased costs of American health care. First among these has been our traditional model of insurance (VandenBos, 1983). In the United States, health insurance has developed largely as a passive risk-sharing system, based on a casualty model of insurance. Later, we describe alternative insurance models used in other countries.

Health planning has been, as Stuart Eizenstat put it, "ad hoc. There are bursts of initiative that come, like Medicaid. But they come without any real planning, without fully recognizing how they fit in with other similar programs" (in Bevan, 1982, p. 1129). Our de facto health care system has, over the years, had a number of inflationary features added, such as cost-based reimbursement, fee for service, and incentives that favor inpatient care. Employee health costs were also tax-exempt to the corporation (and to a lesser extent, the consumer), making consumers less price sensitive and the health care market relatively "income/price inelastic."[1]

Certain of America's health-related values have also been implicated in our high and rising health care costs: (a) Health care is viewed as a basic human right in this country; (b) our traditional model of health care has been authoritarian—the prototypic paternalistic doctor and passive patient, as in "doctor knows best," and "doctor's orders"; and (c) the matter of health-care resource consumption has been largely based on the philosophy that "if some is good, more must be even better."

Greater access to providers and broader insurance coverage has spurred more resource utilization and therefore costs. The National Center for Health Statistics has estimated that one third of the increase in health care costs from 1965 to 1980 was due to an increase in services provided (VandenBos, 1983). In reviewing major changes in health services, Aiken and Marx (1982) found that new benefits consistently stimulate greater demand for services than originally anticipated and that new categories of

---

[1]Income/price elasticity is a term used in economics to describe how buying changes as a function of changes in the price of the product and/or the income of the purchaser. Thus, when inelastic, buyers will not change their behavior much when their income rises and/or the price of the product falls.

patients not originally considered to need them suddenly claim those services as a right.

Many groups involved have begun to look at new overall methods of funding and insuring health (and mental health) care. Comparison between the funding bases for the United States and Great Britain has been resurrected with the new sensitivities of the 1980s. In the United States, we ration the first dollar of health care cost but insure later dollars (Merrill, 1987). Catastrophic insurance is the most extreme form of this type of insurance. Designed to reimburse only for the most serious disorders, it is one of the most expensive forms of health insurance (Zook, Moore, & Zeckhauser, 1981). The English system, on the other hand, reimburses the first dollar but not necessarily the last. The English national health system thus provides free care for initial treatment but does not guarantee payment for expensive treatment—dialysis, for example. The choice of the United States to insure last dollar costs results in the irony that early (and inexpensive) detection and treatment of progressive disorders is not reimbursable for indigent citizens, but they can get very expensive care once their health has deteriorated sufficiently.

American values regarding health are being reexamined. Debate issues include the following: Is health care a right or a privilege? Where should the focus of responsibility and choice be placed—on the patient or the physician? What kind of health care rationing is appropriate and how should it be implemented? Next we highlight a few of the main themes of our rapidly changing world of health policy and practice.

HIGHLIGHTS OF THE HEALTH CARE REVOLUTION

In this section, we review (a) some initial primitive cost containment efforts, such as patient-oriented risk shifting and provider-oriented risk capitation; (b) the organizational restructuring by providers that ensued, such as corporatization, diversification, and vertical integration; and (c) certain emergent features of this decade's pro-competitive market, including the imperfect supply–demand relationship, regulated markets, and changing power bases.

Cost-Containment Efforts

The current press for less expensive but adequate health care is felt by the full range of interested parties: third party payers, large employers, the government, and consumers. Indeed, large employers may be choosing self-insurance and creating their own comprehensive health plans. The government is considering both insurance cuts and incentives designed to make consumers more responsible for health care and maintenance. The consumers are angry at what they perceive as exorbitant medical charges (Rundle, 1987).

Two primary approaches have dominated efforts at cost containment: risk shifting and risk capitation. In each case, the initiating agent has been the insurers, both public and private.

Risk shifting. Changes in reimbursement schemes (such as higher premiums and deductibles) reflect the shifting of financial risk from insurers and employers to consumers. Risk shifting is an attempt to hold down inflation by shifting responsibility for excess cost from the third party payer to the recipient of health care. The consumer is presumed to be in a better position to oversee costs, that is, to judge if physician A, who charges a higher fee, is more cost effective than physician B, who charges a lower fee. Most of the risk shifting to date has been oriented toward cost shifting (e.g., rebates, rewards to users of cost-containing health plans, vouchers, and competitive bidding). This risk shifting is patient oriented in that the patient takes more risks for high costs. Risk shifting contributes to a change in the power base, a topic we will return to later.

Risk capitation. Supplementing risk shifting is the trend toward capitation (putting a ceiling on the indemnity). The most prominent example of this approach is Medicare's prospective payment system (PPS), in which reimbursement for health care is fixed in advance of treatment. PPS is based on diagnosis-related groups (DRGs) to adjust for case mix, and incorporates outlier payments for special cases requiring elongated treatment. Under PPS, a hospital or other provider organization must manage treatment efficiently, so that costs do not exceed the reimbursement "caps" for the treatment they agree to provide. If treatment costs are less than the known cap, those savings go to the provider; if they are greater, the providers bear the loss. Thus, PPS represents not only risk capitation but also a shift of risk—from insurer to provider. Most surgical and medical episodes for Medicare patients are already reimbursed under PPS.

There are many potential variations on risk shifting and capitation. The cost-containment efforts discussed above are the primitive early efforts by insurers and government to stem the rising costs of health care. The health care industry has also responded to the new challenges in fiscal management by rapid organizational restructuring.

The Health Care Industry's Response: Restructuring the Medical–Industrial Complex

Risk spreading and horizontal integration through corporatization. The expanding size of corporations in the medical–industrial complex has been facilitated by the inflationary, progrowth health care market of the last decade. The access to greater capital by incorporation permits the acceptance of more risk. Also, a potentially greater economy of scale by a larger corporation allows horizontal growth—capturing a larger market share of a given service or product. Two forms of corporatization are having substantial impact in the rapidly changing world of the health care marketplace. One is the rapid aggregation of providers into preferred provider organizations (PPOs), health maintenance organizations (HMOs), independent practice associations (IPAs), and the like. Corporatization's economy of scale in all of these situations permits safer and more profitable spreading of risks associated with case mix, size of population served, caseload, and other variables. The organization of providers into fiscally managed plans has been occurring so extensively and rapidly that it is commonly predicted that nearly all providers will be practicing in such a fashion within a matter of years.

The second form of corporatization is that of private hospital chains, which purchase large numbers of hospitals nationally and internationally. In the last 15 years or so, there has been an exponential growth in the number of hospitals purchased by hospital chains. This growth has slowed recently for several reasons. However, a small number of hospital corporations could very well own the majority of hospital beds in the United States in the next few years. One of the principal advantages of hospital chains is their corporate access to very large amounts of capital and the resulting economies of scale such access makes possible.

Risk diversification and vertical integration. Economic factors and antitrust regulations conspire to limit the extent of corporate growth in a given part of the market. The larger corporations have of late employed other strategies of growth—risk diversification and vertical integration.

By investing in more than one sector of products or services in the medical–industrial complex, a health care corporation can spread its risks across very different sectors, such as hospitals, hospital supplies or equipment, pharmaceuticals, testing laboratories, nursing homes, or insurance companies. Particularly in times of uncertainty and rapid change, this is a sound business strategy for a large corporation. Considerable risk diversification is occurring at present, with perhaps the most high risk/high yield activities involving mergers between hospital and insurance corporations.

In recent years, American Medical International has started a new insurance company, and Hospital Corporation of America has combined with Equitable Insurance Company to form a new corporation (Equicor). Exactly how well these mergers will work is not yet clear because profit margins of hospital chains and insurance companies depend, to some extent, on opposing market factors. That is, when a given patient stays a long time in a hospital, the hospital profit margin increases, but the profit margin of the insurance company decreases. Traditional conflicts between insurance companies and hospital corporations will probably continue, but in the board rooms of these newly merged corporations. Because of the capitalization involved—billions of dollars for each of these mergers—these new companies will play an important, albeit somewhat unpredictable, role in health policy in the future.

Vertical integration is a term used in marketing and economics to describe complex systems that link resource development, manufacturing, distribution, and consumption (Brown & McCool, 1986). For example, food chains, when vertically linked, subsume owner-operated farms, processing plants, and distribution systems and may provide the food in a variety of forms, such as meal services and restaurants. A health provider system, when vertically integrated, provides all levels and all intensities of service to all health care consumers in a definable group (a county or a corporation, for example). In this sense, merely owning different service modalities in different parts of the country, as in the mergers of hospital chains and insurance companies, is a form of diversification, not vertical integration. In the private sector, the Chrysler Corporation took a large step toward vertical integration in founding its self-insured plan.

One critical feature of vertical integration is that the corporate entity that delivers cost-effective care keeps the money saved. The Chrysler Corporation, with its Health Committee of the Board of Directors under the leadership of Joe Califano (1986), has taken strenuous measures to decrease the cost of health care for its employees, retirees, and their families. As a self-insured corporation, it is Chrysler that retains the benefits of such decreased cost. If the cost-cutting attempt fails, it is also the Chrysler Corporation Health Plan that is at risk.

The transformation of the American health care system has been rapid and extensive, and it is by no means over. The field has already been reshaped both by changes in the funding of health care and changes in the organizational behavior of the increasingly large players (sometimes referred to as the "Supermeds" or the "Exxons" of the health care industry). In this "era of fiscal incentives" (Bovbjerg, Held, & Diamond, 1987), we see the widespread acceptance of managed health care plans, with the inevitable consequences of increased managerial control and organizational complexity.

The Procompetitive Market of the 1980s

Our nation has clearly swung, in most areas, toward a more freely competitive market in the Reaganomics of the 1980s. In health care, it is alleged that free competition among providers, in concert with free consumer choice and accountability (read "cost sharing"), will provide the best quality of health care at the cheapest price. In this view, marketplace economics, not government regulation, should shape our health care system. The stimulated free market of the current period reduces the authority of the professional provider and places new responsibilities on the buyer of health care services (Rodriguez, 1985). In this context, several phenomena are salient.

The imperfect relationship between supply and demand. Most economists agree that health care does not follow the usual laws of supply and demand in the marketplace. In particular, it has been found that the more health providers present in a given setting, the greater the costs not only for the system as a whole but also for the individual patient.

The imperfect linkage between supply and demand and health care costs applies to hospitals as well as to individual providers. Robinson and Luft (1987) examined hospital competition (defined as the number of hospitals within 24 kilometers of a given hospital) for all U.S. general hospitals in 1982. Controlling for wage rates, case mix, state regulations, and hospital teaching roles, hospitals with the most competition charged 26% more than those with the least competition for the same services. Competition in the marketplace for health services not only did not bring down costs but in fact increased them.

Why is that? There are several reasons. Competing hospitals are competing for patients, often marketing themselves with special "extras" to attract patients (e.g., nicer waiting rooms or floral services). They also compete for physicians—not only in direct salaries but also in indirect costs such as clerical help, parking, and the like. Finally, hospitals in a competitive environment often market themselves by promoting their high technology equipment. For example, when a hospital purchases nuclear magnetic resonance (NMR) apparatus, competing hospitals are likely to do so as well, driving costs up by competitive redundancy. Robinson and Luft referred to this phenomenon as a "medical arms race," which leads to cost-increasing acquisition of new technology attractive to both patients and physicians.

There is not a very close link between the services flowing from health care providers and the money flowing from patients back to the provider, according to Reinhardt (1987). He presented data showing that charges for a given medical procedure are (a) greater in the United States than they are for the same procedure in neighboring Canada by a factor of 2.5, and (b) vary by region in this country by a factor of 3. He argued that costs of care are rising despite greater provider competition and a growing surplus of health resources (e.g., beds).

The argument for a freely competitive, price-sensitive market presumes that consumers are well-informed and capable of rational choice regarding competing services. But patients in medical crises are often anxious and unlikely to assess rationally the range of health service packages offered to them. Further, in an authoritarian doctor–patient interaction, the potential patient may not be given enough information to make an informed choice. That is, one reason for a somewhat price-insensitive market may be that the consumer is really not in a position to assess the quality of the service product in advance.

Price insensitivity is also increased to the degree that the provider organizations (e.g., the American Medical Association) function as labor monopolies to undercut the free market. Thus, for example, it is typically the provider who sets the fee, monitored only by the judgment of provider peers that the fee is "reasonable and customary," that is, normative.

Normative practices of physicians may significantly determine treatment procedures and costs without necessarily affecting treatment outcome. Thus, there are normative differences in various regions of the country regarding the length of stay for particular disorders, psychiatric or medical. There is no evidence, though, that these reliable regional variations in accepted practice and resource consumption (e.g., length of stay) are in any sense related to treatment outcome (Fuchs, 1974).

American health care providers claimed almost 11% of the GNP in 1985, compared to the 8% to 9% of Canadian and West German GNP that went to providers, or the 6% of GNP for providers in the United Kingdom or Japan (Reinhardt, 1987). Without evidence that the much greater allocation of money to providers in this country results in a corresponding superiority of services or outcomes, one might hypothesize that other countries manage their resources more effectively. Reinhardt made the point more forcefully, proposing that American providers are collusively hiking their charges up to maintain their "Cadillac" life-styles (1987).

For these and other reasons (e.g., our cultural beliefs about guarantees of health care to the needy), the imperfect relationship between supply and demand of health services will always be only a "quasi-market." As such, economic and political restraints on the market will affect health services and their costs. Peer review organizations (PROs) are one existing mechanism. Additional government action may be needed to regulate such cost-related activities as (a) unnecessary duplication of high technology equipment in a given geographical area, (b) unnecessary and inflationary advertising and marketing in the health care marketplace, and (c) other spurious cost-raising factors associated with "normative practice."

Monopsonistic (single-buyer) marketpower and self-regulation by the large private and public buyers. The government is not the only, or even the primary, source of regulation of the health care industry. We have already discussed the corporatization of the industry and the rapid growth of private hospital chains and their mergers. We point here to a relatively new phenomenon, the self-insured corporation. Under the Employee Retirement Income Security Act (ERISA), self-insured corporations are legally exempt from state premium taxes, some state regulations (e.g., freedom of choice), and the reserve requirements of insurance companies. Full self-insurance entails substantial financial risk. It also requires a capacity for large-scale billing and an extensive management information system: Only very large corporations can qualify (e.g., Chrysler). By 1983, 17.5% of the private health insurance market was accounted for by self-insured corporations (Higgins and Meyers, 1986).

There is also a modified form of self-insurance, where the corporation contracts with an outside insurance company to provide billing and other administrative services and to insure the corporation against very large claims. Purchase of these capacities—administrative services and the reduction of risk—allows substantially smaller companies to self-insure. The question of whether this modified self-insurance represents an unintended "loophole" in ERISA has been raised by disenfranchised groups, but it has yet to be tested in federal court. Certainly, this form of self-insurance is growing. By 1983, it constituted another 14.3% of the health care market. Higgins and Meyers (1986) estimated that it may currently be as much as 50%.

Inevitably, self-insured corporations have shown increasing intolerance of unjustified costs and increasing self-regulation to contain them. The Chrysler Corporation in particular has developed firm and clear watchdog mechanisms to reduce its health care costs (Califano, 1986). This private sector regulation should lead to decreased inpatient care, substitution of outpatient care for inpatient care for many disorders, decreases in service intensity, improvement in documentation of outcomes of services, and a decrease in the availability of inefficient services.

To date, these corporations have employed only a "moderate" form of utilization review, most typically by provider peers. We suspect, however, that ultimately these review mechanisms will be tougher and less dependent on judgments of typicality and normativity of a particular service. That is, we predict corporations in the future will insist on service outcome as a primary criterion. The utilization review committee might well ask not only, "Was the service provided a medically reasonable service to provide under the circumstances?" but also, "Was the outcome obtained also reasonable and cost-effective?"

Given their size, the emphasis of the private self-insured companies on costs makes them major players in health care. Their arrangement involves a single buyer, representing all the consumers (i.e., company employees). A single buyer has considerable market power, particularly when bargaining with competing physicians (as in the case of the British National Health Service [NHS], which represents all British citizens in negotiating what providers will be paid). This monopsonistic (single buyer) market power in the private sector will, we predict, enable dramatic damping of rising health care cost—to the degree that there is competition among providers.

Monopsonistic procurement practices are especially effective when there is vertical integration in the buying entity. Such practices are increasingly attractive to both the self-insured corporations and the public insurers, that is, Medicare and Medicaid. In Medicare, demonstrations are planned that will pool funds for inpatient and outpatient care for a defined population. A single public entity will establish systems of managed care for that population and develop waivers for care (Mechanic, 1987). This public entity will thus be empowered to control resource allocations in the full range of (vertically integrated) community-care systems, and of course, also be accountable for health care and its budget.

The changing power base underlying health policies and practice. Health policies and practices have historically been under the control of providers (particularly physicians, of course). This is changing, in large part as a result of a national press for restricting the variety and extensiveness of treatment unless justified by outcome. "In the absence of evidence that more is better, pressures for cost-containment will almost certainly dictate that less is good enough" (Higgins & Meyers, 1986, p. 25). The prospective payment system is a reflection of the power shift: The buyer, not the provider, sets the cost. Traditionally, providers were free to set their own practice norms and fees in this country—a seller's market. It is now, and will continue to be in the forseeable future, a buyer's market.

Management information systems linking cost, clinical services, and outcomes will become typical. With such systems, the controllers of the systems become powerful. Through easy oversight of practice, the controllers can track "good" or "bad" providers or services (defined by cost or outcome criteria). Already pre-admission certification, second opinion, and concurrent or ex post facto review of a provider's treatment restrict provider autonomy in treatment management. As Rodriguez (1985) has noted, today's "cookbook medicine," embodied in DRGs and other economic algorithms, is aversive to providers, but third party payers use it because of the lack of efficacy data provided by professionals.

In the provider–patient exchange, power is shifting toward the consumer or consumer representative. In the initial movements of the private sector, the power base is shifting from providers to corporate officials and oversight boards, not necessarily provider-controlled, whose decisions are based on evidence that the treatment is needed and cost effective. A power shift from seller to buyer may also occur in the public sector, if accountability for use of health care resources rests with a single public entity representing a specific patient population. With a power shift, we would expect more internal regulation, facilitative of monopsonistic consumer choice.

IMPLICATIONS FOR MENTAL HEALTH

Each of these aspects of the health care revolution has implications for mental health services and policy. Let us review our predictions for health care and then look more closely at mental health.

Overall, immense changes are taking place. We predict that public and private cost-containment efforts, in tandem with rapid restructuring of the industry and growing consensus about the limits of free marketplace competition should lead to declining provider autonomy, increasing integration of services, increasing emphasis on treatment outcomes, increasing management purview and control, changing power bases, and (eventually) more consumer control via government and administrative decree. This extraordinary restructuring of our nation's health care system is needed, is occurring, and will continue for some time.

How will the trendsetters in the health care revolution see mental health care within the overall system? We suspect they will conclude that trends in the mental health sector have essentially followed those in the larger health care delivery system—more providers, more users of their services, and greater costs. The work force of mental health professionals (e.g., psychiatrists, clinical psychologists, social workers, and psychiatric nurses) increased from 23,000 in 1947 to 121,000 in 1977, a greater than fivefold increase in 30 years (Mechanic, 1980). The number of psychiatrists and licensed psychologists per 100,000 members of the population increased by a factor of 10 over a 30-year period (Cummings & Duhl, 1987).

Greater access to providers and greater insurance coverage has spurred more resource utilization and therefore costs in mental health as well as health. Thus, although the percentage of the U.S. population using professional mental health services increased from 14% to 26% in the period between 1957 and 1976 (the critics will say), the level of well-being in the population at large did not change (Kulka, Veroff, & Douvan, 1979), a finding repeatedly observed in health. The most seriously mentally ill still have not been adequately served (Mechanic, 1987). When Chrysler Corporation provided better mental health coverage to its employees, annual use of such services rose more than six times—and their costs almost seven times within four years ("Califano Speaks," 1984). Recall that about a third of the increased cost of health services is due to increased services per capita.

Mental health is by no means a small piece of the pie. By 1980, mental illness was the third most expensive category of disorders, accounting for more than $20 billion of health care expenditures (Mechanic, 1987). By 1983, the direct and indirect costs of mental illness, exclusive of alcoholism and drug abuse, were estimated to be almost $73 billion (Harwood, Napolitano, & Kristiansen, 1983). In 1981, 23% of all hospital days in the United States were accounted for by mental disorders (Kiesler & Sibulkin, 1987).

Psychologists and other mental health professionals do have counterarguments for this expected "new" view of mental health services. For example, if mental health services are needed, the fact that they also cost should be neither a surprise nor a primary concern. The same could be said of surgical services. Further, mental health services, when added to an existing system of health care, can reduce health care utilization and costs (e.g., Jones & Vischi, 1980). A service can add costs to a system and still be cost effective. Psychologists have made these points repeatedly over the years (e.g., Kiesler, 1980).

However, the fact that psychologists have arguments in their favor is less important than the fact that they will be required to make them convincingly (yet again)—and to an entirely new, powerful, and less knowledgeable audience, the superplayers of the health care revolution.

These public policy changes will affect mental health ultimately. For example, currently treatment for the bulk of mental and emotional episodes in the Medicare population remains exempt from PPS (and is funded on a modified fee-for-service basis). In part, this was due to lobbying efforts by the psychiatric and psychological organizations, who argued that length of stay in the hospital (the largest cost factor in mental health care) could not be adequately predicted by DRGs. At the time, investigators were able to predict only 12% to 16% of the variance in length of stay with DRGs and other patient and treatment information available (English, Sharfstein, Scherl, Astrachan, & Muszynski, 1986; Frank, Lave, Taube, Rupp, & Goldman, 1986). In our own work on general hospitals, however, we account for 35% of the variance in length of stay for mental disorder diagnoses (MDC-19) and 66% for alcohol and drug abuse related disorders (MDC-20) in Medicare patients (Kiesler, Simpkins, & Morton, 1987).

A recent study of PPS on psychiatry in Ohio found that operating on PPS treatment guidelines has cut average length of stay by two hospital days, just as it has done for nonpsychiatric (medical and surgical) episodes (Thienhaus & Simon, 1987). We have reviewed the arguments for and against the use of a DRG-based PPS for psychiatric services elsewhere (Kiesler & Morton, 1988). We suspect these and other recent findings might well reopen this debate.

Even if they do not, risk capitation through a PPS is an influential prototype. Medicare serves as a model for other insurers in both the public and private sectors (DeLeon, VandenBos, & Cummings, 1983). At last report, nine states required DRGs for all forms of treatment and reimbursement, Medicare-related or not. In short, PPS is gaining momentum in health care outside of Medicare and will, in some form or other, be a salient force in the future. The continued resistance of mental health providers to national PPS rates will likely have an ironic consequence—further erosion of mental health benefits in insurance plans (Jencks & Goldman, 1987).

Some of these changes could have a positive effect on psychology and mental health. Take the concept of vertical integration, for example. In the public sector, Dane County in Wisconsin is vertically integrated. That is, there is an attempt to channel all public funds to one central point in a delivery system (e.g., Test, 1981). Cost-effective care depends partly on proper financial incentives from which those delivering cost-effective care keep the savings. Thus, when the Mendota Mental Health Center succeeds in diverting a patient from a more expensive state mental hospital to a less expensive community-based rehabilitation program, the Center retains the cost savings for potential use with other patients. Similar changes are taking place in other states. Incentives for cost-effective care are not present in most systems of mental health care, although they are in systems that are vertically integrated. Given the "era of fiscal incentives," we expect more vertical integration in the mental health services marketplace of the future.

The health care revolution is an attempt to wrest control of the health system and its costs from professionals. Health policy has always dominated mental health policy, often unwittingly (Kiesler, 1980). Even if mental health were never explicitly considered, psychologists and other mental health professionals would be seriously affected by these events. Consider psychologists' attempts to deliver services under Medicaid, for example. A policymaker focused on cost containment would obviously view this effort very differently than one primarily concerned with an expended need for cost-effective services.

One might also expect monopsonistic buyers from private corporations to be less sympathetic to including sophisticated mental health services in an overall package than experienced professionals from the more traditional public sector have been in the past. Just as mental health has made inroads in developing knowledgeable policymakers, the power is shifting to a new group, one much less sophisticated about mental health needs and services.

As mentioned, the restructuring of our health care system is needed, is occurring, and will continue. Each element, from vertical integration to monopsonistic buyers to the outcome demands of the private sector, will affect psychology in both practice and research. What can and should psychology do about them? This is a question of a responsible role for psychology in health and mental health policy.

IMPLICATIONS FOR RESPONSIBLE PUBLIC POLICY

When we discuss public policy, we mean at one level to imply use of public funds—for direct payment of services, as an incentive to tilt a system in a particular direction (e.g., use of public funds or tax incentives to build a hospital), or as a means to subsidize certain sites within the system (e.g., state hospitals or community mental health centers). In addition, public policy can refer to the need to regulate the private sector as it affects the public (e.g., insurance plans, hospital practices, or benefit packages of self-insured corporations or Blue Cross/Blue Shield).

The primary, overriding goals of public policy for psychology remain what they have been historically: to ensure adequate access of the public to quality care, delivered with accountability and cost effectiveness. These are the major goals as well for such citizen groups as the National Mental Health Association. But responsible public policy becomes a more complex undertaking in a restructured, more cost-conscious health care system. Our primary policy priority at present must be the development of systems of organization and funding that permit more optimal resource allocation.

In an era of health care rationing, our public policy concerns center on the overall distribution of our health care resources. Reinhardt (1987) requested "elegant algorithms" to direct services from those who get too much to those who do not get enough. Thier (1986) called for a technology for assessing quality of care per dollar spent, or the degree to which access to care is determined by medical need versus ability to pay. Mechanic (1987) stressed the critical need to clearly define needs and priorities for mental health systems design. All have emphasized the efficiency or effectiveness of these systems. These are the same old public policy goals—but with a twist: the necessity of a top-down analysis for responsible public policy.

Top-down analyses imply inspecting the system of care as a whole, linking it to the public interest, and considering changes in the overall system. Conversely, bottom-up analyses imply a concern with elements of the overall system in isolation, without regard for the interaction among elements of the system. A broad, top-down, nonpartisan perspective on health care could ensure that professional psychology will maintain a publicly responsible public policy. Indeed, a top-down perspective is necessary for establishing both what public policy is or should be, as well as the challenges and opportunities for professional psychology in the "health care revolution." Only by simultaneously attending to the rapid developments in policies regarding Medicare reform, the emergent policies of the self-insured employers, and the restructuring of the hospital industry, for example, can one establish the problems at their interfaces.

The boundaries between public and private policy in the future settings of marketplace competition are new and ambiguous, and the questions for public policy are more complicated. Which changes are most beneficial to consumers? Which of those changes can best be implemented by the private sector? Where are public funds needed, and under what conditions, if any, should they be used to stimulate private sector services and activities?

The conflicting motives of profit and public service are also newly configured in the competitive, fiscally driven health care marketplace. At the business level, we are both less tolerant of poorly managed public health care and newly alarmed at the growing number of homeless and other indigent individuals who "fall through the cracks" of systems designed for them or for others.

OPPORTUNITIES FOR PSYCHOLOGY IN THE PUBLIC INTEREST

The major question is not whether the changes in health care delivery are occurring. They are. The major question is whether psychologists will see the opportunity, analyze it in a publicly responsible way, and develop unique contributions to this changing world.

Psychologists have several advantages for use in the public interest: (a) an empirical orientation emphasizing outcomes, which can allow them to overcome professional biases; (b) expertise not traditionally allied with medicine and with hospital care; (c) emphasis on both prevention and the concept of wellness; and (d) knowledge about the effect of the environment on behavior and well-being. These strengths could be comparative advantages to be used in the public interest. Taken together, we argue that these strengths should enable psychologists to take the lead in formulating responsible public policy.

The solution for providing adequate health care for a more reasonable cost lies in changing the incentive systems: to deemphasize professional care where possible and to substitute alternative treatments, to change the "life-styles" of American consumers (their health attitudes and behaviors), to encourage an efficiency-oriented health care market in the private sector, and at the same time to ensure that the poor, the elderly, the underemployed, and the unemployed receive equally sophisticated incentives and supports. The underserved populations will continue to require advocacy, and the rapidly changing care arena must be monitored vigilantly to ensure that savings are obtained by changing consumers' health behaviors and by lowering unnecessary hospital and medical professional costs, and not by depriving the underprivileged of adequate care.

Service Sites

Care outside a mental hospital is likely to be the wave of the future because it is more effective and can be less expensive, especially if nonprofessionals are amply used (Kiesler, 1982; Kiesler & Sibulkin, 1987). Large corporations, both insurance corporations and hospital chains, are recognizing this, and it is probably only a matter of time before they implement these strategies in large insured populations. Both self-insured large corporations and hospital chains merged with insurance companies are building on the empirical fact of the cost-effectiveness of nonhospitalization. They will increasingly use hospitals only for short emergency care, coordinated with subsequent alternative care outside the hospital. Whether currently owned hospitals can remain full with such a policy is more a question of the size of the insured population than the practice of the hospital.

Several aspects of the new systems of care require creative engineering of services and research on service delivery. For example, new service sites are increasingly represented in alternatives to hospitalization, such as health maintenance organizations, employee assistance programs (EAPs), nursing homes, and alcohol and substance abuse rehabilitation programs. The continuing and overarching issues are embodied in policy-relevant research on needs, outcome, service delivery systems, and resource allocation.

Health maintenance organizations. HMOs have been the original model for nontraditional, cost-effective care. Medical offset effects, in which the use of psychological services decreases the cost and use of physical health services, have largely been found in HMOs or similarly organized service delivery systems (Jones & Vischi, 1980; Shemo, 1985). Their salaried providers are not likely to elongate treatment as much as fee-for-service providers (Mechanic, 1979). HMO plans and HMO membership size have tripled in the last five years, so that there are now 650 plans covering 28 million people (Rundle, 1987). It is projected that HMO memberships will reach 50 million by 1993 (Inglehart, 1984) and that the majority of Americans will be in price-competitive plans by the early 1990s (Ellwood, 1985). More than half of the nations's practicing physicians are already allied with HMOs or similar plans (Rundle, 1987), and the "oversupply" of physicians expected in this decade (whose numbers will increase 70% from 1980 to 1990) are expected to be even more involved in new forms of service delivery organization (Flinn et al., 1987).

The notion of a different style of organization and incentives at the margin favoring brief treatment should, on a priori grounds, attract psychologists to be very involved in HMOs. They have not been, but they should consider HMOs as a potential opportunity.

Employee assistance programs. EAPs and other "workplace wellness" initiatives represent another opportunity to design workplace incentives for health and to demonstrate the cost-effectiveness of various prevention, promotion, and specialized EAP efforts. Here, too, the field is dominated by those from other disciplines, and many of the experimental efforts in this arena have been inadequately researched (Conrad, 1987). Although not fully a missed opportunity, health programs for the workplace have developed under others' guidance, and whether psychologists can influence this area adequately remains to be seen.

Nursing homes. Nursing homes are proliferating as structured care for the elderly evolves, offering new opportunities for creative professional policy. Public awareness is quite recent here, and there is ample evidence that the mental health delivery system will increasingly involve program and policy in nonhospital settings for elderly persons. The number of elderly individuals with mental disorders in nursing homes is increasing, well beyond the increase of elderly individuals in the population at large (Kiesler & Sibulkin, 1987). In the care of elderly individuals, we will see perhaps the most interesting and productive interfaces of public and private sector policies, partly stimulated by Medicare reform.

Alcohol and drug abuse rehabilitation programs. These programs make up yet another area that has developed without a strong presence from psychology. Hospitals and units within general hospitals specializing in such treatment have proliferated in recent years, and policy-related activity has been great. DRGs for alcohol and substance abuse disorders have already been modified to reflect treatment procedures (similar to DRGs for surgery), and such specialized treatment units are no longer exempt from PPS (as of October 1987). Whether treatments in these specialized units are effective is not the issue here. The point here is that preliminary and large-scale mapping of the treatment ecology and economy for these diagnoses has already been proceeding at a brisk pace, largely led by physicians, alcohol and drug abuse specialists, and others. This is another opportunity for psychology.

Underserved Populations

The number of chronically ill individuals has increased predictably, given known demographic trends. Goldman, Gattozzi, and Taube (1981) estimated about 2.4 million chronically mentally ill individuals nationally; 1.7 million of them have severe, prolonged disability. These patients consume 43% of the direct costs of mental illness, with the bulk of these funds going to nursing homes and state and county hospitals (Talbott & Sharfstein, 1986). Yet, the quality of this service sector is poor. There is a great need for integrated, community-based services for this population (Mechanic, 1987).

There is also a growing number of Americans, perhaps 37 million (Mechanic, 1987), who are presently uninsured altogether. Some of them are homeless; some are only partially employed or employed by smaller companies who offer no health benefits. This large group has been lost in the policy discussion and represents another compelling reason for top-down analysis focused on the interface of private and public sector policies. They represent an increasingly grave policy concern.

There is growing consensus that there is not only an underserved population, but an overserved one as well—both relative to medical need and relative to the utilization rates of others. Many concerned with resource allocation have suggested the need for redistribution of health care to ensure an efficient national health system in aggregate. However, other strategies for improving resource allocation are under discussion. Use of mental health services to offset other medical costs of overutilizers, in tandem with greater incentives to ensure that funds follow patients who are underserved is but one example. Use of treatments that demonstrably reduce relapse or recidivism is another.

Research Issues

There is a variety of research opportunities of major importance to responsible health and mental health policy of the future. Such research would undergird the challenge of designing an effective health care system.

Needs assessment. Needs assessment is not a new area for psychology, but there are newly critical questions at present surrounding such issues as access to care, the ability of patients to make informed choices, and the adequacy of private and public monopsonists' needs assessments for the populations they represent.

Outcome studies. Such studies have a heightened urgency, as planners and policymakers scrutinize hard data more shrewdly for information on effectiveness and cost (McGuire & Frieman, 1983). Clinical researchers of the future will have impact to the degree that they design and report the research in a broader context. Minimally, future outcome studies should include a description of the organizational and policy context in which treatment and outcome occur. This information is necessary for evaluating the incentives and alternatives available to patients, providers, and funders—quite apart from the specific treatment under consideration. For maximized policy relevance, outcome studies should include cost information, so that health care planners can evaluate treatment outcomes in terms of direct and indirect financial impact. With a growing awareness that added costs at the margin do not necessarily improve the quality of care received, the challenge to outcome studies is not just "does it work?" but "can you beat this?"

Service systems research. Such research is a critical area for policy impact in health or mental health care. Independent variables of special interest include continuity of case management, integration of nonhealth components (e.g., housing and social services) with the health care delivery component, the degree to which funds follow the patient (vs. the services or providers), and the use of incentives within the system to obtain and sustain effective care across the board. Given its vast scope and central policy relevance, this research may be the most challenging of the research enterprises.

Resource allocation. Resource allocation represents a final area of needed research and policy discussion. Research on DRG configurations or on various potential facets of PPS are exemplars (Jencks & Goldman, 1987). Such research is already well underway, will continue for some time, and will have major impact on the distribution of quality and quantity of health care. Dealing with both the psychometrics of diagnosis and the economics of treatment, this kind of research has great salience to the issues of error, equity, and power, as we have discussed earlier.

We have listed a few of the areas where constructive efforts on behalf of a well-designed national health care system are needed. The public needs include sophisticated delivery of care in the full range of new service sites and focused attention on delivery of care to the growing number of underserved individuals. The quality of the emergent care system is largely dependent on current and future research on needs, treatment outcome, delivery systems, and resource allocation. We argue that these represent exciting opportunities for psychologists and that their greatest assets are those most called for in the present redesign of our country's health and mental health delivery systems.

Traditional thinking about health and mental health services is under fire. Systems of service delivery—not independent practitioners operating at an *individual* level—will dominate future policies. Psychology's focus must be on its role in a total system of service delivery. The rapidly changing health care context requires a reorientation by organized psychology if it is to develop responsible public policy. A top-down perspective emphasizes the organizational and economic systems, relates psychology to health and not just mental health, and attends to the efficacy and cost of health services.

Graduate Education

There are nearly as many future professional psychologists already enrolled in graduate training as there are currently in the work force. Most of them are destined to work in the new service sites, under the new reimbursement and organizational policies developing now. If academic trainers fail to shape this next generation to take a leadership role in the new service delivery contexts, future psychologists may well be consigned to only a minor technician's role in systems designed by others.

A top-down analysis of health care delivery, entailing liberal seasonings of health economics and policy analysis, would be an important perspective to provide to the professional psychologists of the future. Required courses might include health economics, health and mental health policy, health law, and epidemiology. One might see required reading from *Inquiry*, *The Milbank Quarterly*, *The Journal of Health Economics*, *Health Care Management Review*, *The American Journal of Psychiatry*, *The New England Journal of Medicine*, *Medical Care*, and *The Journal of Policy Analysis and Management*. These are important journals for mental health policy, and we both know professional psychologists and graduate students who would not recognize the names of several of them. Policy researchers also need a broader array of methodological and statistical techniques than commonly found in graduate curricula in psychology, including large-scale sampling issues, multiple regression, and the mathematical modeling involved in econometrics and the policy sciences. It is important to keep in mind that all policy analysis and research is, by definition, interdisciplinary in nature. To the extent that psychology graduate students are only learning about psychology and its data and perspective, they are ill-prepared for analytical or empirical work in mental health policy. Outcome research must be underscored for these trainees as well. Already it is apparent that brief, demonstrably effective treatment and prevention techniques are favored in the new cost and efficacy consciousness. Trainers must go further and emphasize the economics of resource use as a dimension of treatment, as well as the need for more general short- and long-term measures of efficacy (such as medical cost offsets, recidivism/relapse analysis, and criterion variables such as cardiovascular incidence). The research likely to have the greatest impact on the nature of practice in the future will be top-down analyses, outcome research, and policy research emphasizing economics and epidemiology for systems of care.

Extraordinary and needed changes are occurring in health and mental health service delivery. The health care revolution, already well under way, is challenging traditional modes and systems of care. New and powerful forces, particularly from the private sector, are redefining health care all the way from its overall organization to the basic relationship between provider and patient. These events are simultaneously a threat to traditional views and practice and an exciting opportunity to consider alternative futures.

REFERENCES

Aiken, L. H., & Marx, M. M. (1982). Hospices: Perspectives on the national policy debate. *American Psychologist, 37,* 1271–1279.

Bevan, W. (1982). Human welfare and national policy: A conversation with Stuart Eizenstat. *American Psychologist, 37,* 1128–1135.

Bovbjerg, R. R., Held, P. J., & Diamond, L. H. (1987). Provider–patient relations and treatment choice in the era of fiscal incentives: The case of the end-stage renal disease program. *The Milbank Quarterly, 65,* 177–202.

Brown, M., & McCool, B. (1986). Vertical integration: Exploration of a popular strategic concept. *Health Care Management Review, 11*(4), 7–19.

Califano, J. A., Jr. (1986). A corporate Rx for America: Managing runaway health cost. *Issues in Science and Technology, 2*(3), 81–90.

Califano speaks on health care costs at Gracie Square celebration (1984, August 3). *Psychiatric News,* p. 14.

Conrad, P. (1987). Wellness in the workplace: Potentials and pitfalls of work-site health promotion. *The Milbank Quarterly, 65,* 255–275.

Cummings, N. A., & Duhl, L. J. (1987). The new delivery system. In L. J. Cummings & N. A. Cummings (Eds.), *The future of mental health services: Coping with crisis* (pp. 85–98). New York: Springer.

DeLeon, P. H., VandenBos, G. R., & Cummings, N. A. (1983). Psychotherapy: Is it safe, effective and appropriate? *American Psychologist, 38,* 907–911.

Ellwood, P. (1985, June). *The HMO summary.* Excelsior, MN: Interstudy.

English, J. T., Sharfstein, S. S., Scherl, D. J., Astrachan, B., & Muszynski, I. L. (1986). Diagnosis-related groups and general hospitals psychiatry: The APA study. *American Journal of Psychiatry, 143,* 131–139.

Flinn, D. E., McMahon, T. C., & Collins, M. F. (1987). Health maintenance organizations and their implications for psychiatry. *Hospital and Community Psychiatry, 38,* 255–262.

Frank, R. G., Lave, J. R., Taube, C. A., Rupp, A., & Goldman, H. H. (1986). *The impact of Medicare's prospective payment system on psychiatric patients treated in scatter beds* (Working Paper No. 2030). Cambridge, MA: National Bureau of Economic Research.

Fuchs, V. R. (1974). *Who shall live? Health, economics and social choice.* New York: Basic Books.

Goldman, H. H., Gattozzi, A. A., & Taube, C. A. (1981). Defining and counting the chronically mentally ill. *Hospital and Community Psychiatry, 32,* 21–27.

Harwood, H. J., Napolitano, D. M., & Kristiansen, P. L. (1983). *Economic costs to society of alcohol and drug abuse and mental illness, 1980.* Research Triangle, NC: Research Triangle Institute.

Higgins, C. W., & Meyers, E. D. (1986). The economic transformation of American health insurance: Implications for the hospital industry. *Health Care Management Review, 11*(4), 21–27.

Inglehart, J. K. (1984). HMOs (for-profit and not-for-profit) on the move. *New England Journal of Medicine, 310,* 1203–1208.

Jencks, S. F., & Goldman, H. H. (1987). Implications of research for psychiatric prospective payment. *Medical Care, 25*(9, Suppl.), 542–551.

Jones, K., & Vischi, T. (1980). Impact of alcohol drug abuse and mental health treatment on medical care utilization: Review of the research literature. *Medical Care, 12*(Suppl. 17).

Kiesler, C. A. (1980). Mental health policy as a field of inquiry for psychology. *American Psychologist, 35,* 1066–1080.

Kiesler, C. A. (1982). Mental hospitals and alternative care: Non-institutionalization as potential public policy for mental patients. *American Psychologist, 37,* 349–360.

Kiesler, C. A., & Morton, T. L. (1988). Prospective payment system for psychiatric services: The advantages of controversy. *American Psychologist, 43,* 141–150.

Kiesler, C. A., Sibulkin, A. (1987). *Mental hospitalization: Myths and facts about a national crisis.* Newbury Park, CA: Sage.

Kiesler, C. A., Simpkins, C. G., & Morton, T. L. (1987). *Predicting hospital length of stay for psychiatric inpatients: The HDS data.* Unpublished technical report.

Kulka, R. A., Veroff, J., & Douvan, E. (1979). Social class and the use of professional help for personal problems, 1957 and 1976. *Journal of Health and Social Behavior, 26,* 2–17.

McGuire, T. B., & Frieman, L. K. (1983). Reimbursement policy and cost-effective mental health care. *American Psychologist, 38,* 935–940.

Mechanic, D. (1979). Physicians. In H. E. Freeman, S. Levine, & L. G. Reeder (Eds.), *Handbook of medical sociology* (3rd ed.). Englewood Cliffs, NJ: Prentice-Hall.

Mechanic, D. (1980). *Mental health and social policy* (rev. ed). Englewood Cliffs, NJ: Prentice-Hall.

Mechanic, D. (1987). Correcting misconception in mental health policy: Strategies for improved care of the seriously mentally ill. *The Milbank Quarterly, 65,* 203–230.

Merrill, J. C. (1987). The emperor's new clothes: Unraveling the myths about rationing. *Inquiry, 24,* 105–109.

Reinhardt, U. E. (1987). Resource allocation in health care: The allocation of lifestyles to providers. *The Milbank Quarterly, 65,* 153–176.

Robinson, J. C., & Luft, H. S. (1987). Competition and the cost of hospital care, 1972–1982. *Journal of the American Medical Association, 257,* 3241–3245.

Rodriguez, A. R. (1985). Current and future directions in reimbursement for psychiatric services. *General Hospital Psychiatry, 7,* 341–348.

Rundle, R. L. (1987, October 6). Medical debate: Doctors who oppose the spread of HMOs are losing their fight/Public seems much angrier about high health costs than any erosion of care. *Wall Street Journal.*

Shemo, J. P. (1985). Cost-effectiveness of providing mental health services: The offset effect. *International Journal of Psychiatry in Medicine, 15*(1), 19–30.

Short, T., & Goldfarb, M. G. (1987). Redistribution of revenues under a prototypical perspective payment system: Characteristics of winners and losers. *Journal of Policy Analysis and Management, 6,* 385–401.

Talbott, J. A., & Sharfstein, S. S. (1986). A proposal for future funding of chronic and episodic mental illness. *Hospital and Community Psychiatry, 37,* 1126–1130.

Test, M. A. (1981). Effective treatment of the chronically mentally ill: What is necessary? *Journal of Social Issues, 37,* 71–86.

Thienhaus, D. J., & Simon, S. E. (1987). Prospective payment and hospital psychiatry. *Hospital and Community Psychiatry, 38,* 1041–1043.

Thier, S. O. (1986). Health policy: The critical issues. *Issues in Science and Technology, 2*(3), 3–6.

Uyeda, M. K., & Moldawsky, S. (1986). Prospective payment and psychological services. *American Psychologist, 41,* 60–63.

VandenBos, G. R. (1983). Health financing, service utilization, and national policy: A conversation with Stan Jones. *American Psychologist, 38,* 948–955.

Zook, C. J., Moore, F. D., & Zeckhauser, R. J. (1981). "Catastrophic" health insurance—a misguided prescription? *The Public Interest, 62,* 66–81.

4

LEGAL POLICY ANALYSIS AND EVALUATION

MICHAEL J. SAKS

A few years ago I was having lunch with two law professors from fairly traditional legal backgrounds and with an economist interested in the law. The economist and I had been invited to explain to the legal scholars what we, from our respective viewpoints, saw to be the shortcomings of law and legal scholarship. The economist summed up his case by suggesting, in essence, that "the law is policy analysis without benefit of theory." My view was that the law's principal problem was that it is "policy analysis without benefit of data."

I will save for another occasion discussion of whether evidence or theory is more fundamental, whether one of them can ever really exist without the other, or whether one can get into more trouble trying to be serious about theory without bothering about data, or trying to be serious about data without bothering about theory.[1] Instead of fighting with each

Reprinted from *American Psychologist*, 44, 1110–1117. Copyright 1989 by the American Psychological Association.

This chapter is based on the address given for the 1987 award for Distinguished Contributions to Psychology in the Public Interest, presented at the 96th Annual Meeting of the American Psychological Association, Atlanta, Georgia, August 13, 1988.

I acknowledge the interdisciplinary research grant support provided by University House and the University of Iowa, which facilitated work on this article.
[1]The economist, of course, had in mind a particular theory or family of theories that he believed to be correct without rigorous empirical testing, although in principle these theories would be subject to disconfirmation through empirical testing.

other about with shortcoming was more serious, the economist and I tacitly agreed that the law surely would benefit from more of both theory and data because for most of its life it had muddled along without much of either.

What I want to do here is to develop the idea that "the law is policy analysis without benefit of data," to discuss the problems the law runs into as a result of that deficiency, and to consider the prospects for improving the situation. My goal is to encourage empirical research among social scientists and legal scholars on legal policy issues (Saks & Baron, 1980).

The law is an extremely important practical activity that typically is informed by little more than guesswork. Few aspects of our lives escape legal facilitation, guidance, sufferance, discouragement, prohibition, or sanction.

Legal policy concerns the content and method of regulation of the transactions between buyers and sellers, of the safety of cars and planes, or of the food we eat, or of the essential absence of regulation of organizations such as the American Psychological Association (APA) or of my freedom to write and of APA to publish this criticism of the law. Why stop with such mundane matters? The law also defines, for various purposes, when life begins and ends, and such definitions affect how the world functions. For example, a change in the definition of death can change whether life insurance is paid, who is held criminally liable for a death (the attacker who put the decedent in a hospital or the physician who turned off the life support apparatus), and whether organ transplantation will flourish or shrivel. Under the traditional definition of death (which is cessation of respiration and circulation; see *Commonwealth v. Golston*, 1977), fewer organs would be available for transplant than under the newer brain death definition. Thus, even in choosing definitions, the law does not make abstract and indifferent choices; it concerns itself with the likely impact of those choices on our society.

One might think that the vitally important issues with which the law deals would demand the highest quality of information and thought. However, the law is casual about such information. It is not casual in one sense because expert witnesses are sworn in and their testimony is recorded verbatim and sometimes scrutinized by opponents, but it *is* casual in the sense that lawyers, judges, and legislators are not sure what information is relevant, where to find it, or how to evaluate it. The process of receiving information is steeped in ceremony and ritual. The process of digesting and applying that information is a far more uncertain enterprise.

The law and its practitioners are careful, thoughtful, and rigorous about many things, but those things do not include the nature of social and behavioral phenomena, cause and effect relationships, or the effects of the interventions made by the law. In those areas, the law lacks rigor. Legislative acts usually will withstand judicial review if they are not flagrantly irrational and if the legislators had some minimal basis for believing that their solution to a problem would work.[2] Courts sometimes receive information about policy-relevant empirical phenomena through witnesses or briefs or through their own review of relevant literature. However, they are more likely simply to imagine what the answer might be and to assume that to be correct.

The substantive rules that make up the law and the procedural rules that specify how the law will carry out its work have been developed, for the most part, by rigorless examination of evidence, by intuition, and by guesswork. Sometimes this is excused by saying that the law's principal concern is symbolic: The law announces what it seeks to accomplish. Whether it in fact accomplishes those things is secondary. The primary issue is that for which the law stands.

ILLUSTRATIONS

I want to illustrate the kinds of problems that are engendered because the law lacks a tradition of seriously informing itself about empirical questions, as well as skill in interpreting and criticizing empirical claims.

Illustration 1: Reforming the Insanity Defense

The exact content of the insanity defense has been debated for many decades. Measurement of the *effects* of different insanity defenses has received considerably less attention. In any event, by 1980 the majority of states and the federal courts had adopted the American Law Institute's Model Penal Code rule[3] as the best alternative. All that changed in 1982, however, when John Hinckley shot President Reagan and was acquitted by reason of insanity. Then the whole country set about to change the insanity defense rules (Low, Jeffries, & Bonnie, 1986, p. 663), presumably so that if that incident occurred again, John Hinckley would be locked up in prison rather than in St. Elizabeths Hospital.

The insanity acquittal of John Hinckley seems to have suggested to many legislators that many defendants were escaping punishment by way of the existing insanity defense rules.

---

[2]This is known as the rational relationship test; it is the least stringent standard by which courts evaluate the constitutionality of a statute. The courts do have stricter standards that they apply in certain kinds of cases.

[3]According to the code,

> A person is not responsible for criminal conduct if at the time of such conduct as a result of mental disease or defect he lacks substantial capacity either to appreciate the criminality [wrongfulness] of his conduct or to conform his conduct to the requirements of law. (Model Penal Code §4.01).

Pasewark and Pasewark (1982) surveyed Wyoming state legislators concerning their estimates of the frequency with which the insanity defense is raised by criminal defendants and their estimates of the frequency with which the defense succeeds in winning an acquittal. On average, the legislators believed the defense was raised in their state 44 times as often as it actually was and that it succeeded 3,000 times as often as it actually did.

This study provides an illustration of a legislature (one that almost certainly is not alone) that lacked a good description of the nature and magnitude of the problem it had undertaken to repair. It also illustrates the power of a single salient incident to drive policy that will affect numerous other cases in the future. As with other human decision-makers, the intuitive estimates of legislators of the magnitude of various problems are affected by such things as cognitive heuristics (Tversky & Kahneman, 1982; for legal applications see Saks & Kidd, 1981; in the case of insanity defense reform, thanks to John Hinckley, the availability heuristic). Their magnitude estimates in turn affect which problems they decide to address and what they decide to do about these problems. Because these legislators apparently mistakenly believed that many more defendants availed themselves of the insanity defense and many more juries granted insanity acquittals than was actually true, they presumably "fixed" the problem with more extreme reforms than they might have if they knew the actual magnitudes.

An argument can be made that the insanity defense is unrelated to the practicalities of what a criminal justice system exists to do and that the insanity defense exists largely for symbolic reasons—namely, to define who ought to be excused of responsibility for criminal acts—thereby keeping the criminal law from overstepping its own moral foundations. Accordingly, the number of defendants who would or would not be acquitted under any particular insanity defense is beside the point. Therefore, I would be complaining about ignorance of facts that play no real part in the policy to be adopted.

Undoubtedly, that view is held by some legal scholars, but it plainly is not held by the many legislators who were moved to change the law because of a widespread perception among themselves and their constituents that the insanity defense provided too large an escape hatch for defendants. For them, the practicalities of the law's effects played at least as much a part as the principles for which the law stands as a symbol.

Thus, this example also illustrates that the perceptions of constituents stand as vitally important data for legislators. Suppose a legislator comes to believe, through a conscientious examination of the evidence, that "X is true," but the legislator's constituents mistakenly believe that "X is not true." How ought that legislator to resolve the tension between those competing beliefs (Wildavsky, 1979)?

Illustration 2: Fixing "the Liability Crisis"

In the past three years, virtually every state in the United States has passed new laws limiting the ability of plaintiffs to recover damages from those they believe injured them. These reforms were prompted, according to the Tort Policy Working Group of the U.S. Department of Justice (1986), by

> a dramatic change in . . . the *availability* and *adequacy* of liability insurance. Where insurance is available . . . premium increases of *several hundred percent* over the last year or two have become commonplace. . . . The Working Group was particularly struck by the extraordinary growth over the last decade of the number of tort lawsuits and the average award per lawsuit. (pp. 1–2; emphasis in the original)

Virtually every observer and commentator has concluded (or simply assumed) that there has in fact been a "rapid upsurge in tort litigation" and in the size of awards ("Editor's Notes," 1986). The question is whether this perception is veridical.

These conclusions generally rest on three bases: anecdotes, unadjusted aggregate data, and cause–effect inferences that are taken as true without any testing. (See Danzon, 1985; Galanter, 1986; Saks, 1986a; and Saks, 1986b, which form the basis for the following discussion.)

Even if the anecdotes were true—and many of them are untrue—one can dismiss them for the same reason one can dismiss any anecdotes. They simply do not provide sufficient evidence to make the case one way or the other. Surely there *are* instances in which plaintiffs who should lose actually win or cases in which they win more damages than they should. Surely there are false positives as there are in any decision-making system.

Deciding among policy choices, however, requires at least an assessment of the ratio of those false positives to the false negatives (those who are entitled to compensation but who do not receive any). And one must determine the ratio of all erroneous decisions to correct decisions. Studies providing data relevant to these issues indicate uniformly that false negatives predominate in the system; that is, people entitled to compensation who receive too little or none at all are far more numerous than people not entitled to compensation who do receive it.

Anecdotes about "winners" in the "tort lottery," however, are more accessible and memorable than stories about the more numerous losers who never bring claims, settle for less than they need, or lose at trial. The few statistical studies of medical malpractice injuries, suits, and compensation reveal the following scenario: Out of every 1 million patients, approximately 8,000 will suffer an injury due to malpractice. Eight hundred will seek compensation, usually by bringing suit, and 320 will receive some kind of compensation. Thus, of the injured who would be entitled to some kind of compensation for their injuries, over 90% never are heard from by an insurance company, and 96% are never paid anything by an insurance company. The more interesting research question for those who want to understand human behavior in the tort system, then, is not why people sue, but why so many people do not sue (cf. Harris et al., 1984). Critics and reformers may be correct that the tort litigation glass is twice as full as it was a decade ago, but they ignore the fact that it is still more than 90% empty.

The unadjusted aggregate data to which I refer show many inconsistencies, but consider the part of that picture that has most excited legislatures in the past few years: rising numbers of tort filings, more trials, more winning cases by plaintiffs, and rising awards. The trouble with such numbers is that one cannot know what they mean if one does not compare them with some meaningful base. For example, if the base rate of injuries is rising (more product injuries, more medical malpractice injuries, or more serious or more costly injuries), then nothing in the legal system has really changed if there is a proportionate increase in filings, trials, and awards.

In many of the studies providing the data on which the law has relied, not even controls for population growth have been employed. Even population, however, is a crude proxy for an injury base rate. Why assume that the same proportion of the population is injured each year? There have been demographic shifts (a grayer population is a more vulnerable one). Products and services have grown safer in some respects and more dangerous in others. Similarly, awards have been controlled—if at all—only for overall inflation, but the largest chunks of a damage award are for medical expenses and lost earnings. Medical costs have been rising at a much faster rate than the consumer price index (CPI). In the past generation, Americans' real income has approximately doubled. Awards that merely track these increases would be no increases at all.

Before one can tell how much change has occurred and begin to identify the causes, one needs to remove from the picture all the phantom changes—the confounds, noise, and systematic error. Methodologists and statisticians know that task cannot be done perfectly, but so far legal policymakers have not attempted such analysis at all.

Like the insanity defense example, the tort reform example also illustrates the law's lack of a good description of the nature and magnitude of the problem it busily is fixing. Additionally, there is confusion about effects and their causes, and statistical mirages sometimes are treated as reality. That is, the law is not sure whether something is really changing or not, and if something has changed, the law does not know what has brought about the change. In all of this confusion, legislators do not know that they do not know.

Illustration 3: Sentencing Guidelines

In the area of imposing punishment on those convicted of crimes, there is great concern that judges have been inconsistent. Examples can be presented of defendants who have been convicted of the same crimes and have similar histories, but who have received widely differing sentences (Frankel, 1973). If Americans agree on little else in criminal justice policy, surely they would agree that convicts who have similar records and have been convicted of similar crimes should receive similar sentences.

This issue, although so simply posed, generates a whole series of questions that can be answered only quantitatively. First one needs to know how big this problem is, and that calls not only for measuring sentences but also for controlling apparent differences in sentencing due to variables that reasonably justify different sentences, such as prior criminal record, use of a gun in the commission of the crime, and so on. If one were to find that impermissible variables explain differences in sentencing (such as race or gender producing sentence surtaxes or discounts), one probably would want to be sure to resolve the problem. (I say "probably" because in 1987 the Supreme Court concluded in *McClesky v. Kemp* that preserving discretion in the criminal justice system was so important that it could be purchased at the price of executing murderers of Whites disproportionately more often than the murderers of Blacks.)

One then would want to look at the unexplained variation and ask if it is large enough to do something about. Some error variation in sentencing (or anything else) is unavoidable. Is the amount of variation so small that it cannot be reduced further? Is it greater than is tolerated in decisions of comparable gravity? Shari Diamond (1983) has shown that the consistency of federal judges in sentencing (to a term of incarceration vs. release) is as good or better than the diagnoses of physicians and the funding recommendations of National Science Foundation grant reviewers. Still, the law may conclude that this is more variation than we care to live with. Being as good as physicians and scientists may not be good enough for the law. There is symbolic value in "doing something" even if what one is doing accomplishes nothing in real terms.

Once policymakers know that there is something that warrants fixing and is fixable, they must try out some remedies and measure their effects. Do such changes reduce race-based disparities? Do they increase the consistency of different judges at different times sentencing similar defendants?

One interesting and popular idea for limiting unwanted variation that has been invented is known as "[voluntary] sentencing guidelines." This method takes into account certain features of the crime and the defendant's background and yields a table that enables judges to find the recommended range within which the defendant's sentence shall fall. The "voluntary" aspect of sentencing guidelines is that if the judge does not believe that the guideline sentence is appropriate, the judge is free to impose a longer or shorter sentence. The idea behind this method was that it structured judges' discretion without rigidly constraining them. It allowed them to use their judgment to tailor sentences to individual cases but would keep them from being too idiosyncratic. Inventors and adopters expected that the amount of unwanted disparity in sentencing would decline.

A number of state and local courts adopted this interesting idea. One important question remained: Did the guidelines reduce disparity? Empirical evaluation of voluntary sentencing guidelines found them to have no impact at all on the sentencing behavior of judges (Rich, Sutton, Clear, & Saks, 1982). Without empirical evaluation, this technique might have grown ever more popular and entrenched, until an awareness slowly grew, perhaps a generation or a century from now, that it might not be working. Then it would be replaced by a new solution, which might or might not work.

This particular story has a potentially happy ending.[4] The evaluation research identified possible improvements for this reform, so that in an amended version it might accomplish its goals.[5] Some jurisdictions that were planning to adopt the original version changed their minds, and others adopted improved versions. Most prominently, the U.S. Congress adopted the guidelines approach and created a U.S. Sentencing Commission to develop and deploy them (Comprehensive Crime Control Act of 1984). Whether by luck or awareness of the shortcomings of the previous incarnations of guidelines, this version included some of the improvements suggested by the evaluation researchers: (a) Notably, departures from the guidelines must be accompanied by a written opinion explaining the basis for the departure (18 U.S.C. 235, §3742), and (b) sentences are subject to review by a higher court (18 U.S.C. 235, §3742). Thus, sentencing judges must take the guidelines seriously. Still, evaluations of the effects of these not-so-voluntary guidelines on sentencing in federal courts would need to be undertaken.

---

[4] It also has at least one potentially disastrous ending. The Commission's guidelines generally involve more incarceration for longer periods of time than has been the past practice. If nothing else, this will create additional pressures on already overcrowded prisons—some calculations suggest large increases in the prison population. However, the Commission declined to create any solutions to this likely problem (see, e.g., Ogletree, 1988).

[5] For example, the guidelines were based on an aggregate empirical description of past sentencing behavior of the affected judges. This aggregation produced an average sentence that may have seemed too low to some judges and too high to others; thus both ignored it. Perhaps the best way to develop the ranges was not to examine past behavior but to have the judges meet and argue their way to a consensus, or to have a representative authority do the arguing and reach a consensus. In addition, judges may have been too free to depart from the guidelines. When they issued a sentence outside of the guidelines, judges were supposed to provide a written explanation of their choice. Almost no judges prepared those written explanations. Defendants whose sentences were outside the guidelines and were given an unsatisfying reason or no explanation had nowhere to go with their complaints. The sentences were unreviewable.

This illustrates (as if an illustration were necessary) the need for empirical testing of the effects of legal interventions (or decisions not to intervene) in the society or in the workings of the law itself. Good ideas do not always work, and sometimes they make matters worse rather than better.

Illustration 4: Federal Rules of Civil Procedure

A far more profound example of the law's failure to empirically evaluate the effects of its interventions is provided by the Federal Rules of Civil Procedure. These Rules were an important and in some ways dramatic innovation in how the process of civil litigation was to be carried out. These rules govern the conditions under which people have access to the courts, the party structure of cases, the pretrial process, and the conduct of trials. Last year marked the 50th anniversary of the adoption of these rules. At the same time that their anniversary was being celebrated, there was controversy and pressure for change. A recent survey indicates that state and federal trial judges in the United States are now nearly unanimous in blaming the discovery process for undesirable expense and delay in litigation ("Poll of Judges Released," 1988).

Consider these questions: What sorts of data do these judges have on which to base their conclusions concerning what problems exist and what features of the rules cause those problems? If the problems do indeed exist, as is widely believed, why weren't these shortcomings (or developing trends) recognized decades ago? Although several answers are possible, one that is certainly true is that no one was watching in any systematic way. Appreciating the benefits of the federal rules was largely a matter of faith, and detecting their negative effects was something that occurred, if at all, by casual observation. No one was systematically measuring and monitoring the performance of the system. Charles Wright, one of the foremost scholars of civil procedure, wrote in 1967, "We know very little about how present procedures work. We know even less what changes might produce future improvement" (p. 578).

Laurens Walker (1988) recently has reviewed every empirical study done on these celebrated and maligned Rules of Civil Procedure. The studies number fewer than three dozen. If one sets the methodological standards above case studies, the number drops to a mere handful. (I should say, parenthetically, that social psychologist Saul Kassin's 1985 study of Rule 11—judicially imposed sanctions for abuses of the legal process by attorneys or their clients—is one of the best of the studies.)

To avoid repeating the ignorance of the past, Walker has proposed a system of "restricted field experiments." Walker envisions that these would be true experiments and would be restricted in the sense that only a relative few of the federal district courts would be involved in any given study.

Consider the astonishing cost society has been willing to endure up to this point: either in rules that are not accomplishing their intended purposes for a quarter of a million federal civil cases per year or are doing so in unnecessarily costly ways. If Walker's proposal or one similar to it were to be adopted, the acquisition of knowledge about the functioning of the litigation system would accelerate. Serious defects would be detected more often than a few times in a century, and more improvements could be tested in shorter spans of time and without burdening the entire system.

Illustration 5: Lexogenic Injury

Iatrogenic injuries are those produced by the healer. Lexogenic injuries involve social harm produced by the law. Healers do not intend to injure their patients, yet some of the thickest tomes in the library are on medical iatrogenics (e.g., D'Arcy & Griffin, 1986). Many treatments once thought to be "good ideas" turned out to be worthless or more harmful than the condition they were intended to cure (Bunker, Barnes, & Mosteller, 1977). Empirical evaluation of the effects of the law will, undoubtedly, produce parallel knowledge of good ideas that in operation resulted in more harm than benefit.

Here are three examples of laws that are still popular, but that may be doing more harm than the good that was expected of them.

1. *Drug laws*. The first federal law restricting the possession and use of drugs was the 1914 Harrison Act. Within six weeks of its effective date, criminal activity by drug users was reported to have increased, the cost of drugs rose, and a black market in illegal drugs was born (Brecher, 1972; "Mental Sequelae," 1915). The Harrison Act and its successors have modified our drug laws dozens of times in the intervening 75 years. With each revision, the resources put into drug law enforcement grew larger, the penalties grew tougher, and the problem grew worse. As a number of scholars have long suggested and as several mayors of major U.S. cities (LaFranchi, 1988) recently have joined them in suspecting, our drug laws may be an example of the law turning a small problem into a major one.

2. *Juvenile courts*. A second example is the use of juvenile courts to assume jurisdiction over delinquent children. The idea is that children who are thought to be in need of supervision will benefit from judicial intervention in their lives. In research comparing delinquents who were referred for official attention (at least of whatever kind was offered by the courts studied) versus those who were returned to their families, Farrington (1977) found that those receiving more official supervision later became more rather than less involved in criminal activity. Because the study lacked random assignment, alternative explanations are possible, such as that the judges could tell which children were more serious risks and retained jurisdiction over them. Even taking Farrington's findings as only suggestive,

however, they provide some cause for concern. Can we assume that our most well-intended "treatments" work, rather than being counter-productive? Might we, by labeling children and placing them in contact with delinquent subcultures, produce more harm than help? We need to know the answer.

3. *Reduction in the size of civil juries.* In the 1970s numerous states reduced the size of civil juries to eight or six in order to save a modicum of time and money. However, reduction in the size of a decision-making group increases the error variance in its decisions, both the decision of whether to find liability and the determination of the size of damage awards (Saks, 1977). The decision to reduce the size of juries has almost certainly played some part in the "liability crisis" discussed earlier by increasing the unpredictability of trial outcomes (Saks, 1986b) and, in turn, making the process of settlement more difficult.

Perhaps some lawyers and many politicians will regard the cost in embarrassment to them and to the law, and possible loss of citizens' faith in the law, as prices too high to pay for the knowledge of what works and what does not. I would answer that the cost of not knowing may be greater. In any event, a preference for ignorance about the law's workings runs counter to our culture's grain, and the institutionalization of a preference for ignorance would reduce the law to a grand deception.[6] If the law's experience with evaluation is anything like that of medicine, we are likely to find that good, bad, and worthless ideas occur in roughly equal proportions. We cannot know, of course, which are which until they are tested. Until that is done and done well, we live with the benefits, harm, and waste of all of them.

THE LARGER PROBLEM AND THE PROSPECTS FOR IMPROVEMENT

Is this any way to run anything as important as the justice system? Earlier in this decade Harvard President Derek Bok outlined what he saw as major shortcomings in legal training, practice, and scholarship. It is noteworthy that he was the former dean of the law school whose work he, as Harvard's chief executive, undertook to criticize. Bok (1983) wrote,

> Law schools have done surprisingly little to seek the knowledge that the legal system requires. Even the most rudimentary facts about the legal system are unknown or misunderstood. . . . We ignore the social sciences at our peril. . . . Scholars in schools of public policy and

---

[6]That is, the society is persuaded that the law does what no one has verified that it does, and attempts at verification are discouraged. I do not claim that this is what in fact goes on; I do claim that those who eschew empirical evaluations of the law encourage such a world, whether intentionally or inadvertently.

education develop more sophisticated methods of program evaluation that could help implement sunset laws or detect the secondary or tertiary effects of legal rules on human behavior. . . . As yet, this work is largely overlooked by our great schools of law. (pp. 581–582)

He concluded by urging legal scholars to get involved in such research and, indeed, to direct such work:

Law professors cannot stand idly by and expect others to investigate their problems. Social scientists have not done much of this work in the past nor will they in the future. If the necessary research is to go forward, legal scholars must help organize it and participate in it, albeit with the aid of interested colleagues from other disciplines. (p. 582)

Bok was not the first lawyer to suggest that those in the areas of the law and legal scholarship undertake such policy assessment research. By the first quarter of the 20th century, the early legal realists were already arguing for it and doing it. In 1931 in the *Harvard Law Review*, Karl Llewellyn[7] wrote about

the conception of law as means to social ends and not as an end in itself; so that any part needs constantly to be examined for its purpose, and for its effect, and to be judged in the light of both and of their relation to each other. (p. 1236)

When legislation is enacted, it is regarded by its authors as the solution to whatever problem needs to be solved. Little remains to do but celebrate. To an empirical researcher, however, the effective date of a new law marks the induction of the independent variable and the mid-point of the work of designing and conducting a study to gather the data to find out the extent to which the new law made the situation better or worse or stimulated new problems that need solving. Accordingly, Llewellyn demanded that there be "an insistence on evaluation of any part of law in terms of its effects, and an insistence on the worthwhileness of trying to find these effects" (p. 1237).

With such long and esteemed support for the idea of empirically evaluating legal policy, why has there been so little research of this type? The heart of the problem, I suspect, is that lawyers and social scientists come from two different cultures (cf. Snow, 1959; also see Melton, Monahan, & Saks, 1987): The law, and most of the people who enter the law, had their intellectual upbringing in the humanities. Law students are typically smart people who do not like math. The quantitative, empirical social and behavioral sciences exist in another world.

The methods of legal education and practice more closely resemble those of the humanities. Their focus is on the examination and manipu-

---

[7]Note that Llewellyn was writing 7 years *before* the adoption of the Federal Rules of Civil Procedure.

lation of ideas through reflection and argument. In legal education, case facts are disposed of quickly at the outset of discussion and then are manipulated through "hypotheticals": Students are asked to assume a modified set of facts and the serious work of exploring or testing the limits of doctrine continues. In that world, doctrine is the figure; facts are the ground. Such evidence as there is comes from some text that is believed to be important to the debate and perhaps even authoritative. As Harry Kalven once explained this method, most legal policy debates are resolved through a heated exchange of quotations. The idea of going out and obtaining data to resolve those issues that are empirical often does not enter the minds of legal policymakers.

When such notions do enter their minds, most legal scholars quickly recognize that they do not have the skills to carry out empirical work or a strong sense of the logic of drawing inferences from data or challenging claims about the state of empirical reality (see Lehman, Lempert, & Nisbet, 1988). Striking examples exist of brilliant and energetic legal scholars who found that to answer the questions they wanted to ask, they had to acquire empirical research skills or find collaborators who had such skills. These include many of the early legal realists and in recent times, such examples as Walker (Thibaut & Walker, 1975), Baldus (Baldus & Cole, 1980; Baldus, Pulaski, & Woodworth, 1986), and Chambers (1979). However, these legal scholars stand as notable exceptions, not a trend. By their inclination, training, and talents, lawyers want to examine ideas for all their nuances. I do not mean to suggest that this set of intellectual skills is unimportant. Good lawyers and legal scholars bring impressive analytic tools to problems, and there are enough problems that require precisely this kind of thinking to keep them all quite busy. These tools, however, are only a part of what is required to produce correct answers to policy questions.

Perhaps worse for the law, it has no technology for evaluating its substantive rules or itself. Without social science skills, it cannot do what Llwellyn or Bok urged it to do. To be sure, it invites witnesses to legislative hearings, and judges take judicial notice of legislative facts (or social authority, see Monahan & Walker, 1988) or receive briefs. However, the law has no rigorous notion of what to make of what it receives. Embarrassingly, it often is reduced to judging the message by the messenger or by the number of messengers.

The other culture, social science, has its own shortcomings that keep its practitioners from doing the empirical work that lawyers are not doing. Most social scientists have little appreciation of the breadth and content of the law. They do not know what issues are most worth pursuing. In large part that may explain why the topics that law and psychology scholars have addressed are so limited. They are not likely to study what they do not know about. Moreover, many social and behavioral scientists tend to overlook the normative dimensions of a problem, assuming that the values they subscribe to are the consensus values and that the central problem is bringing about the agreed-upon goals. Often, however, deciding on those goals is at least as difficult as figuring out how to achieve a goal once consensus is reached. The social scientists' emphasis on the empirical means that they often will feel stymied and frustrated by the normative tensions and uncertainties that provide much of the law's greatest intellectual excitement.

The problem is to bridge these two cultures, and I have little expectation that it will happen soon. The law will go on muddling through, which will waste much time, energy, and resources and produce some amount of injustice and other misery. Perhaps mercifully, without a control group, most people will not even know what is broken, so it will not be noticeable if it does not get fixed. In fact, many things will get fixed—even if they were not broken, and that will give everyone the feeling that progress is being made. If Llwellyn and Bok could not change the law from a sophisticated and high stakes guessing game to a more empirically sure-footed enterprise, I have little expectation that I can do it with this article.

What I do hope to do, however, is encourage more social scientists to pursue more projects in legal policy. (See Appendix A at the end of this article for a brief list of topics that await study.) More legal scholars and social scientists will have to become friends and teach each other about their respective fields. Together, they must keep reminding the law and society about the worthwhileness of discovering the law's effects.

REFERENCES

Baldus, D., & Cole, J. W. L. (1980). *Statistical proof of discrimination.* Colorado Springs: Shepard's.

Baldus, D., Pulaski, C. A., & Woodworth, G. (1986). Arbitrariness and discrimination in the administration of the death penalty: A challenge to state supreme courts. *Stetson Law Review, 15,* 133–261.

Bok, D. (1983). A flawed system of law practice and training. *Journal of Legal Education, 33,* 570–585.

Brecher, E. M., and the Editors of *Consumer Reports* (1972). *Licit and illicit drugs.* Mount Vernon, NY: Consumers Union.

Bunker, J. P., Barnes, B. A., & Mosteller, F. (Eds.). (1977). *Cost, risks and benefits of surgery.* New York: Oxford University Press.

Chambers, D. L. (1979). *Making fathers pay.* Chicago: University of Chicago Press.

Commonwealth v. Golston, 373 Mass. 249, 366 N.E.2d 744 (1977).

Comprehensive Crime Control Act of 1984, 28 USC 58 §§991–998.

Danzon, P. (1985). *Medical malpractice: Theory, evidence, and public policy.* Cambridge, MA: Harvard University Press.

D'Arcy, P. F., & Griffin, J. P. (1986). *Iatrogenic diseases* (3rd. ed.). New York: Oxford University Press.

Diamond, S. S. (1983). Order in the court: Consistency in criminal court decisions. In C. J. Scheirer & B. L. Hammonds (Eds.), *The Master Lecture Series: Vol. 2. Psychology and the law* (pp. 119–146). Washington, DC: American Psychological Association.

Editor's notes. The liability crisis: Who's to blame? (1986). *Manhattan Report,* 6, 2.

Farrington, D. P. (1977). The effects of public labelling. *British Journal of Criminology, 17,* 112–125.

Frankel, M. E. (1973). *Criminal sentences: Law without order.* New York: Hill and Wang.

Galanter, M. (1986). The day after the litigation explosion. *Maryland Law Review, 46,* 3–39.

Harris, D., MacLean, M., Genn, H., Lloyd-Bostock, S., Fenn, P., Corfield, P., & Brittan, Y. (1984). *Compensation and support for illness and injury.* Oxford, England: Clarendon Press.

Harrison Act, Ch. 1, 38 Stat. 785 (Dec. 17, 1914).

Kassin, S. (1985). *An empirical study of Rule 11 Sanctions.* Washington, DC: Federal Judicial Center.

LaFranchi, H. (1988, May 20). Declaring a truce in war on drugs gains supporters. *The Christian Science Monitor,* p. 1.

Lehman, D. R., Lempert, R. O., & Nisbet, R. E. (1988). The effects of graduate training on reasoning: Formal discipline and thinking about everyday-life events. *American Psychologist, 43,* 431–442.

Llewellyn, K. (1931). Some realism about realism. *Harvard Law Review, 44,* 1222–1264.

Low, P. W., Jeffries, J. C., & Bonnie, R. (1986). *Criminal law.* Mineola, NY: Foundation Press.

McCleskey v. Kemp, 479 U.S. 806, 107 S.Ct. 1756 (1987).

Melton, G. B., Monahan, J., & Saks, M. J. (1987). Psychologists as law professors. *American Psychologist, 42,* 502–509.

Mental sequelae of the Harrison law. (1915, May 15). *New York Medical Journal, 102,* 1014.

Monahan, J., & Walker, L. (1988). Social science research in law: A new paradigm. *American Psychologist, 43,* 465–472.

Ogletree, C. J., Jr. (1988). The death of discretion? Reflections on the Federal Sentencing Guidelines. *Harvard Law Review, 101,* 1938–1960.

Pasewark, R. A., & Pasewark, M. D. (1982). The insanity plea: Much ado about little. In B. Bloom & S. Asher (Eds.), *Psychiatric patient rights and patient advocacy: Issues and evidence* (pp. 101–128). New York: Human Sciences Press.

Poll of judges released at Yale Law Conference. (1988). *Yale Law Report, 34,* 25.

Posner, R. A. (1986). *Economic analysis of law* (3rd ed.). Boston: Little, Brown.

Resnik, J. (1984). Tiers. *Southern California Law Review, 57,* 837–1035.

Rich, W. D., Sutton, L. P., Clear, T. R., & Saks, M. J. (1982). *Sentencing by mathematics: An evaluation of the early attempts to develop and implement sentencing guidelines.* Williamsburg, VA: National Center for State Courts.

Risinger, D. M., Denbeaux, M. P., & Saks, M. J. (1989). Exorcism of ignorance as a proxy for rational knowledge: The case of handwriting identification "expertise." *University of Pennsylvania Law Review, 137,* 731–792.

Roehl, J. A., & Cook, R. F. (1985). Issues in mediation: Rhetoric and reality revisited. *Journal of Social Issues, 41,* 161–178.

Saks, M. J. (1977). *Jury verdicts: The role of group size and social decision rule.* Lexington, MA: Heath.

Saks, M. J. (1986a). In search of the "lawsuit crisis." *Law, Medicine & Health Care, 14,* 77–79.

Saks, M. J. (1986b). If there be a crisis, how shall we know it? *Maryland Law Review, 46,* 63–77.

Saks, M. J., & Baron, C. H. (Eds.). (1980). *The use/nonuse/misuse of applied social research in the courts.* Cambridge, MA: Abt Books.

Saks, M. J., & Kidd, R. F. (1981). Human information processing and adjudication: Trial by heuristics. *Law and Society Review, 15,* 124–160.

Sander, F. E. A. (1976). Varieties of dispute processing. *Federal Rules Decisions, 70,* 111–134.

Snow, C. P. (1959). *The two cultures and the scientific revolution.* Cambridge, England: Cambridge University Press.

Thibaut, J., & Walker, L. (1975). *Procedural justice: A psychological analysis.* Hillsdale, NJ: Erlbaum.

Tversky, A., & Kahneman, D. (1982). *Judgment under uncertainty: Heuristics and biases.* New York: Cambridge University Press.

Tyler, T. R., & Lind, E. A. (1988). *The social psychology of procedural justice.* New York: Plenum.

U.S. Department of Justice. (1986). *Report of the Tort Policy Working Group on the Causes, Extent and Policy Implications of the Current Crisis in Insurance Availability and Affordability.* Washington, DC: U.S. Department of Justice.

Walker, L. (1988). Perfecting federal civil rules: A proposal for restricted field experiments. *Law and Contemporary Problems, 51.*

Wildavsky, A. (1979). *Speaking truth to power: The art and craft of policy analysis.* New York: Little, Brown.

Wissler, R. L. (1986). *Disputants' assessments of the process and outcome of mediation and adjudication.* Unpublished doctoral dissertation, Boston College.

Wright, C. A. (1967). Procedural reform: Its limitations and its future. *Georgia Law Review, 1,* 563–585.

APPENDIX A

Some Unstudied and Understudied Areas for Psychology and Law Research

Explaining the substantive law. Why are the substantive rules of law (torts, contracts, property, criminal law, etc.) what they are rather than something else? Those rules have changed and evolved over time; can those changes be explained? This is one of the most theoretically important aspects of the scholarly study of law. So far it has been dominated by philosophy and economics. Philosophical scholarship in law is not so much explanation but an analysis of what the rules "should" be, normatively. Economic explanations will seem more familiar to psychologists. Economic explanations offer theories that purport to explain the evolved rules by way of certain economic theories, which for the most part are a mixture of a fairly simple incentive psychology coupled with the concept of efficiency. Surely the other social and behavioral sciences have theories that can compete with economic explanations of law. (See R. Posner, 1986.)

Legal procedures. A good deal of social psychological research on the law consists of studies of procedure, but most of this research is limited to various aspects of trials. This work could be expanded in a variety of directions. Studies could be done on aspects of other settings, such as administrative procedures of government agencies; how problems are defined, information gathered, solutions found, and laws written in the legislative branch; and decision making in the executive branch. Research could be done on other aspects of the trial process, notably rules of evidence. A more complete and comprehensive study could be conducted on how the procedures adopted by the law work (or could work better). (Concerning such expansion in the area of procedural justice, see Tyler and Lind, 1988.)

More process, less outcome. Much of the existing psychological research on decision making in the law focuses on the accuracy of decision outcomes. We need to develop a body of research that teaches us more about the process of the law: How do people react to various processes, and what do different processes accomplish or seek to accomplish for litigants and for society? (For an essay on such possibilities by a legal scholar, see Resnik, 1984.)

Alternative dispute resolution. Although alternative dispute resolution (ADR) is the rage in some quarters, more theoretical and practical research on alternatives is needed. We know little about the precise features of disputes that would suggest using one type of alternative rather than another (Roehl & Cook, 1985; Wissler, 1986; cf. Sander, 1976, who recognizes the questions, but guesses at the answers). Such knowledge would permit us to have appropriate (rather than merely alternative) dispute resolution. Moreover, one of the most notable things about ADR is how resistant people are to actually using it. Why? That question also needs research.

Empirical underpinnings of law. The law is built on a deep foundation of empirical assumptions about human behavior—so much so that most legal practitioners and scholars are unaware of the assumptions. Many normative arguments are supported by unrecognized empirical assumptions. Consider this example: "If we allow euthanasia for the terminally ill who request death, that will put us on a slippery slope and we will end up killing the merely sick or retarded or old." What is the evidence that slippery slopes actually exist or that the law cannot draw lines that stick? A great many important projects would consist of identifying and empirically testing the law's vast bedrock of empirical assumptions. Although this is a commonly discussed theme of law and psychology, we have done very little of it. What has been done for eyewitness identification can be done for a thousand topics at least as important.

Developing expertise about experts. The same kinds of studies to which psychiatric and clinical psychologist expert witnesses have been subjected (regarding the reliability and validity of diagnoses and predictions) can be done for many other kinds of experts. What made these studies appropriate for behavioral scientists interested in the law was less the fact that the subjects of the studies were themselves members of the professional branch of behavioral science and more that they were behaving: making judgments, predictions and postmortems on the basis of certain evidence. This same basic kind of activity is engaged in by fingerprint experts, toxicologists, handwriting experts, real estate appraisers, ballistics experts, medical examiners, and so on. Those fields have done little to study the reliability and validity of their own decisions because carrying out such studies is more commonly done by behavioral scientists and statisticians. What empirical research has been done indicates a wide range of accuracy and error within and between those various fields. The law would benefit from knowing how probative the testimony of those experts is, but without empirical testing, they cannot know. (For a review of the empirical research on handwriting expertise, see Risinger, Denbeaux & Saks, 1989.)

5

PSYCHOLOGY IN THE PUBLIC INTEREST: WHAT HAVE WE DONE? WHAT CAN WE DO?

M. BREWSTER SMITH

This is an interesting time for psychologists because all the critical problems of our times (including the remaining threat of nuclear war, political injustice, the increasing gap between the affluent and the impoverished, and environmental disasters) have their psychological aspects, experimental and behavioral. Of course, none of these problems is essentially psychological; the problems and the possible ways of coping with them (I don't say "solutions") transcend professions and disciplines. We should be applying ourselves to developing and promoting psychological contributions toward coping with the catastrophic problems. This is surely the most fundamental context in which to consider the public interest.

Any attempt to advance the public interest is inherently political. In American Psychological Association (APA) politics we are experiencing the head-on clash between the two major interest groups within our Association, both pursuing their legitimate guild interests: the clinical practitioners, who now hold the majority, and the scientist-academics, now in the minority. My strongest commitments are to the "third force" in APA,

Reprinted from *American Psychologist, 45,* 530–536. Copyright 1990 by the American Psychological Association.

This chapter was presented as a Distinguished Contributions to Psychology in the Public Interest Award Address, at the meeting of the American Psychological Association, New Orleans, LA, August 14, 1989.

the groups self-identified with the public interest. That is a much weaker force than the guild interests generate, but it *requires* an APA with both scientists and practitioners to sustain it.

My aspiration here is to take a sounding as to what APA has accomplished in the name of the public interest, what has *not* been accomplished, and what challenges are presently before us. Although we can find valid reasons for satisfaction in our record, we have no grounds for complacency. Our public interest activities have been most successful when they have also advanced the individual and group interests of socially disadvantaged categories of our membership. Our other attempts to promote psychology in the public interest have been more controversial, and *in toto* they have been less effective. In order to understand this pattern of differential success and perhaps get beyond it, we must give serious thought to what we mean and *can* mean by the "public interest." Identifying the public interest in general and in psychology is no simple matter, and in a serious sense it is intrinsically political. Like all political issues, it involves a continuing, ongoing process and is never finally resolved. So I will end by defending a prominent place for *advocacy*—specifically, advocacy for public interest issues—in APA politics.

ACCOMPLISHMENTS IN THE PUBLIC INTEREST

As a major association in the social and behavioral sciences, APA has been a leader in advocacy for the rights of the disadvantaged, and a role model in action on their behalf. The concerns of disadvantaged categories of our own membership have mobilized the APA to take the lead in aligning psychological competence with justice. This enterprise has a long history, but for most purposes we can go back to Kenneth B. Clark, whose legacy to APA from his 1971 presidency was the Board of Social and Ethical Responsibility for Psychology (BSERP). BSERP nurtured APA's advocacy and modeling roles in regard to ethnic minorities, women, disabled and handicapped persons, and gays and lesbians. BSERP spun off committees and boards, each of which (with one exception that I will discuss later: the Committee on Children, Youth, and Families) represents the call for justice from a particular disadvantaged category of APA members.

Advance in justice comes in small packages, and it is very much to the credit of APA that in advancing justice toward its own disadvantaged members, it has played a visibly useful role in national affairs. In 1952 we refused to hold our convention in racially segregated locales. In 1977 we refused to meet in states that had not ratified the Equal Rights Amendment (ERA), taking a financial risk by abrogating standing contracts. (This was a more divisive issue among APA members than our stand against racial segregation, but in referendum a majority supported the Board's action.)

As a major sponsor of large national meetings, APA was very effective in getting convention hotels to make their facilities accessible to physically handicapped individuals. More recently, APA has been a national leader in pressing for government support of the counterattack on AIDS and in marshaling the competence of psychologists to help cope with the crucial behavioral aspects of prevention and treatment.

In all of these public interest concerns, justice as most of us would conceive of it is congruent with the self-interest of major segments of our own membership. Black, Chicano, female, gay, lesbian, and physically handicapped psychologists have had to suffer unfair deprivations within their own discipline and profession and Association; thus, the actions that they have mobilized APA to take in its own affairs and in the world outside are energized substantially by their own group interests (and other members' empathy with them). It should be no surprise that the "public interest" activities of APA have worked best when group self-interests converged with justice. Again, with the exception of the Committee on Children, Youth, and Families, these *are* the public interest concerns that have become built into the board and committee and even the divisional structure of APA.

The boards and committees that represent these interests make an immense difference to their constituencies and play an important role in putting psychology in the service of justice. When the APA was recently in tight financial straits and board and committee meetings were being rationed severely, this aspect of public interest psychology suffered badly. The conventional wail that boards and committees drain APA dollars made no sense. The cost was a miniscule fraction of the APA budget; the gain from these board and committee activities has been large in sustaining APA's humane role, in making APA worth belonging to.

TROUBLESOME TOPICS AND DIFFICULTIES

It is the other set of topics, social issues not specifically linked with justice to ourselves as APA members, that have been most troublesome for APA governance. These include our involvement with protest against the Vietnam War, our endorsement of the Nuclear Freeze, our stand against corporal punishment in the schools and against aversive interventions in behavioral modification, and our positions on international human rights, among others. *Should* APA take stands on social issues beyond the promotion of psychology as a science and as a profession? Does our concern with human welfare, legitimated by the preamble to our by-laws, warrant our intrusion into affairs outside the small world of APA? There never has been agreement about it. Our perennial debates about "advocacy" have cleaved us along rather traditional lines of liberal versus conservative, and radical versus reactionary. The controversy about APA's advocacy role never goes away and is never settled. I think there are intrinsic reasons why it never *can* be settled, and it might improve the quality of our political discourse if we could share more common understanding as to *why*.

Behind the many different concrete ways in which the issue continually arises in APA are two underlying difficulties. One is a general feature of modern American culture in which American psychologists participate—our extreme individualism (accentuated during the Reagan years), in which the pursuit of self-interest or group interest is taken for granted and altruistic concerns are discounted cynically as naive or self-deceptive. Self-interested activity seems almost always to be unquestionably legitimate, in the APA as elsewhere; it is activity supposedly in the public interest that has trouble justifying itself. With the popular doctrines that psychology has exported concerning reinforcement and exchange theory, which seem to give scientific authority to self-interestedness, psychology has even been part of the problem.

The prevailing suspicion regarding public interest advocacy is also grounded in sound reasons for skepticism, which comprise the second, more fundamental difficulty. Who is to decide what is the public interest? On the one hand, we are all subject to the self-serving bias that warps our perception of our private self-interests so that we see them as also being in the public interest. From Charlie Wilson's "What's good for General Motors is good for the country," it is not very far to "What's good for advancing psychological science is good for humanity," or, "What's good for the practice of psychology is good for mental health." And, apart from the self-serving bias, we hold divergent views of what is right and proper, so each of us defines the public interest implicitly or explicitly according to our own lights in a different way. People who are absolutely sure that they know what the public interest is, the "true believer" types, do a lot of damage, as we know all too well. The damage does not necessarily come just from the religious fundamentalists who claim they have a pipeline to God's truth, though they have indeed become very difficult.

INDIVIDUALISM AS A PROBLEM

Let me go back to the problem of individualism, which was accentuated in the "me" epoch with considerable help from both my humanistic and my behavioristic colleagues. In cross-cultural perspective, American culture is really over the edge in its individualistic ethos, and the costs to people that this extreme orientation entails are increasingly visible. Enthusiastically promoted from on high in the Reagan years, our accentuated individualism has given rise to a degree of corruption in American public life that has little precedent, even in the rotten splendors of the Gilded

Age. (Reagan's appointees have been wrung out through the courts; the Pentagon procurement scandal, the Wall Street inside trading scandal, and the savings and loan scandal, which cost billions of dollars, were being followed as I wrote this by the scandal in the Chicago futures market and by charges of bribery in the previously lily-pure Federal Drug Administration about generic drugs. The scandals continue!) Unashamed predatory self-interest is becoming visible to the victimized public, and I hope that perpetrators will be held to account—and that an overdue pendulum swing is occurring.

More than just a pendulum swing is needed for humane values to prevail. It is good that psychologists and other social scientists are beginning to provide a thoughtful critical base, in touch with our science though hardly derived from it, that supports a view of what is possible for people in society that is different from the hedonistic individualism with which psychologists have mainly been identified hitherto. I am thinking, of course, of Robert Bellah and his colleagues in sociology and philosophy (Bellah, Madsen, Sullivan, Swidler, & Tipton, 1985), whose book, *Habits of the Heart*, reached a large audience, taking contemporary America to task for giving precedence to individualism over community in the explicit values in terms of which Americans justify themselves. (The self-accounts of the psychotherapeutic subculture were treated roughly in Bellah et al.'s book.) I am thinking of the early essay by Ed Sampson (1977) that pointed out the degree to which unrecognized individualistic assumptions pervade American psychology and of his recent manifesto relating his analysis to the current world situation (Sampson, 1989), of Paul Wachtel's (1983) powerful criticism of the individualist tradition in psychology and psychoanalysis, of Barry Schwartz's (1986) reexamination of "human nature," and of the important critique of *Psychology's Sanctions for Selfishness* provided by Michael and Lise Wallach (1983), now followed by their courageous new attempt to break through the bad choice between liberal relativism and authoritarian absolutism in *Rethinking Goodness* (1990). I also have Seymour Sarason's numerous contributions (e.g., 1986, 1988) in mind. In the past, our influential social critics have come from the humanities, the other social sciences, and psychoanalysis—not from psychology. Cheers for the emergence of strong and clear critical voices from our own ranks!

As I understand and resonate to the message being put forth by these colleagues, they are telling us that we psychologists have given the sanction of science uncritically to implicit individualistic values that are, of course, preempirical, not legitimately accessible to "scientific" support on such lines. The pursuit of self-interest, of self-development and self-actualization as the primary ends of existence has not been dictated by firm psychological knowledge but arises from our having been shaped by particular features of our culture in their historical vicissitudes. To the extent that the psychology we "give away" (Miller, 1969) has supported the basically selfish trend in our times (the word *narcissistic* is too fancy and entails too much bad theory!), I hope that we may now be getting into a position in which we psychologists are not a major part of the problem.

WHAT IS THE PUBLIC INTEREST?

Granted, then, that the individualistic orientation that psychology has shared with its environing culture has made us complacent about letting guild interests and special group interests dominate APA politics and that psychologists are now beginning to pose a fundamental challenge to this feature of our culture, there remains the second difficulty: How are we ever going to discover or define the public interest? Like the rest of you, I have strong intuitions as to what the public interest is, in psychology and in the world at large, and I act on them in my political participation in the APA and in local and national politics. Like everybody else, especially members of the Public Interest Coalition in APA, I *know* what is in the public interest! Because I also know, however, that my conviction that I know is not to be trusted (it will not be trusted by others, so I should not trust it myself), I have to back away from my commitments in order to consider the broader issue of how to discover and define the public interest.

Of course, there is no simple solution: I will have to wind up favoring an open politics that gives voice to competitive claims, and expects only temporary resolutions of them. Whatever *can* we mean by the public interest? In trying to come to an answer that could satisfy others besides myself, I looked back to a respected commentator, Walter Lippmann, from a generation before mine who wrote very persuasively about *The Public Philosophy* (1955). As a political commentator and social theorist, Lippmann began his discussion of "What is the public interest?" by writing, "We are examining the question of how, and by whom, the interest of an invisible community over a long span of time is represented in the practical work of governing a modern state" (p. 41). Let me extract from what Lippmann (1955) wrote over three decades ago, which is not irrelevant to issues in contemporary psychology:

> In ordinary circumstances voters cannot be expected to transcend their particular, localized and self-regarding opinions. . . . In their circumstances, which as private persons they cannot readily surmount, the voters are most likely to suppose that whatever seems obviously good to them must be good for the country, and good in the sight of God.
>
> I am far from implying that the voters are not entitled to the representation of their particular opinions and interests. But their opinions and interests should be taken for what they are and for no more. They are not—as such—propositions in the public interest. . . .

Let us ask ourselves, How is the public interest discerned and judged? . . . [W]e cannot answer the question by attempting to forecast what the invisible community, with all its unborn constituents, will, would, or might say if and when it ever had a chance to vote. There is no point in toying with any notion of an imaginary plebiscite to discover the public interest. We cannot know what we ourselves will be thinking five years hence, much less what infants now in the cradle will be thinking when they go to the polling booth.

Yet their interests, as we observe them today, are within the public interest. Living adults share, we must believe, the same public interest. For them, however, the public interest is mixed with, and is often at odds with, their private and special interests. Put this way, we can say, I suggest, that the public interest may be presumed to be what men [we would now say *people*] would choose if they saw clearly, thought rationally, acted disinterested and benevolently. (pp. 41–42)

In modern mass democracies, Lippmann thought, the challenge to political leadership is to promote the public interest so conceived in dialogue with the many voices of private and special group interests. He saw the modern record as poor and attributed the crisis in 20th century democracies to attrition of what he called the "public philosophy" as a shared underlying political ideology, his phrasing for the Natural Law doctrine of the Enlightenment. In his words, it amounts to

the postulate that there is a rational order of things in which it is possible, by sincere inquiry and rational debate, to distinguish the true and the false, the right and the wrong, the good which leads to the realization of human ends and the evil which leads to destruction and to the death of civility. The free political institutions of the Western world were conceived and established by men who believed that honest reflection on the common experience of mankind would always cause men to come to the same ultimate conclusions. (p. 134)

Do you perceive Lippmann, as I read him, anticipating recent intellectually fashionable writers on the conservative side, such as Alasdair MacIntyre (1981) and Alan Bloom (1987)? In *After Virtue*, McIntyre traced the present plight of moral philosophy, with its cacophony of voices and loss of moral meaning, to the collapse of the Aristotelian tradition as sustaining and sustained by a moral community—the collapse of the public philosophy in Lippmann's sense. Bloom's best-selling jeremiad against the liberal relativism of the world of American colleges and universities, *The Closing of the American Mind*, explicitly sought to restore the reign of natural law as a frame for personal philosophy. For that matter, Bellah et al. (1985) in *Habits of the Heart* introduced their critique of contemporary American culture, according to which commitment and community as intrinsic sources of human value suffer in our excesses of what they term *utilitarian* and *expressive individualism*, by reminding us how the Biblical and Republican traditions moderated our individualistic tendencies in public life at America's origins. They too are nostalgic for the "public philosophy."

As you may have guessed, so am I! I share their yearning for community and their discontent with anomic relativism (though I may weigh more heavily than they the favorable shift in the balance of human values that came about for most of us when so many people left the arduous and spiritually destructive poverty of traditional rural life and the narrow constraints of Main Street for the broadened vistas and healthier prospects of the modern world). All the same, I do not think we can retrieve the old Enlightenment faith, at least as Lippmann phrased it, by any fiat of Jamesian "will to believe." Our faith in the two pillars of modern thought since Descartes, reason and empiricism, has been too deeply shaken. In fact, we do live in a multicultural nation in a multicultural world, in which the older certainties are moot. There are liberating advantages to our intellectual and moral situation, just as there are heavy human costs. But we cannot wish our situation away. Future generations, if they survive the life-threatening world problems of which we are already aware, might reemerge into community in the old style after a new Dark Age, which some of our true believers are promoting, but the community of traditional consensus is beyond our deliberate reach. A good many modern psychologists, I among them, would be among the last people to believe that, by reason and evidence, we could or should all arrive at the same conclusions.

In other words, I cannot defend as tenable for our time the public philosophy that Lippmann called on to justify the public interest. For better or worse, we are stuck in a pluralistic society and world in which there is little prospect of our agreeing on first premises about abortion, the meaning of gender, or any of the things about which people seem still to be ready to fight, including religion and nationhood. Nevertheless, I want to endorse the essence of his conception of the public interest and to argue that even without consensus on fundamentals, we can do much better than is usual for us by trying, in our leadership and individually, to emphasize informed, rational, disinterested, benevolent decision making. Just as in our scientific roles we should and mostly do act *as if* there were truth "out there" that we only have to be clever enough to discover (whether or not the constructivists are right, that is surely the only pragmatically justified stance for scientists to take), so in our personal, political, and psychologist roles we also do well to act *as if* there were objective right and wrong, better and worse, choices and policies. We are surely mistaken if we have the presumption to believe we are *absolutely* right about our own choices, just as we are mistaken if we are sure about the absolute truth of our factual beliefs. But we are adrift as persons and useless as citizens if we do not try to find and pursue the right and if we do not take our own convictions—and those of our opponents—seriously as attempts to advance the right and give it reality. We become literally "demoralized."

As I see it, the least common denominator of politics is the negotiation of competing self- and group interests. At its best, politics is the arena in which different conceptions of the right—of justice and the public interest—get threshed out, modified, mutually accommodated, and negotiated with the various special interests. Politics so conceived never settles issues, but it contributes centrally to the quality of human life at least as it has been experienced in the Western tradition. Psychologists generally are not used to thinking along these lines. (For access to the intellectual sources on which this way of thinking is based, I am most indebted to Hannah Arendt, 1958, and Isaiah Berlin, 1978.) I hope we can come to "give away" a psychology that is more concordant with this way of thinking. And I hope we can apply it to thinking about the public interest, as APA policy and action bear on it.

THE POLITICS OF PUBLIC INTEREST IN THE APA

I will now leave these underlying issues of philosophical perspective, which are hard to discuss persuasively despite their importance, and return to the public interest politics of APA. First, I will continue my consideration of APA advocacy on public interest issues. Then I will discuss the public interest aspect of psychologists' major guild commitments as scientists and as professionals.

Conservatives in academic science have time and again parted company with the Society for the Psychological Study of Social Issues (SPSSI; Division 9 of APA) types to insist that APA respect a sharp separation between psychologists' and citizens' roles in regard to advocacy on issues other than the promotion of guild and (sometime) member-category interests. They have argued that the APA, and its members when they speak as psychologists, should only present the conclusions of our scientific research, only on the basis of *data*. Only when we have solid data have we a right to speak as psychologists, they insist, and our advocacy should be restricted to summarizing and interpreting the data "objectively." I cannot agree. "Data" are seldom conclusive, and data are not our only or even necessarily our most important contribution to the public interest, although it is great when we have conclusive data. Kiesler (Kiesler & Sibulkin, 1987) has some very important data that help redefine the public interest in hospitalizing mentally ill persons. But the role of data is mostly different. In the area of international conflict and peace, our major contributors—Urie Bronfenbrenner (1961), Ralph White (1970), and Morton Deutsch (1983)—have had their largest impact through the use of their research to *reframe* the problem of international conflict. They do not prove a policy issue; they employ research to illustrate or dramatize a view of the conflict process that focuses on the symmetrical, mirror-like enemy images that develop, which tend to exacerbate and escalate the conflict, rather than focusing exclusively on the evil of the adversary, as is common even in national councils of policy. Such contributions open important options for policy discussion, although they do not involve definitive conclusions that are firmly based on data. They have been influential in the past, and appropriately so (Smith, 1986).

I think there is also much misunderstanding about the actual role of APA in "advocacy." In the Council of Representatives, much heat has been generated over the years by resolutions proposing that APA endorse one or another policy position. Rarely do such resolutions have real-life effects that justify their cost in organizational strain. They may be worth the cost, however, when they instruct the activity of APA staff specifically or when there are organizations and constituencies outside the APA that are in place to use them (as, for example, with APA's position, taken in 1975, against corporal punishment in the schools). APA can usually advocate more effectively for public interest matters along lines similar to its support for guild issues: providing relevant information and testimony in close liaison with the government's legislative and executive branches and disseminating public information skillfully. This is not at all in the same realm as passing resolutions!

APA *has* gone substantially beyond our guild interests and the special interests of our own disadvantaged categories of members in ways that do not strain our internal politics, in spite of the contrary broad characterization I have made of our public interest activity. A prime example is the relatively recent BSERP Committee on Children, Youth, and Families that I have already mentioned (but its establishment *was* a motherhood issue that was hardly debatable!) APA might still do much more by way of research and advocacy on behalf of children, so many of whom are poor. Among the divisions of APA, there is especially SPSSI (Society for the Psychological Study of Social Issues), which had a prior independent existence before the reorganization of the APA after World War II and has consistently advocated broadly conceived public interest concerns in APA and at large. Members should also know that APA's policy staff, well equipped to represent APA in the national political process, regularly address public interest issues as well as guild issues. When I was preparing this article, I read in the newsletter of Division 34, Population and Environmental Psychology, the following statement from its president, Ralph Taylor (1989), after his participation in the 1989 Division Leadership Conference:

> As a member of APA who has felt in the past that the organization was not applying research to policymakers as much as it should, I find

recent developments in the PID [Public Interest Directorate] *extremely* heartening. These activities also point up the substantial clout that APA is capable of having. (p. 3)

Presumably, Taylor was particularly impressed by the careful, scrupulous, and effective representation that APA made to Surgeon General Koop concerning the inconclusive research evidence about the psychological effects of abortion on women, although there was a trend suggesting that abortion causes minimal trauma.

OUR GUILD ISSUES: PROFESSIONAL AND SCIENTIFIC

Public interest issues have received much attention in APA politics, but I have no doubt that it is how APA handles its guild issues—of psychology as a science and profession—that has the greatest impact on the public interest, however we may interpret it. What we do as a science, what we do as a profession, makes a difference to the public weal. It can even be harmful; it is often neutral; we all hope that it makes a positive contribution. I have long argued that our guild concerns, whether scientific or human service-oriented, ought to be compatible with promoting the public interest. At a minimum, they should be at least orthogonal, though because of our self-serving bias, a degree of skepticism about such claims is always in order. APA's advocacy roles are so heavily focused on guild interests that scrutiny of their compatibility with the public interest is highly desirable and inherently political.

Because my own affiliations are closer to the scientific than to the professional wing of psychology, I tend to give psychological science a relatively clean bill of health in terms of its involvement with the public interest. I do believe that the development of psychological science is mostly in the public interest. As a long-term SPSSI member, I am delighted when competent science-oriented psychologists devote themselves to attacking problems to which contributions should be humanly important. I worry that insufficient scientific attention is being paid to the psychological aspects of the world-shaking issues of war and peace and environmental pollution and depletion, the essential life and death issues that I mentioned at the outset, and to the causes and consequences of poverty, which underlies so many human problems. But I am just as delighted when others are so captured by their intrinsic sense of direction in basic research that such an applied focus would seem immoral to them. I am worried about the ethics of experimentation with humans and with animals, especially when dubious practices of deception became normative for a whole subfield, as they did for a while in social psychology, but I think our record is mostly good. Under current regulative pressure, it seems to me that the risk of losing important knowledge that may ultimately help people (and other animals!) probably exceeds the risk of damaging ethical violations. Our ethics of research are becoming too bureaucratic, at the cost, perhaps, of becoming less internalized.

On the professional side, I also believe that a strong and responsible profession of psychology is in the public interest. But continued warfare with psychiatry over issues of turf—essential guild interests—may be to the disadvantage of the troubled people we claim to serve, who suffer from the heavy cutting of government funds that have supported both psychiatry and psychology. I think our reflex rejection of anything labeled as a "medical model" is self-serving and wrong. Many problems of "mental health" that properly concern us also have their medical aspects. And I do not like our recent single-minded focus on the financial aspects of practice—third party payments, health insurance, medicare, and the rest. It is all justifiable and understandable, but it somehow blocks out the *service* values that may have been a little more prominent earlier on, though not so prominent as in social work, which seems to have undergone a similar value transition.

CAN PSYCHOLOGISTS GIVE *PRO BONO* SERVICE?

Psychologists got into professionalized human service too late to emulate the earlier *pro bono* traditions of medicine, now in attrition in the era of Medicaid and Medicare. Unlike earlier medicine and even contemporary law, psychology has *no* tradition of *pro bono* practice, even though the concept is endorsed in our formal ethical code. On the science side, which includes scientist-practioners, there is normative pressure to contribute to peer reviewing of papers and research proposals. On the clinical side, I see no equivalent.

I am not suggesting that clinical practitioners take on charity cases paternalistically; we have outgrown that era. Rather, psychologists might take initiative to provide consultation, *not* guidance and control, to the burgeoning realm of self-help and volunteer organizations (see Jacobs & Goodman, 1989). It has seemed to me for a long time that self-help and volunteer programs are *the* most constructive development imaginable in the field of mental health. For people with problems in living, there simply cannot be enough professionals or even paraprofessionals to treat patients on a one-to-one basis (Smith & Hobbs, 1966). The widespread replication of these mutual support systems clearly is based on real merit. They will not necessarily or perhaps often want the help of psychologists even if we proffer it, but with genuine concern and respectful tact, professional psychologists can surely make a valuable contribution to them—on a *pro bono* basis. Psychologists might also find ways of involving themselves more actively, for example, in evaluating the effectiveness of differently organized programs and in stimulating the trial of new models. In my limited range of direct acquaintance, I know of a community suicide-prevention hotline that benefited greatly from the volunteered aid of a psychologist who developed training materials and contributed largely to the recurrent training of new cohorts of telephone volunteers. There are surely many examples of such contributions, but they have not become a normative component of professional careers in psychology.

CONCLUSIONS

In closing, let me draw together the complex issues that we have been considering. However we may conceive of the public interest, the ways in which scientists and professionals in psychology pursue their guild interests have more effect on the public interest than any activities that they carry out explicitly in its name. Let us be sure that our guild activities at least do not harm the public interest, and let us hope that we do better. Understandably, APA has met with most success in its public interest activities when they converge with the special interests of justice to particular disadvantaged segments of our membership. Our record in other areas of advocacy is more mixed, but we have used our strong presence with the executive and legislative branches of the federal government effectively on matters not tied to our guild concerns. May these efforts continue!

When we ask ourselves, what *is* the public interest, our attempts to generate informed, reasonable, disinterested, and benevolent answers will not automatically produce consensus. Open political debate about divergent interpretations of the public interest is good for the APA. Because there can be no valid claims to absolute truth about the public interest, it is the best we can do. However, as we debate these issues, I hope we can bear in mind the urgent problems of human survival and social justice that I noted at the outset. The Reagan years, which I despise, have made us too accustomed to acquiescing in human (and biological) disaster. Psychologists have much to contribute in recreating a more humane and sustainable world. The APA can do much more to facilitate it. I hope that APA will continued its involvement in public interest issues in our national politics and that psychologists, as members of APA and the American Psychological Society and individually, will keep in touch with public issues that affect the lives of people and become politically active on the side of justice and human welfare.

REFERENCES

Arendt, H. (1958). *The human condition.* Chicago: University of Chicago Press.

Bellah, R. N., Madsen, R., Sullivan, W. M., Swidler, A., & Tipton, S. M. (1985). *Habits of the heart: Individualism and commitment in American life.* Berkeley: University of California Press.

Berlin, I. (1978). Does political theory exist? In I. Berlin, *Concepts and categories: Philosophical essays.* London: Hogarth Press.

Bloom, A. (1987). *The closing of the American mind.* New York: Simon & Schuster.

Bronfenbrenner, U. (1961). The mirror image in Soviet-American relations: A social psychologist's report. *Journal of Social Issues, 17*(3), 45–56.

Deutsch, M. (1983). The prevention of World War III: A psychological perspective. *Political Psychology, 4,* 3–32.

Jacobs, M. K., & Goodman, G. (1989). Psychology and self-help groups: Predictions on a partnership. *American Psychologist, 44,* 536–545.

Kiesler, C., & Sibulkin, A. E. (1987). *Mental hospitalization: Myths and facts about a national crisis.* Newbury Park, CA: Sage.

Lippmann, W. (1955). *The public philosophy.* Boston: Little, Brown.

MacIntyre, A. (1981). *After virtue: A study in moral theory.* Notre Dame, IN: University of Notre Dame Press.

Miller, G. A. (1969). Psychology as a means of promoting human welfare. *American Psychologist, 24,* 1063–1075.

Sampson, E. E. (1977). Psychology and the American ideal. *Journal of Personality and Social Psychology, 35,* 767–782.

Sampson, E. E. (1989). The challenge of social change for psychology: Globalization and psychology's theory of the person. *American Psychologist, 44,* 914–921.

Sarason, S. B. (1986). And what is the public interest? *American Psychologist, 41,* 899–905.

Sarason, S. B. (1988). *The making of an American Psychologist: An autobiography.* San Francisco: Jossey-Bass.

Schwartz, B. (1986). *The battle for human nature: Science, morality, and modern life.* New York: Norton.

Smith, M. B. (1986). War, peace, and psychology. *Journal of Social Issues, 42*(4), 23–38.

Smith, M. B., & Hobbs, N. (1966). The community and the community mental health center. *American Psychologist, 21,* 499–509.

Taylor, R. B. (1989). From the president. *Population and Environmental Psychology 34 News, 15*(2), 1–3.

Wachtel, P. L. (1983). *The poverty of affluence: A psychological portrait of the American way of life.* New York: Free Press/MacMillan.

Wallach, M. A., & Wallach, L. (1983). *Psychology's sanction for selfishness: The error of egoism in theory and therapy.* San Francisco: Freeman.

Wallach, M. A., & Wallach, L. (1990). *Rethinking goodness.* Albany, NY: New York State University Press.

White, R. (1970). *Nobody wanted war: Misperception in Vietnam and other wars.* Garden City, NJ: Doubleday-Anchor.

II

PSYCHOLOGICAL SCIENCE
AS A POLICY RESOURCE

INTRODUCTION

A RENEWED NEED FOR RESEARCH ON THE SCIENCE OF PUBLIC POLICY

PAMELA EBERT FLATTAU and WILLIAM HOWELL

Psychologists have long understood that the research they conduct is of interest and use to the public. A key to the successful use—and further support—of psychological research is thought to be the "informed decision maker."

In the 1970s, a small band of applied scientists actively explored the process by which decision makers at national, state, and local levels acquired information for purposes of policy and planning, and related studies looked into the uses that were made of scientific findings during the course of the policy process. For the most part, those earlier studies—some of which are included in this section—suggested that scientists could be assured of the effective use of their findings for policy and planning if the scientists played a more active role in the communication of that information.

Attentive to the need for informed decision making, numerous professional societies, including the American Psychological Association (APA), decided about two decades ago to strengthen channels of communication between scientists and policymakers in a number of ways. For example:

- The American Association for the Advancement of Science (AAAS) established the Congressional Science Fellowship program, placing doctoral level scientists in U.S. congressional offices for a period of public service; the APA soon joined the AAAS in providing support for that effort.

- Cognizant of the important role an "informed public" plays in the support for and use of science, awards were given—and continue to be given—by a number of organizations to science writers and entertainers for their accurate and lively portrayals of advances in science and—in the case of psychology—for their exploration of sensitive psychological issues through publications, radio, television, or film.
- Professional journals, such as *American Psychologist*, started to devote sections of their journals to the exploration of public policy issues in an effort to keep readers informed of policies and programs affecting them as professionals.
- More emphasis was placed by the scientific community on the direct communication of science to policymakers through the increased participation of scientists—including psychologists—in influential advisory roles, whether at the national, state, or local level.

There is every indication that society stands today at a major crossroads in the public understanding and use of psychology. Advances in scientific psychology continue in many areas, both basic and applied. However, major changes are taking place in the perceived utility of the very programs and policies in which psychologists, among others, have had a special interest.

It is not clear, furthermore, that today's decision makers will invite scientific input in the same spirit that such input was solicited two or three decades ago. In a way, a new policy paradigm has emerged, offering a unique opportunity for applied scientists to take a fresh look at the science-and-public-policy interface as it affects and involves psychology. New policy studies might well lead to the conclusion that other strategies are needed for strengthening the connection between science and public policy decision making beyond those initiated two decades ago.

To facilitate a renewal of research on the science of public policy, we consider first what we have learned from those earlier policy studies and then consider the extent to which those studies apply to the contemporary policy scene.

WHAT HAS BEEN LEARNED FROM PAST STUDIES OF PUBLIC POLICY

The editors of this volume have assembled in this section an impressive collection of previously published articles by psychologists whose findings we have summarized in four recurrent themes. The first of these concerns access to information:

> Policymakers regularly receive a wide variety of scientific and technical information, which they apply in shaping social and scientific policies and programs.

The chapters by Weiss and Weiss (see chap. 8) and by Maccoby et al. (see chap. 9) make this point, as do several of the others. It is safe to say that advances in information technology have greatly increased access to such input since these articles appeared (in 1981 and 1989, respectively) and that the trend will continue well into the future. A key issue raised by Weiss and Weiss, however, concerns the way in which policymakers actually *use* such information in making policy decisions—a process that appears quite different from that to which scientists are accustomed.

The second theme follows directly from the application process issue, and it has implications for the role scientists might play in ensuring a policy impact from their research.

> The information provided by scientists for policy and planning will be interpreted in a political context that cannot be ignored.

Archer and his colleagues (see chap. 10; first published in 1992) poignantly underscore the challenges that contemporary scientists can expect to encounter in the course of conducting policy-relevant research and making that research available for policy and planning. Although the scenario depicted in their chapter addresses the formation of "energy policy," there is every reason to believe that scientists working in other policy areas have shared the experience documented by Archer. Of course, the failure of researchers to understand the process by which their findings might influence policy, or in some cases even to understand the problems to which their work might be usefully applied, is a continuing concern. Bevan's chapter (see chap. 7; first published in 1980) makes this point, along with the argument that scientists must become more adept at communicating the value of their work in the public or political arena.

There are risks, then, associated with participation in contemporary public policy debates. Perhaps the greatest risk for a scientist is the potential for ethical problems related to the act of "guiding" decision makers:

> To whom are social scientists responsible? What emphasis should be placed on propositions about human behavior relative to the action implications that flow from them?

These questions were posed by Caplan and Nelson in 1973 (see chap. 6) and pertain today. The answers are no easier to come by today than they were 20 years ago. Policymakers are making new interpretations of the utility of research by social and behavioral scientists whether scientists like it or not. For Caplan and Nelson, there is a serious danger that the behavioral emphasis of psychology encourages policymakers to seek *individual* rather than *institutional* solutions to social problems and thus to misuse the information. The implication is that scientists should do what they can to minimize the risk of misapplications of science.

The final theme simply recognizes that science exists in a very different political world today than it did several decades ago, when policymakers generally accepted research as a worthy endeavor and scientists devoted most of their attention to it.

> A *"professionalization of science"* has evolved over the years, replete with the emergence of national organizations and an increasing awareness within the research community that science must inform public policy. It is not clear, however, whether individual scientists are becoming better prepared to fulfill this role.

Former APA President William Bevan (see chap. 7) offers a thoughtful analysis of the changes that took place in the social and political climate in which science operated through the 1970s. Considering the ongoing nature of public policy debates, we share Bevan's hope that succeeding generations of psychologists have been—and will continue to be—more attuned to the history and appropriate uses of science by policymakers than their predecessors.

However, as Weiss and Weiss (see chap. 8) point out, it is not always "scientific criteria" that determine how scientific information will be used in the end, and it is not clear whether contemporary planners and policymakers are more likely to be sensitive to the intrusion of "extrascientific criteria" into the decisions they will make.

THE OBLIGATION OF PSYCHOLOGISTS AS SCIENTISTS IN A POLICY ENVIRONMENT

In order to assure that psychological science is serving—and serving appropriately—as a resource for policy and planning, a contemporary review is needed of the "science-and-public-policy" process. As a profession, psychologists need to focus attention on the issues raised 20 years ago by the authors whose chapters are found in this section, if only to make certain that the next generation of scientists—like those contributing to the chapter by Archer and his colleagues—are prepared for the challenges they will confront in the course of making their work available to the public for policy and planning.

Some of the issues we believe merit consideration by our profession derive from the following considerations:

- How do today's decision makers gain access to the latest research and thinking in psychology? What might be done to improve that access for purposes of policy and planning?
- How well-informed are psychologists about the political context within which the research and information that they contribute will be interpreted and used? How might deficiencies in their understanding best be addressed?
- How much agreement exists within the psychological science community regarding the proper role for researchers in ensuring appropriate application of the knowledge they generate? What are the alternative strategies, and how can they be implemented?
- How well are young psychologists being prepared to cope with the social and ethical responsibilities inherent in the conduct and communication of publicly supported research, especially that of a more "socially relevant" nature? What could or should be done to improve the situation?

Attentive readers may well find other, salient conclusions to draw about the science-and-public-policy interface from the chapters that follow. We look forward to a renewal of professional interest in this topic, and we believe that the authors who paved the way 20 years ago for the new debate provided an important professional service to all psychologists.

6

ON BEING USEFUL: THE NATURE AND CONSEQUENCES OF PSYCHOLOGICAL RESEARCH ON SOCIAL PROBLEMS

NATHAN CAPLAN and STEPHEN D. NELSON

There is considerable encouragement, support, and pressure today for behavioral scientists to direct their attention away from the preoccupations of their vigorously irrelevant past and to engage in work with more obvious social utility. This move from peripheral functions at the edge of society to the more central activities of organized social planning enjoys the official sanction of two important study groups (Brim et al., 1969; National Academy of Sciences, 1969) and the promise of favorable future financial support as exemplified by the National Science Foundation Research Addressing National Needs (RANN). Increased federal funding for "applied" research is already evident. Riecken (1972) reported that from fiscal year 1968 to 1971, the total federal expenditures for "basic" research in the

Reprinted from *American Psychologist*, 28, 199–211. Copyright 1973 by the American Psychological Association.

An earlier version of this chapter was presented at the annual meeting of the American Psychological Association, Washington, D. C., September 1971. The chapter is supported in part by Grant MH 19313 to the authors from the National Institute of Mental Health, United States Public Health Service.

The authors wish to express their appreciation to Joyce Kornbluh for her help in preparing the manuscript.

social sciences grew from \$116 to \$141 million, while federal expenditures for "applied" research during that same period grew from \$134 to \$257 million.

Those of us who have long felt that the social sciences have not met their social responsibility welcome this upsurge of interest in the problems of society. On the other hand, becoming useful is not as simple a matter as it might first appear. The application of psychological findings and thought to the improvement of societal functioning and human welfare is fraught with many potential problems. Our purpose here is to discuss some meta-issues that raise doubts and uncertainties about the possible consequences of applying psychological thought and research—and the behavioral sciences in general—to the problems of society. We do this in hopes that both psychology as a profession and society as a whole may avoid potential pitfalls and unanticipated negative consequences that may ensue from injudiciously moving the orientation of psychology as a science into the public arena as a means for dealing with the problems that beset society.

To delimit the domain of "relevancy" with which this article is concerned we should emphasize three things: (a) in this article we deal with *social* policy and not other types of public policy issues; (b) our interest is in social policy at the national level, with nationwide implications; and (c) we are concerned with social problems and problem behavior—various kinds of so-called social pathology.

The discussion of these issues is organized into two parts. The first part deals with what may be called the "person-blame" causal attribution bias in psychological research on social problems. By this we mean the tendency to hold individuals responsible for their problems. Our concern is with (a) psychologically oriented research that focuses on "person-centered" characteristics (those that lie within the individual), while ignoring situationally relevant factors (those external to the individual); and (b) the tendency to attribute *causal* significance to person-centered variables found in statistical association with the social problem in question. Published research reports are used to illustrate this bias. In this section of the article we also discuss the social action implications of this person-blame bias and two major reasons for its prevalence among psychologists.

In the second part of the discussion we explore the utility and applicability of psychological thought and research to social problems within the framework of the issues raised in the first part of the discussion. Particular attention is given to the political implications and partisan advantages of person-blame interpretations and how unintended functions served by such a bias in causal attribution may become ends in themselves if well-meaning researchers continue to regard social research as if it were a neutral competency.

PROBLEM DEFINITIONS AND CAUSAL ATTRIBUTION BIAS IN PSYCHOLOGICAL RESEARCH

The Importance of Problem Definitions: Person Versus Situation

We have chosen to concentrate on problem-defining activities for three closely linked reasons.

1. First, what is done about a problem depends on how it is defined. The way a social problem is defined determines the attempts at remediation—or even whether such attempts will be made—by suggesting both the *foci* and the *techniques* of intervention and by ruling out alternative possibilities. More specifically, problem definition determines the change strategy, the selection of a social action delivery system, and the criteria for evaluation.

Problem definitions are based on assumptions about the causes of the problem and where they lie.[1] If the causes of delinquency, for example, are defined in *person-centered* terms (e.g., inability to delay gratification, or incomplete sexual identity), then it would be logical to initiate *person-change* treatment techniques and intervention strategies to deal with the problem. Such treatment would take the form of counseling or other person-change efforts to "reach" the delinquent, thereby using his potential for self-control to make his behavior more conventional. Or if it seemed that person-centered impediments at the root of such "antisocial" behavior were too deeply ingrained or not amenable to routine help (e.g., causes such as birth order position or an extra Y chromosome), it would then follow that coercive external control techniques (e.g., confinement or possibly medical solutions) could be instituted. Under such circumstances, it

---

[1]The reader should be forewarned that in the discussion to follow, a constant-sum model of causality is used, which assumes in its weakest form that person-centered causes and situation-centered causes are inversely related (i.e., the more one type of causal factor is shown to operate, the less the other type is assumed to operate, in bringing about particular outcomes). In its most extreme form, this model would assume that person-centered and situation-centered causal factors are dichotomous and mutually exclusive (i.e., if one type of factor is shown to be causally operative, it is assumed that the other type does not operate at all). The authors labor under no such simplistic notions and are well aware of the complexities of causal interpretation and multidetermined outcomes. The arguments in this article follow this simpler model, however, because of (a) the tendency of the public to think in such either-or terms with respect to causality, and (b) the eagerness of political actors to take advantage of that tendency.

Further, because we are dealing with the public phenomenology of causality, the article necessarily blurs two concepts that would be carefully distinguished in a more rigorously analytical article. These are the concepts of (a) the *cause* of an event or condition, which according to the scientific ideal can be factually and empirically ascertained and then communicated in a purely descriptive, nonevaluative fashion; and (b) *responsibility* for an event or condition, which includes both credit and blame and, as these words suggest, is more evaluative and value laden, based on certain normative assumptions including an evaluation of the event and, in the case of personal or group agents, intentionality. There is an even sharper analytical and often empirical distinction between these two concepts and a third, that of responsibility for changing an undesirable event or condition.

could be argued with impunity that those officially defined as delinquent would have to relinquish autonomous control over their behavior and other rights in the service of the common good. Thus, where person-centered interpretations provide the foundation on which corrective intervention is based, little need be done about external factors since they would presumably be of lesser or no etiological significance in the determination of such behavior.

If, on the other hand, explanations are *situation-centered*, for example, if delinquency were interpreted as the substitution of extralegal paths for already preempted, conventionally approved pathways for achieving socially valued goals, then efforts toward corrective treatment would logically have a *system-change* orientation. Efforts would be launched to create suitable opportunities for success and achievement along conventional lines; thus, existing physical, social, or economic arrangements, not individual psyches, would be the targets for change.

The way a problem is defined determines not only what is done about it, but also what is *not* done—or what apparently need not be done. If matrifocal family structure is argued to be the basis for deviancy, nonachievement, and high unemployment, then opportunity structure, discriminatory hiring practices, and other system defects would appear less blameworthy as the causes of poverty. Likewise, if it can be shown that the use of nonstandard speech interferes with the ability to mediate thought and consequently is the cause of poor performance on formal academic tasks, then such a person-blame explanation would remove pressure for structural and institutional changes in the educational system to raise the educational levels of persons from "linguistically deficient" backgrounds. If leniency during child rearing could be shown to be characteristic of student activists, then their system-antagonistic actions could be discredited as the ravings of immature and spoiled children. If, on the other hand, we found that the dissidents are more likely to be cognitively correct about the issues in question than nondissidents or counterdissidents, then there would be reason to seriously consider their recommendations for change.

Whether the social problem to be attacked is delinquency, mental health, drug abuse, unemployment, ghetto riots, or whatever, the significance of the defining process is the same: *the action (or inaction) taken will depend largely on whether causes are seen as residing within individuals or in the environment.* Thus, because the remedies proposed reflect the definition of the problem, it is crucial that the causal inferences made by problem identifiers, social policy planners, and professional change agents—anyone who plans and guides large-scale action programs—be based on accurate and comprehensive information. Sartre, in *Saint Genet*, said it in a way that illustrates not only that how you define something determines what you do about it, but also that what you do about a problem also defines it: "Action, whatever it be, modifies that which is in the name of that which is not yet."

2. Such definitions, once legitimated and acted upon, tend to define the problem indefinitely, irrespective of their validity. Once in effect, they resist replacement by other definitions. Program administrators and professional change agents develop a vested interest in maintaining established definitions since their very jobs, status, power, and the employment of subordinates may depend on those definitions being accepted as correct. If intervention fails, the problem definition and the delivery system are seldom held responsible. Instead, the responsibility for failure may be avoided by locating blame in the target group and by interpreting that failure as a further sign of the seriousness of the "pathology" being dealt with. As far as we know, no recent large-scale action program has been put out of business because research has shown its failure to fulfill its intended goals.

Also, to the extent that a problem definition conforms to and reinforces dominant cultural myths and clichés (e.g., Horatio Alger), as indeed most definitions must in order to become widely accepted, its change or replacement will be stubbornly resisted. Furthermore, people tend to conform to public definitions and expectations; even if there are doubts regarding their accuracy, they at least provide people with a publicly defined role and definite image of who they are and what is expected of them. Still further, of course, many groups have economic and political interests in seeing that certain definitions are accepted over others (e.g., the business community with regard to the causes of unemployment). In the context of such pressures, an invalid person-centered problem definition often has its most pernicious effect: it can convince the target population of its blameworthiness as alleged.

Thus, problem definitions take on a life of their own; they set in motion a variety of social and psychological forces which give them important functional significance. Consequently, to question established definitions is to challenge important institutions and belief systems that have their origins in those definitions.

3. In view of the federal funds being invested in evaluations of social intervention efforts, it bears emphasizing that effective evaluation depends on linking program outcomes to the presumed causes of the problem behavior. Thus, a precise and explicit diagnosis of the problem is an indispensable preliminary to good program evaluation. Many different forces shape human behavior, and if remedial intervention fails to produce intended effects, it may be impossible to know the reasons for failure, that is, whether because of the limited changeability of the target population, whether the level of intensity of the treatment was inadequate to produce

an effect, or whether the treatment program was inappropriate because it was premised on invalid problem definitions and incorrect assumptions about the causal factors involved.

In the foregoing we have described why problem definitions are crucial in determining what is done or not done about social problems and, more specifically, how person-blame definitions may deflect attention and energies away from important situational determinants, often to the detriment of those supposedly being helped. The significance of this discussion resides in the fact that regardless of the type of problem and the intent of the investigator, the findings of psychologically oriented research lend themselves more easily to person-blame than to system-blame interpretations of the problem. In consequence, such research frequently plays an integral role in a chain of events that results in *blaming people in difficult situations for their own predicament*. This article focuses on the processes by which this takes place and the implications for "problem" subgroups, the profession, and society as a whole.

Person-Centered Preoccupation and Causal Attribution Bias of Psychological Research

It is often at the problem definition stage in the social policy formulation process that social scientists either volunteer, or are called on, to be helpful. It is expected that we will provide expert and unbiased information, but the meaning of "unbiased" is not identical for the consumers and the producers of social science information. To the knowledge user, it may mean (*a*) that the problem will be viewed from all vantage points and that the interpretation offered will depend on an assessment of a sufficient variety of competing hypotheses that reflect the complexity of the issues, and/or (*b*) that the new information does not challenge established definitions.

To the social science knowledge producer, on the other hand, "unbiased" is defined in terms of the canons of scientific methodology. However, there is a characteristic that distinguishes psychology from other disciplines, and while this distinction may or may not be a bias in a technical, methodological sense, the fact that the chief focus of interest for psychologists is on person-centered variables has a definite biasing effect on the *inferential potential* of the findings when used as a premise on which to base later action for "corrective" change. Psychologists study individuals and in particular their mental states: their thoughts, attitudes, motives, intrapsychic equilibrium, etc. Moreover, we prefer to view these factors as independent variables, that is, antecedent and causal in relation to other behavior; and while we may pay lip service to external factors influencing behavior and agree that man to a large degree is a simulator of his environment, when it comes to the actual study of that man and why he behaves as he does, we are more likely to limit our search for etiological evidence to what goes on between his ears and to ignore or exclude from consideration a multitude of external impingements that could justifiably be hypothesized as causal.[2]

The law of the instrument. When psychologists turn their attention to social problems, we see something akin to what Archibald (1970) called the "clinical orientation" to the utilization of social scientific knowledge, which she characterizes as assuming that "if the shoe doesn't fit, there's something wrong with your foot." The reasons for this parochial perspective are understandable. To begin with, it is an occupational expectancy that the psychologist would want to demonstrate the applicability of his skills and services. Kaplan (1964) called this widely observed tendency the Law of the Instrument: give a small boy a hammer, and suddenly he discovers that everything needs hammering. Train a person in psychological theory and research, and suddenly a world disastrously out of tune with human needs is explained as a state of mind. As we shall see presently, the probability of locating cause in variables outside one's area of familiarity or expertise is not great. "It comes as no particular surprise to discover that a scientist formulates problems in a way which requires for their solution just those techniques in which he himself is especially skilled [Kaplan, 1964, p. 31]." The difficulty is that, as Kaplan says, "The price of training is always a certain 'trained incapacity': the more we know how to do something, the harder it is to learn to do it differently [p. 31]."

Evidence of the person-centered bias in psychology with regard to social problems. To illustrate the intrapersonal preoccupation of psychologists studying social problems, we examined the first six months' issues of the 1970 *Psychological Abstracts* (Volume 44, Numbers 1–6, plus the semiannual index). We took as an example the research dealing with black Americans, who represent the largest, most visible, and most frequently studied group in a problematic relationship to the rest of society.

The following criteria were used for deciding whether a particular abstract should be included in the categorization:

1. We selected those items that either mentioned blacks specifically or were included under the index heading "Negro."

---

[2] Our assertion is not inconsistent with, nor should it be confused with, Carlson's (1971) recent claim of a "generalist" bias in personality research (i.e., the tendency to concentrate on the effect of different experimental conditions on individuals, irrespective of individual differences). Her claim is relevant to a particular area of academic psychology, while we are concerned with the psychologist's research orientation to social problems. While the claim of her insightful and persuasive paper may be valid for the area to which she refers, we are convinced that quite another viewpoint is adopted when the psychologist turns toward the real world and its problems.

2. Abstracts from clearly nonpsychological journals (such as those for sociology, political science, etc.) were excluded, not because such journals are not of interest to psychologists, but because psychologists are less likely to publish in them.
3. Because our interest is in American psychology, abstracts were included only if they appeared in a journal published in the United States or if the author was based in the United States.
4. PhD dissertations were excluded.
5. Because we are concerned with psychological research, only data-based research studies were used. We excluded case reports, review articles, and general discussions of the topic.

We sorted each abstract that met the above criteria into categories based on (a) the types of variables studied (i.e., person versus situation) and (b) the causal relationships between them as interpreted by the authors. We found a total of 69 items that could be meaningfully categorized. The categories, together with the percentage of the abstracts that fell into each of them, are presented in Table 1.

Authors of Category 1 studies, containing 15% of the research articles, reported an association between a problem characteristic and a personal characteristic and concluded that the personal characteristic is the cause of the problem. Thus, this category of studies lends itself most readily to person-blame interpretations. Category 2, containing 19% of the studies, also permits such interpretations, especially among those readers (whether social scientists or not) who do not concern themselves with the finer points of the logic of causal proof. While the authors of such studies make no explicit causal inferences regarding two correlated variables, the nature of the person-centered variables is such that a causal relation seems so plausible that the reader is easily led to conclude that the cause of the problem is psychological. Studies of the kind in Category 8, into which 48% of the studies fall, can also be pressed into service for person-blame interpretations of social problems, especially in view of the fact that a majority of such studies which could be compared cross-racially put blacks in an unfavorable light. Of the 33 abstracts which fell into this category, 14 reported unfavorable comparisons of blacks to whites, 2 showed blacks' performance as better than whites', and 6 reported no differences. (Eleven could not be evaluated cross-racially.)

Categories 4, 5, and 7 are amenable to system-blame interpretations of social problems. Of these, only Category 4, with 16% of the articles, contains any entries. It is noteworthy that no studies were found in Cat-

TABLE 1
Distribution of Types of Causal Attribution in Research on Black Americans Found in *Psychological Abstracts*, 1970, *44*, No. 1–6

Category	Variable type	Type and direction of association	Variable type	% of abstracts
1	Personal characteristic[a]	Causal →	Problem characteristic[b]	15
2	Personal characteristic	Correlation ↑	Problem characteristic	19
3	Personal characteristic[b]	Causal ↓	Problem characteristic[a]	0
4	Situational or environmental characteristic[a]	Causal →	Problem characteristic[b]	16
5	Situational or environmental characteristic	Correlation ↑	Problem characteristic	0
6	Situational or environmental characteristic[b]	Causal ↓	Problem characteristic[a]	3
7	Both personal and situational characteristics[a]	Causal →	Problem characteristic[b]	0
8[c]	Group membership (e.g., black or white)	Correlation ↑	Personal characteristics	48
9	Group membership (e.g., black or white)	Correlation	Situational characteristics	0

[a]Independent variable.
[b]Dependent variable.
[c]To illustrate the difference between Category 8 and Categories 1 and 2, let us take a hypothetical example. If a study merely documented the existence of an alleged "deficit" in blacks as compared to whites, it would fall into Category 8. If, however, the study tried to relate an alleged "deficit" among blacks (e.g., in standard English language skills) to another socially relevant "problem" of blacks (e.g., educational underachievement), then it fell into either Category 1 or 2 depending on whether a causal relation was specified or not.

egory 7, which is often held up as a model for social psychologists to follow.[3]

Although this is admittedly a crude way of measuring fairly complex phenomena, the picture that emerges is one of psychologists investing disproportionate amounts of time, funds, and energy in studies that lend themselves, directly or by implication, to interpreting the difficulties of black Americans in terms of personal shortcomings. Combining Categories 1, 2, and 8, we see that 82% of the classifiable psychological research dealing with black Americans reported in the six months of *Psychological Abstracts* under study are of this sort. It should be clearly understood that we do not condemn this preoccupation in and of itself, but rather because it overlooks the importance of other kinds of forces that operate on black

---

[3]Despite our emphasis on the necessity of acknowledging the causal role played by environmental factors, we do not believe that this is enough, for even explanations that employ situational factors can be twisted into playing a person-blaming role. Ryan (1971) eloquently described such interpretations:

> Victim-blaming is often cloaked in kindness and concern, and bears all the trappings and statistical furbelows of scientism; it is obscured by a perfumed haze of humanitarianism . . . and those who practice this art display a deep concern for the victims that is quite genuine. . . . Its adherents include sympathetic social scientists with social consciences in good working order, and liberal politicians with a genuine commitment to reform. . . . They indignantly condemn any notions of innate wickedness or genetic defect. "The Negro is *not born* inferior," they shout apoplectically. "Force of circumstance," they explain in reasonable tones, "has *made* him inferior". (pp. 6–7)

Whereas earlier, more conservative ideologies attributed the position of blacks in society to intrinsic or inherent defects, the new ones described by Ryan stress environmental causation.

> The new ideology attributes defect and inadequacy to the malignant nature of poverty, injustice, slum life, and racial difficulties. The stigma that marks the victim and accounts for his victimization is an acquired stigma, a stigma of social, rather than genetic, origin. But the stigma, the defect, the fatal difference—though derived in the past from environmental forces—is still located within the victim, inside his skin. With such an elegant formulation, the humanitarian can have it both ways. He can, all at the same time, concentrate his charitable interest in the defects of the victim, condemn the vague social and environmental stresses that produced the defect (some time ago), and ignore the continuing effect of victimizing social forces (right now). It is a brilliant ideology for justifying a perverse form of social action designed to change, not society, as one might expect, but rather society's victim. (pp. 6–7)

Ryan argues persuasively that it is not personal defects produced by past environmental influences that account for blacks' social and economic position in society, but rather the present and continuing effects of situational forces acting upon individuals who, given the same opportunities as most of the rest of us, would do equally well or poorly. This is certainly a credible hypothesis and one as worthy of scientific testing as any other.

Another closely related question demonstrates the inadequacy of simply acknowledging that situational forces play determining roles in the emergence of social problems. This is the question of whether particular problems produced by the social structure are inherent in that structure and occur inevitably because of internal contradictions within the structure, or whether instead they are merely mistakes or unforeseen consequences, perhaps caused by significant but essentially random processes. The answer to this question will have profound implications for the policies proposed, for if the problems are seen as manifestations of the essential nature of the system as it normally operates, then policies that go farther to fundamentally restructure the system will be proposed.

Americans, and thereby reinforces the negative labeling of a group already politically and socially vulnerable.[4]

The occupational orientation of psychologists and its effects. A second major reason for this preoccupation with person-centered variables pertains to career gains. There is little chance for a career-conscious psychologist to become successful by helping people who are not. But it is possible to enhance one's own position among colleagues by conducting "relevant"

---

[4]As with telephone books, reading *Psychological Abstracts* can be instructive in ways not intended by those who compiled or organized it. Some peripherally relevant observations: (*a*) Although *Psychological Abstracts* abstracts articles from the journal *Social Problems* (roughly, sociology's counterpart to SPSSI's *Journal of Social Issues*), there is no category by that name or any variation of it in the subject index. (*b*) In the format outline used by *Psychological Abstracts*, the areas of crime, juvenile delinquency, and drug addiction are among those grouped under the subheading of Behavior Disorder within the division of Clinical Psychology—again illustrating the bias of the field. (*c*) Perhaps reflecting their missionary zeal, Mental Health and Psychological Services listings can be found under the index heading Social Movements. (*d*) Even in the act of trying to select social problems areas with which to illustrate our thesis, our assertion was substantiated. Almost all "problems" listed are those of individuals or conventionally defined categories of persons. One searches in vain for serious treatment—whether as dependent, independent, or merely correlated variables—of social *system* variables as they may relate to those psychological variables with which psychologists ordinarily concern themselves. Examples of social system variables that one might expect to play a role of some consequence are the following: the concentration of wealth and power, unequal educational or occupational opportunity, particularistic dispensation of justice at the hands of the police and the judicial system, national budgetary priorities for destructive as compared to social welfare purposes, and the militarization of the economy. (Psychologists should not be singled out for criticism on this point, since until recently the standard sociological works on "social problems," "deviance," and the like, have also focused to a large extent on individuals, for example, crime, juvenile delinquency, alcoholism, suicide, etc.) Possible exceptions might include organizational (i.e., business and industrial) analysis and occasional use of variables that represent summaries of individual "problems" or problem behavior (e.g., crime rates, the magnitude of poverty in the United States, etc.). Another possible exception involves the uncharacteristic analysis of certain kinds of problem behavior (e.g., riots) in terms of a "system breakdown." For cogent critiques of this often misused concept, see Coser (1956) and Buckley (1967).

Finally, we share with the reader a few items which came to our attention in our search of the abstracts. Admittedly, these are the more extreme examples of the tendencies to which this article refers, but it must be recognized that they differ only in degree and not in kind. The subject index description of a dissertation study (No. 564) concerned with attitudes toward "handicapped groups" reads as follows: "public vs. private attitudes toward stutterers & cerebral palsied & blind & Negroes." A study of conscientious objectors (No. 677) belonging to a fundamentalist religious sect showed "extraordinary inhibition of aggression" on their part, on the basis of MMPI scale scores which were "higher than *other* federal prisoners or *noncriminals*" (authors' italics). A shallow understanding of the roots of urban disorders was evident in two other reports. One author investigating "use patterns & the effects of mass media" on black ghetto residents (No. 3570) stated that his results support the hypothesis that "open communication channels would lessen the tendency to riot." The second report (No. 2248), summarizing four studies of the Detroit riots, reported that results "revealed an obvious lack of communication between the black and the power structures. . . . It is suggested that psychiatry be used to further understand these matters." Showing that no bit of common wisdom is immune from the scrutiny of empirical investigation, another author (No. 2191) evaluated inner-city black youths' sense of rhythm, tonal memory, and other musical talents, finding them "markedly deficient" by test standards (although he holds out the possibility that such "standardized testing programs" may be inappropriate for such populations). "Suicide, and white reformatory girls' preference for Negro men" was the subject of an article (No. 8798) which concluded that this preference results from both groups' rejection by society and feelings of worthlessness. The abstract of an article entitled "The Irrational in Economic Behavior" (No. 6825), although vague, suggested a focus on the individual consumer's irrationality and contained no hint of any recognition of such forces as ubiquitous advertising and a need-creating, redundant economy which may induce persons to act counter to their own best interests.

research as a means for pursuing theoretical rather than applied interests, while at the same time contributing to the profession as a whole by offering explanations and solutions within the paradigms of a particular discipline.

It is the good will and approval of our colleagues in the scientific community, not that of the target population members affected by our work, that get us ahead. A social scientist's findings may provide or influence the underlying assumptions on which "corrective" programs affecting thousands or perhaps millions of persons will be predicated. It is ironic, then, that his career gains will depend more on his contribution to the advancement of his discipline from studying applied problems than on the success or failure of those programs.

This would not be a cause for such serious concern if, as tends to be the case in academic psychology, the only risk is that of bad or incorrect theory. But, what is good for science and the individual scientist may not be good for those on whom the research is based. As we have recently seen, to talk of hereditary and environmental effects on intelligence (long a concern of psychologists) means one thing when discussed in terms of its relevance to psychological theory, but quite another when applied to those in a problematic relationship to the rest of society (cf. Jensen and his critics in *Environment, Heredity, and Intelligence*). Similarly, to focus on the role of different nuclear family units and their consequences on childhood development is one thing when discussed on theoretical grounds and another when applied to real groups living under extraordinarily difficulty circumstances (cf. Moynihan's *The Negro Family* and the ensuing controversy).

The repercussions of our research findings—the views of the world they inspire or perpetuate—may seem like epiphenomena to us, but they are often painfully real for those affected by them. Thus, psychology as a profession has special reason to consider a more balanced approach in the selection of variables for the study of social problems. In addition to the usual reason for acknowledging the necessity of such an approach, namely, that any discipline-bound approach to any given social problem is at best only partially correct and at worst just plain wrong, psychologists have added reason to show caution: person-blame explanations of social problems, *whether valid or not*, hold the potential for reinforcing established stereotypes and thereby perpetuating the condition of the "problem" group.

A closely related set of incentives further contributes to the psychologist's bias toward person-centered research on social problems. It is based, in part, on Becker's (1970) notion of a "hierarchy of credibility":

> In any system of ranked groups, participants take it as given that members of the highest group have the right to define the way things really are. . . . From the point of view of the well socialized participant in the system, any tale told by those at the top intrinsically deserves to

be regarded as the most credible account obtainable. . . . And since
. . . matters of rank and status are contained in the mores, this belief
has a moral quality. We are, if we are proper members of the group,
morally bound to accept the definition imposed on reality by a super-
ordinate group in preference to the definitions espoused by subordinates. . . . By refusing to accept the hierarchy of credibility, we
express disrespect for the entire established order. (p. 18)

Thus, when authorities offer person-blame explanations for particular social
problems and make research funds available, suddenly one's disciplinary
outlook, career gains, and socially acceptable behavior all converge for the
psychologist. By investigating a social problem in terms given him, a *mutually beneficial exchange relationship* is established: the researcher is rewarded
both materially and in terms of prestige (in addition to remaining a "proper
member of the group") by using the tools of his trade; while on the other
side of the exchange, officialdom stands to have its preferred interpretation
buttressed by the respectability of "scientific data."

Little has been said in this section about the political and social
context of psychological research on social problems for the purpose of
illustrating the implications of such research, independent of other considerations. Even under the most ideal conditions of a conscientious, well-
meaning, responsive government and populace, on the basis of psychological research, person-blame definitions of social problems would be the
likely outcome. Given the actual nature of government and the political
process, however, this outcome is made even more certain, except that the
consequences are likely to be less benign for the "problem" group. In the
next section we will consider these broader issues in order to understand
(*a*) why person-centered research findings lead so quickly to person-blame
public interpretations, and, in turn, (*b*) the social and political conditions
favorable for the emergence of, and the uncritical willingness among policy
planners to embrace, person-blame interpretations.

UTILITY OF PERSON-BLAME PROBLEM DEFINITIONS

Problem Identification

Every society attempts to characterize its deviant segments as problematic, and therefore as candidates for change, sometimes because they
represent a breach of norms and folkways, and at other times for purely
political or interest-based reasons. But the social scientist who becomes
"relevant" seldom questions already established problem definitions, or the
wisdom behind the process that leads to the identification of so-called
social problems. Nor does he question whose ends are served by the entire
definitional process and by his participation in that process. Instead he

waits in the wings until the problems have been selected for attention. Only then does he become involved, as if accepting as given that (a) whatever becomes identified publicly as a social problem is a genuine problem, derived from universally recognized truths; and (b) the problem is of such priority that it deserves attention over other problems that go unattended or unrecognized.

Why does one kind of poverty concern us, and another does not? Why do we constantly study the poor rather than the nonpoor in order to understand the origins of poverty? Why do we study nonachievement among minority group members as undesirable behavior, but do not study exaggerated profit motive among "successful" businessmen as a form of deviance? Why do we study the use of marijuana as a "drug problem," but not federal government involvement in the drugging of "minimal brain dysfunction" (MBD) children in our grammar schools? Why is it illegal to be a "wetback" but not to hire one (cf. Bustamante, 1972)?

These kinds of questions are rarely raised. Yet the social scientist should understand that by his involvement *qua* scientific authority in research, treatment, and planning operations, he has—consciously or unconsciously, explicitly or implicitly—lent credibility and legitimation to a given problem as publicly defined and the treatment program launched to deal with that problem.

Certain groups within society become continually stigmatized as problem groups (e.g., migratory workers, mental patients, blacks, the poor) because they are visible and accessible, but, most especially, because they are vulnerable to the social scientist for research purposes. In this sense the criteria by which social scientists select "problem" groups for study are not unlike the criteria by which the wider culture selects certain groups as scapegoats. Indeed, the former process often follows the lead of the latter. Nonachieving lower income children are more identifiable and accessible as a research population than are greedy "entrepreneurially motivated" slum landlords, for example, and they command far less countervailing power and resources than do the landlords. Thus, there is much person-centered research data to justify initiating a program such as Head Start (all of the data suggesting, essentially, that it is the child who fails, rather than the school and the educational system). But, by contrast, there is a lack of data on landlords, bankers, and city officials who permit building code violations that would justify using them as targets for person-change treatment efforts.

Moreover, just as we must concern ourselves with whose problem definition we are being asked to validate, we must constantly examine what is *not* being done. Social ills which are ignored through oversight, ignorance, or deliberate non-issue-making may be as important as those "problems" that become issues. Dubos (1970) said:

The greatest crime committed in American cities may not be murder, rape, or robbery, but rather the wholesale and constant exposure of children to noise, ugliness and garbage in the street, thereby conditioning them to accept public squalor as the normal state of affairs. (p. 14)

These issues are of particular concern at this time because of the rise of interest in social indicators. It would be expected that those charged with the responsibility of conducting such research would use this opportunity to participate in identifying social problems and thereby make the study of social indicators something more than social seismology. But this seems unlikely, judging from Bauer (1969), as one of the movement's main advocates:

The decision to observe a phenomenon implies a decision to be responsible for it, if such responsibility is within one's own power. . . . It is wisdom, not cynicism, to urge caution in extending diagnostic measures of social phenomena beyond the system's capacity to respond to the problems which are unveiled. (p. 67)

Contrary to the Dubos position, Bauer implies that something becomes a social problem only if it is politically feasible to deal with it. As long as such attitudes prevail among the leaders of the social indicator movement, there should be no question as to whose welfare and interests—dominant political and economic interests, or the wider society—will be served by the selection and gathering of social indicators. If social scientists choose to be morally indifferent social bookkeepers and leave the selection of indicators and their use in the hands of others, then, to use Biderman's (1966) term, social "vindicators" would be a better name for such measures. If our apprehensions are confirmed, these vindicators will take the form of person-blame data collected for the political management of guilt and culpability.

Blame Displacement and the Use of Social Scientists

Whether or not the problems we study are true social problems, or whether they deserve the attention that they receive vis-à-vis other social ills, is open to debate. However, a more serious and less obvious danger is *the use of social science and social scientists to displace the blame for prior political and technological failures.* Such failures are often the end result of a series of short-run political and technological accommodations for which there may no longer be either short- or long-term political and technological, or social solutions. But because breakdowns in the political-economic system produce serious social *consequences*, social scientists are called on to deal with these so-called "social" problems. Their involvement carries with it the implication that socially undesirable behavior *is the problem*, rather than the inevitable by-product of political trade-offs and technological fixes, thereby distracting attention from the real causes. Kramer (1970) succinctly warned: "Never forget that your research may seem like an end in itself to you, but to rank outsiders with other agendas, it may be a means to other goals [p. 32]."

To a substantial extent, transportation, public housing, education, environmental pollution, possibly even drugs, and many other such problems associated with the management of urban life fall into this category. Public housing problems provide a good example. At the early planning stages the important decisions about such housing are often based solely on political and technological grounds, for example, the level and timing of appropriations, the selection of sites, the choice of building materials and design, and production methods. It is only after the housing is completed and people do not want to live in it, or are afraid to live in it, or those who live in it do not behave in some desired way, that public housing becomes viewed as a problem requiring social science expertise, and thereafter becomes publicly defined as a "social" problem. The "problem" behavior may in fact be a straightforward reaction to external realities in the immediate environment. But, by a process of causal inversion, the victims of poor planning become treated as if they were the cause of the situation in which they find themselves.

The Negotiation of Reality[5]

Perhaps one of the more important but subtle political advantages of person-blame research is that it can permit authorities to control troublesome segments of the population under the guise of being helpful, even indulgent. Normally one would expect that those who control power and resources would be unrelentingly noncooperative with system-antagonistic "problem" groups. "Cooperation" with such groups is possible, however, if a person-blame rather than system-blame action program can be negotiated. Thus, they can be "helpful" as long as the way in which the target group is helped serves the interests of those offering assistance. Under these circumstances the definitional process remains in the control of the would-be benefactor, and "help" will be forthcoming as long as the public definitions of the real problem behind the system-antagonistic acts are explained in person-centered terms.[6] The system-antagonistic poor become "deserving" of help only if they accept personal blame for their social and economic position in society; that is, because of personal impediments, they

---

[5]The phrase is borrowed from Scheff (1968).
[6]Scheff (1968) discussed analogous relationships between psychotherapists and their patients, and between defense lawyers and their clients.

would be unable to effectuate personal and social goals even under the most ideal conditions. Otherwise, they remain "undeserving" of help and are ignored or controlled through the exercise of negative sanctions.

For example, in 1969, a group of Indians occupied and attempted to reclaim Alcatraz Island shortly after its use as a prison facility had been discontinued. They argued that it should rightfully be returned to them since it was in effect surplus federal land. The government refused to recognize the legitimacy of their claim and made it exceedingly difficult for the group to survive on the island, Finally, after two years, the Indians were forcibly removed.

These events in San Francisco Bay contrast with a similar incident on the opposite coast. In the summer of 1970, a small group of blacks landed on Ellis Island in New York Harbor and attempted to claim it because, like Alcatraz, it was federal land no longer being used. They were immediately threatened with expulsion, and the illegality of their actions was made public. After several days of negotiation, however, authorities agreed to provide a major drug rehabilitation center on the island, and the dispute was settled.

The outcomes on Alcatraz and Ellis Island might have been reversed, however, if the Indians had agreed to the establishment of a treatment center for alcoholism among Indians (thus adding credibility to a stereotyped person-blame explanation to account for their social and economic position in America), and if the blacks had denounced white repression and demanded to use Ellis Island as the base for establishing an independent black nation.

We do not mean to appear unduly alarmist by implying that every problem group, particularly those who are system antagonistic, has a rendezvous with a deviancy label, nor that the social sciences will inevitably become insidious political arms of the state, nor that the government will go to the extreme of hospitalizing its political opponents as mentally ill. We have not come to that, nor are we likely to, at least not in the near future. We should realize, however, that the potential for manipulation of problem definitions for purely political ends, while now only partially realized, could become a fully exploited reality.

SUMMARY AND CONCLUSIONS: TRUTH OR CONSEQUENCES

Causal Attribution Bias

We have demonstrated the existence of a person-centered preoccupation and causal attribution bias in psychological research which, when applied to social problems, favors explanations in terms of the personal characteristics of those experiencing the problem, while disregarding the possible influence of external forces. Because of the ominous prospects that can ensue from the narrowly circumscribed range of action possibilities derivable from person-centered data, there is reason to question whether such findings would be a suitable foundation for the development and promulgation of ameliorative programs.

Because these issues are complex and their implications are far reaching, we should caution the reader against possible misinterpretations. First, we are not concerned with which academic disciplines have a hegemony over truth. We are not saying that person-centered variables are less valid or etiologically less important than situational variables in accounting for social problems. Second, we do not object to psychologically oriented research on social problems because it offends our sense of egalitarianism by documenting individual or group differences. Such differences may or may not exist, but that alone is not our concern here. Third, the reader should not conclude that we are blindly enamored of an approach that stresses environmental factors to the exclusion of person-centered factors. That would be an error in the opposite direction.[7] Instead, our concern is not with the truth of propositions about human behavior so much as with their social, political, economic, and human consequences.

Functions of Person-Blame Research

Although the initial intent behind the use of psychological research and analysis on social problems may have been an effort of responsible government to be responsive to human needs, because the data psychologists provide stress person-centered impediments to account for societal

---

[7]A dogmatic system-blame orientation has its own dangers, in addition to also being part of the truth. Just as such an orientation once liberated man from supernatural or biological conceptions of his destiny, it may now become increasingly repressive of man's initiative and spirit. Reifying environmental factors as causal agents may deny, and thus have the effect of dampening, the autonomy and dynamism of the individual (Gouldner, 1970). This raises the serious question of people's attitudes toward their responsibility for their behavior. Unless counteracted in some way, an excessively system-blame perspective carries with it the potential for providing the individual with a ready explanation for avoiding responsibility for his own behavior.

One of the most serious philosophical and psychological problems of our age may be to provide a view of man and his surroundings that recognizes the validity of situational causality without leaving the individual feeling helpless and unable to shape his fate. Part of that view will have to contain a more complex and sophisticated view of causality than the implicit constant-sum model that most people seem to hold (i.e., the more my environment is responsible for my outcomes, the less responsible I am, and vice versa). But until that state is reached, social scientists, especially those concerned with environmental determinants of behavior and thought, have a responsibility: we must recognize that much of our work holds the potential for further eroding an already changing social order and crumbling value system; and, therefore, it may be argued that we have an obligation to put something better in the place of that which we help destroy. It is in this spirit that Miller (1969) suggested that perhaps the most radical activity that psychology can undertake is to build a new image of man, more valid and hopeful than those of the past, and to freely dispense that image to anyone who will listen.

problems, they serve other ends as well. We have distinguished at least five latent functions of person-blame interpretations of social problems.

1. They offer a convenient apology for freeing the government and primary cultural institutions from blame for the problem.

2. Since those institutions are apparently not the cause of the problem, it may be legitimately contended that they cannot be held responsible for amelioration. If they do provide such help, they are credited with being exceedingly humane, while gaining control over those being helped, through the manipulation of problem definitions in exchange for treatment resources.

3. Such interpretations provide and legitimate the right to initiate person-change rather than system-change treatment programs. This in turn has the following functions: (*a*) it serves as a publicly acceptable device to control troublesome segments of the population, (*b*) it distracts attention from possible systemic causes, and (*c*) it discredits system-oriented criticism. Some of these functions were illustrated in a recent, much publicized address to correctional psychologists by Judge David Bazelon (1972):

> Why should we even consider fundamental social changes or massive income redistribution if the entire problem can be solved by having scientists teach the criminal class—like a group of laboratory rats—to march successfully through the maze of our society? In short, before you respond with enthusiasm to our pleas for help, you must ask yourselves whether your help is really needed, or whether you are merely engaged as magicians to preform an intriguing side-show so that the spectators will not notice the crisis in the center ring. In considering our motives for offering you a role, I think you would do well to consider how much less expensive it is to hire a thousand psychologists than to make even a miniscule change in the social and economic structure. (p. 6)[8]

4. The loyalty of large numbers of the well-educated, melioristic-minded nonneedy is cemented to the national structure by means of occupational involvement in "socially relevant" managerial, treatment, and custodial roles required to deal with those persons designated as needing person-centered correction.

5. Person-blame interpretations reinforce social myths about one's degree of control over his own fate, thus rewarding the members of the great

---

[8]A few academics have pointed with undisguised glee at what they perceive to be an inherent contradiction in claims variously attributed to radicals, students, and various other critics. On the one hand, they assert, the social sciences are accused of being "irrelevant" and inconsequential; yet, on the other hand, they are also accused of being power serving. How can these both be possible? The apparent inconsistency vanishes when one recognizes that the two charges pertain to different domains, the first to those academic and theoretical issues that occupy most of the space in journals and many texts, and the second to the realm of social problems and public issues, in the ways demonstrated by this article. We regard both charges as being more accurate than false.

middle class by flattering their self-esteem for having "made it on their own." This in turn increases public complacency about the plight of those who have not "made it on their own."

The major conclusion that can be drawn from the above is that *person-blame interpretations are in everyone's interests except those subjected to analysis.*

Assuming that person-blame interpretations can produce the political benefits described above, the provocative question of function versus intent must be considered. Are these effects merely unforeseen consequences of decisions made for purely humanitarian reasons, or are they the products of decisions made deliberately with these political gains in mind? The more conspiratorial view would argue that such outcomes are intended, while the more benign view would hold that they are both unintended and unanticipated. Both views probably have elements of truth, but each misses the mark to some degree.

Unquestionably, conscious and deliberate use has been made of person-blame arguments, buttressed by psychologically oriented research, with a view toward protecting the established order against criticism. Although those who have relied on person-blame arguments in these ways have been associated with dominant economic, social, and political institutions, it must be emphasized that others in these same institutions have not been and would not be engaged in such activities.

Following Ryan (1971), we suggest that for most persons (including psychologists and other social scientists) who subscribe to person-blame interpretations of social problems, the functions that such explanations serve are indeed unintended and probably even unsuspected as yet. These interpretations derive largely from epistemological biases and "blinders" deeply embedded in cultural beliefs that favor person-centered interpretations of either success or failure. Citing Mannheim (1936), Ryan states that while such belief systems distort reality and serve specific functions (namely, maintaining the status quo in the interests of particular groups), the distortion is neither conscious nor intentional. Thus, in the main, person-blame interpretations have the function, but not necessarily the intent, of serving the interests of the relatively advantaged segments of the society.

In conclusion, we would like to turn our attention to the legitimacy and appropriateness of the volatile issues raised in this article, such as (a) what is the relative emphasis the social sciences should place on the truth of propositions about human behavior, on the one hand, and the action implications, often political, that flow from them, on the other; (b) to whom are social scientists responsible and to whom should they be responsible; and (c) more generally, what is the proper role of science and of individual scientists with regard to research on "relevant" social issues? Increasingly we will have to face such issues, both as individuals and as a profession, and the quality of our solutions will not be improved by postponing the discussion. The purpose of this article was to show why we must be wary of uncritically accepting the idea that the promotion and dissemination of social science knowledge are intrinsically good, moral, and wise. The sooner we recognize that such knowledge is not truth divorced from the realities of time, place, or *use*, the better will be our chances of making a truly responsible contribution to societal improvement.

REFERENCES

Archibald, K. (1970). Alternative orientations to social science utilization. *Social Science Information*, 9(2), 7–34.

Bauer, R. (1969). Societal feedback. In B. Gross (Ed.), *Social intelligence for America's future*. Boston: Allyn & Bacon.

Bazelon, D. L. (1972). Untitled. Address to the American Association of Correctional Psychologists' Conferences on "Psychology's Roles and Contributions in Problems of Crime, Delinquency and Corrections." Lake Wales, Florida, January 20. (Mimeo)

Becker, H. S. (1970). Whose side are we on? In W. J. Filstead (Ed.), *Qualitative methodology: Firsthand involvement with the social world*. Chicago: Markham. (Orig. publ. in *Social Problems*, 14, 239–247 [1967].)

Biderman, A. D. (1966). Social indicators and goals. In R. Bauer (Ed.), *Social indicators*. Cambridge, MA: M.I.T. Press.

Brim, O. G., et al. (1969). *Knowledge into action: Improving the nation's use of the social sciences*. (Report of the Special Commission on the Social Sciences of the National Science Board) Washington, DC: National Science Foundation.

Buckley, W. (1967). *Sociology and modern systems theory*. Englewood Cliffs, NJ: Prentice-Hall.

Bustamante, J. A. (1972). The "wetback" as deviant: An application of labelling theory. *American Journal of Sociology*, 77, 706–718.

Carlson, R. (1971). Where is the person in personality research? *Psychological Bulletin*, 75, 203–219.

Coser, L. (1956). *The functions of social conflict*. Glencoe, IL: Free Press.

Dubos, R. (1970). Life is an endless give-and-take with earth and all her creatures. *Smithsonian*, 1, 8–17.

Environment, heredity, and intelligence. (1969). (Compiled from the *Harvard Educational Review*. Reprint Series No. 2) Cambridge, MA: Harvard Educational Review.

Gouldner, A. (1970). Toward the radical reconstruction of sociology. *Social Policy*, May/June, 18–25.

Kaplan, A. (1964). *The conduct of inquiry*. San Francisco: Chandler.

Kramer, J. R. (1970). The social relevance of the psychologist. In F. Korten, S. W. Cook, & J. I. Lacey (Eds.), *Psychology and the problems of society*. Washington, DC: American Psychological Association.

Mannheim, K. (1936). *Ideology and utopia*. (Trans. by L. Worth & E. Shils) New York: Harcourt, Brace & World.

Miller, G. A. (1969). Psychology as a means of promoting human welfare. *American Psychologist, 24*, 1063–1075.

National Academy of Sciences (1969). Behavioral and Social Sciences Survey Committee. *The behavioral and social sciences: Outlook and needs*. Englewood Cliffs, NJ: Prentice-Hall.

Riecken, H. W. (1972). Social change and social science. Address in the Science and Public Policy Series, Rockefeller University, January 26. (Mimeo)

Ryan, W. (1971). *Blaming the victim*. New York: Pantheon.

Scheff, T. J. (1968). Negotiating reality: Notes on power in the assessment of responsibility. *Social Problems, 16*, 3–17.

7

ON GETTING IN BED WITH A LION

WILLIAM BEVAN

The lion and the calf shall lie down together, but the calf won't get much sleep.

Woody Allen, 1977

The times, as Bob Dylan says, they are a-changin'. In fact, for academic science in its relationship to the federal government, the times have been changing since the mid-1960s, as any thoughtful observer of that particular contemporary scene can readily attest. Still, the largest number of scientists within the American academic community continue to view their world, plan their work, and indoctrinate their students precisely as they did during the heady days following World War II and during the space race with the Russians, when federal support for science increased at an annual rate of

Reprinted from *American Psychologist*, 35, 779–789. Copyright 1980 by the American Psychological Association.

This essay summarizes several themes on which I have spoken and written repeatedly in the course of the last decade. I have tried deliberately, for stylistic reasons, to keep formal citations to a minimum. The statistical data I discuss are readily available from published reports of the National Science Foundation, the National Academy of Sciences, the American Council on Education, the Council of Graduate Schools, the National Center for Education Statistics, the Fact File of the *Chronicle of Higher Education*, and similar publications. The literature on the Lazzaroni is rather limited; the best introduction is probably that of Miller, Voss, and Hussey (1972). Haberer (1969) provides an excellent discussion of the Cartesian and Baconian conceptions of science. Those concerned with the issue of federal regulation will find three recent collections (Hobbs, 1978; Holton & Morison, 1979; Seabury, 1979) and a chapter by Finn (1978) of interest.

12% and we all complained that it wasn't 15. Today, in contrast, federal support for science, in even the most optimistic scenario, will fail to match inflation.

In making this comparison I do not mean to suggest that science is at present being badly treated. Nor am I playing the doomsayer. We have had enough of that already. Rather, the theme of this essay is quite simple and straightforward. Times have changed. Scientists can no longer expect to receive the repeated large-scale increases in public funding they enjoyed in the 1950s and 1960s, nor the uncritical public approval that lay behind such actions. If they are concerned for the continued health of their enterprise and for its value as a public good—if, indeed, they are only interested in making the most of their opportunities as individual practitioners of science—they will have to perceive more clearly than they do now their *collective* status as a special interest group, and they will have to appreciate better than they do now the political dynamics of an era dominated by a plethora of special interest groups. Moreover, they will have to understand more fully why the particular changes that have come to affect them have in fact occurred and to recognize more precisely those alternatives in attitude and behavior that, as a consequence of change, now best ensure their goals as a community. No amount of complaining about an ungrateful or misunderstanding public, no manner of wishful thinking, will usher back the golden age.

OF PRINCES, PATRONS, ETC.

My kingdom is as wide as the world. I go forward always, freeing spirits and weighing worlds, without fear, without compassion, without love, and without God. Men call me Science.

Gustave Flaubert, 1874

For science is—like virtue, its own exceeding great reward.

Charles Kingsley, 1874

Science, the new nobility!

Arthur Rimbaud, 1873

Academic science in America from its earliest days has been dominated by a single vision of the proper ideology and role of the scientist. It is that vision put forward by René Descartes (1951) in his *Discourse on Method.* In a phrase, the goal of science is the valid conceptualization of Nature on a grand scale. The proper strategy for success is the all-consuming commitment of the individual mind. From this perspective comes a whole set of specific attitudes that define, at least in the pure case, the Cartesian scientist's relationship to work, to colleagues, and to the nonscientific public and its institutions. One's own individual attack on Nature is what one sees as personally most real. Doing science is like running a race, and one's colleagues in the field can therefore only be viewed as strong competitors. Science is, to use Price's (1977) useful term, a *consumption good* to be pursued because it is intrinsically worthwhile. The typical scientist is pessimistic about the lay public's ability and indifferent to its need to understand science. Moreover, the principle of public accountability is not really understood in the same way as it is by people in public life. Rather, any scrutiny on the part of the public or its institutions tends to be viewed as an unjustified intrusion. The search for Truth takes precedence over all other considerations; therefore science is inevitably ethically neutral. Finally, the public is perceived as having only one role, that of patron. It can assist the scientist in his or her lonely quest in only one acceptable way: It can—indeed, it should—provide financial support, but must otherwise stay clear of the enterprise.

Over the years academic scientists in the United States, when needing public support, have directed their attention primarily toward the executive branch of government. Their style has for the most part been informal and where possible has been shaped to exploit *personal* relationships. Illustrative cases abound. Among the more instructive is that of the Lazzaroni. These were a small, informally organized, mid-19th century group led by Louis Agassiz. Their chief interest was in establishing a national science of high quality, in gaining public recognition for the importance of basic research, in securing government patronage, and incidentally, in consolidating their own personal control over the entire process. Existing as a "supper club" within the newly emerged American Association for the Advancement of Science (AAAS), they made the association a vehicle for power through the influence they had on the drafting of its initial constitution, through their subsequent shaping of its legislation, and by seeing that their members held key positions within its governance structure. But the Lazzaroni did not confine themselves to the affairs of the AAAS. Agassiz, with the aid of those in the group among the Harvard faculty, undertook to transform the university from an undergraduate college to a professionally oriented postbaccalaureate institution—first through a scheme that involved persuading the governor of Massachusetts to take control of the university on behalf of the state and then, when this strategy failed, through an attempt to divert the recently appropriated federal land-grant funds to the university, a scheme that also failed.

A third area of Lazzaroni politics centered on the founding of the National Academy of Sciences. Agassiz and his collaborators had long coveted a national organization to which membership would be by invitation and that would relate to the federal government in the way that the older European academies related to their aristocratic patrons. This time Agassiz, with a trusted subset of the group and with the cooperation of a sympathetic senator from Massachusetts, prepared a bill that was rushed through Congress in the closing hours of its 1863 session. The bill created the

National Academy of Sciences (NAS) and named its incorporators. All of the Lazzaroni were included, and the first president, vice-president, and foreign secretary (Agassiz) were drawn from their ranks. But the federal research funds that Agassiz had hoped the creation of the academy would bring about were not forthcoming. Indeed, the NAS failed to exert any significant influence on national policy until the period during World War I when the formation of the National Research Council brought representatives of the broader scientific community into a variety of governmental advisory roles.

If the Cartesian perspective has dominated American academic science, it has not been the only available philosophy. The conception of science advanced by Francis Bacon (1870–1872) in the *Novum Organum* and the *New Atlantis* stands in striking contrast to that of Descartes. Science is viewed as a social enterprise, a cooperative activity within a professional community marked by a clear-cut division of labor but bound by a single shared altruistic commitment to the promotion of human welfare. Thus, in this view science is, to use Price's (1977) contrasting term, an *investment good*. It has no intrinsic social value, but gains value only as its outcomes give rise to beneficial application. This is the view predominantly held by nonacademic scientists. It is also the reason most often advanced for the public support of academic science. I have yet to hear a public official seek support for science as a consumption good, and when scientists themselves talk about science in such terms it is almost always to assert an ideal. Indeed, when they now seek the approbation and the financial support of the nonscientific world, it is difficult to differentiate those who are Cartesian from those who are Baconian in perspective. On such occasions, basic research is justified either by specific anticipated applications or by the potential for practical outcomes that result from serendipity. I believe that the circumstances of our times increasingly relegate the Cartesian ideology and lifestyle, at least in their early, uncompromising forms, to science's past. Moreover, the Cartesian and Baconian philosophies need not be placed in opposition. Given the increasing interdependence of science and technology, given the division of labor that is the hallmark of the Baconian community, and given tolerance on both sides, the two contrasting perspectives, when properly applied, can in fact reinforce each other.

OLD CREDOS AND NEW SOCIAL BARGAINS

There ain't no such thing as a free lunch—

Crane's Law

Neither the Cartesian nor the Baconian view of science as a social enterprise is adequate for today's world. Both emerged during the 17th century, an era quite different from the present. The governments of France, Holland, and England were monarchies, and serving the state meant serving the interest of an individual patron, the King. (Out of such a history may well have emerged the long-standing—and, I think, ultimately regrettable—habit on the part of the scientific leadership of acquiescing to the state whenever a confrontation of values occurs.) Now, however, science is, willy-nilly, a large-scale social force, and the good of the many has increasingly become the paramount question. Science three hundred years ago was an avocation practiced by an affluent elite as a means of satisfying personal curiosity. While it required ingenuity, it required little technical skill. It was an activity pursued by individuals. Today it is a profession and a means of earning a livelihood, requiring in the main great technical sophistication. It is most likely to be a team effort. The Cartesian goal of public support for basic inquiry now gains justification by the rapidly growing interdependence of science and technology. Increasingly, success in high technology depends on sophisticated science and vice versa. Meanwhile, the Baconians among us largely persist in an innocent view of science as unadulterated good and in a simplistic conception of the science–government relationship as a mutually reinforcing partnership of means and ends.

To understand fully the character of the current science–government relationship, one must understand its history, particularly that of the post-World War II period. According to Blissett (1972), the institutional development of American science strongly reflects the evolution of political power in this country. He describes the latter in terms of three successive political forms: the liberal state, the bureaucratic state, and the postindustrial state.

In the earliest period, government had only a limited interest in science. In the liberal state, powers were narrowly defined and carefully circumscribed, and as a result, science was an activity of the private sector. Though there were, of course, instances of the government's involvement in science, a formal relationship waited for the creation of the National Academy of Sciences at the time of the Civil War, and major involvement did not occur until the period of World War II. Meanwhile, the emergence of large-scale industrialization at the end of the 19th century stimulated the appearance of the bureaucratic state. During the shift toward public ownership in the 1930s, the regulatory function of government expanded, and the bureaucracy became well established. With the advent of World War II, involvement of the scientific community in matters of government concern followed the traditional pattern for the bureaucratic state. Scientists were recruited into government service, resources were supplied, and overall goals were set. However, operational decisions were largely left to advisors from the private sector.

This strategy persisted into the postwar period. If science could play an important part in winning the war, surely, government decision makers reasoned, it could play an equally important role in winning the peace. As the scale of government involvement in science increased, administrative mechanisms specific to science were created: the Office of Science and Technology, the Federal Council for Science and Technology, the President's Science Advisory Committee, the offices of scientific research of the various military services, the extramural programs of Health, Education, and Welfare, and the National Science Foundation. This signaled a major policy change. While decision making for science continued to be largely in the hands of scientists, control shifted from the private to the public sector. As levels of funding grew in the 1950s, increasingly broad considerations, many beyond the domain of science itself, had an impact on funding decisions. Scientists became increasingly financially dependent on particular agencies and were thus inevitably drawn into the policy politics of those agencies.

More recently scientists have faced still another shift in power. Out of the brokering activities of the bureaucratic state, new spheres of influence—political consortia of private corporations, federal agencies, public interest groups, and so on—have emerged. (For example, Blissett, 1972, enumerates the complex of organizations concerned with pesticide policy: large chemical companies, the Departments of Agriculture and the Interior, the Food and Drug Administration, the Public Health Service, the Environmental Protection Agency, and a number of public interest groups.) Because the politician in the postindustrial state understands that scientific and technical knowledge is power, these topically oriented institutional complexes become the basic units of political power. They maintain their status by accumulating resources and by using them for their own protection and growth. Thus, science is no longer simply a way of satisfying the curiosity of the individual scientist: It has become a means of accumulating political power by particular interest groups.

Some years ago Toulmin (1966) expressed the view that in the postindustrial state science constitutes a tertiary industry, that is, an industry that serves to employ institutional resources rather than to produce raw materials or manufactured goods. If Toulmin is correct, then we should soon see science incorporated into other institutions of society, tied more closely to technology, and ultimately, along with technology, subjected to an increasingly wide range of political pressures. When this occurs, programs to implement public policy will replace grants and contracts as the mechanism for allocating public resources to science. We are in fact already seeing such a trend in the recent legislative actions of Congress and in the list of projects selected for support each year by the various executive departments of government.

A WORLD OF FOCUSED ISSUES, DIMINISHING DOLLARS, AND BUREAUCRATIC OVERSIGHT

Neither life nor liberty nor sacred honor are safe while the legislature is in session—

Revere's Canon

The world in which academic scientists must live for the immediate future, and in some of its aspects quite likely for considerably longer, is different from any they have ever before known. It is marked by a dominating politics of specific issues, a complex of factors—many in their derivation totally independent of science—that spell financially troubled times. More-over, they spell rapidly increasing governmental regulation that, if scientists are not vigilant, could, in my view, become seriously debilitating.

Will Rogers once remarked that this country has come to feel the same when Congress is in session as when a baby gets hold of a hammer. Certainly, despite the fact that the quality of the individual members of Congress is probably better than it has ever been before, the performance of Congress as a whole has never been worse. Here we are six years after the energy crisis, and we still don't have a coherent national energy policy. Other examples are readily apparent. Every member of Congress seems bound to be assertive on every issue, and the enactment of even the sim-plest bill has become a highly complex, uncertain, and protracted affair. In short, near anarchy prevails. This state of affairs, it seems to me, stems at least in part from the increasing influence of a substantial number of nar-rowly preoccupied special interest groups—something quite different from the politics of special privilege that has been with us since the invention of our particular form of government. Don't get me wrong. It is not the fact of self-interest that worries me, for after all, all politics has some self-interest at its base. Admittedly, the problems confronted are often issues that legislatures have never before had to confront. And their advocates, both pro and con, for the most part appear not to be persons seeking either money or broad political power. But their concerns are excessively narrow in form, and as protagonists they usually do not politically compromise themselves by making common cause with advocates of other issues. And it is precisely these characteristics that bother me, for the modern special interest zealot too often fails to recognize either the genuine complexity of the questions at issue when placed in the broader context or the fact that political victories are not ultimately always real solutions. Furthermore, special interest activists are skillful fund raisers and evangelists. Political-action committees, lobbies, and sublobbies proliferate. In the last few years alone over two thousand such organizations have come into existence. The rise of the modern specific-issue movement has brought about not only the fragmentation of Congress but also an unhealthy centralization of power within the bureaucracy of the executive branch. Again, examples are easily found.

One example will suffice. When Mr. Califano became President Carter's first Secretary of Health, Education and Welfare, he consolidated in one *appointed* official—himself—the decision-making prerogatives formally held by ten regional directors and presumably of all the officials under them. Now I am not unmindful of the impervious indifference to social needs wrought of a tenured bureaucracy or of the commonly held view that responsiveness can be enhanced through the consolidation of executive power. But such a consolidation of power causes me anxiety because with it can come the attitude that any institution of society, either public or private and willing or not, can be dragooned as an instrument of narrow political purpose, whether such action is in the broader public interest or not.

It is undeniably true that specific-issue politics has produced many significant social advances. Indeed, many could have been accomplished in no other way. However, as the rather intense language of the preceding paragraph has undoubtedly suggested, I worry that we may now be getting too much of a good thing, that the political fragmentation which has accompanied special-issue politics has now reached the level of being counterproductive to the greater public good. Be that as it may, it seems to be manifestly clear that neither the political indifference of the Cartesian scientist, born of a patron-oriented psychology, nor the naive idealism of the unreconstructed Baconian can be conducive to the survival of that particular cluster of interests which characterizes science, no matter how humane. When the Science Policy Act of 1976 reaffirmed the Congress's view of science as a national resource, academic scientists once again lost their claim to the principle of self-determination, which has been among their more important sustaining convictions.

Academic science faces problems in part because the academic enterprise as a whole faces problems. I need not dwell on these in great detail. All of us are acutely conscious of the effects of inflation. A decade ago the cost of living increased at an annual rate of about 4%; today it is almost 20%. Academic institutions cannot pass on these increased costs to their clientele quite as easily as can institutions in the business sector. About two thirds of institutional costs relate to people, and faculty salaries have significantly failed for some time to keep up with increases in the consumer price index. (Over the period 1967–1968, the latter increased 120% while salaries increased 75%.) Just as serious is the fact that institutions face increasing constraints on financial aid for academically promising students. In my own university our commitments from general operating funds have increased by 125% in the last several years, and we still cannot meet the level of student need we recognize. In the past decade we have experienced a 200% increase in the cost of library books and a 300% increase in the cost of journals. Last year our energy costs doubled even though we reduced consumption significantly.

The pressures of inflation are complicated by the demographic outlook as regards both students and faculties. By the mid-1980s, the pool of 18-year-olds from which colleges and universities will draw the majority of their classes will have shrunk by 16%; by the early 1990s, it will be down 25% from current levels. Moreover, patterns of enrollment are changing. A decade ago almost half of the nation's high school graduates attended college or university. By the mid-1970s, the proportion had dropped to a third, and had women not started to enroll in larger numbers we would have experienced even greater losses. Already the population growth rate in the country is less than zero, and whatever the broader geopolitical implications of this may be—salutary or otherwise—the decline in population represents bad news for higher education given the assumptions on which our colleges and universities presently operate.

Dropping enrollments represent an impediment, but only one, to maintaining viability in the faculty. It has been a standing rule of thumb for research universities that the proportion of the faculty which is tenured not exceed two thirds. The national average for faculty members holding doctorates is already over 70%, and in many institutions, including some of our most distinguished, it is significantly in excess of 80%. By the mid-1980s, the national average is expected to exceed 80%. Meanwhile, the median age of tenured faculty members is 47 years, and only about 40% are over 50. Unless there is a drastic change in employment philosophy, something that is highly unlikely, this can only mean increasingly fewer appointments. In the mid-1960s, there were 26,000 new faculty appointments each year. At present the rate is roughly half the earlier level, and by the late 1980s it will have dropped to 4,000. Although the total unemployment of scientists is still small relative to that of the work force in general (for the behavioral sciences overall, it is 2.4%, and for psychologists, the American Psychological Association reports, it is fortunately only 1%), there is ample anecdotal evidence that a trend toward greater unemployment is taking place. Academic jobs are harder to find and are taking longer to obtain. One can only ask rhetorically with the balladeer, "Where have all the flowers gone?"

Academic scientists face constraints that are arguably more severe than those faced by faculty members in general. The monumental expansion of academic science in the 1950s and 1960s was made possible by direct subsidies for equipment and facilities. By the early 1970s, appropriations for facilities had virtually ceased, except in the case of large-scale development projects with specific and immediate mission goals. The National Science Foundation, for example, is receiving fewer facilities dollars now than it did even in the mid-1970s. In an extensive and by now widely cited study of academic science, Smith and Karlesky (1977) report that equipment is worn and in many cases obsolete and that facilities are in various states of disrepair.

The inability to compensate for normal wear and tear is one thing. The failure to keep abreast with the rapid growth that is occurring in the versatility and power of scientific instrumentation is quite another matter and one that is far more serious. In a 1978 editorial in *Science*, Philip Abelson, that magazine's editor, estimated that progress in instrumentation in the natural sciences advances by a factor of 10 every five years. Thus equipment that is ten years old is, with few exceptions, obsolete. Meanwhile, he calculated that for every professor and graduate student doing research in chemistry (his field), only about $1,000 per year is available to purchase equipment. One biomedical scientist friend of mine regularly sends his students to West Germany to gain access to instruments not available to them in the United States. Though I suspect I could not make the same case for psychology across the board—at least in absolute terms—my many conversations with laboratory colleagues in various parts of the country suggest that in our own way we are in similarly unfortunate straits. The National Science Foundation, beginning with a 1979 appropriation, will fund a program of regional instrumentation to meet the needs of academic science for larger scale modern instrumentation. But for the present and foreseeable future, this is totally inadequate to the demonstrated need for physical support, and if a broader and more comprehensive answer is not soon provided, the quality of graduate education in many, if not most, of the sciences may be irreparably harmed.

My concerns thus far have been with the economy and the increasing degree of constraint it is placing on the perpetual process of growth and renewal that most academic scientists view to be essential to the well-being of their enterprise. As great as our problems in this arena may be, they are not, in my view, our most serious. Greater concern, I fear, must be reserved for the intrusion of the federal government into the affairs of the academic community. It is easy, I know, to cry wolf. But the evidence grows in persistent fashion. For example, the cost of compliance with the ever-increasing number of federal regulations—some general and some tailored specifically for the educational sector—is reaching major proportions. In the decade from 1965 to 1975, these overall costs escalated between 1,000% and 2,000%. My own university provides a typical example. In the 1960s costs of compliance were negligible. Today they exceed 2 million dollars annually. In 1939 the Federal Register devoted 5,000 pages to the publication of regulations, proposed or adopted; in 1978 the comparable page allotment was 61,000 pages. Currently some 87 separate federal agencies are engaged in the enforcement of regulations. They employ in excess of 100,000 people, and the top 30 expend some 3 billion federal dollars each year.

The consequences of such regulation involve, in my view, much more than simply an added burden on our institutional budgets and an expansion of our institutional bureaucracies. At the level of the individual, they have diverted scholars from their laboratory benches and writing tables and have forced them to become bookkeepers and managers. At the level of the institution, they have transformed the quality of academic life. Process has become more important than human relationships. Where we were once communities of colleagues who lived by a simple set of implicit rules centering about our shared interests, values, and goals, we are now closer to being collections of individuals who function separately within a rigid network of formal controls and contractual arrangements. More than this, there have been violations of the freedoms that the academician has traditionally enjoyed. The most intensive regulation has been fiscal, but there are also growing threats to academic freedom as such. The first attempts at legislation directed toward the potential hazards of DNA research, had they been successful, would have closed down the laboratories and created chaos in the field. Four or five years of intense concentration by scientists on educating policymakers have finally given DNA researchers enough elbow room to get on with their work.

The same kind of struggle occurs over experimentation involving the use of human subjects. While safeguards are certainly essential, some constraints are downright silly. They cause, at the least, unnecessary inconvenience when experimental procedures are manifestly benign and, indeed, make it impossible to do certain kinds of studies even when the risk is highly speculative. These rules share a common characteristic with much of the regulation that now applies to science. They lack a necessary modulation. Much of their effect is like hitting a fine cello with a baseball bat.

The broader academic community faces other intrusions. The Buckley Amendment to the 1974 Family Rights and Privacy Act, when it appeared, severely hampered the ability of academic institutions to maintain and transmit candid evaluations of their students by giving the student access to these evaluations and the right to prevent their disclosure. The Health Professions Educational Assistance Act of 1976 proscribed the right of medical schools to select and deal with their own students, faculties, and even curricula. Although the 1977 amendments to this act have reduced the requirements concerning the admission of Americans already enrolled in medical schools abroad, they still impose greatly on the curriculum. Similarly, the new GI Bill passed in 1976 to extend educational benefits to Vietnam veterans contains provisions that govern classroom attendance, the proportion of veterans in individual classes, the scheduling of classes, institutional policies on grading, the assignment of credit, and even the reporting of information on students who are not veterans, although the institutional records of the latter are presumably protected by the new laws on privacy.

The history of government–university relationships is a long one. Universities were first chartered in the 13th century. The Puritans had hardly settled the Massachusetts Bay Colony when they established Harvard College with public, among other, funds. For most of the ensuing years the relationship between higher education and government in America has been congenial and mutually beneficial. Indeed, the specter of an intrusive, constraining federal government and the emergence of what some see as a burgeoning managerial bureaucracy that is itself, as noted earlier, immune to management date from as recently as the early 1960s. Moreover, colleges and universities are peculiarly vulnerable to regulation because most institutions—and certainly all the major ones—are sorely dependent on federal money. When 25% to 50% of one's total operating budget comes from government sources, it is difficult to resist attempts at government control. Clark Kerr once described the American university as a public utility, and public utilities are, obviously, by their nature regulated industries.

I should make clear that I am not an "autonomy freak." I do not count myself among those who insist that institutions of higher learning should be totally exempt from regulation. It is manifestly clear that the intent of the regulatory legislation directed toward the Academy is benign; one need only survey the goals behind it—equality of opportunity, human rights, safety—to be convinced of that fact. Moreover, much that we now find confining came about in response to neglect or abuse of these goals by members of the academic community itself. The antipathy of the Nixon White House and the oratorical excesses of certain members of Congress notwithstanding, I certainly refuse to believe that there is in this country a conscious plot to restrict academic or scientific freedom as such. The reasons for regulation, and for the danger of overregulation, are complex. As I have just noted, we have brought some regulations upon ourselves through our failure to understand both the meaning of public accountability and the depth of the government's commitment to social equity. And some regulations, of course, result from our lack of political influence as a community of interest, our inability to support organized political action, our Cartesian preoccupation with the individual qua individual, and our feeling that political action is somehow degrading. Even where regulations have been friendly, we have lacked the clout necessary to protect our community from unnecessarily burdensome breadth or detail.

We understand but often forget that from the very beginnings of America's history as a nation, we have viewed our institutions of higher education as instruments of national purpose. Thus, in an era of dominating bureaucracies one should not be surprised if government bureaucrats assume colleges and universities and the various activities they encompass to constitute collectively one giant laboratory for the implementation of social policy. Since World War II the relationship between the government and the Academy has been contractual. During the war, universities, through the mechanism of research contracts, contributed much of the technology that aided in bringing hostilities to a successful conclusion. After the war our colleges and universities undertook, under the provisions of the GI Bill of Rights, to provide advanced education for veterans on an unprecedented scale. But the contractual model that is the legacy of those days is a model for predictable outcomes and is simply not suited to the flexibility now needed for effectiveness in many aspects of the academic enterprise. Such is particularly the case in scientific research, where great leaps forward are frequently the result of following unplanned leads and insights. Much of the scientist's unhappiness in recent years has come from the need to resist the straitjackets of the bureaucratic mind while trying to capitalize on the serendipity inherent in the scientific process.

The effort to find a strategy that will meet the intent of public-accountability policies and educate the public about the necessary risks of creative scholarship will not be easy, nor will it be short-lived. The psychology of the contract brings with it the scrutiny of anything that approaches some threshold of critical size. When agency budgets reach the billion-dollar mark, as have the budgets of both the National Science Foundation and the Alcohol, Drug Abuse, and Mental Health Administration, one can expect widespread and constant surveillance. Furthermore, federal laws are almost always written for the general case, and to prepare the countless modulations needed to accommodate the individual instance with equity is a difficult, if not insurmountable, task. Thus, we should not be too surprised to find the government, as Bailey (1978) wittily put it, "using an industry-oriented bulldozer to weed an academic garden" (p. 109). Finally, it is in the nature of the government to regulate; so it is inevitable that when government is big, the penchant to regulate will be strong and its rationalization little more than the ready assertion of lofty principles.

In a society as complex as ours, there is always the possibility that institutionalized values will clash. Moreover, the overriding quality of some values will be self-evident, in which case academic institutions have no alternative but to seek ways of serving them while doing minimal disservice to others. Certainly in those instances in which, for example, the outcomes of scientific research have a reasonable likelihood of serious physical or psychological damage, the possibility of regulation must be honestly and squarely faced. The latter notwithstanding, essential institutional values will still need to be protected in the face of external political and social pressure; academics must be prepared to fight for their preservation at any cost.

A case recently brought by the Department of Health, Education, and Welfare (Forsham v. Califano) and now pending before the Supreme

Court provides an instance in point. The matter at issue concerns whether *raw* data collected in federally funded research projects are the private property of the researcher or are agency records and hence available to anyone under the authority of the Freedom of Information Act. How free can responsible scientists be if raw data must be surrendered to anyone, regardless of his or her ability to understand and interpret them? The right of free inquiry—whether in the classroom or in the laboratory—is the foundation on which our intellectual scholarship is built, and long experience has made clear to academics that the Academy has been greatest when it has insisted upon the responsible pursuit of such inquiry. Long experience has also made clear that in the United States rights are not abridged suddenly or in full-scale fashion. Rather, we are now coming to realize that abridgment is the kind of incursive process, gradual and often inadvertent, that requires constant vigilance if the integrity of both the scientific and the academic enterprise is to be preserved.

BARGAINING WITHIN AN IDEOLOGY OF LIMITS

The contract between society at large and the Academy—the learned professions and the institutions in which they work—is being rewritten. The stakes in renegotiation are high.

Brewster Denny, 1978

After preaching the gospel of science as a consumption good for some 30 years, I have reluctantly come to the conclusion that such a philosophy by itself is neither humane nor realistic and is therefore not viable. "If science ever was," as Holton (1979) writes, "a charismatic profession dominated by abstract spirits, those days are gone forever" (p. 229). Even the best friends of science have consistently justified the public support of science in investment terms. Viewed in such terms, basic research as a publicly-sponsored enterprise must be defined as a high-risk activity underwritten by a promissory note of indefinite term. What most academic scientists seem never to have understood is that such notes are always subject to payment on demand and rarely with just a simple accumulation of interest. If they are going to preserve the integrity of the basic research undertaking under such a social contract, scientists are going to have to take a more active interest in and become more knowledgeable of the nature of the process of making public policy than has heretofore been the case. Engagement must be realized in both institutional individual terms. Like any other special interest group operating in an era of special interest politics, scientists must be prepared to engage in open debate. But they must first put their own house in order. As Barzun (1978) has recently pointed out, if the professions, including science, are to survive with anything like the freedom they have enjoyed in the past, their one hope is in the recovery of mental and moral force.

As befits their fundamental philosophical commitment, they must place their own special concerns within the broader context of the greater public good. They must give greater attention to the prudent use of public resources. Though scientists must assert their *real* needs with greater clarity and effectiveness, they cannot afford to make unrealistic and unwarranted demands. They must renew their commitment to the collective honesty that is, above all, their sustaining principle. They must be willing to explore the implications of their work with the widest perspective possible, and they must assess risks alongside benefits. Most important, they must not *over*sell the likelihood of practical research outcomes. Nothing will hurt public confidence in science more than unfulfilled promises. To talk of putting one's house in order is to imply the development of self-regulatory systems that are policed with no fraternal hand, no concession to public relations. Whether these can ultimately work effectively on the large scale is a matter of honest doubt. But in any event they warrant a serious effort.

As academic scientists contemplate the next decade of the science–government relationship, they need to adopt a new metaphor. During the "golden years" between the end of World War II and the middle 1960s, most of us developed the pleasant habit of thinking and speaking of our agency sponsors in terms of the accommodations of a marriage. In any era marked by an ideology of limits, it is more realistic to think in terms of a negotiated treaty. Successful marriages are said to be built on mutual trust; successful treaties are based on mutually recognized self-interest. Treaties are also based on mutually shared goals and values, if nothing more than a mutually recognized interdependence and a willingness to negotiate differences. Finally, they involve an arrangement between equals in which neither member can afford to take the other for granted.

Academic scientists are also going to need to acquire a better understanding of the mechanisms and strategies by which policy is established. Certainly it is important that they know what the policy processes are and what they are not. Many, for example, would probably be surprised if not disturbed to realize that policy hardly ever exists as a totally explicit, completely rational, clearly formulated, and fully comprehensive set of statements—that, indeed, policy is more often than not nothing more than what a particular bureaucrat elects to do about a particular matter at a particular time. With a view toward greater grass-roots understanding and involvement, scientists at the level of the university department could well take more seriously the need to analyze the policy process in the context of specific issues as well as the need to teach their students about science, politics, and government as social consensual systems and about how these systems interact in the modern world. If MIT can create a College for

Science, Technology, and Society, surely other universities can at least organize an appropriate course or seminar and persuade their science departments of the wisdom of graduate student participation. While it is certainly true that many colleges and universities both monitor and involve themselves in the federal legislative process on an everyday basis, it is equally true that the largest number remain relatively indifferent to such matters. Even those that participate actively do, for the most part, an abysmally poor job of keeping their faculties properly informed.

The Washington-based organizations that coordinate the interests of the scientific and higher education communities need to create more vigorous and more effective lobbies for the overlapping constituencies they represent, particularly in the case of the scientific societies. I am fully aware of the fine job being done in the legislative arena by the American Psychological Association, the Association for the Advancement of Psychology, the American Physical Society, the American Chemical Society, the American Association for the Advancement of Science, and a few others like them, but they constitute a very small proportion of the well over three hundred scientific societies that exist as national organizations. None, I would submit, have yet fully learned the value of political alliances. Most often they operate singly or in very small consortia. Certainly they have not yet learned to a significant degree the advantages of joining with groups outside their area of specialized interest. Indeed, social and behavioral scientists have not even learned how to make common cause with natural scientists and engineers. It is important to remember that the private sector comprises many different communities, and all—the corporate community, labor unions, public interest groups, and others—are potential political allies. Even more fundamental than the lesson of cooperative action is the need to recognize that effective political action is an expensive undertaking and to display a willingness to place our resources in significant amounts behind our convictions.

In addition to political intervention, there are a number of other useful activities that our scientific societies would do well to initiate. They can organize workshops in the policy process for those of their members who wish to acquire a background for participating in public affairs. They can devote a larger proportion of their annual programs to sessions that deal with the interface between science and government. They can create special seminars for the intensive study of particular legislative issues. They can arrange person-to-person advisory services for individual members of Congress. They can conduct seminars on a regular basis for appropriate members of Congress and their legislative aides. They can establish research units with the capability of providing the background information and carrying out the analytic studies that are essential to formulating an effective legislative posture. They can insist on a vigorous program of testimony before congressional committees. They can engage in informal dialogue with members of Congress and their staffs over the long course that it takes to transform a legislative proposal into law. Finally, they can devote more serious effort to educating their memberships in the grass-roots expression of policy positions. Grass-roots consciousness raising and political action more often than not are the ingredients that make the difference between success and failure in the pursuit of a political objective. At present, it is common practice for some of the federal granting agencies to hire academic scientists to work for several years as program officers. It would be worthwhile for the societies to arrange similar rotations, either in the Congress or on society staffs, for work in the field of science policy, with the rotators then returning to campus to help in the education of their colleagues.

As scientists contemplate the possibility of greater government intrusion into their workaday lives, they will, I believe, benefit from learning, both as individuals and as a community, the truth of the old admonition "Neither flatter wealth nor cringe before power." They will recognize the ultimate benefit of saying no when principle is threatened, even if this means a possible loss of funding. Such a drawing of the line by leading American medical schools, when confronted by the provisions of the Health Professions Educational Assistance Act of 1976, precipitated the more palatable conditions of the Act's 1977 amendment. But perhaps the most important lesson scientists can learn is that given the way we govern ourselves in this country, it is not a matter of who *should* decide a policy question but who *will*.

Policy directions are set through dint of persistence, political skill, and political influence, and if scientists have any suspicions about the untoward nature of their bed partner, they had better realize that there is no third party in the bed to create their defenses for them. Governments by their inherent nature continue to grow, to become more complex, and thus to intrude, to monopolize, and to centralize. As we have all learned in recent years, it is incumbent upon the governed, in their own best interest, to harbor a healthy skepticism about the intentions of their government, to insist constantly on the distinctions between legitimate need and demand, and to resist encroachment on the rights of the individual or the group except when it is manifestly essential to the advancement of the overall public good.

Academic science, like every other sector of American life, will get the kind of government it deserves. If government regulation exceeds the bounds of fair treatment or otherwise violates individual and group rights, it will be because scientists have neglected to educate government about those rights, have failed to resist unwarranted intrusions with the necessary effectiveness, or both. Some years ago Justice Brandeis observed that the citizenry should be most on its guard when the government's purposes are beneficent. "The greatest dangers to liberty," he said, "lurk in insidious encroachment by means of zeal, well meaning but without understanding" (quoted in Gardner & Reese, 1975, p. 208). There can be few in the scientific community who fail to understand that the public at large, whether it so wishes or not, has a major stake in the consequences of modern science and its attendant technology. It is therefore perfectly proper for the public to express interest in these consequences and apply protective controls when these are fully understood to be needed. But the history of science provides enough examples of the way in which well-intentioned regulators from the time of Galileo to the present have threatened the well-being of our enterprise to underline the importance of eternal vigilance on everyone's part. The time for hand wringing is over. Now is the time to come to terms with reality and to do so with courage and with a commitment to preserve what is important for science and for the common good.

REFERENCES

Abelson, P. H. Obsolete instrumentation at universities. *Science*, 1978, *200*, 1111.

Bacon, F. *The works of Francis Bacon* (Vols. 3 and 4, J. Spedding, R. L. Ellis, & D. D. Heath, Eds.). London: Longmans, 1870–1872.

Bailey, S. K. The peculiar mixture: Public norms and private space. In W. C. Hobbs (Ed.), *Government regulation in higher education*. Cambridge, Mass.: Ballinger, 1978.

Barzun, J. The professions under siege. *Harper's*, October 1978, pp. 61–68.

Blissett, M. *Politics in science*. Boston: Little, Brown, 1972.

Denny, B. C. Renegotiating the society–academy contract. *Science*, 1978, *201*, 677.

Descartes, R. *A discourse on method and selected writings* (J. Verton, Trans.). New York: Everyman's Library, 1951.

Finn, C. E., Jr. *Scholars, dollars, and bureaucrats*. Washington, D.C.: Brookings Institution, 1978.

Gardner, J. W., & Reese, F. G. *Know or listen to those who know*. New York: Norton, 1975.

Haberer, J. *Politics and the community of science*. New York: Van Nostrand Reinhold, 1969.

Hobbs, W. C. *Government regulation of higher education*. Cambridge, Mass.: Ballinger, 1978.

Holton, G. From the endless frontier to the ideology of limits. In G. Holton & R. S. Morison (Eds.), *Limits of scientific inquiry*. New York: Norton, 1979.

Holton, G., & Morison, R. S. (Eds.). *Limits of scientific inquiry*. New York: Norton, 1979.

Miller, L., Voss, F., & Hussey, J. M. *The Lazzaroni: Science and scientists in mid-nineteenth century America.* Washington, D.C.: National Portrait Gallery, 1972.

Price, D. de S. An intrinsic value theory for basic and "applied" research. In J. Haberer (Ed.), *Science and technology policy.* Lexington, Mass.: Lexington Books, 1977.

Seabury, P. (Ed.). *Bureaucrats and brain power: Government regulation of universities.* San Francisco: Institute for Contemporary Studies, 1979.

Smith, B. L. R., & Karlesky, J. J. *The universities in the nation's research effort.* New Rochelle, N.Y.: Change Magazine Press, 1977.

Toulmin, S. The complexity of scientific choice: II. Culture, overheads, or tertiary industry? *Minerva,* 1966, *4*(2), 155–169.

8

SOCIAL SCIENTISTS AND DECISION MAKERS LOOK AT THE USEFULNESS OF MENTAL HEALTH RESEARCH

JANET A. WEISS and CAROL H. WEISS

Decision makers and social scientists behave as though social science research makes a genuine contribution to public policy. Decision makers keep paying for research at the respectable level of over a billion dollars a year (National Research Council, 1978). Social scientists keep doing research in the hope that their results will—someday—make a difference (Useem, 1976). But if the two groups are in harmony at this global behavioral level, many observers believe that they diverge in their views of how and why research can be useful to policymakers (e.g., Parloff, 1979; Shaffer, 1977; Stier, 1975).

In this article we compare the views of social scientists and decision makers. Our first objective is to see whether the two groups agree about whether social research is useful and, if so, what makes it useful. The extent of agreement about the determinants of usefulness is central to such issues as planning and funding programs of research, allocating responsibility for disseminating research results, and devising strategies to improve the contribution of research to intelligent policymaking.

Reprinted from *American Psychologist*, 36, 837–847. Copyright 1981 by the American Psychological Association.

    This chapter is based on research funded by the National Institute of Mental Health. The authors are grateful to Michael J. Bucuvalas for his contributions to the research reported here and to Donald R. Kinder for insightful criticism.

The comparison also has implications for the occasionally recriminatory relationship between researchers and decision makers. Many social science researchers have characterized this relationship in classic intergroup terms. Caplan, Morrison, and Stambaugh (1975), for example, conclude from their study of 204 high-ranking federal executives that "social scientists and policy makers operate in separate worlds with different and often conflicting values" (p. x). In a paraphrase of C. P. Snow's distinction between the two cultures of science and the humanities, Caplan et al. label this the "two communities" problem, emphasizing the differences between the perspectives of social scientists and decision makers.[1] The differences between the two groups and the circumstances of their contact with each other seem to have created mistrust and suspicion. Social scientists see themselves as rational, objective, open to new ideas, and committed to truth and standards of evidence; they see decision makers as partisan, action oriented, indifferent to evidence, irresponsible in their pursuit of quick fixes, and reluctant to consider new ideas (Coleman, 1972; Scott & Shore, 1974). On the other side of the fence, decision makers see themselves as pragmatic, action oriented, responsible, and informed in the ways of the world; they see social scientists as naive, jargon ridden, oriented to esoteric academic concerns rather than to accomplishment, and irresponsible in their neglect of practical realities (Caplan et al., 1975; Wilson, 1978).

These mutual stereotypes almost certainly contain some grain of truth; they almost certainly are some part caricature. Here we mount a search for accurate intergroup understanding by comparing the responses of the two groups to questions about each other and about the role of social science research in public policy. Our second research objective is to assess the degree to which the two groups misunderstand each other and the implications of their real or imagined disagreements for their judgments of the usefulness of research.

OVERVIEW OF METHODOLOGY

One hundred fifty-five decision makers in the field of mental health and 100 social scientists were interviewed at length about the characteristics of research that make some studies more useful than others for making decisions about mental health policy, programs, or operations. The sample was stratified to include representatives of five major groups that use, con-

---

[1]Caplan et al. (1975) use the term *policymaker* to refer to federal executives at levels from assistant secretary to Civil Service Grade 14 who "are in policy-influencing positions" (p. viii). We use *decision makers* to describe the same group of federal executives and officials of comparable authority in state and local governments. Because the decision makers we interviewed shape basic policy and program decisions, the terms policymaker and decision maker are equally appropriate descriptions. We use decision maker throughout for the sake of consistency.

duct, and fund mental health research: (a) 51 federal-level decision makers at the level of branch chief or above in the National Institute of Mental Health (NIMH), National Institute of Drug Abuse (NIDA), National Institute for Alcohol Abuse and Alcoholism (NIAAA), and Alcohol, Drug Abuse, and Mental Health Administration (ADAMHA), with responsibilities for policy or program planning; (b) 52 state-level decision makers in 10 state departments of mental health at the level of deputy director, deputy commissioner, or director of such functional areas as drug abuse, mental retardation, community services, and so on; (c) 52 local-level decision makers who were directors or chiefs of service in 52 mental health centers, clinics, and hospitals located in the same 10 cities as the state mental health departments and in the Washington, D.C., area (where we were interviewing federal respondents) and New York City (where our office was located); (d) 50 principal investigators of NIMH, NIDA, and NIAAA research grants and contracts (excluding biological research) who worked in or near the 10 state capitals, Washington, D.C., or New York City; (e) 50 members of 12 peer-review committees that review basic and applied research applications for NIMH, NIDA, and NIAAA, also selected by location in or near a city where we were already interviewing. The decision makers cooperated graciously with our research needs. Of 172 eligible respondents who were invited to participate in the study, 155, or 90%, completed interviews with our staff. Interviewing the two groups of social scientists proved more difficult. We had to approach 163 eligible researchers and review committee members to complete 100 interviews, for a response rate of 61%.

Why this sample? We had originally considered including decision makers in the Congress, the White House, and the Office of the Secretary. During the pretesting, however, we found that people at upper levels were neither informed nor interested in research on mental health services, modalities of care, organization of service delivery, and related issues that are the focus of research studies funded by ADAMHA institutes. Their responsibilities extended to global direction of policy and allocation of resources but not to detailed supervision of the structure of service delivery or to shaping new initiatives in program or treatment. Such policy choices were the responsibility of the federal, state, and local officials—whom we in fact interviewed. We included members of research review committees, who pass on proposals for funding social science research on mental health, because they play a critical role in decisions about which research gets done. We included principal investigators of mental health studies because they shape and do the work with which we are concerned.

The comparison between this group of decision makers and this group of social scientists is important because it juxtaposes two highly knowledgeable subsamples. Those social scientists who serve on ADAMHA review committees and who have federal research funding are probably more sophisticated about social research than a random sample of mental health researchers would be. Decision makers whose jobs require choices about how to make a difference in the emotional and spiritual lives of citizens are probably more sophisticated about social research than a random sample of the Senior Executive Service would be. But if a researcher is studying ways to get minority group members into treatment or how peer groups influence teenage drug use (to pick two examples from the studies we used), who should pay attention to the research? The bulk of mental health research is aimed at precisely the group of decision makers we interviewed. A senator's evaluation of a study does not matter very much when the study concerns ways in which mental health professionals reach out into the community. The Congress has only remote influence over these issues. Our sample has direct authority over such decisions. To them, mental health policy is their life's work.

Interviews were conducted by two professional interviewing firms. Each interview lasted approximately two hours. Respondents were asked about their attitudes toward research, their experience with social science, and their jobs and professional training. Each respondent also read two actual research reports that we had condensed to two-page abstracts. Altogether we used 50 studies listed in the 1973 catalog of ADAMHA research grants and contracts. In an effort to match research studies to respondents' areas of expertise, we selected two studies out of the pool for each respondent. Respondents then rated the research abstract for the usefulness of the research to their work; its technical quality, political acceptability, objectivity, and compatibility with users' values; and a variety of other factors. Respondents also answered open-ended questions about the most appropriate users of the studies, what would make each study more useful, critical barriers to the use of research, and other issues. See C. H. Weiss (1980) for a complete description of the interview schedule.

To analyze differences between the perceptions of the 155 decision makers and the 100 social scientists, we compared the two groups in four ways: (a) their reports of obstacles to the use of mental health research; (b) their responses to open-ended questions about why some studies are more useful than others; (c) their ratings of particular research characteristics for their importance in making a study useful; and (d) the match between their ratings of characteristics of the actual research studies they read during the interview and their ratings of the usefulness of those studies.

OBSTACLES TO USE

Respondents agreed or disagreed on a 4-point scale with 27 statements about the relationship between research and policymaking. These items elicited opinions about obstacles to the effective use of research in mental health. Responses are shown in Table 1, roughly categorized for purposes of discussion into obstacles located in the environment of researchers, in the environment of decision makers, and in linkage systems. In their responses to the first set of items, decision makers seemed to be alert to the constraints of university departments, the academic reward system, and other institutional arrangements that make it difficult for researchers to do interdisciplinary, problem-oriented (and thus presumably more useful) research. Researchers recognized the same problems with roughly the same frequency. Neither group saw the political timidity or competence of researchers as serious problems, although both agreed that some contractors may bias their findings to please their funders. Two thirds of the decision makers reported that social science can make a real contribution to public policy, and a still larger proportion of the social scientists agreed.

In their responses to the second group of items, researchers were more pessimistic than decision makers about obstacles located in the environment of decision makers. While there was general agreement on many of the problems, social scientists perceived all such obstacles to be more severe than did decision makers. If one assumes that decision makers know their own environment better than do social scientists, then the significant differences in this group of items suggest that social scientists exaggerate the politicization of research use and the resistance of decision makers. This pattern offers an illuminating contrast to the first category in Table 1. There we see that decision makers understand the constraints on social scientists in much the same way that social scientists understand these constraints. Furthermore, they exhibit substantial support for the competence of researchers and the value of their research. However, in the items about the policy environment, we see that social scientists do not appear to understand the decision makers' world as well as the decision makers understand theirs.

As the third set of items in Table 1 suggests, decision makers are more impressed than researchers with problems in the linkage systems. More often than researchers, they reported that research program officers, who influence the kind of research that is initiated and funded, are poorly informed about decision makers' needs and have few incentives to select issues of major importance to decision makers. Decision makers also claimed that review of research proposals by outside panels tends to neglect considerations of policy relevance. On their side, social scientists reported that the contract mechanism for funding research leads to poorer research quality.

In spite of these fine-grained differences, the major story in Table 1 is that decision makers and social scientists agree on the importance of the various obstacles. The Spearman rho correlation between the rank orders of the two groups is .86. Most striking is the strong consensus that social

TABLE 1
What Are the Obstacles to the Use of Research for Policy Making?
Percentage Agreeing With Each Statement

Obstacles to use	% decision makers (n = 155)	% social scientists (n = 100)	t(253)
Obstacles located in researchers and their environment			
Interdisciplinary research is discouraged by university departments.	74	64	2.88**
Academic reward system discourages decision-oriented research.	68	72	.05
Contractors slant findings to please decision makers.	65	64	.81
Research institutions do not reward policy research.	54	54	.76
Political values of researchers bias research.	38	34	2.15*
Social sciences are too limited to make a contribution.	32	24	2.88**
Researchers try to avoid political controversy.	31	36	1.66
Most able researchers are uninterested in policy research.	29	34	.82
There is no such thing as research in the public interest.	17	10	1.66
Obstacles located in decision makers and their environment			
Agencies should implement good research even when this would reduce their budgets.	82	85	2.73**
Decision makers ignore information contrary to their own ideas.	75	86	5.46***
Policies are arrived at by politics, not research.	72	85	3.99***
Decision makers cannot define research needs.	68	75	1.70
Agencies ignore findings contrary to their policies.	67	82	4.20***
Agencies have limited options for action.	61	65	1.30
Most decision makers believe research contributes.	54	33	4.08***
Rapid change in policy issues makes research irrelevant.	39	19	5.39***
Obstacles located in linkage systems			
Lack of communication between researchers and decision makers is a major obstacle.	82	85	1.67
Funders do not know decision makers' needs.	69	46	4.60***
Funders do not forecast information needs.	67	65	.18
Funders do not disseminate results.	64	59	1.32

continues

TABLE 1 (Continued)

Obstacles to use	% decision makers (n = 155)	% social scientists (n = 100)	t(253)
Obstacles located in linkage systems			
Contract research trades speed for quality.	51	73	6.09***
Funders have no incentives to aid decision makers.	51	33	3.75***
Outside review panels neglect the relevance of research.	48	37	3.16**
Other opinions			
Good research should be used even when politically controversial.	83	81	.26
One study is not enough to base a decision on.	72	75	.34
Nothing is so practical as good theory.	38	56	6.07***

*$p < .05$. **$p < .01$. ***$p < .001$.

science can and should contribute to intelligent policymaking. Also important are the agreements about what is and is not an obstacle to that contribution and about the strengths and limits of research.

WHAT MAKES RESEARCH USEFUL?

Another angle on these issues comes from responses to the question, "In general, what do you think makes some social science studies more useful than others for decision making in mental health?" The open-ended responses were sorted into categories by two coders working independently. In cases of disagreement between the coders, a conference resolved the dispute, so that final categories were based on 100% agreement. Multiple responses were permitted and were common. The most frequent responses to this question appear in Table 2, with the percentage of respondents whose answers fell into each category. In Table 2 we again find considerable agreement between researchers and decision makers about what makes some research studies more useful than others. According to both groups, research studies are most useful when they deal with a topic of particular relevance to decision makers, when they examine variables that decision makers can do something about, and when they are written clearly.

The general agreement continues in Table 3, which reports respondents' views about how to make particular studies more useful. After reading an abstract of 1 research report (out of the sample of 50 research reports

TABLE 2
In General, What Makes Some Studies More Useful Than Others? Most Frequent Responses

Decision makers	Social scientists
Topic of study of particular relevance or interest (28%)	Study looks at variables that decision makers can do something about (42%)
Study looks at variables that decision makers can do something about (23%)	Topic of study is of particular relevance or interest (16%)
Population studied is of particular interest to user (18%)	Information presented is especially usable (14%)
Study is on time for pending decisions (13%)	Study deals with high-priority topic of great social concern (13%)
Report is understandably written, not overly technical (12%)	Report is understandably written, not overly technical (13%)
	Research is disseminated, available, accessible to people (13%)

Note. Multiple responses were coded.

used in the study) and answering questions about its usefulness, respondents were asked, "What would make this study more useful to decision makers?" Again, the open-ended responses were coded into categories by two independent coders and all discrepancies were reconciled. Note that codes had to be constructed to accommodate responses referring to 50 different research reports. Each respondent answered twice because each evaluated

TABLE 3
What Would Make This Study More Useful to Decision Makers? Most Frequent Responses

Decision makers	Social scientists
If the conceptualization of the problem were better, less superficial, more comprehensive (29%)	If the conceptualization of the problem were better, less superficial, more comprehensive (40%)
If the report presented more information on methods, subjects, definitions, etc. (27%)	If the report presented more information on methods, subjects, definitions, etc. (27%)
If the study had included a follow-up or replication to check on findings, make results more generalizable (18%)	If they had drawn the sample differently, had a larger sample, better response rate (21%)
If they had drawn the sample differently, had a larger sample, better response rate (15%)	If the analysis and interpretation of the data were better done (20%)

Note. Multiple responses were coded.

2 particular studies out of the total pool of 50. Table 3 shows the most frequent responses.

As in Table 2, the level of agreement between decision makers and social scientists is striking. The most common response for both groups was that the study at hand would be more useful if it were better conceptualized. The second most frequent response was that the report did not contain enough information about methods, sampling, operationalizations, and so on for them to make confident recommendations for improvement. This response may be due in part to the fact that respondents read two-page abstracts rather than full study reports. But it is consistent with the pervasive concern with methodology shown in the other frequently mentioned items. And this close link between methods and usefulness was made by decision makers as well as by researchers. Just over 1% of the decision makers' responses to this question were concerned with political or administrative ways to make the study more useful, while 72% of their responses dealt with improvements in methodology such as development of recommendations, sampling, analysis, design, and measures. (This is not to deny the importance of political and administrative concerns; they surface elsewhere in the interviews.)

These open-ended responses provide additional evidence that the two groups hold similar views about the uses of social science research. The responses of decision makers, at least at these levels, look very much like the responses of social scientists, both in their general sense of what makes research useful and in their analyses of particular studies. From these two questions, we see that both groups spontaneously generate two sorts of criteria for assessing usefulness: the quality of a study's methodology and the fit of the study to the needs and interests of potential users.

CHARACTERISTICS OF USEFUL RESEARCH

To compare responses along a broader range of criteria, we asked respondents to tell us how important 26 characteristics of a research study would be, ranked on a 5-point scale from *essential* to *undesirable*. For the 155 decision makers, the question read, "How important are each of these characteristics to you when you choose to use a research study?" For the 100 review panel members and researchers, the question read, "How important are each of these characteristics to decision makers when they choose to use a study?" Here we find major disagreements between the two groups, with 21 of 26 items showing statistically significant differences. Responses to these items appear in Columns 1 and 2 of Table 4, and the test of significance between Columns 1 and 2 appears in Column 3.

The strongest disagreements—where the group means are a full unit apart—concern the political acceptability of research results and the de-

TABLE 4
Importance of Research Characteristics for Usefulness

Research characteristic	SS reported importance[a] (1)	DM reported importance[a] (2)	t[b] (3)	DM revealed importance[c] (4)	Rank order difference[d] (5)
Recommendations supported by data	3.9	4.5	7.97***	.46	-4.5
Objective, unbiased	3.5	4.3	8.46***	.35	-10.0
High-priority issue	4.2	4.1	1.24	.28	-13.5
Adds to practical knowledge	4.0	4.1	.84	.46	-2.0
Findings consistent, unambiguous	3.5	4.0	5.27***	.45	-2.5
Technical quality high	3.4	3.9	6.28***	.49	5.5
Direct implications for action	4.1	3.9	2.03*	.49	5.5
Manipulable variables	4.1	3.9	2.08*	.43	-2.0
Generalizable	3.6	3.8	2.59**	.39	-1.0
On time for decision	3.8	3.8	.75	.39	-1.0
Adds to descriptive, causal, or theoretical knowledge	3.1	3.7	7.70***	.48	8.0
Raises new issues	2.9	3.6	9.46***	.29	-1.5
Comprehensive set of independent variables	2.9	3.6	8.06***	.45	5.5
Quantitative data	3.2	3.6	5.09***	.31	.0
Applicable within existing programs	3.5	3.4	1.45	.47	11.5
Explicit recommendations	3.8	3.4	4.91***	.24	-5.5
Inexpensive to implement	3.4	3.2	2.39*	.08	-9.0
Statistically sophisticated	2.6	3.1	5.58***	.26	-1.5
Targeted, few dependent variables	3.2	3.0	1.66	.22	-3.0
Implies need for major change	2.3	2.9	5.88***	.28	3.0
Challenges assumptions	2.1	2.8	9.03***	.19	-1.5
Compatible with user ideas	3.6	2.8	7.40***	.26	2.0
Consistent with previous knowledge	2.9	2.7	2.77**	.29	8.5
Politically acceptable	3.6	2.6	10.80***	.18	.0
Findings unexpected/novel	2.2	2.4	2.88**	.13	.0
Supports user position	3.2	2.1	14.30***	.28	9.0

Note. SS = social scientist; DM = decision maker.
[a]Rated on a 5-point scale.
[b]Difference between social scientists and decision makers in reported importance.
[c]The revealed importance score is the Pearson correlation coefficient between the respondents' rating of each characteristic for a specific research study and the rating of the usefulness of that research study.
[d]Difference between decision-maker reported importance (Column 2) and revealed importance (Column 4).
*p < .05. **p < .01. ***p < .001.

sirability of research that supports the potential user's position. Social scientists think these characteristics are much more important to decision makers than decision makers think they are. These results reinforce the finding shown in Table 1 that social scientists believe that the policy world is more politicized than decision makers think it is.

Table 4 also shows that social scientists think that such research characteristics as compatibility with user ideas, manipulable variables, explicit recommendations, and direct implications for action are significantly more important to the usefulness of research than decision makers think they are. The social scientists evidently place greater emphasis on immediate practicality than decision makers do. Social scientists do *not* think that scientific concerns—such as recommendations that are supported by data, objectivity, consistent and unambiguous findings, technical quality, generalizability, a comprehensive set of independent variables, quantitative data, or additions to descriptive, causal, or theoretical knowledge—are central to decision makers. Decision makers think they are. Many more decision makers than our social scientists would imagine report that raising new issues, implying a need for major change, and challenging existing assumptions are useful characteristics of research.

These differences show an unexpected pattern. Compared with decision makers, the social scientists place more emphasis on political and instrumental concerns. Compared with social scientists, decision makers place more emphasis on scientific merit, objectivity, and new ideas.

Perhaps each group takes for granted the specialty of its own domain. Social scientists, attuned to the primacy of scientific considerations, may be particularly sensitive to any intrusion of extra-scientific criteria in research matters. Similarly, decision makers, who are accustomed to bureaucratic bargaining and political decision rules, may be especially alert to the objective, scientific, and systematic qualities which distinguish scientific research from other data that enter the policymaking process. A plausible explanation for the results is that each group takes its own accustomed criteria for granted; they are the "ground." The less familiar standards of the other group take on more importance; they are the "figure." Thus decision makers emphasize methodological considerations and social scientists stress politics.

USEFULNESS OF ACTUAL RESEARCH STUDIES

It is hard to know how seriously to take the decision makers' self-reports of what they find useful. That people believe in all sincerity that a factor influences their judgment of usefulness does not necessarily mean that the factor *does* influence their judgment (Nisbett & Wilson, 1977; Ross, 1977; Slovic, Fischhoff, & Lichtenstein, 1980). To increase our confidence that the portrait which decision makers paint of themselves is accurate, we compared their reports of which characteristics make research useful in general with the characteristics that covaried with their judgments of the usefulness of research in particular cases. We were also interested in comparing social scientists' estimates of what makes research useful in general with what decision makers find useful in particular cases.

Each of the 255 respondents read 2 studies out of the total pool of 50. Thus we had at least 10 independent evaluations—6 by decision makers and 4 by social scientists—of the usefulness of each study. Each respondent also rated the 2 studies on the 26 characteristics listed in Table 4. We were thus able to compute a Pearson correlation between the degree to which a study possessed each research characteristic and how useful it was rated. These correlations show how strongly each of the research characteristics is related to decision makers' judgments of usefulness. Column 4 in Table 4 presents the correlation coefficients, which indicate the "revealed" importance of the 26 research characteristics to the decision makers. Because these indicators emerge from the decision makers' judgments of actual research, they provide a check on the decision makers' reports in Column 2 of what they find useful in social science research.

Several things can be noted from Table 4. First, compare Columns 2 and 4. The decision makers' self-reports of the importance of the 26 research characteristics in Column 2 match quite well with the revealed importance of the characteristics in action in Column 4 ($r = .69$). On the whole, the revealed importance of the research characteristics is consistent with decision makers' self-reports, lending those reports substantial credibility. For example, decision makers reported that politically acceptable findings are not essential components of useful research. We were skeptical. But as we see toward the bottom of Column 4, very little of the variation in decision makers' judgments of the usefulness of particular studies can be explained by the political acceptability of their findings. The decision makers' account seems to be confirmed.

In some cases there are discrepancies between self-reports and reactions to research. Column 5 of Table 4 shows the difference between the rank order of the characteristics in their reported importance (Column 2) and in their revealed importance (Column 4). Some characteristics were reported to be much more important (Column 2) than they turned out to be in the evaluations of actual research (Column 4). Whether a study dealt with a high-priority issue, was objective and unbiased, and was inexpensive to implement—all these were less important in action than decision makers had claimed. Other characteristics were more important in their impact on real evaluations than decision makers claimed in self-reports. These included whether research results were applicable within existing programs, supported users' positions, were consistent with previous knowledge, and added to descriptive, causal, or theoretical knowledge.

Column 5 of Table 4 also shows where the decision makers' self-reports are on target. Some of the claims which social scientists were most skeptical about—that decision makers value research which implies the need for major change, value high technical quality, but do not much value political acceptability—are supported by the decision makers' judgments of which actual studies were most useful.

A similar analysis might be done to compare social scientists' reports of what decision makers find useful (Column 1 of Table 4) with what decision makers really do find useful (Column 4). The correlation between the social scientists' estimates of the importance of the various research characteristics and the revealed importance of the characteristics to decision makers is a respectable .44, less accurate than the .69 correlation for decision makers but hardly out of the ball park. Indeed, the social scientists predicted the importance of some research characteristics more accurately than did the decision makers. As the social scientists suspected (in Column 1), objectivity is actually less important to decision makers (in Column 4) than decision makers think it is (in Column 2). Social scientists also reported correctly that "compatible with user ideas" and "supports user position" are moderately important characteristics in revealed effect on decision makers, although decision makers' self-reports had relegated them to the bottom of the list. On other items the social scientists misgauged the situation. They underestimated the importance to decision makers of "high technical quality," "adds to descriptive, causal, or theoretical knowledge," and "comprehensive set of independent variables." They overestimated the importance of "high-priority issue," "explicit recommendations," "inexpensive," and "politically acceptable."

Thus, Table 4 shows that decision makers' self-reports about the research characteristics they find useful are for the most part confirmed by their judgments of the usefulness of actual studies. This suggests that social scientists are substantially wrong in some of their estimates of what decision makers find useful in research. Most important, they underestimate the impact of methodological factors and they overestimate the impact of political factors on decision makers' judgments of research.

Disagreement between social scientists and decision makers about the ingredients of useful research may be less important if the two groups agree on the final product. Thus our final check was whether the social scientists and decision makers who read the same studies agreed about how useful they were. We compared the 10 evaluations—6 by decision makers and 4 by social scientists—of the usefulness of each study. The two groups agreed modestly about which studies were more useful to decision makers. A conservative estimate of the agreement is the intraclass correlation coefficient, $r_i = .25, p < .05$.

TWO COMMUNITIES REVISITED

Are social scientists and decision makers two communities with distinct perspectives on social research? Our data suggest that, at least in mental health, two communities exist primarily in the minds of social scientists. Contrary to the expectations among our researchers, decision makers in this study evaluated research and the research-to-policy connection in very much the same ways that the researchers did. The two groups agree modestly about the usefulness of particular studies. They even agree (also modestly, $r_i = .30, p < .05$) about the methodological quality of particular studies. When asked about how research studies can be more useful, decision makers point to the same factors that social scientists do. As a group, decision makers regard scientific and methodological merit to be an important component of usefulness; they place high value on new knowledge (practice *and* theoretical); they believe that social science has a great deal to contribute to their work. Such findings are more credible because they emerge not only from direct self-report but also from decision makers' reactions to actual research.

These results raise two questions. First, why is there relatively little difference in the ways that social scientists and decision makers evaluate social research? Second, why do social scientists think that differences exist?

The similarities in the perspectives of the two groups may be due in part to the professionalization of the field of mental health. Our 155 decision makers were highly trained, with 45 PhDs and 36 MDs in the group. Because such training took place in a university setting, most of the decision makers had some exposure to research; over half had written up a piece of social research at some point in their professional careers. When we look at the sample of researchers, we see that the professionalization works both ways. Many of the social scientists are relatively knowledgeable about the world of mental health policy and program. By our design, all 100 had some link to the federal mental health agencies. As it happened, over a quarter had also held full-time jobs in federal, state, or local government. In light of these shared experiences, it seems less remarkable that decision makers and social scientists sound so much alike when they talk about research.

It is possible that this level of sophistication (and hence this conclusion) is unique to the field of mental health. This is an empirical question. But our guess is that few groups of decision makers are so illiterate as researchers suppose. Similar results may obtain in any domestic policy arena where decision makers are responsible for keeping up with new professional developments and changing social realities. As the delivery of government services becomes increasingly professionalized and decision makers are increasingly educated in universities instead of on-the-job, familiarity with research and researchers seems likely to become a more central tool in the policymaking repertoire. In Orlans's (1971) terms, social science has already become a language of discourse, a way to define our common and contradictory purposes, a mode of social reporting, and a way to think about what is happening in the world. Literacy in such a language seems likely to spread through government as the issues on the public agenda become more complex and resistant to conventional solutions.

But in spite of this evidence of shared experience and similarity of views, our researchers perceive some major differences between themselves and the decision makers in their notions of usefulness. Something clearly obstructs their ability to see that decision makers are not indifferent ideologues, but instead are responsive to the very qualities they most value in their own work. The obstruction, we think, is a difference between the two groups in what is meant by *using* research for policymaking.

As we saw in Tables 1 and 4, the social scientists think that use of research is a rare event, that political and bureaucratic processes are primary obstacles to use, and that useful research makes explicit recommendations, has direct implications for a course of action, adds to practical knowledge about the operation of policies and programs, and is compatible with the ideas and values of the potential user. They seem to think research is useful when it provides clear-cut, practical prescriptions for action that a decision maker is likely to follow. The implicit definition of *use* is short-term, instrumental, and oriented to specific problems and decisions; it sound like social engineering.

This inference is supported by the social scientists' open-ended responses to the question, "In what ways do decision makers in the field of mental health use social research?" As a group, the social scientists thought that decision makers—if they used research at all—used it in direct instrumental ways, for making particular choices or for justifying previously held positions.

When decision makers were asked the same question, they generated a much longer and richer list of ways to use research. This is consistent with their reports that a more diverse set of research characteristics and environmental factors contribute to usefulness. As we have seen, decision makers find high-quality, objective research useful, even when it challenges conventional wisdom or the political status quo. Raising new issues is actually rated a highly desirable feature of useful research. Decision makers' definition of *use* seems to accommodate the social scientists' problem-solving notion, but extends to a more comprehensive range of functions. It seems to include such uses for research as bringing new ideas to public attention, framing or conceptualizing problems, keeping up with professional developments, finding out what is happening in other states or agencies, legitimating budget allocations, attacking established policies, or lobbying for new programs.

Research need not be practical, explicit, feasible, and noncontroversial to be useful in these ways; in this context the decision makers' claim to value new ideas and technical merit comes to seem quite sensible. Because researchers assume that use of research is instrumental, they assume that decision makers value only research that lends itself to instrumental use. But the decision makers appear to have less constrained assumptions about how research may be used. Thus, they see many more research characteristics as contributing to usefulness, and they regard such obstacles to use as political controversy, limited options, and bureaucratic inertia with more equanimity.

The discrepancies between the two definitions of *use* help us to interpret the similarities and differences between the social scientists and the decision makers. Both groups value social science. But the two hold somewhat different expectations about how that value will be realized. The same differences explain why the social scientists misperceive the attitudes of decision makers. The social scientists are right that decision makers rarely use research directly and instrumentally, as solutions to particular dilemmas. (For evidence on this point, see Knorr, 1977; Rich, 1977; Weiss & Bucuvalas, 1977.) But they move from this correct premise to the conclusion that the only way for research to be more useful is for it to be better suited to direct instrumental use. It is here that the social scientists part company with the decision makers. The decision makers agree that they seldom use research instrumentally. But they conclude that instrumental use is only one of many ways in which social science evidence and ideas can contribute to public policy. Trapped in their own assumptions, social scientists easily infer that decision makers fail to use research instrumentally because they do not want to use research at all. The image of decision makers as dominated by politics and resistant to research is thus created and sustained.

What the researchers have neglected in their analyses are the multiple channels by which social science evidence and ideas may affect the behavior of decision makers. If they understood the full range of uses, the multiple points of access through which their research may work its influence on any given policy or program, they would realize how and why decision makers are more receptive to social science than conventional wisdom has predicted. Even better, they could muster some optimism about the value of their work that is realistically grounded in knowledge of their potential audiences.

REFERENCES

Caplan, N., Morrison, A., & Stambaugh, R. J. (1975). *The use of social science knowledge in policy decisions at the national level.* Ann Arbor: University of Michigan, Institute for Social Research.

Coleman, J. S. (1972). *Policy research in the social sciences.* Morristown, NJ: General Learning Press.

Knorr, K. D. (1977). Policy makers' use of social science knowledge: Symbolic or instrumental? In C. H. Weiss (Ed.), *Using social research in public policy making.* Lexington, MA: Lexington Books.

National Research Council. (1978). *The federal investment in knowledge of social problems.* Washington, DC: National Academy of Sciences.

Nisbett, R. N., & Wilson, T. D. (1977). Telling more than we can know. *Psychological Review, 84,* 231–259.

Orlans, H. (1971). The political uses of social research. *Annals of the American Academy of Political and Social Science, 384,* 28–35.

Parloff, M. B. (1979). Can psychotherapy research guide the policymaker? A little knowledge may be a dangerous thing. *American Psychologist, 34,* 296–306.

Rich, R. F. (1977). Uses of social science information by federal bureaucrats. In C. H. Weiss (Ed.), *Using social research in public policy making.* Lexington, MA: Lexington Books.

Ross, L. (1977). The intuitive psychologist and his shortcomings. In L. Berkowitz (Ed.), *Advances in experimental social psychology* (Vol. 10). New York: Academic Press.

Scott, R. A., & Shore, A. (1974). Sociology and policy analysis. *American Sociologist, 9,* 51–59.

Shaffer, L. S. (1977). The Golden Fleece: Anti-intellectualism and social science. *American Psychologist, 32,* 814–823.

Slovic, P., Fischhoff, B., & Lichtenstein, S. (1980). Perceived risk. In R. Schwing & W. Albers (Eds.), *Societal risk assessment: How safe is safe enough?* New York: Plenum Press.

Stier, S. (1975). Psychology and public policy. In S. Nagel (Ed.), *Policy studies and the social sciences.* Lexington, MA: Lexington Books.

Useem, M. (1976). State production of social knowledge. *American Sociological Review, 41,* 613–629.

Weiss, C. H. (1980). (with contributions by M. J. Bucuvalas). *Social science research and decision making.* New York: Columbia University Press.

Weiss, C. H., & Bucuvalas, M. J. (1977). The challenge of social research to decision making. In C. H. Weiss (Ed.), *Using social research in public policy making.* Lexington, MA: Lexington Books.

Wilson, J. Q. (1978). Social science and public policy: A personal note. In L. E. Lynn (Ed.), *Knowledge and policy: The uncertain connection.* Washington, DC: National Academy of Sciences.

REFERENCES

9

THE ROLE OF PSYCHOLOGICAL RESEARCH IN THE FORMATION OF POLICIES AFFECTING CHILDREN

ELEANOR E. MACCOBY, ALFRED J. KAHN, and
BARBARA A. EVERETT

The relationship between researchers and policymakers is essentially an uneasy one. Policymakers sometimes see researchers as impractical, and may be skeptical about policy recommendations coming from researchers who seem not to understand the complexities of achieving a consensus among rival constituencies or administering programs once they have been legislated. Researchers, on the other hand, often see policymakers as disingenuous and too willing to compromise on matters where compromise does not seem justified on the basis of research evidence. Frustrations can go so deep that informed people throw up their hands and conclude that rational decision making on a societal level is impossible, at least on certain issues (see Steiner, 1981). Yet when a variety of political and social forces converge with empirical findings at a crucial moment in time, research has a clear impact on policy. This article considers the relationship of research to the other elements involved in formulating policy affecting children.

At the outset we should note that "policy research" is not a distinct category. Much of the research drawn upon in public policy formation was not intended for that purpose. Research can be utilized for identifying needs, for setting new objectives, for clarifying what works and what does

Reprinted from *American Psychologist*, 38, 80–84. Copyright 1983 by the American Psychological Association.

not, or for understanding the nature of the phenomena that give rise to a problem or set limits on its solution. In pursuing these questions, policy-makers draw on a wide variety of data sources, including statistical series; descriptive studies of institutions or life circumstances of different segments of the population; evaluation studies which compare the alternative consequences of different interventions; and basic research such as studies that clarify cognitive development or analyze family interaction and socialization. All these kinds of research become "policy research" when utilized during one of the steps in the policy-formation process.

Public policies affecting children are formed and implemented in an intensely political atmosphere. Overarching political and economic ideologies are involved, as are pressures from interest groups. Policy formation occurs in legislative committees, in offices of the executive branches of national, state, and local governments, and in public, private, and semi-private service agencies, boards, and commissions. Outcomes inevitably reflect compromises between conflicting values of various constituencies, and the role played by research depends on what groups are involved and how they are aligned. Consider, for example, the following policy questions, all of which are currently under active debate:

1. When parents abuse or neglect their children, should their legal rights be terminated quickly, so that their children can be placed in permanent adoptive homes? Or should the rights of natural parents be protected against arbitrary bureaucratic action by providing a variety of judicial restraints on removal and a slower decision process that calls for efforts to reconcile the child with the natural parents?

2. Should the public welfare structure be geared toward providing support at home for impoverished mothers of young children, or should it be designed to enable these mothers to work (e.g., by providing day care)?

3. Should federal funds to support day care be made contingent on providers' meeting certain quality standards? If so, who should formulate the standards, what should they require, and how should compliance be monitored?

4. What standard should the law apply in awarding custody of children in contested cases when both parents are judged fit? Is a general "best interest of the child" standard workable? Should there be a presumption for joint custody? Or for maternal custody when the child is "of tender years"?

5. What are the costs and benefits of preschool education programs, particularly for children at risk for subsequent school failure? Is it more efficient to invest in remedial education at

later ages, or does the impact of later interventions depend on earlier ones?

6. Should handicapped children, or children who are slow learners, be put into special education classes or kept in mainstream classrooms? If minority children are overrepresented among slow learners, does this have any implications for which solution should be chosen? (See Heller, Holzman, & Messick, 1982.)

7. In programs designed to detect health problems as early as possible, should children be "screened" for emotional and behavioral problems as well as physical ones? Should screening be done even if no mechanism exists for treating disorders once they are detected?

8. Should physicians be required to inform parents when teenagers are treated for venereal disease or provided with contraceptive information?

9. What should be the responsibility of police, courts, social agencies, and schools with regard to children who are truant from school or run away from home? Under what circumstances, if any, should such children be put in secure detention? (See Handler & Zatz, 1982.)

All of these questions involve value choices. In considering any of them, information is needed from a variety of knowledge areas, so psychological research is only one source of relevant data. There are psychological studies that bear on all these issues and many more, and their findings have played a part in the debates. Whether a particular piece of research is drawn upon, however, depends greatly on its timing in relation to various aspects of the sociopolitical climate. A finding that will fall on deaf ears at one time may become salient at another. For example, an early report on the sexist bias in school textbooks (Child, Potter, & Levine, 1946) was virtually ignored, whereas similar reports appearing in the 1970s, when feminist concerns had become focal, received widespread attention and were used in efforts to reform the content of textbooks in the interests of greater gender equity.

Although available knowledge is frequently not utilized because the political climate is not receptive to it, the reverse situation may also occur. That is, a piece of information may be badly needed to allow policy formation to proceed, so that when this information becomes available it is quickly taken up and acted upon. An instance of this kind is reported in detail in the National Research Council (NRC) report, *Making Policies for Children* (Hayes, 1982). One of the case studies in this report deals with federal standards for day care (Issue 3 above). The NRC analysis shows that although legislation passed in the late 1960s called for the establishment of such standards, the process of formulating them was stalemated for many years. Many experts in early childhood education wanted to require that the ratio of adult caregivers to the number of children being cared for should be high, but it soon became clear that if federal funds to support day care were made contingent on care centers' having high ratios, many existing facilities would have to go out of business and the overall child care system would be weakened. A national study of the factors contributing to favorable outcomes of day care was commissioned. When the results of this study showed that the staff–child ratio was relatively unimportant compared to other factors, a leading element in the policy dilemma was resolved, and it became possible to proceed with the development of federal standards. Although this process has recently become moot (because of channeling federal funds for the support of day care into block grants to states, thus foreclosing the federal role in standard setting), at one point in the process there was a high state of readiness to receive and utilize the findings that the National Day Care Study happened to provide.

There is an issue in the area of divorce and custody where policy formation is perhaps too ready to receive a specific research finding. Legal scholars studying custody cases have recognized that judges are in a poor position to make good decisions in most cases of contested custody. They are looking for an easy formula which will short-circuit the painful and time-consuming adjudication process that now exists, and have moved quickly toward a presumption for joint custody. The studies of divorce and its impact on children (Hetherington, Cox, & Cox, 1982; Wallerstein & Kelley, 1980) have shown that children in maternal custody fare better if they are able to maintain contact with their fathers after the divorce. In their eagerness to find a way to simplify the decision process for judges, legal scholars have interpreted these findings as though they constituted evidence for joint custody in contested cases, which (in our opinion and that of the researchers being cited) they do not. We may presume that if negative findings on the feasibility of joint custody in contested cases emerge as time goes on, it will be much more difficult for them to get a hearing. Thus when research is "needed" by a powerful interest group, as it was in the day-care standards case, it may contribute greatly to the policy-formation process by breaking a deadlock. But this state of readiness may result in research being used prematurely or inappropriately.

The results of the National Day Care Study may have been particularly salient because they ran counter to conventional wisdom about the importance of child–staff ratios. A similar recent instance comes from testimony by Greenberger (1983) on legislation designed to foster adolescent employment. Greenberger reported studies showing that contrary to common belief, teenage employment may *not* foster the long-range occupational achievements of youth. This testimony coincided with the interests of an important interest group (organized labor) that opposed the revision of child labor laws, with a resulting strong impact.

Research is a continuous process, whereas legislation tends to be episodic. New results may call for modifications in programs that drew upon earlier research when they were established. The recent reforms in legislation having to do with adoption and foster care (P.L. 96-272, 198) provide a case in point. This legislation rests on a considerable research base. Surveys and descriptive studies, as well as testimony and some data concerning the experiences of children in institutions and foster homes, suggested that too many children were remaining in long-term foster care without positive results or with detriment. Clearly, not enough was being done to free them for adoption, to strengthen their natural homes, to seek to return them to their parents, or to avoid taking them away in the first place. Reform thus combated well-defined and documented evils. But the reform embodied remedies (strongly backed by financial sanctions) that were not yet documented by research. We do not know whether the subsidized adoptions supported by the new law will be better for children than long-term foster care. And we do not know whether the required efforts to return children to their natural homes will be a successful alternative. Research is now beginning to cast doubt on how successfully children can be reunited with some abusing or neglecting parents, and to show comparatively good outcomes from foster care. These new studies do not detract from the need for reform in our adoption and foster-care procedures, but they do illustrate the problem faced by legislators when research documents the existence of problems but has only begun to explore possible solutions.

The case of the Head Start and Follow Through programs illustrates some of the difficulties of integrating the slow cumulation of research knowledge with the differently timed policy-formation process. Head Start was one of the first social programs to have a requirement for evaluation built in to its founding legislation. At the outset, Head Start instructional programs for preschoolers were put in place with extraordinary haste, and evaluation began before a shakedown period could occur. An early study (Westinghouse, 1969) very nearly killed the program. This study reported that although there had been some health gains for children served by the program, intellectual gains (assessed primarily through IQ scores) were small and temporary. The report came in just before President Nixon's first message to Congress in 1969. He had planned to give an unqualified endorsement to Head Start, but changed the message toward a more neutral position on the basis of the Westinghouse study. The momentum of the program faltered, and Head Start was rescued by pressure from parents and other child advocates in spite of, rather than because of, research. Gradually, replicable positive findings from evaluation studies of early educational intervention programs began to come in. Two reports published in 1975, one generally positive (Stallings) and one showing few sustained effects (Miller & Dyer), illustrated some of the complexities of conducting such evaluations. It was not until 1982 that a monograph became available summarizing some positive long-term outcomes from 12 different early-intervention studies (Lazar & Darlington, 1982). The reports by this consortium are not without their critics: the high attrition rates raise questions; one cannot be sure to what extent teachers in the later grades were aware of the children's early educational histories; and the achievements of "model" programs may not generalize to widely disseminated programs. For our present purposes, however, we will set these questions aside, and consider some of the lessons that have emerged from the history of this and other evaluation research. In this summary, we draw on a National Research Council report on the evaluation of early-childhood programs (Travers & Light, 1982). Some of the major lessons are:

1. Immediate effects and delayed effects of a program may be quite different, and early effects may not be good predictors of later effects. These facts pose problems for the utilization of research results in the policy-formation process, since policy formation often has its own timetable, geared to the politics of election cycles and to the cycles for reauthorization of specific legislation.

2. Different instructional programs have been shown to have different outcomes. Thus there is no way in which an omnibus set of interventions of the sort involved in Head Start and Follow Through can be pronounced successful or unsuccessful. It is necessary to ask which program element is successful with respect to which outcome.

3. Assessment of intervention programs must include evaluation of the degree to which planned programs have actually been implemented. Implementation varies by site and program, and quite often failures to achieve gains via an intervention program have not meant that the program was ineffective; rather, failures have stemmed from the fact that a program was never actually put into place.

4. The verdict with regard to the effectiveness of a program depends heavily on the outcome measures selected for study. (a) Long-term positive effects of early intervention programs have been shown in terms of lower rates of absence from school, lower rates of repeating grades or being assigned to remedial classes, and greater incorporation of academic values into self-concepts. If research attention had been confined to gains in IQ or improvements in achievement scores on specific academic tests, the impact of the programs would have been greatly underestimated. (b) It has been repeatedly noted

that the impact of early interventions on social–emotional development has not been adequately assessed. The problem here is not merely a psychometric one having to do with a lag in test development. Rather, it reflects a lack of basic knowledge concerning the cross-age stability and predictive validity of various aspects of social–emotional functioning— knowledge that would guide both the selection of measures and the design of programs (Travers & Light, 1982). (c) The choice of outcomes depends on values. Legislators are understandably interested in getting demonstrations of short-term effects within their terms of office, but researchers can sometimes get them to attend to the values entailed in longer-term outcomes. The reverse also applies: Advocates are often concerned with establishing programs that involve intervening in childhood so as to lower the subsequent rates of juvenile delinquency, mental illness, or economic dependency. It has been argued that we have been overly preoccupied with such outcomes and that we ought to be concerned with the impact of programs on children's concurrent "quality of life" (assuming that this can be defined and measured).

The impact of a piece of research depends greatly on its timing, its scope in relation to the policy issue at hand, and its concordance or discordance with political forces. It is also true that the degree of agreement among researchers makes a difference. When studies come up with divergent findings, protagonists for various points of view comb through the research literature and select items that best support their own position. They also take as much advantage as possible of any critique of the opposition's research base. In a sense, researchers limit their own effectiveness by reporting nonreplications of other people's findings or mounting heavy methodological critiques of studies that might otherwise play a useful role. It has been suggested that they should attempt to come to some sort of agreement among themselves in advance of public discussion, rather than being caught in the embarrassing position of testifying on both sides of a debate. It seems to us that complexities, critiques, and even contradictions are an inevitable part of the scientific process. Researchers cannot suppress findings, nor can they refrain from criticizing flawed studies. There will always be solid evidence to support more than one side of a debate. We see no way in which researchers can speak with a single voice. It may be hoped, however, that they will be responsibly aware of the ways in which their findings may be interpreted, and try to restrain distortions in the application of their work whenever possible.

Even when there is a reasonably high degree of consensus among researchers and other experts, their knowledge does not always have an impact on policy implementation. If researchers want their work to be utilized on behalf of children, they need to be aware of the timetable governing the decision-making process in legislative and administrative bodies, and they must take the initiative in making their information available at appropriate times. In addition, they will sometimes have to consider how adequate the organizational structure of legislatures and executive offices is for the utilization of information. Is there an appropriate committee in Congress, or an office or agency in the executive branch, that is clearly required and empowered to carry out the policy-formation process with respect to children's issues? Continuous vigilance on the part of informed citizens is necessary if such agencies are to be created, maintained, and given the support necessary to carry out their tasks.

In the long run, we believe, the continuing accumulation of findings from both basic and applied research may have its major impact by influencing the thinking of many people who form the political climate. We have a representative form of government, and both legislators and administrators are responsive to inputs from informed members of their constituencies. With this fact in mind, it becomes important that researchers not only continue to do good work but also translate their findings into readable English and disseminate them not only to legislators and administrators but to influential members of the lay public. These persons can then act in an informed way as a constituency on behalf of children.

REFERENCES

Child, I., Potter, E. H., & Levine, E. M. (1946). Children's textbooks and personality development: An exploration in the social psychology of education. *Psychological Monographs, 60*(3, Whole No. 279).

Greenberger, E. (1983). A researcher in the policy arena: The case of child labor. *American Psychologist, 38*, 104–111.

Handler, J. F., & Zatz, J. (1982). *Neither angels nor thieves: Studies in deinstitutionalization of status offenders.* Washington, D.C.: National Academy Press.

Hayes, C. D. (Ed.). (1982). *Making policies for children: A study of the federal process* (National Research Council report). Washington, D.C.: National Academy Press.

Heller, K. A., Holzman, W. H., & Messick, S. (Eds.). (1982). *Placing children in special education: A strategy for equity* (National Research Council report). Washington, D.C.: National Academy Press.

Hetherington, E. M., Cox, M., & Cox, R. (1982). Effects of divorce on parents and children. In M. Lamb (Ed.), *Non-traditional families.* Hillsdale, NJ: Erlbaum.

Lazar, I., & Darlington, R. (1982). Lasting effects of early education: A report from the Consortium for Longitudinal Studies. *Monographs of the Society for Research in Child Development, 47,* 1–139.

Miller, L. B., & Dyer, J. L. (1975). Four preschool programs: Their dimensions and effects. *Monographs of the Society for Research in Child Development,* 40(5 & 6, Serial No. 162).

Stallings, J. (1975). Implementation and child effects of teaching practices in Follow-Through classrooms. *Monographs of the Society for Research in Child Development,* 40(7 & 8, Serial No. 163).

Steiner, A. Y. (1981). *The futility of family policy.* Washington, D.C.: Brookings Institution.

Travers, J. R., & Light, R. J. (Eds.). (1982). *Learning from experience: Evaluating early childhood demonstration programs* (National Research Council report). Washington, D.C.: National Academy Press.

Wallerstein, J. S., & Kelley, J. B. (1980). *Surviving the breakup: How children and parents cope with divorce.* New York: Basic Books.

Westinghouse Learning Corporation & Ohio University. (1969). *The impact of Head Start: An evaluation of the effects of Head Start on children's cognitive and affective development* (Executive Summary). Report to the Office of Economic Opportunity [EDO 36321]. Washington, D.C.: Clearinghouse for Federal Scientific and Technical Information.

10

MAKING RESEARCH APPLY: HIGH STAKES PUBLIC POLICY IN A REGULATORY ENVIRONMENT

DANE ARCHER, THOMAS F. PETTIGREW, and ELLIOT ARONSON

In the wake of the "energy crisis" of the late 1970s, we were asked by the California Public Utilities Commission (PUC) to undertake an assessment of the ambitious energy conservation programs run by California's four major energy utilities. Although diverse in nature, the utility programs generally promoted minor architectural changes (e.g., insulation), encouraged conservation behavior (e.g., using electricity in "off-peak" hours), and emphasized conservation information and attitudes (e.g., knowledge about appliance efficiency). The intent of the PUC review was to assess current efforts in order to improve future utility programs.

Although new to the regulatory environment, our group had extensive experience in evaluation and policy research. We hoped that this background would complement insights from the behavioral sciences (e.g., Stern & Aronson, 1984) to make our analysis useful. Despite bright auspices, our two-year effort proved far more conflicted than we anticipated. Instead of the creative partnership with the utilities that we had hoped

Reprinted from *American Psychologist*, 47, 1233–1236. Copyright 1992 by the American Psychological Association.

This chapter was sponsored by the Social Psychology and Public Policy Research Group and was supported by the Division of Social Sciences at the University of California, Santa Cruz. We wish to thank our younger colleagues Scott Coltrane, Larry Condelli, Mark Costanzo, Barbara Curbow, Marti Gonzales, Beverly McLeod, Gary Rolison, Larry White, and Suzanne Yates for their assistance in the project whose history is described here.

for, we found ourselves in an increasingly adversarial relationship. The potential for conflict in the evaluation role has long been recognized (e.g., Weiss, 1972), and we are far from first to discover that evaluation is an unloved profession. At the same time, our experience seems unique for two reasons: (a) the high stakes involved (approximately a quarter of a billion dollars in annual program costs); and (b) the complex "regulatory triangle" linking our evaluation group, the utilities, and our "client" (the state PUC) that compounded the adversarial climate. Both factors played a role in the unfolding history of our project.

FIRST PROBLEMS

Our work began when the PUC assembled documents on 200 utility programs and studies and transferred this material to us for review and evaluation. It immediately became clear that our expectations poorly fit the utility documents. We had anticipated doing a meta-analysis to identify which types of interventions were most effective. We intended to assess effect sizes and other measures of program impact (Rosenthal & Rubin, 1982), and had even drawn up forms to summarize these data. As it turned out, these preparations were in vain. Basic data essential for meta-analysis (means, standard deviations, etc.) were absent from the utility reports. This is of course a reflection on our own naivete, as well as a comment on utility research.

There were also other, more serious problems. The utility reports had little or no evidence linking utility programs to actual conservation behaviors, instead emphasizing "softer" outcome variables such as citizen abilities to recall utility advertisements. In addition, the reports overlooked major threats to validity, such as secular trends in attitudes (e.g., generally increased concern about conservation), economic conditions (e.g., dramatic fuel price increases), lack of appropriate comparison groups, reliance on self-reported behaviors, and multiple unprotected statistical tests. A summary of the methodological problems we found is contained in White et al. (1984). Suggestions for improved programs are included in Archer et al. (1987), Condelli et al. (1984), Coltrane, Archer, and Aronson (1986), and Costanzo, Archer, Aronson, and Pettigrew (1986).

In general, the problems we encountered reflected a troubling gulf between academic standards for research design and applied practice. Clearly, money was not the problem. The utilities routinely conducted surveys with samples as high as 25,000, and one ineffective program was defended by a utility staff member as having a budget of "only" $100,000. Utility research was endowed, therefore, with resources rare in academic research. The gulf appeared instead to involve a different research culture in the utilities, in which artifacts, controlled comparison, spuriousness, and other kinds of issues dear to the hearts of academic researchers, seemed not to exist. For example, there were programs in which no control group was used, allegedly so that all customers or dealers could be included. Such cases clearly called for "waiting list" control groups, yet the utility documents revealed no awareness that these approaches existed.

CONFLICT AND CONFRONTATION

We rapidly realized that our report would be highly critical of some utility programs (while praising others), and that our conclusions were likely to produce conflict. Although the utilities enjoy a monopoly or near monopoly over energy sales, they are private companies with proprietary secrets, a fierce concern for corporate image, substantial advertising budgets, and a profit-making orientation. At the same time, their income depends on rates set by a nominally independent body (the PUC) operating in the public interest. Whatever its merits, this arrangement ensures that public information critical of the utilities could be seen as a threat to future rate decisions.

As anticipated, the draft version of our report was not welcomed. Initial responses to the draft report were obtained in separate face-to-face meetings with representatives of each utility. These meetings were held squarely in the midst of the regulatory triangle—in PUC offices with PUC staff present. Utility representatives had both general and specific criticisms. For one, they challenged our credentials by arguing, quite correctly, that no member of our group was in advertising or had advertising experience. A second major criticism was that we were "ivory tower" academics trying to apply esoteric standards of "pure" science to the real world. We found this criticism curious, because our suggestions (e.g., control groups, measurement of behavior and not merely attitudes, not relying solely on self-reports, etc.) seemed to us anything but new or difficult.

The flavor of the confrontations can be illustrated by example. Because one of our conclusions was that the effectiveness of advertising in changing conservation behavior had not been demonstrated, we urged that the utilities consider pilot programs in which conservation devices (e.g., water heater blankets) were simply given to consumers. This met with withering resistance from the representatives of one utility, despite the fact that this same utility had concluded that the distribution of conservation devices would be less expensive than the extensive advertising they had been conducting. The utility's lawyer asserted that give-away programs would constitute illegal and unfair competition with retail merchants who sell conservation devices. Although we lacked legal expertise, we countered by noting (a) that another utility already had successful device give-away programs, and (b) that any unfair competition problems could be solved by having the utility provide rebates that consumers could use to purchase conservation devices from retail locations, thereby making retailers happy. At this point, the lawyer conceded that such programs were in fact not illegal, but he added, without further explanation, that the utility still opposed give-away programs.

This illustrates the adversarial climate that characterized our meetings in the regulatory triangle. We came to believe that the substance of our criticism and recommendations was incidental to the combative response of the utility representatives. Instead, the mere fact that our review was critical came to dominate meetings. The goal of the utilities was simple: to undermine the potential impact of the report, using any arguments necessary. The utilities seemed bent on preventing any criticism from entering the PUC record in order to minimize any possible fiscal damage at later rate hearings.

FINAL REPORT AND AFTERMATH

After receiving oral and written comments from the utilities, we revised our report and submitted it to PUC staff. Because we are external to the PUC, the impact of our report is a matter of conjecture. We expected little voluntary change on the part of the utilities, but—connected to our report or not—changes somehow occurred. In the years following our report, utility conservation programs gradually but unambiguously changed in the direction of our recommendations. These programs have shifted toward (a) conservation device give aways, (b) rebates to spur adoption of efficient appliances, (c) subsidies to retrofit low income homes, (d) proven device installations as dependent variables for program evaluation, and (e) a diminished role for mass advertising as an independent variable. Although these changes constituted our central recommendations, whether this policy drift was directly related to our report is impossible to say.

STRUCTURAL ANALYSIS OF THE REGULATORY ENVIRONMENT

Although initially unprepared for the fray of the regulatory triangle, we eventually rose (or perhaps sunk) to the challenge. As one group member described it, it was as if we had been invited to a dance only to find ourselves in a mud wrestle; once there, however, we found that we did not want to lose. All participants in these exchanges knew that our group would be writing a report for the PUC and, given the unpredictability of the regulatory process, no one could be certain of the effects such a report could have. As a result, interactions with utility representatives had strikingly different qualities depending on whether PUC staff were present. In the presence of PUC staff, for example, the representative of one utility responded angrily with an impassioned defense of his utility's work. After the session, however, with the PUC staff safely out of hearing range, this same person said, "I'm surprised you guys weren't much more negative—those programs were real 'cripples,' but they were done before I joined the company."

The regulatory triangle seemed to limit the types of effects we could have. Although we had hoped to contribute to improving future programs through positive, collegial interaction with the utilities (what we call the *influence model*), the presence of PUC staff in our meetings magnified utility hostility to any criticisms we reported. In our adversarial drama, the PUC staff began to play the role of judge, the utilities the role of defendant, and we, consciously or not, the role of prosecuting attorney.

In the social psychology of the regulatory triangle, the first priority of the utilities became the containment of any influence on our part. From their perspective, the need was to manage the situation, to minimize prospective damage (Gamson, 1968). The utilities could not concede any of our criticisms without seeming to confess that they had received compensation (in the form of prior rate increases) for ineffective programs. For example, one utility initially had us meet with its conservation staff but soon changed representatives; subsequently, this utility was represented by a high-level company attorney. This appeared to reflect a corporate decision that the first priority had to be the defense of the company image rather than, as we had hoped, the idealistic improvement of company conservation programs. In response, our perspective also changed. We moved from an influence model of change to a *power model*. We concluded that any improvement in conservation programs would have to be mandated rather than voluntary, and we began to focus our hopes on the PUC.

COULD IT HAVE BEEN DIFFERENT?

Faced with increasingly adversarial conflict, we frequently wondered whether the experience could have been different. Were there, we wondered, different structural arrangements or different tactics that could have produced less conflict? These are obviously important questions for future policy researchers, and several alternatives are considered in turn.

1. *No written report.* Another researcher told us she had a similarly adversarial experience with utility companies in another state. We asked her if anything could have mitigated this conflict. After a moment's thought, she said that it might have been better if she had not written a final report. Because the report becomes a public document, and also a potential indictment, it inevitably becomes the focus of the evaluatee's

apprehension. As an alternative, this researcher recommended meeting with staff from the evaluated organization for oral (not written) discussions of how programs might be improved. In our case, it is not clear that an oral report would have worked; we evolved from an influence to a power model precisely because cooperative change seemed impossible. In other instances, however, an oral report might be effective, and seems certain to reduce conflict.

2. *Formative rather than summative evaluation.*. The PUC's summative focus (on the dollars saved by conservation programs) multiplied conflict. Under California's regulatory environment, utilities were reimbursed for conservation programs to the extent that they could be shown to have saved energy. This put enormous weight on utility estimates of saved energy, and these estimates frequently could not bear close scrutiny. For example, utilities sometimes assumed that some hypothetical portion (e.g., 5%) of all consumers were following a conservation advertising tip (such as doing laundry in off-peak hours); these figures were then multiplied by the estimated energy savings to calculate the dollar value of energy "saved" by each program.

Mandating summative outcomes invites such poor science. A far preferable regulatory environment would be one in which utilities are compensated for all completed programs whose designs meet PUC guidelines. These guidelines could require certain design features (e.g., control groups, behavioral dependent variables). This principle applies to all policy arenas—"means idealism" (Campbell, 1969, 1988) should be the goal, to avoid the potential distortions inherent in "ends idealism" focused only on how much a given dependent variable moves.

3. *Prospective rather than retrospective report.* The focus on past utility programs maximized utility defensiveness and did not by itself provide the PUC with the information it really needed: prospective guidelines for future utility conservation programs. In hindsight, it would have been preferable if the PUC had asked us to examine documents and records on past utility programs in order to construct a policy blueprint for future utility programs. Again, this principle seems generally applicable to other policy settings; a prospective orientation minimizes defensive conflict.

4. *Utility as client.* It is worth pondering how our experience would have differed if the PUC had not been our client. Had we been retained by the utilities, it is conceivable that we could have pursued an influence strategy, rather than rely ultimately on the coercive power of the PUC. Assuming utility conservation staff were committed to effective programs and valid evaluation, a constructive working relationship might have been easier to achieve away from the glare of PUC scrutiny. A general principle here might be to search for innovative structural arrangements—for example, the PUC could have hired us to provide consulting directly to the utilities.

5. *Supporting our report.* Even when our report was complete, we were faced with tactical decisions. We were asked by PUC staff to delay making our report public while PUC staff reviewed its analysis and recommendations. This request reflected apprehension about the potentially controversial nature of our report. Just as the utilities were apprehensive that our report would embarrass them by concluding that programs for which they had been compensated were ineffective, PUC staff may have been worried that they might share in this embarrassment as the public agency that had approved these programs. We agreed to a delay, but fixed a date by which we would regard the report as a public document. In the same vein, we reminded PUC staff of our mutual agreement that we would be free to publish the substance of what we had learned, as long as confidential or proprietary utility secrets were not disclosed. A general principle is that academic norms do not apply; policy researchers must clarify what rights (if any) they have to the data and analyses they collect.

A COLLISION OF CULTURES

In retrospect, it is clear that the conflict we encountered was an inevitable by-product of three colliding cultures: the basic research world of the academic, the dollar-driven corporate world, and the routinely adversarial world of public regulation. These worlds are poorly matched in many ways. The academic world values (or at least pays lip service to) criticism, and the conclusions of most scholarly research projects have no fiscal consequences. By contrast, in the corporate world, decisions are often associated with enormous costs, leading to fierce defense of past expenditures and thin-skinned hostility to suggested improvements. Finally, in the adversarial world of public regulation, the fear of perceived impropriety is endemic. Just as regulated monopolies depend on looking good in front of their regulatory agency, the regulatory agency is itself apprehensive at any suggestion that public funds may have been fruitlessly spent. For both the regulated and the regulator, this amplifies enormously sensitivity to all criticism and, particularly, to public criticism.

We experienced the collision of these three cultures in the regulatory triangle. Our conflict with the utilities was played according to two sets of incompatible rules: methodological rules drawn from academic research, and legalistic rules unique to the adversarial world of regulated corporate monopolies. Our experience teaches that conventional evaluation criteria cannot be presumed to function in a scientific vacuum free of strong conflicting forces, but also that conflict is not necessarily incompatible with desirable change.

REFERENCES

Archer, D., Pettigrew, T. F., Costanzo, M., Iritani, B., Walker, I., & White, L. T. (1987). Energy conservation and public policy: The mediation of individual behavior. In W. Kempton & M. Neiman (Eds.), *Energy efficiency: Perspectives on individual behavior* (pp. 69–92). Washington, DC: American Council for an Energy-Efficient Economy (ACEEE).

Campbell, D. T. (1969). Reforms as experiments. *American Psychologist, 24,* 409–429.

Campbell, D. T. (1988). The experimenting society. In E. S. Overman (Ed.), *Methodology and epistemology for social science: Selected papers* (pp. 290–314). Chicago: University of Chicago Press.

Condelli, L., Archer, D., Aronson, E., Curbow, B., McLeod, B., Pettigrew, T. F., White, L. T., & Yates, S. (1984). Improving utility conservation programs: Outcomes, interventions, and evaluations. *Energy, 9,* 485–494.

Coltrane, S., Archer, D., & Aronson, E. (1986). The social psychological foundations of successful energy conservation programmes. *Energy Policy, 14,* 133–148.

Costanzo, M., Archer, D., Aronson, E., & Pettigrew, T. F. (1986). Energy conservation behavior: The difficult path from information to action. *American Psychologist, 41,* 521–528.

Gamson, W. A. (1968). *Power and discontent.* Homewood, IL: Dorsey Press.

Rosenthal, R., & Rubin, D. B. (1982). Comparing effect sizes of independent studies. *Psychological Bulletin, 92,* 500–504.

Stern, P., & Aronson, E. (1984). *Energy use: The human dimension.* New York: Freeman.

Weiss, C. H. (1972). *Evaluation research: Methods of assessing program effectiveness.* Englewood Cliffs, NJ: Prentice-Hall.

White, L. T., Archer, D., Aronson, E., Condelli, L., Curbow, B., McLeod, B., Pettigrew, T. F., & Yates, S. (1984). Energy conservation research of California's utilities: A meta-evaluation. *Evaluation Review, 8,* 167–186.

III

PUBLIC HEALTH AND PUBLIC PRIORITIES

INTRODUCTION

BALANCING EXPERTISE WITH PRACTICAL REALITIES

RUSS NEWMAN and TRUDY VINCENT

Although psychologists have been involved with the public policy process and have dealt with policymakers for quite some time, recent years have witnessed unprecedented involvement on the part of those in the profession in shaping public policy. This trend has been the result of both the increased relevance of psychological knowledge to a wide spectrum of the policy-making arena and the increased influence of public policy on the practice and the profession of psychology. In turn, psychologists have needed to become much more skilled and sophisticated in their ability to interact with policymakers, not an easy process for those in a profession that tends to be introspective and focused on internal rather than external issues.

Perhaps the biggest task for psychologists in influencing public policy has been the need to learn to communicate effectively with nonpsychologist policymakers. Among the most significant components of this task is the ability to translate complex psychological concepts and data into "bottom-line" pragmatic terms that will be useful to policymakers. This task is made all the more difficult for those in a profession that has not historically articulated its knowledge base to individuals outside of the profession.

The difficulties of the communication and translation tasks, however, are understandable. The knowledge and database that has been amassed within psychology is replete with complexities, subtleties, and shades of gray, thus making it quite difficult to simplify information. Also, oversimplification of information may be more problematic in the end than not simplifying this complex material enough. Yet, unless this task is accomplished, psychology's expertise will have little utility in the policy arena. Balancing the theoretical or academic nature of the expertise, knowledge, and data collection with the practical realities of the policy-making process is critical to improved communication with policymakers. More important, maintaining the optimal blend of scholarship and pragmatism will maximize the impact psychology is able to have on the development of public policy.

Less visible than psychology's work to affect public policy in the legislative arena—although incorporating many of the same tasks—is the profession's expanding work in the judicial arena. In this area, psychology has typically relied upon *amicus curiae*, or "friend of the court," briefs to influence judicial decision making and judicial policy. This usually entails providing scientific or clinical information uniquely within the scope and expertise of psychology in order to inform decisions on related legal questions (e.g., validity of psychological injury or damages in liability actions; the capacity of neuropsychologists to testify to the presence or etiology of organic injury). In recent years, however, judicial advocacy—defined as use of the courts or legal system to advance psychology's objectives—has been expanded beyond the use of *amicus* briefs. In particular, developing or supporting "test" litigation has been increasingly employed in an effort to influence public policy consistent with psychology's advocacy agenda. Whether through civil litigation (e.g., antitrust) cases or criminal prosecution (e.g., health care fraud and abuse), judicial advocacy has become a strong complement to legislative advocacy in the public policy arena.

The chapters in this section provide a very interesting sampling of some ways in which psychologists have attempted to get involved in influencing public policy. In his chapter (see chap. 11), Tremper argues that organized psychology's most effective method of achieving its public policy objectives may be filing *amicus curiae* briefs in strategic legal cases. He supports his argument with three points: (a) filing *amicus* briefs requires fewer resources while achieving potentially more dramatic results; (b) the judiciary may be more receptive to "underdog" positions than other branches of government; and (c) filing briefs does not jeopardize tax-exempt status in the same way as lobbying the legislative branch does.

On the other hand, as Tremper points out, the effectiveness of the APA's briefs has been difficult to assess, particularly if case disposition is the outcome measure. Whereas in some cases it has been clear that the APA's brief has been quite influential in the determination of outcome, in other cases the role of the brief seems to have been educative but ultimately less influential.

The relative efficacy of intervention in the judicial branch versus lobbying the legislative branch is a question that remains to be answered. We would argue that, particularly in the current political climate, all avenues of influence must be fully utilized if the interests of psychology are to be effectively represented.

The VandenBos chapter (see chap. 16) and the DeLeon, O'Keefe, VandenBos, and Kraut chapter (see chap. 14) both make the case that the profession of psychology must be more actively involved in the public policy arena. The DeLeon et al. article is an interesting description of one method of involving psychologists in the policy-making process. The chapter describes the formation of a policy-oriented committee within the APA whose purpose was primarily to "develop an appreciation . . . for the complexities of formulating public policy" as well as educate guest speakers to the potential contributions psychologists could make to policy formulation within both the legislative and executive branches. Although the description of these efforts is informative, readers should not overlook an equally important lesson that can be drawn from this article: the considerable time and energy necessary to effectively influence public policy. Taking the time to be informed about policy issues that influence one's profession is important, but it is only the first step; taking the time to effectively follow up in such a way that these activities have resonance is crucial to successful influence.

The VandenBos chapter (see chap. 16), written more than a decade later, provides greater detail about the role that psychologists can and, he argues, must play in the formation of policy that directly influences the future of the field. Within the context of the health care reform debate, VandenBos provides a very useful description of the areas where mental health professionals have a stake in policy making and the efforts they must make to ensure some control over this country's health and mental health policy. VandenBos' thorough treatment of the many ways in which psychologists should involve themselves in policy making serves to emphasize the time and energy involved if those in the field hope to influence the outcome of crucial policy decisions.

Chesney's chapter (see chap. 15) addresses the role that health psychology must play in dealing with the human immunodeficiency virus (HIV) as a public health problem. This chapter underscores the important contributions made by psychologists toward understanding the AIDS epidemic, and it raises important questions about how psychologists will rise to future challenges posed by this disease.

Although Chesney does not explicitly address the role of psychologists in influencing public policy in the area of AIDS prevention and treatment, there are few areas in the field of public health where psychologists have a clearer contribution to make. The unique knowledge that psychologists have gained about AIDS prevention is clear and straightforward enough that it should be relatively simple to communicate to policymakers. Convincing them to translate this information into policy, given the controversial nature of the debate around AIDS prevention, may be the greater challenge. On the other hand, in the current political climate, the ability to prove the cost-effectiveness of any behavioral intervention is paramount; these arguments are more easily made with regard to AIDS prevention than most other interventions.

The final two chapters in this section are the most provocative of the group because they raise important issues about the pitfalls of getting involved in policy making. For example, it is commonly accepted that social scientists must "boil down" research findings in order to communicate them effectively to policymakers. Woodhead, using early childhood intervention research as an example, raises questions about the risks entailed in oversimplification and the responsibility of psychologists to ensure the validity of the inferences drawn from their research.

Fischhoff, describing his own experiences in the field of environmental policy, also explores the dangers inherent when complicated social science research outcomes are used in the formation of public policy. He addresses not only the ways in which policymakers may misrepresent data, but also the ways in which scientists and their work may be shaped by their entry into the world of policy making.

Taken as a whole, these chapters provide both a compelling argument and a cautionary note for psychologists contemplating entry into the public policy arena. The task will be arduous, the rewards intermittent, and the dangers and temptations insidious—but the potential for making a difference for both the profession and the public is great.

11

ORGANIZED PSYCHOLOGY'S EFFORTS TO INFLUENCE JUDICIAL POLICY MAKING

CHARLES R. TREMPER

As one might infer from the section titled "Psychology in the Public Forum," which appears frequently in the *American Psychologist*, organized psychology has a substantial interest in government policy making. Spurred initially by a desire to bring psychological expertise to bear on the political process, the American Psychological Association has pursued a course of involvement in governmental affairs consistent with maintaining professional and scientific impartiality (DeLeon, O'Keefe, VandenBos, & Kraut, 1982; Takanishi, DeLeon, & Pallak, 1983). In the process, an ever-growing cadre of psychologists has developed a sophisticated sense of how to influence legislative and executive policy making (Maccoby, Kahn, & Everett, 1983). Relatively little attention has been paid, though, to what may be organized psychology's most effective method of achieving its public policy objectives: filing amicus curiae briefs in strategic legal cases.

Participation as amicus curiae, literally "friend of the court" (O'Connor & Epstein, 1982a), entitles an organization such as the American Psychological Association (APA) to submit an amicus brief, a stylized in-

Reprinted from *American Psychologist, 42,* 496–501. Copyright 1987 by the American Psychological Association.

The author deeply appreciates the assistance of Patrick DeLeon, Jack Donahue, Donald Bersoff, and Gary Melton in explaining the mechanics of the APA amicus participation process and providing relevant materials.

strument for combining facts, law, and logic as needed to present judges with the most compelling argument for adopting whatever position the filer advocates. Filing amicus briefs can be a powerful method of advancing the policy agenda of professional psychology because the judiciary has come to play such an important role in formulating public policy with ramifications for the profession (Berger, 1977). Not only may the substance of judicial opinions affect psychology (for example, by defining standards of professional care or ruling on the validity of discriminating against people with mental disabilities), but the very process of adjudication also may have significant ramifications for psychology if judges commend or disparage psychology (Bersoff, 1986; Monahan & Loftus, 1982).

Confined for most of judicial history to extraordinary cases, the use of amicus briefs is now an almost standard feature of precedent-setting litigation (O'Connor & Epstein, 1982a). For many advocacy organizations, amicus participation has become the primary means of pursuing their policy objectives (Bradley & Gardner, 1985). Although APA is organized for scientific and professional, rather than advocacy purposes, it has followed the trend toward routinized amicus participation. During the 1985–1986 Supreme Court term, APA was active in a record 10 cases, while filing an additional six briefs in lower courts.

AMICUS BRIEFS AS INSTRUMENTS FOR ADVOCACY

Assessing the effectiveness of amicus participation requires a close examination of the briefs, their intended objectives, and the resulting judicial opinions. Using this methodology, researchers have concluded that amicus briefs have substantial effects in at least some cases. Meltsner (1973) credited the legal arguments the National Association for the Advancement of Colored People (NAACP) made in briefs presented in death penalty cases for a favorable decision in the *Furman v. Georgia* (1972) case that suspended executions in the United States. O'Connor and Epstein found that the amicus briefs filed by organizations promoting the interests of women (1983a), labor (1982b), and conservatives (1983b) contributed significantly to achieving those interest groups' objectives. Similar successes have been reported for amicus participation by organizations representing Blacks (Greenberg, 1977) and members of fundamentalist religions (Pfeffer, 1981). Whether the findings from these studies of amicus participation by advocacy organizations hold for the amicus activity of professional organizations such as APA has not been reported.

Given their potential impact on landmark judicial decisions, amicus briefs offer several advantages over other methods of influencing governmental policy. Campaigns to lobby legislative or administrative branches tend to require the mobilization of both substantial resources and a large or very vocal constituency (Berry, 1984). The amicus route, on the other hand, offers the prospect of more dramatic results with the expenditure of fewer resources (Bradley & Gardner, 1985; O'Connor & Epstein, 1983a). Participating in litigation may be particularly attractive for APA because the judiciary tends to be more receptive than the other branches of government to "underdog" positions (O'Connor & Epstein, 1983a; Pfeffer, 1981). Although APA may be an "upperdog" according to Bradley and Gardner's (1985) criteria of having adequate financial resources and a sophisticated membership, it takes the side of the "underdog" frequently enough to have led United States Senator Orrin Hatch to comment that psychologists risk being perceived as "a group on the fringe of social normality who are promoting social deviance" (Hatch, 1982, p. 1035).

A very practical reason APA and similar organizations may prefer to pursue their social policy objectives through the judiciary is that filing briefs does not jeopardize their tax exemption under Section 501 (c) (3) of the Internal Revenue Code (1986). To maintain this highly desirable tax status, an organization must not devote a substantial portion of its activities to attempting to influence legislation. No such limitation applies to attempting to influence judicial decisions.

THE AMICUS PROCESS

In filing an amicus brief, an organization must comply with a specialized set of court rules, the most important of which pertains to whether the organization will be permitted to file a brief (Stern & Gressman, 1985). The Supreme Court rule governing amici's participation is typical: Applicants must either obtain consent from each party or petition the Court for its permission (Sup. Ct. Rule 36.1, 1986). As a practical matter, that permission will almost always be granted if the applicant represents an otherwise absent perspective or offers to provide specialized expertise (Marvell, 1978). Thus, an organization with APA's credentials can enter almost any case it chooses.

The principal purpose of an amicus brief is to address at least one point of law at issue in the case (Shapiro, 1984). In choosing how to address the legal issues, amici generally seek to supplement rather than duplicate the favored party's presentation (Ennis, 1984). Thus, in most cases, there is some degree of collaboration between amici and parties. On other occasions amici may be neutral with regard to which side wins the case and may wish only to present information to the court so an issue can be decided intelligently.

If amici aim to inform the court on matters other then the governing law, they may insert empirical research findings into the brief. For various reasons, doing so is not always possible, sensible, or effective. Because judges are free to rest their decisions on an understanding of the world gleaned from "the pages of human experience" (*Parham v. J.R.*, 1979, p. 602), brief writers are wary of submitting a brief laden with social science findings at the expense of formal legal arguments (Springer, 1984).

What an organization puts into a brief depends to a great extent on the role of the brief in the organization's overall strategy for influencing the courts. The most important variable here is use of the amicus brief as the sole instrument for influencing judicial policy making or using it as but one technique among many. The chief advantage of limiting participation to filing amicus briefs in appellate courts is that filing a brief requires much less expense and effort than more elaborate strategies (Cowan, 1976). The major disadvantages are that only a small percentage of cases reach the appelate level and the ones that do may have a poorly developed trial record because the litigants did not have assistance initially (McIntosh & Parker, 1986).

APA'S AMICUS STRATEGY

To date, APA has chosen to limit its voluntary involvement in litigation almost exclusively to filing amicus briefs in appellate cases, most often in the United States Supreme Court.[1] The decision to participate emerges from a formalized process designed to take the varied interests of the organization into account and draw on the specialized legal expertise of a few members and advisers.

Although any member of the Association may suggest participation in a case, legal counsel or staff usually first identify cases of potential interest. Upon being notified of such a case, the Executive Officer is responsible for having the case screened by staff and counsel and for obtaining input from boards, committees, and divisions likely to have a special interest in the matter. For any case surviving the initial screening, the next step is review by a case panel of the ad hoc Committee on Legal Issues (COLI). This panel consists of three of the nine COLI committee members plus other APA members representing divisions and state organizations with a special interest in the case. In assessing the desirability of entering a case, panel members are guided by a densely printed, three-page booklet titled "Factors Affecting APA Involvement in Litigation" (1983). These factors include such considerations as presence of a social, moral, or ethical

---

[1]Information for this section was drawn from *American Psychologist* "Reports of the Association" section on Legal and Legislative Issues between 1981 and 1986; memoranda of the APA ad hoc Committee on Legal Issues (COLI); correspondence between APA and the Ennis Friedman & Bersoff law firm; the Association's periodic Reports of Legal Actions of Interest covering the period 1978 to 1986; conversations with individuals having a role in the process of authorizing and submitting APA amicus briefs; the briefs themselves; and the judicial opinions.

reason to become involved; the stance of other organizations with respect to the case; and the state of psychological data relevant to the legal issues. Above all, entry is to be consistent with the objectives of APA as stated in the Association bylaws. After review, the case panel presents the Board of Directors with its decision as to whether APA should enter the case and also may assign a priority relative to other cases the panel has examined.

Because the interests of the membership are diverse, APA sometimes foregoes participation in cases of clear relevance. Lack of consensus about the proper interpretation of testing research, for example, caused APA to decline participation in *Larry P. v. Riles* (1979), even though many psychologists testified independently on the issue of racial bias in intelligence tests (Lambert, 1981).

If COLI does make an affirmative recommendation, the Board of Directors must decide what action to take. Authorizing legal counsel to submit the requisite brief is the standard next step, but alternatives such as permitting another amicus filer to list APA as a cosponsor are possible. Although rarely used, the option also exists for individual divisions to file briefs autonomously, provided they do not purport to represent all of APA. If desired, such action could be taken without following the elaborate review process necessary for full APA involvement.

THE INFLUENCE OF APA AMICUS BRIEFS

Whether any of APA's briefs has been effective is difficult to determine because amicus briefs are part of a complex process comprised of multiple, nonorthogonal factors. Although an evaluation might be conducted using case disposition as a criterion variable, that measure obscures causality. A disposition analysis might be made somewhat more discriminating by focusing on resolution of the particular issue or issues addressed in the brief (O'Connor & Epstein, 1982b), but the possibility of right result for the wrong reason remains. Accordingly, impact analysis of amicus briefs customarily focuses on reference in the opinion to material presented in the brief (O'Connor & Epstein, 1983a; Pfeffer, 1981).

Such reliance is most evident where the opinion explicitly cites the brief. Other indicators of reliance usually are more subtle and less objective, although occasionally so obvious as to border on plagiarism. In a more typical case, reliance might be inferred from citations in the opinion to some of the references discussed in the brief or similarities between the structures of the arguments in the brief and the opinion. In such instances, inferences of effectiveness must rest on a careful reading of not only the amicus brief and the opinion but also of the other briefs filed in the case and the major precedents. Even then an element of conjecture remains in attempting to isolate the amicus brief's unique influence.

Through its amicus participation, APA has attempted to advance "the public interest" in the sense of policies consonant with the organization's fundamental precepts. This broad objective can be resolved for analysis into three principal factors, although in any single case more than one of these three factors may be present (cf. Melton, 1985). Sometimes participation has been motivated by a desire to safeguard the quality and integrity of the profession, which ultimately should redound to the benefit of all society. This use of the courts to advance guild interests has been coordinated with attempts to enhance the profession through legislative and administrative measures, a strategy quite similar to the course pioneered by physicians and attorneys (Larson, 1977; Starr, 1982). A second objective has been to increase the perceived utility of psychology as a basis for policy decisions. Again, this effort has complemented attempts to educate policymakers in other branches of government about the value of psychological research (DeLeon, O'Keefe, VandenBos, & Kraut, 1982). The third goal has been to encourage adoption of policies and practices consonant with the precepts of the organization, such as the cardinal value of autonomy (APA, 1981, p. 633).

Effectiveness in Advancing Guild Interests

The need for APA amicus participation to protect guild interests was particularly acute in *City of Akron v. Akron Center for Reproductive Health* (1983). With the parties focusing their arguments on the central features of the multifaceted abortion statute, a requirement that abortion counseling be provided only by a physician would have gone virtually unchallanged had APA not submitted a brief. The brief that APA did submit on this point quite probably contributed to the Supreme Court's favorable decision. At the most fundamental level, the Supreme Court ruled in favor of APA's position, an especially telling factor in light of the APA brief's singularity. More subtly, the structure of the Court's opinion on this point closely paralleled the brief, cited some of the same references, and listed the same alternative regulations to achieve the state's legitimate interests in assuring competent abortion counseling.

Another case shows the relationship between amicus participation and other methods of influencing governmental policy. APA and the Oregon Psychological Association entered *Oregon v. Miller* (1985) as part of professional psychology's ongoing campaign to protect the confidentiality of communications between psychologists and clients. Although that effort has concentrated on encouraging state legislatures to adopt psychotherapist–patient privilege laws, the possibility that judicial interpretation might constrict or invalidate the privilege prompted resort to the courts. Thus in *Miller*, APA filed an amicus brief in support of a criminal defendant's contention that Oregon's psychotherapist–patient privilege should apply to his having called a mental hospital and told both a receptionist and a psychiatrist that he had just killed a man. APA's participation was vital here because the American Psychiatric Association chose not to defend the privilege, perhaps because doing so would have conflicted embarrassingly with the hospital personnel's conduct in notifying the police. In an opinion mirroring the APA brief's arguments and resting on the same policy rationales, the Oregon Supreme Court adopted APA's interpretation of the privilege.

Differences in the APA's and American Psychiatric Association's guild interests, as well as in their world views, have led to their being aligned on opposite sides of some legal disputes. Even though the American Psychiatric Association did not formally file a brief in one of the cases, the rift is quite evident in the *Rivers v. Katz* (1986) and *Rogers v. Commissioner* (1983) cases dealing with the involuntary administration of psychoactive drugs. In both cases the states' highest courts constrained psychiatrists' authority to administer drugs to certain institutionalized patients. Both opinions drew on the analysis of the APA briefs and referred to the data those briefs contained about side effects of psychoactive drugs and effectiveness of counseling alternatives to medication.

Effectiveness in Increasing the Perceived Value of Psychology for Government Policy Making

In some cases, the principal motivation for APA involvement is the likelihood that the case will have a significant impact on how policymakers regard psychology. As noted previously, policymakers, judicial and otherwise, have not always been quick to embrace the field. To overcome that reticence, APA has entered a number of cases in which the appropriateness of relying on psychological research has been at issue. Although APA has yet to convince the entire judiciary that research can usefully inform decision making, its briefs have been instrumental in averting serious setbacks.

When entering a case for this purpose, APA usually seeks to explain the relevance and validity of social science research that illuminates the core "social facts" of the case (Davis, 1942). In the recently decided case of *Lockhart v. McCree* (1986), for example, the trial court record consisted predominantly of research findings on "death-qualified" juries (see Haney, 1984). Especially because APA members had conducted some of the key studies, the incentive to participate was very strong. In scholarly fashion, the APA brief provided the Supreme Court with a careful analysis of the studies introduced at trial, acknowledging their limitations but nonetheless concluding that they established that death-qualified juries are biased in favor of conviction.

Although the brief received favorable mention in the dissenting opinion, it did not sway the majority. By redefining the question to which the studies were addressed, the Court rendered most of the research inapposite. Nonetheless, the majority regarded the research as sufficiently important to warrant devoting several pages of its opinion to critiquing the studies' methodologies. In the end, the APA's position was neither clearly accepted nor rejected, and the implications for the future role of research in litigation are equivocal (Bersoff, 1987).

A similarly equivocal, although less enigmatic, result occurred in the case of *Metropolitan Edison Company v. People Against Nuclear Energy* (1983). There APA sought to have the Court recognize the relevance of psychological harm to determinations of environmental impact under the National Environmental Policy Act (1969). Again, APA averted a clear defeat in that the Court interpreted the law as requiring a review of psychological effects in appropriate instances. In the context of restarting the Three Mile Island nuclear reactor, however, the Court held that psychological effects did not need to be examined because they did not satisfy the statutory requirement of resulting from an alteration of the physical environment.

The potential for APA briefs to inform judges neutrally about psychological research, rather than to support or oppose particular verdicts, is especially evident in two cases involving criminal defendants who wanted to introduce expert testimony on the battered woman's syndrome. For *Hawthorne v. Florida* (1985) and *New Jersey v. Kelly* (1984), APA submitted briefs explaining that several probative studies of the battered woman's syndrome were methodologically sound and the field as a whole was sufficiently well-developed, despite lack of consensus among researchers, that excluding expert testimony on the subject was an abuse of the trial judge's discretion.

Examination of the opinions in those two cases suggests the briefs served well, though not perfectly, to educate the appellate judges. A majority in *Kelly* rendered an opinion holding the expert testimony to be appropriate for introduction at trial. Textual support for that conclusion closely resembled the discussion of the psychological studies cited in APA's brief. The majority in *Hawthorne* reached the opposite result, but the educative function of the brief was not wholly lost. The dissenting judge explicitly cited APA's brief and accepted its analysis of the admissibility issue, concluding that the relevant criterion was the validity of the methodology used in the studies and not the degree of unanimity as to the findings.

Effectiveness in Fostering Adoption of Policies Consonant With Mental Health and Psychological Well-Being

From time to time, APA also enters cases involving issues in which organized psychology may not have any direct interest, but for which psychological research findings are relevant. Illustrative of these cases are *Bowers v. Hardwick* (1986) and *Thornburgh v. American College of Obstetricians and Gynecologists* (1986). *Hardwick* required the United States Supreme Court to rule on the constitutionality of a Georgia law criminalizing homosexual sodomy. APA's brief, cosponsored by the American Public Health Association, was designed to substantiate the party's contention that the Georgia statute served no legitimate health function, and indeed interfered with preservation of a positive self-image and other mental health objectives. Although four members of the Court found this presentation sufficiently enlightening to cite the APA's brief in their dissent, the majority's conclusion that homosexual sodomy is qualitatively different from any of the activities previously afforded constitutional protection under the rubric of privacy undercut the utility of APA's scientific approach.

APA used its brief in *Thornburgh* (partially reprinted in Interdivisional Committee on Adolescent Abortion, 1987) to present the Court with a discussion of the developmental literature on competence of minors to make abortion decisions. Submission of this brief marked the first time in the decade since adolescent abortion issues have been taken to the Supreme Court that any of the parties or amici had presented the pertinent research, a change in strategy that may be attributable in part to the availability of high quality, issue-specific studies conducted since 1976 (Melton & Russo, 1987; Tremper, 1987). Whether this presentation accomplished its educational mission cannot be ascertained at this time because the Court postponed indefinitely a ruling on the minors' access issue.

Prospects for Continued Influence

APA amicus briefs clearly have become an important and effective technique for furthering the interests of psychologists and promoting public policies consonant with the Association's principles. That very success is likely to facilitate future influence by establishing the organization's credentials and respectability (McIntosh & Parker, 1986). Whether APA can continue along the path it has been traveling will depend on the further evolution of its litigation strategies.

Although the scope of APA's judicial involvement has expanded substantially over the last decade, the process for deciding whether to enter a case remains rather cumbersome, and the exclusive reliance on outside counsel to generate a brief for the organization remains the sole method of effectuating participation. For APA's influence on judicial decision making to be most effective, consideration might be given to streamlining and optimizing the entire arrangement. A step in that direction has been proposed by creating a COLI subcommittee that would screen potential cases before involving the customary case review panels. Under that arrangement, the screening panel members would develop a more comprehensive awareness of the full range of cases coming to APA and could make more informed priority judgments.

Thought also might be given to developing model briefs and litigation guides for recurring issues, such as *Tarasoff* liability (*Tarasoff v. Regents of the University of California*, 1976) and recognition of psychologists as expert witnesses. Availability of these materials for APA members and their attorneys facing lawsuits in the lower courts would extend the reach of APA's legal expertise without requiring either the financial expenditure or formal review associated with full-scale participation.

Perhaps the brightest prospect for greater APA influence on judicial policy-making is the potential availability of a high quality psychological research base generated by the membership. APA has an extraordinary advantage over most organizations wishing to influence the courts because its membership is capable of conducting the very research needed to educate judges about empirical matters at issue in litigation. If more of that research was focused specifically on legal issues in the way the Supreme Court suggested in *Lockhart* (see Bersoff, 1986), published in law reviews to increase its facial appeal to judges (Hafemeister & Melton, 1987; Haney, 1980), and, optimally, targeted to particular judges (Springer, 1984), it would constitute an extraordinarily valuable tool for constructing potent amicus briefs.

To encourage expansion of the already existing research base, APA needs effective methods of identifying legal issues for which psychological studies could be relevant and then stimulating research that will produce results suitable for inclusion in amicus briefs. This might be accomplished through direct collaboration between counsel and researchers, forums at the APA convention, a regular feature in the *American Psychologist*, or other means of coordinating the conduct of research with its dissemination to judicial policymakers. The outcome should be a self-reinforcing cycle of greater judicial reliance on research, more satisfaction among psychologists with the increased social utility of their findings, and further improvements in the research itself.

REFERENCES

American Psychological Association. (1981). Ethical principles of psychologists. *American Psychologist, 36*, 633–638.

American Psychological Association, Ad Hoc Committee on Litigation. (1983). *Factors affecting APA involvement in litigation.* (Available from Office of Legal Affairs, American Psychological Association)

Berger, R. (1977). *Government by judiciary.* Cambridge, MA: Harvard University Press.

Berry, J. M. (1984). *The interest group society.* Boston: Little Brown.

Bersoff, D. N. (1986). Psychologists and the judicial system. *Law and Human Behavior, 10,* 151–165.

Bersoff, D. N. (1987). Social science data and the Supreme Court: *Lockhart* as a case in point. *American Psychologist, 42,* 52–58.

Bowers v. Hardwick, 106 S.Ct. 2841 (1986).

Bradley, R. C., & Gardner, P. (1985). Underdogs, upperdogs and the use of the amicus brief: Trends and explanations. *Justice System Journal, 10,* 78–96.

City of Akron v. Akron Center for Reproductive Health, 462 U.S. 416 (1983).

Cowan, R. B. (1976). Women's rights through litigation: An examination of the American Civil Liberties Union Women's Rights Project, 1971–1976. *Columbia Human Rights Review, 8,* 373–412.

Davis, K. C. (1942). An approach to the problems of evidence in the administrative process. *Harvard Law Review, 55,* 364–393.

DeLeon, P. H., O'Keefe, A. M., VandenBos, G. R., & Kraut, A. G. (1982). How to influence public policy: A blueprint for activism. *American Psychologist, 37,* 476–485.

Ennis, B. J. (1984). Effective amicus briefs. *Catholic University Law Review, 33,* 593–609.

Furman v. Georgia, 408 U.S. 238 (1972).

Greenberg, J. (1977). *Judicial process and social changes: Constitutional litigation.* Saint Paul, MN: West.

Hafemeister, T. H., & Melton, G. B. (1987). The impact of social science research on the judiciary. In G. B. Melton (Ed.), *Reforming the law: Impact of child development research.* New York: Guilford Press.

Haney, C. (1980). Psychology and legal change: On the limits of a factual jurisprudence. *Law and Human Behavior, 4,* 147–199.

Haney, C. (Ed.). (1984). Death qualification [Special issue]. *Law and Human Behavior, 8*(1/2).

Hatch, O. G. (1982). Psychology, society, and politics. *American Psychologist, 37,* 1031–1037.

Hawthorne v. Florida, 470 So. 2d. 770 (Fla. Dist. Ct. App. 1985). Internal Revenue Code, 26 U.S.C. (1986).

Interdivisional Committee on Adolescent Abortion. (1987). Adolescent abortion: Psychological and legal issues. *American Psychologist, 42,* 73–78.

Lambert, N. (1981). Psychological evidence in *Larry P. v. Wilson Riles:* An evaluation by a witness for the defense. *American Psychologist, 36,* 937–952.

Larry P. v. Riles, 495 F. Supp. 926 (N.D. Cal. 1979).

Larson, M. S. (1977). *The rise of professionalism: A sociological analysis*. Berkeley: University of California Press.

Lockhart v. McCree, 106 S.Ct. 1758 (1986).

Marvell, T. B. (1978). *Appellate courts and lawyers*. Westport, CT: Greenwood Press.

Maccoby, E. E., Kahn, A. J., & Everett, B. A. (1983). The role of psychological research in the formation of policies affecting children. *American Psychologist, 38,* 80–84.

McIntosh, W. V., & Parker, P. E. (1986, May). *Amici curiae in the courts of appeals*. Paper presented at the annual meeting of the Law and Society Association, Chicago.

Melton, G. B. (1985). Organized psychology and legal policy-making: Involvement in the post-*Hinckley* debate. *Professional Psychology: Research and Practice, 16,* 810–822.

Melton, G. B., & Russo, N. F. (1987). Adolescent abortion: psychological perspectives on public policy. *American Psychologist, 42,* 69–72.

Meltsner, M. (1973). *Cruel and unusual: The Supreme Court and capital punishment*. New York: Random House.

Metropolitan Edison Company v. People Against Nuclear Energy, 460 U.S. 766 (1983).

Monahan, J., & Loftus, E. (1982). The psychology of law. *Annual Review of Psychology, 33,* 226–293.

National Environmental Policy Act of 1969, 42 U.S.C.A. § 4332.

New Jersey v. Kelly, 97 N.J. 178, 478 A.2d 364 (1984).

O'Connor, K., & Epstein, L. (1982a). Amicus curiae participation in U.S. Supreme Court litigation: An appraisal of Hakman's "folklore." *Law and Society Review, 16,* 311–320.

O'Connor, K., & Epstein, L. (1982b). The importance of interest group involvement in employment discrimination litigation. *Howard Law Journal, 25,* 709–729.

O'Connor, K., & Epstein, L. (1983a). Beyond legislative lobbying: Womens' rights groups and the Supreme Court. *Judicature, 67,* 134–143.

O'Connor, K., & Epstein, L. (1983b). The rise of conservative interest group litigation. *Journal of Politics, 45,* 479–489.

Oregon v. Miller, 300 Or. 203, 709 P.2d 225 (1985).

Parham v. J. R., 442 U.S. 584 (1979).

Pfeffer, L. (1981). Amici in church–state litigation. *Law and Contemporary Problems, 44,* 83–110.

Rivers v. Katz, 67 N.Y.2d 485, 504 N.Y.S.2d 74, 495 N.E.2d 337 (1986).

Rogers v. Commissioner, 390 Mass. 489, 458 N.E.2d 308 (1983).

Shapiro, S. M. (1984). Amicus briefs in the Supreme Court. *Litigation, 10*(3), 21–24.

Springer, J. R. (1984). Some suggestions on preparing briefs on the merits in the Supreme Court of the United States. *Catholic University Law Review, 33,* 593–602.

Starr, P. (1982). *The social transformation of American medicine.* New York: Basic Books.

Stern, R. L., & Gressman, E. (1985). *Supreme Court practice* (6th ed.). Washington, DC: Bureau of National Affairs.

Sup. Ct. Rule 36.1 (1986).

Takanishi, R., DeLeon, P. H., & Pallak, M. S. (1983). Psychology and public policy affecting children, youth, and families. *American Psychologist, 37,* 67–69.

Tarasoff v. Regents of the University of California, 17 Cal. 3d 425, 551 P. 2d 334 (1976).

Thornburgh v. American College of Obstetricians and Gynecologists, 106 S.Ct. 2169 (1986).

Tremper, C. R. (1987). The high road to the bench: Presenting research findings in appellate briefs. In G. B. Melton (Ed.), *Reforming the law: Impact of child development research* (pp. 199–231). New York: Guilford Press.

12

WHEN PSYCHOLOGY INFORMS PUBLIC POLICY: THE CASE OF EARLY CHILDHOOD INTERVENTION

MARTIN WOODHEAD

Analyses of the potential for psychological research to inform public policy are now perennial, especially when the welfare and development of young children is at issue (e.g., Brim & Dustan, 1983; Maccoby, Kahn, & Everett, 1983; Scarr, 1979; Takanishi, DeLeon, & Pallak, 1983). Frequently, discussion centers on the problem of how to communicate research, what dissemination modes to use, and so on. But effective dissemination is not always a problem. Occasionally, the determined efforts of social scientists reap rewards when their research captures the attention of policymakers, politicians, and the public at large and is generally accepted as having made a tangible contribution to the development of policy. On such occasions, attention turns away from problems of communication to issues of responsibility—psychologists' responsibility to ensure the validity not only of their research findings but also of inferences that are drawn for policy. A classic example of this is the controversy that recently emerged about the adequacy of the 1954 Social Science Statement, "The Effect of

Reprinted from *American Psychologist*, 43, 443–454. Copyright 1988 by the American Psychological Association.

This chapter is based in part on research carried out while the author was a Fulbright Scholar in the United States, based at High/Scope Educational Research Foundation, with financial support from the Nuffield Foundation, Great Britain. An earlier version was presented at a Thomas Coram Research Foundation conference at the Institute of Education, University of London, December 1985.

Segregation and the Consequences of Desegregation," which played a significant part in Supreme Court deliberations at the time (Cook, 1984; Gerard, 1983).

The presentation of social science findings about the value of early childhood intervention has not been the subject of anything as formal as a public statement supported by multiple signatories, such as the Social Science Statement, but it has been no less influential. In particular, a series of reports was published between 1977 and 1983 by the Consortium for Developmental Continuity, later renamed the Consortium for Longitudinal Studies, that convincingly demonstrated for the first time that well-planned preschool programs could have a lasting effect on the fortunes of socially disadvantaged (especially Black) youngsters, right through into adult life (Consortium for Developmental Continuity, 1977; Consortium for Longitudinal Studies, 1978, 1983; Darlington, Royce, Snipper, Murray, & Lazar, 1980; Lazar, Darlington, Murray, & Snipper, 1982). These reports were the product of collaboration among investigators representing 11 projects, each a well-planned and carefully researched preschool intervention, adopting an experimental or at least quasi-experimental design. By conducting a joint follow-up in 1976, and again in 1980, the Consortium has been able to provide a comprehensive picture of the extent of long-term effects. At the same time, several of the projects within the Consortium have also reported recent follow-up data independently (e.g., Clement, Schweinhart, Barnett, Epstein, & Weikart, 1984; Gray, Ramsey, & Klaus, 1982).

Data from the Consortium and its constituent projects has served an important function in strengthening public support for early childhood programs for disadvantaged children, notably Head Start. Recently, it has also been cited in broader debate about the case for extending public education to four-year-olds (discussed by Zigler, 1987). It also made up part of the evidence that shaped Public Law 99-457 (Education of the Handicapped Act Amendments, 1986) mandating public education for handicapped infants and preschoolers. Moreover, the impact of this research is being felt not only in North America. Considerable interest in the lessons for policy has been aroused both for other western countries (e.g., Woodhead, 1985) and for the third world (e.g., Halpern & Myers, 1985; Liddell, 1987; Myers & Hertenberg, 1987). The purpose of this article is to review the implications for public policy that have been claimed from this most recent body of early intervention data, focusing particularly on projects within the Consortium.

THE WIDER CONTEXT OF EARLY INTERVENTION RESEARCH

In electing to focus on this particular group of studies, I acknowledge that they are part of a long-standing and broad-based tradition of policy-linked intervention research. For example, early studies attempted to identify the potential to compensate for chronic deprivation (e.g., Goldfarb, 1945; Skodak & Skeels, 1949; & Spitz, 1945). These entailed a relatively profound intervention in the lives of young children. More recent examples include the Milwaukee study carried out during the 1960s (Garber & Heber, 1983) and the Abecedarian Project (Ramey & Campbell, 1987; Ramey, Yeates, & Short, 1984), which has demonstrated the scope for helping prevent developmental retardation through a massive intervention—an intensive all-year day-care program from infancy. A great deal of intervention research has been targetted toward handicapped infants, and there is now a substantial body of evidence about its effectiveness (e.g., Bryant & Ramey, 1985; Guralnick & Bennett, 1987; White, 1986). However, attempts to integrate findings by means of meta-analysis are controversial (e.g., Casto & Mastropieri, 1986; Dunst & Snyder, 1986; Strain & Smith, 1986) and point to the necessity of differentiating statements about effectiveness according to such features as the population studied, the program design, and the intensity of the intervention (Guralnick, 1988).

Although Consortium projects have many features in common with these other intervention-research traditions, they are distinctive in terms of their target population (socially disadvantaged 2- to 4-year-old children), the intensity of their intervention (relatively moderate and potentially generally applicable programs), and their policy relevance (notably, they are seen as providing a proving ground for the principles underlying Project Head Start). In this respect, they are often referred to alongside the substantial number of evaluations of Head Start itself. The earliest major example of such evaluations was the Westinghouse Learning Corporation Study (1969), which has been the most influential (Datta, 1976), as well as the most controversial (Cicirrelli, 1984; Zigler, 1984). Some 1,500 studies of Head Start practice have now been annotated by Hubbell (1983), and these studies provided the data base for a meta-analysis conducted by the Head Start Synthesis Project. Briefly, there is encouraging evidence that children have shown gains in cognitive competence, school readiness, and school achievement that have lasted for three years after they attended Head Start (Harrell, 1983). There is also evidence of positive effects on children's socioemotional development and health status (McKey et al., 1985). However, the aggregation of findings from studies with acknowledged methodological flaws (notably noncomparability of groups) detracts from the potential of this meta-analysis to offer clear messages about Head Start effectiveness (Gamble & Zigler, 1989).

It is against this background that public attention has been directed toward research projects, such as those within the Consortium, that are less severely constrained by the problems of reconciling the rigors of experimental design with the requirements of program implementation and that do, on the face of it, offer unequivocal evidence of early intervention effectiveness. Their credibility rests on the assumption that they share sufficient features in common with regular Head Start programs that it can be presumed they simulate processes that could be readily reproduced within Head Start and similar interventions (Schweinhart & Weikart, 1986, pp. 52–53). A further reason for the salience of these experimental projects is that they have been carried out over such a long period, offering a rare opportunity to examine the impact of an intervention from early childhood into adult life. Indeed, the very existence of such a unique set of data relating to a particular area of public policy is in itself instructive about the political status of early childhood work.

THE POLITICAL STATUS OF EARLY CHILDHOOD INTERVENTION

Few areas of social and educational policy are ever evaluated on such an extended time frame as has been applied to intervention studies. One major reason why researchers have been motivated to carry out such long-term evaluations lies in the relatively marginal status of early childhood programs on the policy agenda. Although universal schooling is taken as a sine qua non of Western civilization, governments have remained ambivalent about the desirability of providing a comprehensive pattern of services to support families with young children. Even when preschool services have been developed, the goals of enhancing children's welfare and their development per se have frequently been subsumed within a more compelling political priority, be it the release of women into the labor force (e.g., as in Britain during two world wars, Tizard, Moss, & Perry, 1976); the furtherance of equal opportunities for working parents (e.g., postwar Swedish day care provision, Berfenstam & William-Olsson, 1974); or as in this case, the pursuit of social egalitarian goals (e.g., through the War on Poverty during the 1960s, Zigler & Berman, 1983; Zigler & Valentine, 1979). By and large, it is these priorities that have shaped the direction of research programs. So, in the case of Head Start, the broad range of potential concurrent benefits to children and families has received relatively little attention, compared with the search for empirical support for the political ideals of the War on Poverty in measurable long-term effects (especially cognitive effects) throughout schooling and on into adult life (Kotelchuck & Richmond, 1987; Zigler, 1976). It is this search, continued over two decades, that culminated in the most recent, apparently unequivocal evidence that early childhood programs might, after all, live up to the promise cherished by the president who initiated the first Head Start program in 1965—"that no American child shall be condemned to failure by the accident of his birth" (President Johnson, quoted in Zigler & Valentine, 1979, p. 20).

This tendency to harness the credibility of early childhood programs to broad and somewhat ephemeral social goals, which on the face of it are far removed from immediate priorities for young children, has had one other consequence. Early childhood advocates have displayed considerable ingenuity in framing their case to address the political imperatives of the day. Thus, when Head Start was initiated in the early 1960s, claims about the long-term value of early intervention were sufficient to justify expenditure by an Administration committed to reduce social and educational inequalities. By contrast, in the late 1970s and early 1980s, even data as strong as those offered by the Consortium would not have had great political significance if the implication appeared to be simply one of increased public expenditure. In this context, the impact of long-term effects data has been greatly enhanced by the presentation of policy conclusions that appear not only to be justified by scientifically derived data but also are politically expedient. Particularly significant have been the use of "real-life" measures (such as employment and delinquency), which when combined with a cost-benefit approach, have led to dramatic claims that, far from being a burden on the public purse, preschool is a sound financial investment. This induced the *Wall Street Journal* to review a follow-up of Perry Pre-School Project children at 19 years of age (Clement et al., 1984), with a feature article entitled "A Head Start Pays Off in the End" (Crittenden, 1984). The article began, "If ever there was a program for the 1980s, a program that addresses the needs for greater productivity and the needs of women and the problem of poverty, it is—are you ready?—preschool education."

Media coverage is only the first indicator of the successful communication of a message. Arguably, it was no coincidence that the year after the first report from the Consortium for Developmental Continuity (1977) was issued, the first substantial increase in Head Start's budget was funded since publication of the Westinghouse report nearly a decade earlier. More remarkable is the fact that steady increases in Head Start's budget were maintained in the unfavorable public-spending climate of the mid 1980s, topping 1 billion dollars by 1985 (Administration for Children, Youth and Families, 1985). One commentator has argued (Datta, 1983a) that the decision to include Head Start as one of the social "safety-net" measures was due, at least in part, to the Consortium investigators' assiduous efforts to convey the message of their evidence to influential politicians of the day.

In short, reports from the Consortium for Longitudinal Studies and its constituent projects certainly count as having been highly successful in making an impact on public policy, and the conclusions they draw are, on the face of it, well-founded in their data. Yet despite the widespread attention being paid to this research, many questions remain inadequately answered that could have a strong bearing on the implications for policy.

This article centers on three in particular: What causal processes could have produced effects over such a long period? What significance does an understanding of possible causal processes have for policy? How valid are the implications that have commonly been inferred from the data?

EVIDENCE OF LONG-TERM EFFECTS

The longest term evidence of effectiveness offered in the Consortium reports is based on data collected in 1980. By that time, children in four of the projects (those directed by Beller, Gray, Karnes, & Weikart) were old enough to have completed high school. In each case, the program group had higher completion rates, a finding that proved to be significant when the data were pooled. Taken together, there was a 15% difference in high school completion rates (Royce, Darlington, & Murray, 1983). These effects were matched by evidence of higher occupational aspirations and expectations among the children and their parents. In view of the numerous other influences on children's progress during the intervening dozen or more years, the discovery of significant effects on these measures seems, on the face of it, fairly convincing evidence that early intervention makes a lasting impact, at least until the end of schooling. The Consortium did report one measure after children had left school, children's success in obtaining employment. For the three projects for which subjects were old enough to make the criterion relevant (Beller, Gray, & Karnes), no direct effects could be discerned on their success in the job market (Royce et al., 1983).

Since the final Consortium report was published in 1983, children in the project directed by David Weikart have been followed up again at 19 years of age (Clement et al., 1984). Indeed, Weikart's Perry Pre-School Project has taken much of the limelight when it comes to arguing the policy implications of early intervention research. Unlike the other Consortium projects, Weikart's study has demonstrated a significant effect of preschool on employment rates for his 121 subjects. Fully 59% of the preschool group were employed, compared with 32% of the control group. Also, Weikart's is the only study showing clear though diminishing effects on scholastic attainment (Schweinhart & Weikart, 1980). Additionally, Weikart has demonstrated significant effects on levels of juvenile crime and arrests, as well as rates of teenage pregnancy. It is these "real-life" measures, along with the employment measure, that have most often captured the public imagination. Preschool intervention is no longer seen as an issue for debate solely among psychologists and educationists; it has now also taken a spotlight in the debates about maternal and child welfare, about youth unemployment, and about the prevention of delinquency (e.g., Farrington, 1985). Publication of such clear-cut findings on a whole series of salient measures, which have been converted into cost-benefit analyses, combined with the indefatigable efforts of Weikart and his team to communicate their findings, accounts for the substantial public attention that has been paid to this single project.

A PROMISE FOR SOCIAL POLICY

Taken together, these findings seem to translate readily into major policy implications for the development of early childhood programs both in the United States and further afield. It is tempting to let the matter rest there, with an apparently watertight case for investment in the early years that promises not only to reduce the incidence of educational failure throughout schooling but also to make measurable impact on many of the social ills that beset advanced industrial countries. Certainly, although there has been a great deal of media discussion of this tantalizing possibility, there has been remarkably little published academic review of the findings, either in terms of research adequacy or in terms of implications for policy (also noted by Datta, 1983b, p. 478, footnote 3; and Haskins & Gallagher, 1984, p. 3). Exceptions include an article by Zigler (1987), in which he challenged the misapplication of preschool intervention data in recent debates abut extending kindergarten programs to all four-year-olds, and my earlier article, in which I attempted to define the limits on generalizability (Woodhead, 1985).

The fact that the academic community has paid relatively little critical attention to this research may, in part, stem from an understandable reluctance to appear to be challenging the scientific base for politically precarious social and educational programs that achieve a great deal for children and families in poverty. However, the consequence is that tacit endorsement is given to conclusions about the power of early intervention that emerge from simplistic interpretation of the message in the data. This may appear politically expedient in the short term, but in the long run it carries inherent dangers. In the first place, it reinforces the political preference to urge single strategy and (relatively) inexpensive educational solutions to complex social and economic problems (Lazerson, 1970). Second, it risks perpetuating the idea that the impact an educational intervention makes on an individual can be understood in isolation from the context in which it occurs. Third, it fails to recognize that there may be features of experimental projects that it is difficult, even impossible, to reproduce in a national social program (including the fact of being experimental and by definition only being available to a particular group of children). Fourth, as Zigler's article reemphasized, it encourages advocates to overstate the case, courting a political backlash if the program does not turn out to fulfill promises made for it (Zigler, 1987, pp. 257–258).

These dangers were well illustrated by the media coverage surrounding publication of Weikart and his colleagues' monograph *Changed Lives* (Clement et al., 1984). The *Wall Street Journal* feature (Crittenden, 1984) has already been mentioned. The national and local press throughout the United States consistently reported data from the Perry Pre-School Project under dramatic headlines, including, for example, "Head Start Saves Children and Money" (1984) and "Head Start Gets a High Grade" (1984). Such reports fudged several by no means trivial issues about the relationship between one carefully planned and maintained experimental project and the 1,200 diverse community-run programs collectively known as Head Start (Besharov & Hartle, 1987; Kotelchuck & Richmond, 1987).

One way of approaching these issues is by asking questions about generalizability. What were the features of the successful programs, and how far are they, could they be, and need they be replicated on a wider scale for early intervention to be effective? Such questions have been examined by Woodhead (1985) and Zigler (1987) and will only be briefly summarized here.

CONSTRAINTS ON GENERALIZABILITY

The two major potential constraints on generalizability are the characteristics (a) of the children and (b) of the early childhood program they attended. The Consortium projects can only offer evidence on the value of preschool education for an extreme group of disadvantaged children. They were in the lowest social class; their parents had little education; and their initial IQs ranged from a mean of 79.0 (Weikart) to 93.6 (Levenstein; see Lazar et al., 1982). A majority of the children were Black, and in four out of the eleven projects, 100% were Black. Those few attempts to evaluate the significance of disadvantage are inconclusive, although they lend some support to the idea that the most disadvantaged groups can benefit most, with the possible exception of the most extreme groups (Di Lorenzo, 1969; Harrell, 1983; Herzog, Newcomb, & Cisin, 1974).

As for the program design, the Consortium projects offer only limited opportunity to make key comparisons. There was a great deal of variability in program designs, including whether programs were home or center based, children's age at entry, length and intensity of program, extent of parental involvement, and curriculum model. Because all the studies showed similar patterns of effect, even though they differed in the extent of that effect, the evidence does not suggest that effectiveness is associated with one single strategy. That does not mean that the approaches are equivalent—they may have quite different patterns of impact, but these did not show up on the relatively gross measures available to the Consortium researchers.

There is also no reason to suppose that it is the end of the story. The failure to show differential effects is undoubtedly partly due to the inadequacy of the designs to answer these questions. One area which has been well tested, and in which a great deal of professional investment has been made, is the choice of curriculum model. Until recently, no long-term effects data had emerged that suggested that one of the rival curriculum models (developmental, instructional, etc.) was superior to another, (e.g., Karnes, Zehrbrach, & Teska, 1974; Weikart, Bond, & McNeil, 1978; Weikart, Epstein, Schweinhart, & Bond, 1978). However, Schweinhart, Weikart, and Larner (1986a) have offered data from an age-15 follow-up comparison of a small sample of children who experienced the High/Scope Cognitively Oriented Curriculum, Direct Instruction approach, or a Traditional Nursery Curriculum (there were just over 20 subjects in each group). They claim that the data indicate a tendency for the direct instruction group to report higher levels of delinquency and poorer family relations than the other groups. However, the validity of this conclusion has been strongly challenged in terms of questions both about methodological limitations of the research and the legitimacy of inferences drawn for curriculum choice (Bereiter, 1986; Gersten, 1986; but see also Schweinhart, Weikert, & Larner, 1986b).

As a general summary, the data suggest that, at least for extremely disadvantaged children, a wide range of early intervention strategies may be effective. This does not necessarily mean, however, that all strategies are effective. Far from it. There are certain distinctive shared features of the Consortium projects that were not systematically tested but that may have accounted for their success. All were carefully planned and implemented; staff were well supported; there were low child to adult ratios (averaging 5:1); and all had a carefully designed program applied within a clear framework of aims. All involved parents actively in the learning process, and some required their active participation in parent programs and home visiting. In the absence of further systematic research specifically examining the impact of these variables, a cautious conclusion for policy would acknowledge that assured effectiveness among the general run of preschool programs may necessitate implementation of minimum standards in some or all of these respects.

However, as noted earlier, the focus of this article is on a different set of issues that have a less obvious but nonetheless important bearing on implications of early intervention research for policy. These are questions about how a moderate intervention during the early years could result in a long-term change in prospects for adult life. What is an appropriate explanatory model? What are its implications for deriving policy both for early childhood and for the rest of the education system through which the former preschool child must progress? One way of approaching these issues is by asking what the policymaker is expected to make of the data.

MODELS OF EARLY INTERVENTION EFFECTIVENESS

The simplest understanding of long-term effects would draw on a "direct effects" model. Ex-preschool children cope more effectively with school and stay on longer because they are more able: Preschool has made them smarter. This view of early intervention is implicit in the catchphrase "an inoculation against failure," although arguably that particular expression has always been more a part of the folklore of early intervention than a serious attempt to understand the process (Klaus & Gray, 1968). In any case, Head Start has never been solely concerned with cognitive goals: "Improving the child's mental processes and skills with particular attention to conceptual and verbal skills" was only *one* of the seven goals for Head Start set by the original planning committee in 1965 (Richmond, Stipek, & Zigler, 1979, p. 317). The others covered physical, emotional, and social development; self-concept; relationships with parents; and patterns and expectations of school success. Even so, the prospects of causing a permanent change in children's cognitive functioning became the principal criterion of many early evaluations, not least because of the ready availability of well-proven psychometric measures in this area (Zigler & Trickett, 1978, p. 790). The broad educational goals of the War on Poverty were "easily translated into 'becoming smarter,' particularly in a nation as infatuated with intelligence test scores as the United States" (Zigler & Berman, 1983, p. 896).

On the face of it, a direct effects model has a number of virtues that might commend it to those responsible for formulating policy. It is easy to comprehend, as well as simple to present in public debate; it is clear-cut, lacking the vagaries and uncertainties that can hinder decision making; it makes for straightforward, apparently scientifically based policy choices between strategies according to their relative effectiveness; and it appeals to a cultural preference for social interventions targeted to effect individual change. Yet there is very little in the evidence to suggest that the long-term effects identified in the Consortium meta-analysis have come about because of marked permanent changes in children's cognitive competencies as a direct result of their attendance at a preschool program. Although the superiority of experimental groups in measured intelligence remained significant and robust (on the criterion of deleting the project with the most significant effect and recalculating the result) for up to two years after completion of the program, the effects rapidly weakened in subsequent years (Lazar et al., 1982, p. 47). In this respect, the message of the data on IQ has not substantially altered since Bronfenbrenner (1974a) concluded that despite promising short-term effects, "By the first or second year after completion of the program . . . the children began to show a progressive decline, and by the third or fourth year of follow-up had fallen back into the problem range of the lower 90's and below" (p. 52; see also Bronfenbrenner, 1979, p. 168).

The implication for an explanatory model is that a direct effect via IQ is clearly not the answer. If the cognitive effects of early intervention wash out during the early grades, they cannot be directly responsible for children's later school progress. One explanation that appealed initially to the Consortium investigators (reported by Lewin, 1977) was that there might be a sleeper effect; although the effects on IQ were no longer manifest, they had not disappeared, but were lying dormant until some process of maturational change or environmental triggering stimulated their reawakening during the later school years. On closer scrutiny, this interpretation seems somewhat implausible (Clarke & Clarke, 1981, 1982; Seitz, 1981), although this does not mean that cognitive abilities do not have a place in an explanatory model, as will become apparent. However, the discussion must turn to other variables in the search for processes that might account for transmission of long-term effects, variables that do not so much reflect permanent change in the child's psychological functioning but rather suggest that a change has taken place in the child's relationship to significant features of the social environment, both at school and at home.

One group of variables in particular can be singled out as offering evidence that an enduring change had taken place in the relationship of program children to the school system. These are referred to by the Consortium as measures of "school competence," comprising "retention in grade" and "referral to special education classes." Although there were variations among the projects, the general pattern was that children who had experienced a preschool program were less likely to be referred to special education and less likely to be retained in grade. Meta-analysis of both variables for all the projects with equivalent data produced effects that were significant and robust for the projects with more nearly randomized designs (Lazar et al., 1982, p. 38). Most important, the effect on special education actually became stronger as children progressed through school, right up to the 12th grade (Royce et al., 1983, p. 439).

How did early intervention affect these indicators of school competence? The Consortium authors themselves offered a plausible explanation:

> When the children entered the first grade, they had positive attitudes toward classroom activities, were able to adapt to classroom procedures, and were able to learn and do the schoolwork. The public school experience, in short, was also positive. The children's positive attitudes toward school were reinforced; they felt competent. In all probability, their teachers identified them as competent and treated them as such. Once set in motion, success tended to breed success, resulting in the program/control differences in school performance. (Lazar et al., 1982, p. 64)

Data from two of the Consortium projects endorse this interpretation, with evidence that subjects received higher teacher ratings for social development, attitudes toward learning, and conduct (Beller, 1974; Schweinhart & Weikart, 1980). It must be emphasized that the performance of these children was quite poor in absolute terms even after preschool. Many program group children were referred to special education (e.g., Gordon, 23%; Gray, 3%; and Weikart, 14%). But without preschool, referral to special education became a very common experience indeed for control group children (Gordon, 54%; Gray, 29%; and Weikart, 28%; see Lazar et al., 1982, p. 32). Presumably, the ex-preschool children escaped that potential failure trap because they projected a more positive image to their teachers and to the school psychologists responsible for referral.

This is where the short-lived cognitive effects may have come in. Bearing in mind Zigler and Berman's warning, if during the early grades these children were seen as smarter as well as more adjusted to the demands of school, this could have been sufficient to trigger a more positive cycle of achievement and expectation (or perhaps more realistically, help prevent the worst aspects of the negative cycle of failure). This effect could carry the child through the later grades, long after the initial cognitive benefits had washed out. The Consortium authors have acknowledged the potential significance of these processes as part of the explanation for the transmission of long-term effects.

> Assignment to special classes in itself *affects* children. They are labelled in their own eyes and the eyes of others. Labels such as "emotionally disturbed" or "mildly retarded" have a life of their own, remaining on children's records for years and potentially affecting each new teacher's expectations for and treatment of a child. (Lazar et al., 1982, p. 58; emphasis added)

However, there are further implications of this line of reasoning that have been much less widely acknowledged; namely that a characteristic of the school context into which children moved *after* participating in a preschool program may have played a significant part in explaining the apparent power of that program to modify those children's fortunes in the long term.

To summarize the analysis so far, early intervention appears to have been effective not because in itself it fundamentally altered children's psychological functioning. Rather, in the short term it appears to have rendered them better able to cope with the demands of schooling at a critical time when their identities within the education system were being established. To use a metaphor from the world of athletics, the process of long-term effectiveness does not appear to be like a marathon 15-year test of the stamina of a single runner. Rather, it resembles a relay race, in which the burst of superior performance in the first runner (such as cognitive abilities and social adjustment) soon fades but not before the baton has been passed to later runners on the team (such as parent and teacher expectations, avoidance of referral to special classes, and so on), each of which transmits and even increases that initial superiority.

To put it another way, within the school system at that time, special education referral and retention in grade appear to have functioned as gateways that steered many disadvantaged children down a pathway of low expectations and achievement. There is nothing inevitable about special education serving these functions. It is nonetheless salutary to note that the originator of one of the IQ tests that has been widely applied as the gatekeeper in this process, Binet, harbored no illusions about the consequences of referral. He noted that "it will never be to one's credit to have attended a special school" (quoted in Lazerson, 1975, p. 50). Arguably, preschool intervention was so effective because in the short-term it acted on gatekeeper variables like IQ.

The significance of this process for the interpretation of early intervention effects can be clarified by analogy with a British educational practice that was common during the postwar period. At that time, the 11+ examination was widely employed to determine whether children went on to a grammar or secondary modern school. During the weeks and months leading up to the 11+, it became common for teachers to coach their children on tasks similar to those in the exam. If a systematic experiment had been set up to evaluate the long-term effects of pre-11+ coaching, it is reasonable to expect that experimental group children would have gone on to perform better throughout schooling and in the final examinations, more frequently gained access to universities, and even been more successful in adult life, compared with control group children who had no particular preparation. What would be the appropriate conclusion from such findings? Would it be that the last few months of primary school are a sensitive or critical period in the formation of children's competencies? Such a conclusion is doubtful. A more plausible explanation would recognize that the primary school program only appeared to have such a profound impact because of its proximity to the 11+ gateway, which would fundamentally shape their future.

The process of early intervention effectiveness is not as straightforward as this 11+ example, but the implication is that the evidence of long-term effects is the product of a more complex and more subtle process than any simple reading of the data would suggest. A good deal of attention has been paid here to the potential importance of referral to special education and retention in grade as transmission pathways that could have transformed short-term effects into long-term outcomes. Many other important transmission pathways are probably unknown because they have not been measured. Those that were identified in the Consortium studies and that appear to be significant pathways include the self-concept and educational attitudes of the children, as well as the attitudes and aspirations of their parents. From interview data collected in 1976, it became clear that ex-preschool children were significantly more achievement oriented, and their parents were more satisfied with their children's progress, even after controlling for their actual progress (Lazar et al., 1982). In short, preschool intervention was affecting children, their teachers, and their parents, both directly (e.g., children were more competent) and indirectly (e.g., the children projected a more positive impression, which modified parental aspirations as well as teachers' decision making).

The perspective that emerges from this analysis recognizes that no social action affects an individual in isolation. The long-term effects of an early intervention cannot be understood without reference to the social context within which that intervention is introduced and within which an individual's subsequent development is enmeshed. The importance of this perspective is increasingly being advocated by developmental theorists. In his review of the relationship between developmental research and public policy, Bronfenbrenner (1974b) appealed for "the study of human development in context" (p. 5) and has subsequently proposed an "ecological" framework for research, of which his hypotheses 48–50 are especially pertinent to this analysis (Bronfenbrenner, 1979, pp. 286–288). An influential collection of articles edited by Richards (1974) drew attention to similar issues, and it has been followed up by a further collection in which, to put it at its simplest, the authors argued "that social context is, at a variety of levels, intrinsic to the developmental process itself; rather than the icing of the cake it is as much a part of the structure as the flour or eggs that may be used to make it" (Richards & Light, 1986, p. 1). At a more theoretical level, this perspective has been described as "social constructionism" (Harre, 1986). A closely related line of argument has been developed by Kessen (1979, p. 819; see also Kessel & Siegel, 1983). Finally, one other expression of this general perspective is particularly suited to the study of intervention effects. The "transactional model" (Sameroff, 1975; Sameroff & Chandler, 1975) has the virtue of recognizing not only that effects are the result of a complex interaction of variables in home and school, throughout the school years and beyond, but also that the children themselves play an active part in the process through the images they project and the self-concept they acquire of themselves, either as competent and motivated, or apathetic, problematic, and unwilling.

POLICY IMPLICATIONS OF LONG-TERM EFFECTS

The potential power of a transactional model to explain the process of long-term effects has been acknowledged by a number of authors of intervention research (e.g., Lazar et al., 1982, p. 30; Schweinhart & Weikart, 1980, p. 5). However, the implications that adoption of such a model might have for policy have received much less attention. As already noted, if a direct effects model were supported by the data, it could provide a clear message for policy. Policymakers would be quite justified in drawing a general conclusion about the value of quality preschool programs in disadvantaged children's development, their power to reduce the need for special education services, and the enduring quality of their effect right through into adulthood. By contrast, in the case of a transactional model, the significance of intervention as the cause of greater competence in school and adult life is not nearly as cut and dried. The long-term significance of any impact it makes on the child depends on the mediation of other processes in family and school. The importance, and even existence, of these transmission pathways will undoubtedly vary from one culture to another and one school system to another. They may even vary between one experimental project and an individual community Head Start, and between one birth cohort and another. Trying to establish the potential of early intervention becomes a little like trying to establish the contribution of heredity. The pressure from policymakers is for an absolute figure, but in social scientific terms it makes little sense. As Campbell (1969) put it,

> Too many social scientists expect single experiments to settle issues once and for all. This may be a mistaken generalization from the history of great crucial experiments in physics and chemistry. . . . Because we social scientists have less ability to achieve "experimental isolation," because we have good reason to expect our treatment effects to interact significantly with a wide variety of social factors many of which we have not yet mapped, we have much greater need for replication experiments than do the physical sciences. (pp. 427–428)

Arguably, one should not even expect results of replication experiments to settle the issue once and for all either. Such is the nature of human development that an identical early experience may be found to result in quite different outcomes according to the cultural context in which it occurred. Cultural context includes not only the constellation of other situational variables that interact with the impact of a specific experience but also the different meanings ascribed to the experience by participants, as well as by those who influence their development.

Clearly, in adopting this perspective, there are dangers of substituting an untenable universalistic model of human development with an extreme culturally relativistic model, which, as Campbell has acknowledged, risks becoming "ontological nihilism" (cited in Edelstein, 1983, p. 52). Thus, it is important to emphasize that this perspective can be translated into a positive agenda for conducting and interpreting research. Brief reference to another area of human development will make the point. In reviewing cross-generational data from three British cohort studies, Wadsworth (1986) argued that differences in cultural attitude toward divorce during different epochs may modify the impact of that trauma on children. Wadsworth cited evidence from a 1946 cohort for which an association was found between the experience of parental separation or divorce during children's first five years and the incidence of criminal convictions among boys by the age of 21. He postulated a series of transmission pathways that might account for this relationship, including the social stigma associated with divorce at that time, which may have altered the relationship of children to significant adults with whom they came into contact. Most important, he recognized that the effect of this transmission pathway might be specific to the era in which these children grew up, during which professionals were encouraged to hold strong expectations that children would be severely adversely affected by the experience.

> Further and more detailed comparison of the cohorts will help to show the relevance of the postulated stigmatizing action of teachers' and community nurses' attitudes, since the prevailing views of the effects of parental divorce and separation on children have changed so much during the time that these three cohort studies have taken place. (Wadsworth, 1986, p. 126)

If this general principle is applied to early intervention data, the central issue for policy becomes whether contextual conditions are in fact similar between the site of data (in this case preschool programs experienced by children growing up in the 1960s) and the site for policy (whether contemporary Head Start or school kindergarten programs in the United States, or preschool in other industrialized or third world countries). If so, it may be reasonable to assume that the magnitude of initial early intervention effects would be as great and that there would be transmission pathways sufficient to transform short-term effects into long-term outcomes. If these conditions were not satisfied, however, serious questions must be raised about the validity of drawing general conclusions for policy. Hypothetically, the magnitude of preschool intervention effects might be attenuated in a setting where one transmission pathway was missing. Of course, they might also actually be amplified if different conditions generated an even stronger transmission pathway.

The case of Latin American countries provides a clear illustration of this. Halpern and Myers (1985) have noted that both the more acute effects of poverty on development and the very different context of schooling might well modify the effects of preschool intervention:

> The conditions of schooling in the developing countries—large classes, few instructional resources, often poorly trained teachers, an inadequate number of "places" in each grade—are such that the newly acquired skills that preschool participants bring to primary school may be less influential than in the US in shaping the course of children's school careers. When *promotion policies are only loosely tied to children's*

abilities, when there is no special education to be "avoided," and when there are resources for only 10 or 20 per cent of primary school participants to complete secondary school, positive long-term effects on the course of children's school careers found in the US may not be replicated in developing countries. (p. 16; emphasis added)

Similar reservations can be made about replicability in Britain, where the most clear discrepancy with the United States is the absence of retention in grade or equivalent referral procedures. What significance that might have for the transmission of preschool effects is a matter for speculation. The question is whether there are equivalent processes in the British school system that might stimulate the contribution of these procedures to the determination of children's success and failure in the American school system.

The lesson from this analysis is that acceptance of a transactional model to account for long-term effects modifies the kind of messages that can be inferred for policy. The Consortium data have yielded valuable information not only about the impact of preschool interventions but also indirectly about the impact of school practices on children's educational progress. A neglected implication of this research is that although it has provided good evidence of the power of early intervention to alter children's life chances, it has also pointed to other strategies that could have been employed to achieve this end, notably the modification of school practices that contribute to the process of failure. The policy significance of this implication has been highlighted by Liddell (1987) in reviewing South African government plans to introduce a preschool enrichment program for Black children based on British and American models. Liddell noted that of the 58% of Black South African children who failed to achieve the required standard during the first four years of schooling, 60% were judged failures by the end of the first year. She concluded that "failure rates might be lessened more effectively by modifications in the Grade One curriculum, rather than by the implementation of preschool enrichment schemes" (p. 129).

In this context, it is worth remembering that for many of those who set up experimental preschool projects in the United States in the 1960s, a belief in the potential of preschool was only part of the motive. The way poor children, especially poor, low ability, Black children were treated within the school system was a source of deep frustration. For example, in 1962 David Weikart was responsible for psychological services in Ypsilanti, Michigan.

> Children unable to learn at the standard rate were seen simply as failures. The major remedy of choice was to require students to repeat grades until they learned the necessary skills. This practice produced, in Ypsilanti, the outlandish result of approximately 50 per cent of all

ninth-graders being from one to five years behind in grade, and a 50 per cent dropout rate with legal school-leaving occurring for some youngsters as early as seventh grade. (Weikart, Bond, & McNeil, 1978, p. 2)

It is notable that Head Start was established in 1965 to provide federal funds directly to local community agencies (and it still does). Perhaps bypassing practices common in the public school system was viewed as an important first step in helping the disadvantaged child. In short, preschool was being justified not only because it could compensate for presumed deficiencies in children's home life but also because it could modify the undesirable effects of deficiencies in the school system. So, although the pragmatic case for early intervention in the Consortium data is certainly a strong one, from a child development standpoint it might be argued, to put it bluntly, that this is evidence for preschool for the worst of possible reasons!

This is not all, however. Insofar as special education and grade retention practices played a significant role in the transmission of long-term effects, then any changes in those practices might alter, and possibly weaken, the measurable long-term impact of preschool intervention. This is not an entirely hypothetical argument. Concern about the experience of disadvantaged children in the school system that was part of the rationale for establishing Head Start in the 1960s was translated during the 1970s into widespread litigation over the inadequacies of educational opportunity for handicapped children, culminating in the implementation of the Education for All Handicapped Children Act in 1975 (Abeson & Zettel, 1977). The requirement of this law that children identified as handicapped receive education in the "least restrictive environment" has discouraged school authorities from widespread use of special education classes, as well as sparking off a new wave of research designed to establish the relative educational merits of special classes versus mainstreaming for children with various categories of handicaps (e.g., Heller, 1982). If these reforms have been effective, then the school context in which contemporary preschool interventions are embedded will be different. The implication is that school procedures prevalent in the 1980s may no longer be reproducing the function that 1960s referral practices served in the transformation of initial preschool effects into long-term outcomes. Consequently, the impact of preschool intervention on the long-term fortunes of disadvantaged children who border on the category of educable mentally retarded might well be weaker than a literal interpretation of data from the Consortium projects would predict.

Thus far, the emphasis of this analysis has been on the policy significance of school procedures that appear to have played a significant part in the transmission of long-term effects. It would be wrong, however, to place too much emphasis on the importance of these variables to the transactional process. They have been discussed at length here because they are so clearly illustrative of a general principle that applies to any attempt to derive general conclusions about the long-term effects of particular experiences. The school procedures discussed here represent only one type of transmission pathway identified in Consortium analyses, and the policy significance of the research does not rest on this set of variables alone.

Another major pathway is via family attitudes to their children's schooling and prospects. The same considerations about deriving policy implications apply to these as well. Clearly, family attitudes have not been subject to such readily discernible shifts as the reforms in policy affecting special education. However, there is some reason to believe that family and community processes may have been particularly sensitively attuned to preschool effects at the time the Consortium projects began their work. Gray, Ramsey, and Klaus (1983) have come closest to acknowledging this. The period of the early 1960s was a special time for poor Black Americans and their families. It was a period of desegregation and civil rights legislation, when the voice of Martin Luther King, Jr., rang in the ears not just of Black Americans but of the world. For Black parents, it was a time of hope, which they focused on their children. Of course, for preschool workers, it was also a time of great optimism; they were initiating their project against the political background of the War on Poverty and the psychological background of optimism about the power of early experience (e.g., Bloom, 1964; Hunt, 1961). Faith, hope, and optimism are difficult qualities to measure, but that does not mean that they should be forgotten when judging the implications of these studies. As Gray (1985) put it, "the times were on our side." Whether they are still so several decades later could have an important bearing on the legitimacy of assuming that what has been achieved through preschool interventions with children born in the early 1960s would be reproduced in the same degree or kind if the experiments were repeated with children born in the 1980s or 1990s.

In short, interpreting the early intervention evidence for policy requires more than recognition of questions about the internal validity of the data (although these also have to be addressed). The focus of this article has been on a different set of issues that arise out of acknowledgment that the effects of early intervention come about as a result of a complex set of interactions between the initial effects of the preschool program and a set of mediating variables in the family and school. Variations in the context of family and school may have a significant impact on the extent of measurable long-term effects of preschool intervention. Consequently, generalizations about the potential of any particular educational or social strategy risk being misleading unless they take full account not only of the features of the strategy itself but also of the cultural and educational system in which that potential is embedded. That lesson applies both within national systems, which vary geographically and are subject to continuous evolution, and across national systems, where the organization of schooling varies, as do the economic and cultural bases on which it is founded.

CONCLUSION

In a frequently quoted analysis of the potential for research-based policy development, Campbell (1969) argued for "an experimental approach to social reform, an approach in which we try out new programs . . . and in which we retain, imitate, modify, or discard them on the basis of apparent effectiveness on the multiple imperfect criteria available" (p. 409). The research reviewed in this article has considerable potential to inform the policy process in the terms in which Campbell anticipated, provided it is recognized that where human development is concerned even an experimental approach can rarely yield definitive universally applicable statements about the extent to which a program is effective.

However, even if it were possible to identify unequivocal messages in this area of research, Campbell's is still a very optimistic view of the relationship that might be established between research and policy. Granted that American politicians and administrators are reported to be more attuned to the messages of research than their counterparts in other countries such as Britain (Sharpe, 1978), these messages are nonetheless rarely translated directly into reforms. More frequently, they are drawn into a complex web of sometimes inconsistent and frequently competing lines of argument, public pressure, and political priority. This process has been illustrated by Zigler (1987) in the movement to extend public education to four-year-olds. He argued that the evidence of early intervention research has been applied, and in some respects misapplied, as part of an educational case for reform that also springs from concern about the failings of secondary schools. These educational lines of argument have also been overlaid by a quite different issue, namely, the problem of responding to parental demands for more adequate day-care services in the early years, which might be partly but not completely resolved by more kindergarten provision.

Arguably, social scientists have never been as remote from the process of informing public policy as is implied by conventional images of dispassionate scientific inquiry. In recent years, however, the relationship between the impartiality of research and the partiality attached to the solutions that are inferred from that research has been extensively reappraised (e.g., Hatch, 1982; Howard, 1985; Robinson, 1984). In this case, psychologists have increasingly been drawn into the policy arena. They are no longer content to merely illuminate social problems or offer solutions to be implemented by others but are actively campaigning for public policies that appear to have been demonstrated by the research to be effective. For instance,

> Equity is still an attainable goal of social policy in the United States. To achieve this goal we may have to use some of the strategies that proved successful in the past and discard others that were not useful. In the realm of child and family policy, this could mean *new roles for scientists* and experts *as advocates*. (Valentine & Zigler, 1983, p. 279; emphasis added)

The strenuous efforts of the Consortium authors to communicate their findings to influential policy figures clearly illustrate this role (Datta, 1983a), as do the carefully coordinated dissemination efforts of the High/ Scope "Voices for Children" project (Haskins & Gallagher, 1984; High/ Scope Educational Research Foundation, 1984).

In the short term, these advocacy efforts have certainly served an important political function in strengthening the lobby for increased expenditure and further development of early childhood programs. They have been offered as powerful empirical support to the popular sentiment that experiences in the early years are formative of personal fortunes in adult life. However, in this article, I have argued that in the long run, the scientific value of this body of research lies in its power to illustrate the inadequacy of such an appealing view of the role of early childhood intervention in attaining the goals of social policy. On the one hand, that view places unrealistic emphasis on the early years as a period for effecting permanent individual change through educational and social programs. On the other hand, it distracts attention from other concurrent and subsequent processes in community and school that interact with experiences in the early years to determine long-term patterns of development. Accordingly, a first responsibility of social science advocacy is to avoid perpetuating and indeed to actively seek to counteract the tendency in public debate to adopt simple deterministic views of the scope for intervention in human development.

The evidence of long-term effects needs to be introduced into public debate within the context of a model of human development that recognizes the many other factors besides the preschool program that contributed to the transmission of its effects and that need to be taken into consideration when interpreting the evidence for policy. In some settings, these factors might not be present, whereas in others, the particular network of influences on child development might suggest an alternative focus for intervention that might prove more fruitful than a preschool program.

One of the problems in communicating the messages of this research is that experimental design in itself encourages disproportionate attention to be directed toward the critical manipulated variable as *the* cause of observed differences between experimental and control groups, no matter how remote in time or nature the outcome measures are from the intervention. Yet failure to communicate a more sophisticated understanding of long-term effects carries certain risks. Expectations are becoming narrowly focused on the apparent power of early intervention to tackle social problems single-handedly. Such expectations are unlikely to be realized in practice. In the long run, this could undermine public sympathies toward early childhood programs, as well as diminishing the credibility of experimental research as a tool of social reform.

REFERENCES

Abeson, A., & Zettel, J. (1977). The end of a quiet revolution: The United States Education for All Handicapped Children Act. *Exceptional Children*, *44*, 115–128.

Administration for Children, Youth and Families. (1985). *Project Head Start: Statistical fact sheet.* Washington, DC: Department of Health and Human Services.

Beller, E. K. (1974). Impact of early education on disadvantaged children. In S. Ryan (Ed.), *A report on longitudinal evaluations of pre-school programs* (Vol. 1, pp. 15–48). Washington, DC: Department of Health, Education, and Welfare.

Bereiter, C. (1986). Does direct instruction cause delinquency? *Early Childhood Research Quarterly*, *1*, 289–292.

Berfenstam, R., & William-Olsson, I. (1974). *Early child-care in Sweden.* London: Gordon & Breach.

Besharov, D. J., & Hartle, T. W. (1987). Head Start: Making a popular program work. *Pediatrics*, *79*(3), 440–441.

Bloom, B. S. (1964). *Stability and change in human characteristics.* New York: Wiley.

Brim, O. G., & Dunstan, J. (1983). Translating research into policy for children. *American Psychologist*, *38*, 85–90.

Bronfenbrenner, U. (1974a). *Is early intervention effective?* Washington, DC: Department of Health, Education, and Welfare.

Bronfenbrenner, U. (1974b). Developmental research, public policy, and the ecology of childhood. *Child Development*, *45*(1), 1–5.

Bronfenbrenner, U. (1979). *The ecology of human development.* Cambridge, MA: Harvard University Press.

Bryant, D. M., & Ramey, C. T. (1985). Prevention-oriented infant education programs. *Journal of Children in Contemporary Society*, *17*(1), 17–35.

Campbell, D. T. (1969). Reforms as experiments. *American Psychologist*, *25*, 409–429.

Casto, G., & Mastropieri, M. A. (1986). The efficacy of early intervention programs: A meta-analysis. *Exceptional Children*, *52*, 417–424.

Cicirelli, V. (1984). The misinterpretation of the Westinghouse study: A reply to Zigler and Berman. *American Psychologist, 39*, 915–916.

Clarke, A. M., & Clarke, A. D. B. (1981). Sleeper effects in development: Fact or artifact? *Developmental Review, 1*, 344–360.

Clarke, A. M., & Clarke, A. D. B. (1982). Intervention and sleeper effects: A reply to Victoria Seitz. *Developmental Review, 2*, 76–78.

Clement, J. R. B., Schweinhart, L. J., Barnett, W. S., Epstein, A. S., & Weikart, D. P. (1984). *Changed lives: The effects of the Perry Pre-School Program on youths through age 19* (Monograph No. 8). Ypsilanti, MI: High/Scope.

Consortium for Developmental Continuity. (1977). *The persistence of pre-school effects.* Washington, DC: Department of Health, Education, and Welfare.

Consortium for Longitudinal Studies. (1978). *Lasting effects after preschool.* Washington, DC: Department of Health, Education, and Welfare.

Consortium for Longitudinal Studies. (1983). *As the twig is bent.* London: Erlbaum.

Cook, S. W. (1984). The 1954 social science statement and school desegregation: A reply to Gerard. *American Psychologist, 39*, 819–832.

Crittenden, A. (1984, November 29). A Head Start pays off in the end. *The Wall Street Journal.*

Darlington, R. B., Royce, J. M., Snipper, A. S., Murray, H. W., & Lazar, I. (1980). Pre-school programs and later school competence of children from low-income families. *Science, 208*, 202–204.

Datta, L. (1976). The impact of the Westinghouse/Ohio evaluation on the development of Project Head Start. In C. Abt (Ed.), *The evaluation of social programs.* Beverly Hills, CA: Sage.

Datta, L. (1983a). A tale of two studies: The Westinghouse/Ohio evaluation of Project Head Start and the Consortium for Longitudinal Studies report. *Studies in Educational Evaluation, 8*, 271–280.

Datta, L. (1983b). We never promised you a rose garden but one may have grown anyhow. In Consortium for Longitudinal Studies, *As the twig is bent* (pp. 467–480). London: Erlbaum.

Di Lorenzo, L. T. (1969). *Pre-kindergarten programs for educationally disadvantaged children: Final report.* Washington, DC: U.S. Office of Education.

Dunst, C. J., & Snyder, S. W. (1986). A critique of the Utah State University early intervention meta-analysis research. *Exceptional Children, 53*, 269–276.

Edelstein, W. (1983). Cultural constraints on development and the vicissitudes of progress. In F. S. Kessel & A. W. Siegel (Eds.), *The child and other cultural inventions* (pp. 48–81). New York: Praeger.

Education for All Handicapped Children Act, Pub. L. No. 94-142 (1975).

Education of the Handicapped Act Amendments of 1986, Pub. L. No. 99-457.

The effect of segregation and the consequences of desegregation: A social science statement. Appendix to apellants' briefs: *Brown v. Board of Education of Topeka, Kansas.* (1953). *Minnesota Law Review, 37*, 427–439.

Farrington, D. (1985). Delinquency prevention in the 1980s. *Journal of Adolescence, 8*, 3–16.

Gamble, T. J., & Zigler, E. F. (1989). The Head Start Synthesis Project: Review and critique. *Journal of Applied Developmental Psychology, 10*(2), 267–274.

Garber, H., & Heber, R. (1983). Modification of predicted cognitive development in high-risk children through early intervention. In M. K. Detterman & R. J. Sternberg (Eds.), *How much can intelligence be increased?* (pp. 121–137). Norwood, NJ: Ablex.

Gerard, H. B. (1983). School desegregation: The social science role. *American Psychologist, 38*, 869–877.

Gersten, R. (1986). Response to "Consequences of three preschool curriculum models through age 15." *Early Childhood Research Quarterly, 1*, 293–302.

Goldfarb, W. (1945). Effects of psychological deprivation in infancy and subsequent stimulation. *American Journal of Psychiatry, 102*, 18–33.

Gray, S. (1985, August). *The early training project.* Paper presented at the annual meeting of the American Psychological Association, Toronto, Canada.

Gray, S. W., Ramsey, B. K., & Klaus, R. A. (1982). *From 3 to 20: The Early Training Project.* Baltimore: University Park Press.

Gray, S. W., Ramsey, B. K., & Klaus, R. A. (1983). The Early Training Project: 1962–1980. In Consortium for Longitudinal Studies, *As the twig is bent* (pp. 33–70). London: Erlbaum.

Guralnick, M. J. (1988). Efficacy research in early childhood intervention programs. In S. L. Odom & M. B. Karnes (Eds.), *Early intervention for infants & children with handicaps: An empirical base.* Baltimore: Brookes.

Guralnick, M. J., & Bennett, F. C. (1987). *The effectiveness of early intervention for at-risk and handicapped children.* New York: Academic Press.

Halpern, R., & Myers, R. (1985). *Effects of early childhood intervention on primary school progress and performance in the developing countries.* Unpublished manuscript. Ypsilanti, MI: High/Scope-U.S. Agency for International Development.

Harre, R. (1986). The step to social constructionism. In M. P. M. Richards & P. Light (Eds.), *Children of social worlds* (pp. 287–296). Cambridge, England: Polity Press.

Harrell, R. (1983). *The effects of the Head Start program on children's cognitive development: Preliminary report of the Head Start evaluation, synthesis and utilization project.* Washington, DC: U.S. Department of Health and Human Services.

Haskins, R., & Gallagher, J. J. (1984). *The Voices for Children Project: A report to the Carnegie Foundation.* Chapel Hill: University of North Carolina, Bush Institute for Child and Family Policy.

Hatch, O. (1982). Psychology, society and politics. *American Psychologist, 37*, 1031–1037.

Head Start gets a high grade. (September 24, 1984). *U.S. News and World Report.*

Head Start saves children and money. (September 19, 1984). *San Diego Tribune.*

Heller, K. A. (1982). Effects of special education placement on educable mentally retarded children. In K. A. Heller, W. H. Holtzman, & S. Messick (Eds.), *Placing children in special education: A strategy for equity* (pp. 262–299). Washington, DC: National Academy Press.

Herzog, E., Newcomb, C. H., & Cisin, I. H. (1974). Double deprivation: The less they have the less they learn. In S. Ryan (Ed.), *A report on longitudinal evaluation of pre-school programs* (Vol. 1, pp. 61–88). Washington, DC: U.S. Department of Health, Education and Welfare.

High/Scope Educational Research Foundation. (1984). *Response to the Haskins and Gallagher report on the Voices for Children Project.* Ypsilanti, MI: Author.

Howard, G. S. (1985). The role of values in the science of psychology. *American Psychologist, 40,* 255–266.

Hubbell, R. (1983). *A review of Head Start since 1970.* Washington, DC: U.S. Department of Health and Human Services.

Hunt, J. McV. (1961). *Intelligence and experience.* New York: Ronald Press.

Karnes, M. B., Zehrbach, R. R., & Teska, J. A. (1974). The Karnes pre-school program: Rationale, curricular offerings and follow-up data. In S. Ryan (Ed.), *Report on longitudinal evaluations of pre-school programs* (pp. 95–108). Washington, DC: U.S. Department of Health, Education and Welfare.

Kessel, F. S., & Siegel, A. W. (Eds.). (1983). *The child and other cultural inventions.* New York: Praeger.

Kessen, W. (1979). The American child and other cultural inventions. *American Psychologist, 34,* 815–820.

Klaus, R. A., & Gray, S. W. (1968). The Early Training Project for disadvantaged children. *Monographs of the Society for Research in Child Development, 33* (4, Serial No. 120).

Kotelchuck, M., & Richmond, J. B. (1987). Head Start: Evolution of a successful comprehensive child development program. *Pediatrics, 79*(3), 441–445.

Lazar, I., Darlington, R. B., Murray, H. W., & Snipper, A. S. (1982). Lasting effects of early education: A report from the Consortium for Longitudinal Studies. *Monograph of Society for Research in Child Development, 47* (195, Serial No. 2-3).

Lazerson, M. (1970). Social reform and early childhood education: Some historical perspectives. *Urban Education, 5,* 84–102.

Lazerson, M. (1975). Educational institutions and mental subnormality: Notes on writing a history. In M. J. Begab & S. A. R. Richardson (Eds.), *The mentally retarded and society: A social science perspective* (pp. 38–52). Baltimore: View Park Press.

Lewin, R. (1977). Head Start pays off. *New Scientist,* 3rd March, 508–509.

Liddell, C. (1987). Some issues regarding the introduction of pre-school enrichment programmes for black South African children. *International Journal of Educational Development, 7*(2), 127–131.

Maccoby, E. E., Kahn, A. J., & Everett, B. A. (1983). The role of psychological research in the formation of policies affecting children. *American Psychologist, 38*, 80–84.

McKey, R. H., Condelli, L., Ganson, H., Barrett, B., McConkey, C., & Plantz, M. (1985). *The impact of Head Start on children, families and communities* (Final report of Head Start Evaluation, Synthesis and Utilization Project). Washington, DC: CSR Inc.

Myers, R. G., & Hertenberg, R. (1987). *The eleven who survive: Toward a re-examination of early childhood development program options and costs* (The World Bank Education and Training Report No. EDT 69). Washington, DC: World Bank.

Ramey, C. T., & Campbell, F. A. (1987). The Carolina Abecedarian Project: An educational experiment concerning human malleability. In J. J. Gallagher & C. T. Ramey (Eds.), *The malleability of children* (pp. 127–139). Baltimore, MD: Brookes.

Ramey, C. T., Yeates, K. O., & Short, E. T. (1984). The plasticity of intellectual development: Insights from preventive intervention. *Child Development, 55*, 1913–1925.

Richards, M. P. M. (Ed.) (1974). *Integration of a child into a social world.* London: Cambridge University Press.

Richards, M. P. M., & Light, P. (Eds.). (1986). *Children of social worlds.* Cambridge, England: Polity Press.

Richmond, J. B., Stipek, D. J., & Zigler, E. F. (1979). A decade of Head Start. In E. F. Zigler & J. Valentine (Eds)., *Project Head Start: A legacy of the war on poverty* (pp. 135–152). New York: Free Press.

Robinson, D. N. (1984). Ethics and advocacy. *American Psychologist, 39*, 787–793.

Royce, J. M., Darlington, R. B., & Murray, H. W. (1983). Pooled analysis: Findings across studies. In Consortium for Longitudinal Studies, *As the twig is bent* (pp. 411–460). London: Erlbaum.

Sameroff, A. J. (1975). Early influences on development: Fact or fancy? *Merrill-Palmer Quarterly, 21*(4), 267–294.

Sameroff, A., & Chandler, M. (1975). Reproductive risk and the continuum of caretaking casualty. In F. Horowitz (Ed.), *Review of child development research* (Vol. 4, pp. 187–244). Chicago: University of Chicago Press.

Scarr, S. (Ed.). (1979). Psychology and children: Current research and practice. *American Psychologist, 34*, 809–1039.

Schweinhart, L. J., & Weikart, D. P. (1980). *Young children grow up* (Monograph 7). Ypsilanti, MI: High/Scope.

Schweinhart, L. J., & Weikart, D. P. (1986, January). What do we know so far? A review of the Head Start Synthesis Project. *Young Children*, pp. 49–55.

Schweinhart, L. J., Weikart, D. P., & Larner, M. B. (1986a). Consequences of three curriculum models through age 15. *Early Childhood Research Quarterly, 1*, 15–54.

Schweinhart, L. J., Weikart, D. P., & Larner, M. B. (1986b). Child-initiated activities in early childhood programs help prevent delinquency. *Early Childhood Research Quarterly*, 1, 303–311.

Seitz, V. (1981). Intervention and sleeper effects: A reply to Clarke and Clarke. *Developmental Review*, 1, 361–373.

Sharpe, L. J. (1978). The social scientist and policy-making in Britain and America: A comparison. In M. Bulmer (Ed.), *Social policy research* (pp. 303–312). London: Macmillan.

Skodak, M., & Skeels, H. M. (1949). A final follow-up study of one hundred adopted children. *Journal of Genetic Psychology*, 75, 85–125.

Spitz, R. A. (1945). Hospitalism: An enquiry into the genesis of psychiatric conditions in early childhood. *Psychoanalytic Study of the Child*, 1, 53–74.

Strain, P. S., & Smith, B. J. (1986). A counter-interpretation of early intervention effects: A response to Casto and Mastropieri. *Exceptional Children*, 53, 260–265.

Takanishi, R., DeLeon, P. H., & Pallak, M. S. (1983). Psychology and public policy affecting children, youth, and families. *American Psychologist*, 38, 67–69.

Tizard, J., Moss, P., & Perry, J. (1976). *All our children*. London: Temple Smith/ New Society.

Valentine, J., & Zigler, E. (1983). Head Start: A case study in the development of social policy for children and families. In E. Zigler, S. L. Kagan, & E. Klugman (Eds.), *Children, families and government: Perspectives on American social policy* (pp. 260–288). New York: Cambridge University Press.

Wadsworth, M. (1986). Evidence from three birth cohort studies for long term and cross-generational effects on the development of children. In M. P. M. Richards & P. Light (Eds.), *Children of social worlds* (pp. 116–134). Cambridge, England: Polity Press.

Weikart, D. P., Bond, J. T., & McNeil, J. T. (1978). *The Ypsilanti Perry Pre-School Project: Pre-school years and longitudinal results through fourth grade* (Monograph 3). Ypsilanti, MI: High/Scope.

Weikart, D. P., Epstein, A. S., Schweinhart, L. J., & Bond, J. T. (1978). *The Ypsilanti Pre-School Curriculum Demonstration Project: Preschool years and longitudinal results* (Monograph 4). Ypsilanti, MI: High/Scope.

Westinghouse Learning Corporation. (1969). *The impact of Head Start: An evaluation of the effects of Head Start on children's cognitive and affective development* (Report to Office of Economic Opportunity). Washington, DC: Clearinghouse for Federal, Scientific and Technical Information.

White, K. R. (1986). Efficacy of early intervention. *Journal of Special Education*, 19(4), 401–416.

Woodhead, M. (1985). Pre-school education has long term effects: But can they be generalized? *Oxford Review of Education*, 11(2), 133–155.

Zigler, E. F. (1976). Head Start: Not a program but an evolving concept. In J. D. Andrews (Ed.), *Early childhood education: It's an art? It's a science?* (pp. 1–14). Washington, DC: National Association for the Education of Young Children.

Zigler, E. F. (1984). Meeting the critics on their own terms. *American Psychologist, 39*, 916–917.

Zigler, E. F. (1987). Formal schooling for four-year-olds? No. *American Psychologist, 42*, 254–260.

Zigler, E. F., & Berman, W. (1983). Discerning the future of early childhood intervention. *American Psychologist, 38*, 894–906.

Zigler, E. F., & Trickett, P. K. (1978). IQ, social competence and evaluation of early childhood intervention programs. *American Psychologist, 33*, 789–798.

Zigler, E. F., & Valentine, J. (Eds.). (1979). *Project Head Start: A legacy of the War on Poverty.* New York: Free Press.

13

PSYCHOLOGY AND PUBLIC POLICY: TOOL OR TOOLMAKER?

BARUCH FISCHHOFF

Psychologists are needed by public policymakers whenever the outcomes of their policies either affect or depend on human behavior (Noll, 1985; Stokols & Altman, 1987). For example, in the context of environmental policy, psychological expertise is needed to (a) determine what people value in outdoors experiences (e.g., as an aid to designing parks or evaluating wilderness areas, Daniel & Vining, 1983); (b) assess the stressfulness of living near hazardous waste facilities, as an input to measuring their environmental impact (Baum & Singer, 1981); and (c) see how noise affects school performance, as a guide to siting freeways or retrofitting sound buffers (Cohen, Evans, Krantz, & Stokols, 1980).

By contrast, psychologists often *seem* needed by policymakers primarily when some of the public's behavior threatens their policies. For example, psychologists were asked (or allowed) to study home energy con-

Reprinted from *American Psychologist*, 45, 647–653. Copyright 1990 by the American Psychological Association.

I would like to thank Lita Furby for her continuing help in understanding these issues. Much of the research cited here was conducted in collaboration with other investigators, particularly Paul Slovic and Sarah Lichtenstein. Their contributions are gratefully acknowledged. They are not, however, to be held responsible for this personal interpretation of the interface between psychology and public policy.

Preparation of this chapter was supported by the National Science Foundation, under Grant No. SES-8715564 to Carnegie Mellon University. The views expressed are those of the author and do not represent those of the Foundation.

servation when a "wasteful" public appeared to be an obstacle to national energy independence (Aronson & O'Leary, 1983; McClelland & Cook, 1980). They were encouraged to study seat belt usage when nonusage increased pressure for mandatory airbags or unpopular seat belt laws (Geller, Paterson, & Talbott, 1982; Robertson, 1983). Economists functioning as psychologists have been paid to ask laypeople what they would pay for environmental improvements in situations in which industries felt they had to pay too much to achieve those changes (Smith & Desvousges, 1986).

On the positive side, any invitation to psychologists reflects a sensitivity to human wants and needs. It offers us, as psychologists, an opportunity to "show our stuff," increasing policymakers' understanding of what psychologists can do. The evidence that we produce ought to be better than the undisciplined speculations that would come in its stead. The funding to create that evidence should enhance the scientific base and public prestige of our profession, attracting better students (and funding) to it.

On the other hand, the terms of these invitations to study the public may be bad for both the public and the scientist. The invitation can harm the public whenever the presenting symptoms (described by policymakers) cast the public in a troublesome (or troublemaker's) role. Indeed, simply by accepting such descriptions, psychologists help undermine the public's political credibility. If they use their expertise to remedy such untoward behavior, then psychologists may shift the political balance against the public's best interest. Even by claiming to explain the public's behavior, psychologists can contribute to a sort of disenfranchisement—by reducing the perceived need to let the public speak for itself.

The terms of these invitations can be bad for science whenever they mislead us regarding the nature of the "problem." We may then be slow to understand what is actually happening, either in the field or in our own data. That means wasting our time and society's resources as well as missing the opportunity to be stretched by the confrontation with a reality outside our labs.

It would, of course, be naive to expect psychologists to be invited to *set* public policy regarding the environment or any other significant issue. Policy-making involves the allocation of resources, a right that is jealously guarded by elected and appointed officials (i.e., politicians and bureaucrats). In one way or another, they justify their actions by claiming to know what the public wants and needs. If they invite us, it is not to share their power, but to fortify it, by fine-tuning programs, anticipating and overcoming resistance, or guiding and legitimizing initiatives.

To some extent, these will be acceptable roles for psychologists. We did, after all, choose a profession rather than the explicit political life. On the other hand, when taking part in public policy issues, we often have greater aspirations than merely being hand servants of good government and efficient markets. We are attracted to issues because we care about their outcomes. We also know that those individuals closest to the locus of decision making have the greatest opportunity to influence its outcome. Scientists who get close can exert influence directly by what they say to policymakers and the press. They may do so indirectly by how they design policy-relevant studies. For example, Executive Order 12291 requires all significant federal actions to be justified in terms of cost-benefit analyses (Bentkover, Covello, & Mumpower, 1985). However, the technical definitions of *cost* and *benefit* used in these analyses do not follow logically from some basic science, but express political values (Campen, 1986; Fischhoff & Cox, 1985). By their choice of definition, the scientists who conduct such studies are, in effect, setting policy. Similar political power accompanies defining the terms of other quasi-scientific research, such as evaluation studies, public opinion polls, or risk analyses (Fischhoff, Watson, & Hope, 1984; Turner & Martin, 1985).

Handling direct political influence responsibly is relatively straightforward. We need to recognize that we have entered the political arena through a back door, realize the limits to our expertise and mandate, and acknowledge when we speak from our hearts rather than represent our evidence. When environmental issues seem too important to be left to environmental policymakers, any path to influence may seem legitimate. However, intellectual hygiene dictates that we recognize where our political agendas abut our research activities—even if we keep that insight to ourselves (Fischhoff, Pidgeon, & Fiske, 1983).

Handling indirect political influence is more difficult. It means examining the political philosophy underlying routine professional work. For example, what concept of *justice* guides the construction of stimuli in studies of perceived equity (Furby, 1986)? What outcomes do we decide to measure when evaluating clinical treatments? How do we describe women who have experienced sexual assaults and, indeed, the assaults themselves (Hindelang, Gottfredson, & Garofalo, 1978)?

In any life, professional or personal, it is hard, but potentially rewarding, to reflect on otherwise unquestioned assumptions. When our assumptions affect other people's fortunes, reflection becomes obligatory. Figuring out how policymakers might use us to further their own agendas can provide particular impetus, and perhaps some cues, to explore who we are. For those who desire the political life, one obvious path is to go where the action is. An alternative is to seek the politics wherever one is already, seeing how one's profession shapes and is shaped by the world.

To these ends, I will describe several episodes involving psychology and environmental policy, asking how well we have been able to create tools to help the public define and pursue its own interests, rather than becoming tools for manipulating the public to others' ends. I draw primarily from my own experiences. Not only is that material most readily accessible, but I can be most candid about the mistakes that I have made.

PERCEIVED RISKS

A critical question in many environmental controversies is "How much does the public know?" If the public understands environmental risks well, then it may be entitled to a more active role in their management. A knowledgeable public should, for example, be taken more seriously when it objects to the siting of an incinerator, the opening of a wetlands to "development," or the denial of information about what has been stored at a waste disposal dump. Not surprisingly, risk management debates are rife with claims and counterclaims about the public's scientific literacy and competence. These claims then are used to buttress proposals for right-to-know laws, consumer protection agencies, referendums, products liability reforms, warning labels, and the like (National Research Council, 1989).

Figure 1 shows one attempt to supplement anecdotal speculation about the public with systematic evidence. It contrasts the estimates of a group of educated laypeople with available public health statistics regarding the annual number of deaths from various causes. It was interpreted as showing two kinds of bias. The first is a flattening of the best-fit curve, relative to the identity line (representing completely accurate judgments). The second is a tendency to over- and underestimate certain death rates, relative to the fitted curve. This *secondary bias* was found to be predicted well by the relative *availability* of deaths from these causes as measured in several different ways (Combs & Slovic, 1979; Lichtenstein, Slovic, Fischhoff, Layman, & Combs, 1978; Tversky & Kahneman, 1973).

Figure 1 has had a remarkable public life, being cited extensively in policymakers' discussions of risk management (e.g., Starr & Whipple, 1980; Upton, 1982). Typically, it has been described as proving the public's ignorance (or even "irrationality") regarding risk issues with the attendant political ramifications. I have heard it described as proving the public's hopeless confusion about risks (e.g., nuclear power) that were not even in the study. Not only were these claims unwarranted by these results, but they went far beyond what could be shown in any single series of studies.

One response to such apparent distortions is to collect the missing data. Thus, one subsequent study found that similar subjects were quite well informed about the annual death rate (to that date) from nuclear power (Slovic, Fischhoff, & Lichtenstein, 1979). A second follow-up study found that making such numerical judgments is sufficiently unusual that whether people seem to overestimate or underestimate these rates depends on methodological details of how the question is asked (Fischhoff &

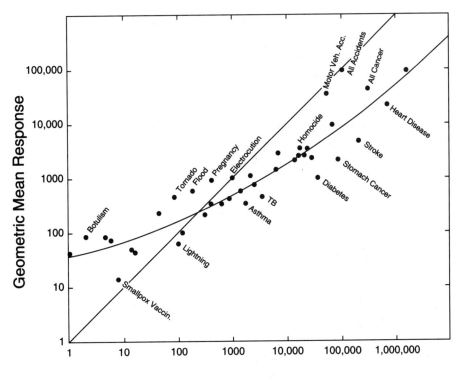

Figure 1. Laypersons' direct estimates of the frequency of various risks. The straight line represents accurate estimation. The curved line fits the subjects mean responses and shows a primary basis of overestimation of infrequent events and underestimation of frequent events. Deviations from the curved line were quite consistent for different groups of subjects and represent secondary biases. These secondary biases are emphasized in the text. Reprinted from "Judged Frequency of Lethal Events," by S. Lichtenstein, P. Slovic, B. Fischhoff, M. Layman, and B. Combs, 1978, *Journal of Experimental Psychology: Human Learning and Memory, 4,* p. 566. Copyright 1978 by the American Psychological Association. Reprinted with permission of the author.

MacGregor, 1983). A third study found that when people think about the "risks" of a technology, they factor in other features, such as its potential for catastrophic accidents as well as its routine death toll (Slovic, Fischhoff, & Lichtenstein, 1980). As a result, Figure 1 shows but a part of the lay public's risk perceptions.

A rather different response is to ask how policymakers reached their misinterpretations. One speculation is that they misunderstand the nature of social science data. Social scientists do not seem needed at all until things get out of hand (e.g., public protest over nuclear power). At that point, we are expected to explain (and perhaps alter) the public's views quickly. One study ought to produce confident conclusions. Alternative explanations need not be sought or tested.

A second speculation is that readers simply saw what they wanted to see in our results. The proponents of beleaguered technologies would like to believe that the central issue in the debate is the magnitude of risks, regarding which they are (or employ) the ranking experts. They would like to believe that *risk* refers to average-year fatalities, a subject on which they have the firmest data, rather than including catastrophic potential, which is hard to estimate. They would like to believe that they can deal with the public at arms' length and inexpensively, through a few social science studies, rather than engaging the public directly.

ACCEPTABLE RISK I

Some light on these speculations might be seen from the responses to a series of studies attempting to sketch a richer picture of the public's attitude toward risky technologies. Its point of departure was a study by Starr (1969) claiming to show, on the basis of historical data, that technologies with greater risks also have greater benefits. In addition, at any given level of risk, technologies whose risks are borne involuntarily have considerably greater benefit. Starr argued that our society works so well that these historical patterns show the risk–benefit tradeoffs that it wants. If so, then policymakers could determine the acceptability of a proposed technology by computing its expected risks and benefits and seeing whether those fit the patterns.

One obvious question about this upbeat interpretation is whether people's perceptions of these risks and benefits correspond to the values that Starr computed. After all, society works on the basis of what it sees, rather than what some expert computes.[1] We asked some publicly involved citizens to judge the current risks and benefits of various technologies (Fischhoff, Slovic, Lichtenstein, Read, & Combs, 1978). Their responses showed no correlation between perceived risks and benefits, indicating that they did not see societal institutions as successfully producing acceptable tradeoffs. This result fits the persistent result of opinion polls, showing the desire for greater environmental protection (e.g., Freudenberg & Rosa, 1984).

When risk levels were adjusted to what our subjects though they *should* be, a willingness to make tradeoffs emerged. In addition, more voluntary risks were allowed higher risk levels. However, voluntariness was not the only qualitative aspect of risk that seemed to justify a double standard. For example, more risk was also tolerable with technologies that were

---

[1]Indeed, the confidence in public risk perceptions implicit in this study seems in striking contrast to the lack of confidence usually expressed by the technical community. Questions have also been raised about the accuracy of Starr's calculations (Otway & Cohen, 1975).

well understood by science and that took their toll one by one, rather than in catastrophic incidents. As a basis for social policy, each of these features expresses quite a different principle. Voluntariness sounds like a civil rights issue; scientific understanding sounds like a question of prudence; how deaths are "packaged" sounds like a macabre question of taste.

These features tend to be highly correlated with one another across technologies, so that it is hard to tell which drives a correlation with the acceptability of risks (Hohenemser, Kates, & Slovic, 1983; Slovic et al., 1980). In order to show these interrelationships, we published Figure 2. It shows a factor analysis of ratings for various technologies on nine qualitative features of risk. This figure and variants of it (e.g., Slovic et al.,

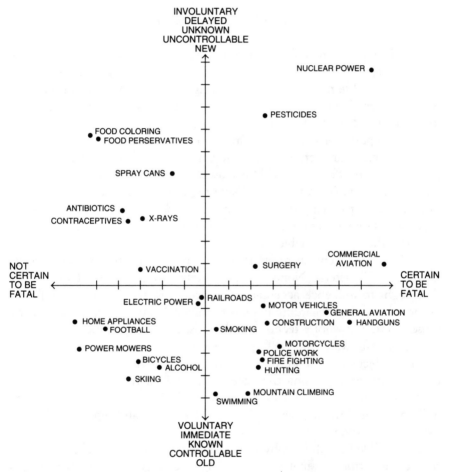

Figure 2. Location of risk items within the two-factor space. Reprinted from "Facts and Fears: Understanding Perceived Risk," by P. Slovic, B. Fischhoff, & S. Lichtenstein. In *Societal Risk Assessment: How Safe Is Safe Enough?* R. Schwing and W. A. Albers, Jr. (Eds.), 1979, New York: Plenum Press. Copyright 1979 by Plenum Press. Reprinted with permission.

1979, 1980, 1984; Vlek & Stallen, 1981) have been cited often. On the other hand, the critique of Starr's (1969) *revealed preference* analysis that motivated it has virtually escaped mention. That critique produced a relatively complex conclusion as well as one that was quite unwelcome to advocates of Starr's "whatever is right" philosophy. By contrast, the figure seems to have functioned as a projective test. In particular, people favoring nuclear power read it as showing the unique (and irrational) "psychological" status afforded their favorite energy technology (Freudenburg & Rosa, 1984). The fact that the judgments of technical experts yield a similar factor structure has done little to dilute Figure 2's contribution to confirming disrespect for the public.

ACCEPTABLE RISK II

Still hopeful, my colleagues and I accepted a contract from the U.S. Nuclear Regulatory Commission (NRC) to analyze possible procedures for setting acceptable risk levels. The resulting report (Fischhoff, Lichtenstein, Slovic, Derby, & Keeney, 1981) was not exactly what the NRC had hoped for. It argued, first, that the concept of acceptable risk was ill conceived: People accept options, not risks. One feature of those options is their level of risk. Even if an option is accepted, it might be rejected in favor of another option offering less risk at reasonable additional cost or more risk along with a sizable cost saving. Assuming that people view risk levels in isolation leads to seeing them as responding inconsistently, sometimes accepting and sometimes rejecting the same risks. (Thus, the more reasonable they are, the less reasonable they seem.)

Our report went on to argue that no policy-making procedure meets all the NRC's criteria. None can adequately accommodate all the factors that ought to influence acceptable-risk decisions. None makes wholly realistic assumptions regarding human behavior. None is "objective," in the sense of offering wholly technical solutions, devoid of political values.

Soon afterward, the NRC proposed a policy so incomplete, unrealistic, and subjective that we had not thought to review it explicitly. It set forth a number expressing the acceptable level of risk for nuclear power (U.S. Nuclear Regulatory Commission, 1982). That number (one in one million) seemed to go down well with the industry and represented a first explicit expression of a safety philosophy by the NRC (which had previously embedded its philosophy in decisions about specific technical issues, such as how thick to make pipes). Our (attempted) contribution to this effort was an analysis of when it made sense to rely on such rigid numbers and how they needed to be specified in order to create meaningful, predictable safety standards (Fischhoff, 1983, 1984). It had little discernible effect.

More surprising than having little impact was being asked to try. What are psychologists doing analyzing the logic and ideology of policy-making methods? In part, we were exploiting a relative vacuum. At any time, there are many more people implementing methods than worrying about their fundamentals. We were invited just to explain the public's behavior, but saw the opportunity to fill a larger role. In part, we were exploiting psychology's unique origins. As a discipline, psychology has roots in philosophy, biology, and sociology (or its predecessors). Each of these pieces is needed to fulfill this role. Perhaps it is also easier (or at least more appealing) to probe the foundations of other professions.

PERCEIVED BENEFIT

Cost–benefit analysis is the name of the game in evaluating many environmental decisions. As a result, any consequence that cannot be evaluated in monetary terms will tend to be ignored. The usual strategy for determining the monetary value of consequences is to look for their evaluation in some marketplace (Bentkover et al., 1985; Smith & Desvousges, 1986). Yet, many significant environmental consequences are not traded anywhere. In order to gain a hearing for consequences such as degradation of landscapes, reduction in visibility, and extinction of noncommercial species, resource economists (e.g., Cummings, Brookshire, & Schulze, 1986; Mitchell & Carson, 1989) have developed a family of survey techniques called *contingent valuation* methods. They ask people to estimate what they would pay, were there a marketplace offering that consequence.

These are very ambitious questions, compared with the rating scales typically used by psychologists. If these questions can be answered meaningfully, then laypeople's enfranchisement has been extended. Their responses would be plugged directly into cost–benefit analyses. On the other hand, if people cannot answer these complex novel questions, then their own responses will misrepresent their values. Insofar as mean responses in a study will be multiplied by the number of people in a county or country, small errors in responses can produce large errors in evaluating an environmental intervention.

Several agencies sponsoring such research have invited psychologists to look over the shoulders of the economists performing it. When asked, we expected that many aspects of the procedure would not ring true, in terms of psychologists' norms (and tastes) regarding how studies should be conducted and analyzed. We were not disappointed (Fischhoff & Furby, 1986; Gregory & Furby, 1987; Kahneman, 1986).

We were surprised, however, by the incompleteness of the economic analysis. Taking the *contingent market* metaphor seriously means presenting subjects with enough detail to clarify what market is intended. However, the investigators neither agreed about the nature of those details nor realized their own lack of agreement. Features that were stressed in one study were unspecified in another. Features essential to making the task meaningful were sometimes noted, other times, ignored. Might economists lack a clear idea of what a market is? Might psychologists be the ones to help them?

In order to review and design contingent market studies systematically, we developed a framework for specifying markets—or, what we more generally called *transactions*, situations in which people might trade a "payment" for a "good" (Fischhoff & Furby, 1988). That payment might be money, but also time or effort, so as to avoid reifying monetary sacrifices. Our framework showed that far more detail is needed to describe a novel market than is presented in any contingent market studies. It may also be far more detail than could even be absorbed by most subjects under the conditions of most interviews. If such a task could be understood, subjects would still face the task of determining their own response to it.[2]

The theoretical challenge at the moment is to understand how people decide what they want when faced by explicit, but unfamiliar alternatives. The practical challenge is to make these tasks meaningful so that people do not misunderstand the question and their answer to it. The policy challenge is to know which market to specify as best representing the issues actually being considered. These challenges are all a part of a developing science of subjective evaluation requiring the skills of psychology and other disciplines (e.g., Fischhoff, Slovic, & Lichtenstein, 1980; Hechter, Cooper, & Nadel, 1993; Hogarth, 1982; Mitchell & Carson, 1989; Thaler, 1980; Turner & Martin, 1985; Tversky & Kahneman, 1981).

CONCLUSION

The details of these experiences reflect the particular niche occupied by the people working in this area. The work might not ever have been funded had the environmental movement not been pressuring industry in the public name. The work might have emerged quite differently had it not been performed largely by investigators living on soft money. That

---

[2]These details include substantive features, such as just what is the consequence (e.g., is visibility measured by haze intensity, visual range, plume, or light extinction?), why is it valued (e.g., what is being seen?), and what is the source of the change. They also include formal features such as how big a change is, when it will begin, how long it will last, and how likely it is actually to be received if the transaction is accepted. Other details include a precise description of the payment and the social context within which the transaction would be conducted (e.g., who else is doing it, what precedents are being set, and who guarantees the transaction). Our ability to comprehend everyday transactions must owe much to the number of details that can go without saying, allowing us to focus on what well-known things are worth to us in terms of well-known payments.

dependence makes one more interested in people with problems severe enough that they might want psychologists' help. It forces one to look for ways to address basic research questions in the context of applied problems. Nonetheless, there seem to be some general lessons for settings in which psychologists confront environmental policy: (a) Expect to make slow progress in understanding the underpinnings of one's own field; (b) expect to fulfill nonpsychological roles; (c) expect one's empirical results to be distorted, both deliberately and inadvertently; (d) expect "amateurs" to try to usurp the need for psychological expertise, replacing our research with their self-serving speculations; (e) expect to stick with a problem long after any financial support has been exhausted; (f) expect conflicts of conscience (and charges of bias) when balancing science and politics; (g) expect to be misdirected by the presenting symptoms described by clients; and (h) expect the temptation to overshoot one's competence.

The final analysis for such involvements might include three questions: Is it good for society? Is it good for psychology? Is it good for oneself? Answering each of these questions requires an appraisal of what has happened and what matters. Personally, I am not unhappy with the overall results of these gambles or of others taken in the same vein (e.g., Fischhoff & Furby, 1983; Furby & Fischhoff, 1991; Lanir, Fischhoff, & Johnson, 1988). However, they were quite different gambles than trying to publish in more conventionally respectable journals. And they might have turned out quite differently.

REFERENCES

Aronson, E., & O'Leary, M. (1983). The relative effectiveness of models and prompts in energy conservation. *Journal of Environmental Systems, 12,* 219–224.

Baum, A., & Singer, J. E. (Eds.). (1981). *Advances in environmental psychology: Vol. 3. Energy in psychological perspective.* Hillsdale, NJ: Erlbaum.

Bentkover, J. D., Covello, V. T., & Mumpower, J. (Eds.). (1985). *Benefits assessment: The state of the art.* Dordrecht, The Netherlands: Reidel.

Campen, J. (1986). *Benefit, cost and beyond.* Cambridge, MA: Ballinger.

Cohen, S., Evans, G. W., Krantz, D. S., & Stokols, D. (1980). Physiological, motivational, and cognitive effects of aircraft noise on children. *American Psychologist, 35,* 231–243.

Combs, B., & Slovic, P. (1979). Newspaper coverage of causes of death. *Journalism Quarterly, 56,* 837–843, 849.

Cummings, R. O., Brookshire, D. S., & Schulze, W. D. (Eds.). (1986). *Valuing environmental goods: An assessment of the contingent valuation method.* Totowa, NJ: Rowman & Allanheld.

Daniel, T. C., & Vining, J. (1983). Methodological issues in the assessment of landscape quality. In I. Altman & J. F. Wohlwill (Eds.), *Behavior and the natural environment* (pp. 39–84). New York: Plenum Press.

Executive Order 12291. (1978, March 23). Washington, DC: Office of the President.

Fischhoff, B. (1983). Acceptable risk: The case of nuclear power. *Journal of Policy Analysis and Management, 2,* 559–575.

Fischhoff, B. (1984). Setting standards: A systematic approach to managing public health and safety risks. *Management Science, 30,* 823–843.

Fischhoff, B., & Cox, L. A., Jr. (1985). Conceptual framework for benefit assessment. In J. D. Bentkover, V. T. Covello, & J. Mumpower (Eds.), *Benefits assessment: The state of the art* (pp. 51–84). Dordrecht, The Netherlands: Reidel.

Fischhoff, B., & Furby, L. (1983). Psychological dimensions of climatic change. In R. S. Chen, E. Boulding, & S. H. Schneider (Eds.), *Social science research and climate change: An interdisciplinary perspective* (pp. 180–203). Dordrecht, The Netherlands: Reidel.

Fischhoff, B., & Furby, L. (1986). *A review and critique of Tolley, Randall et al. "Establishing and valuing the effects of improved visibility in the Eastern United States"* (ERI Technical Report No. 86-8). Eugene, OR: Eugene Research Institute.

Fischhoff, B., & Furby, L. (1988). Measuring values: A conceptual framework for interpreting transactions with special reference to contingent valuation of visibility. *Journal of Risk and Uncertainty, 1,* 141–178.

Fischhoff, B., Lichtenstein, S., Slovic, P., Derby, S. L., & Keeney, R. L. (1981). *Acceptable risk.* New York: Cambridge University Press.

Fischhoff, B., & MacGregor, D. (1983). Judged lethality: How much people seem to know depends upon how they are asked. *Risk Analysis, 3,* 229–236.

Fischhoff, B., Pidgeon, N., & Fiske, S. (1983). Social science and the politics of the arms race. *Journal of Social Issues, 39,* 161–180.

Fischhoff, B., Slovic, P., & Lichtenstein, S. (1980). Knowing what you want: Measuring labile values. In T. Wallsten (Ed.), *Cognitive processes in choice and decision behavior* (pp. 117–141). Hillsdale, NJ: Erlbaum.

Fischhoff, B., Slovic, P., Lichtenstein, S., Read, S., & Combs, B. (1978). How safe is safe enough?: A psychometric study of attitudes towards technological risks and benefits. *Policy Sciences, 8,* 127–152.

Fischhoff, B., Watson, S., & Hope, C. (1984). Defining risk. *Policy Sciences, 17,* 123–139.

Freudenberg, W. R., & Rosa, E. A. (Eds.). (1984). *Public reaction to nuclear power: Are there critical masses?* Boulder, CO: Westview Press.

Furby, L. (1986). Psychological studies of justice. In R. C. Cohen (Ed.), *Justice: Views from the social sciences.* New York: Plenum Press.

Furby, L., & Fischhoff, B. (1991). Rape self-defense strategies: A review of their effectiveness. *Victimology.*

Geller, E. S., Paterson, L., & Talbott, E. (1982). A behavioral analysis of incentive prompts for motivating seat belt use. *Journal of Applied Behavioral Analysis, 15,* 403–415.

Gregory, R., & Furby, L. (1987). Auctions, experiments and contingent valuation. *Public Choice, 55,* 273–289.

Hechter, M., Cooper, L., & Nadel, L. (Eds.). (1993). *The origin of values.* Stanford, CA: Stanford University Press.

Hindelang, M. J., Gottfredson, M. R., & Garofolo, J. (1978). *Victims of personal crime: An empirical foundation for a theory of personal victimization.* Cambridge, MA: Ballinger.

Hogarth, R. (Ed.). (1982). *New directions for methodology of social and behavioral science: Question framing and response consistency.* San Francisco: Jossey-Bass.

Hohenemser, C., Kates, R. W., & Slovic, P. (1983). The nature of technological hazard. *Science, 220,* 378–384.

Kahneman, D. (1986). Comment. In R. O. Cummings, D. S. Brookshire, & W. D. Schulze (Eds.), *Valuing environmental goods: An assessment of the contingent valuation method.* Totowa, NJ: Rowman & Allanheld.

Lanir, Z., Fischhoff, B., & Johnson, F. (1988). Military risk taking and the cognitive functions of boldness in war. *Journal of Strategic Studies, 11,* 96–114.

Lichtenstein, S., Slovic, P., Fischhoff, B., Layman, M., & Combs, B. (1978). Judged frequency of lethal events. *Journal of Experimental Psychology: Human Learning and Memory, 4,* 551–578.

McClelland, L., & Cook, S. W. (1980). Promoting energy conservation in waste-metered apartments through financial incentives. *Journal of Applied Social Psychology, 10,* 19–31.

Mitchell, R. C., & Carson, R. T. (1989). *Using surveys to value public goods: The contingent valuation method.* Washington, DC: Resources for the Future.

National Research Council. (1989). *Improving risk communication.* Washington, DC: Author.

Noll, R. (Ed.). (1985). *Regulatory policy and the social sciences.* Berkeley, CA: University of California Press.

Otway, H. J., & Cohen, J. J. (1975). *Revealed preference: Comments on the Starr benefit–risk relationships.* Laxenburg, Austria: International Institute for Applied Systems Analysis.

Robertson, L. S. (1983). *Injuries, causes, control, strategies and public policy.* Lexington, MA: Lexington.

Slovic, P., Fischhoff, B., & Lichtenstein, S. (1979). Rating the risks. *Environment, 21*(4), 14–20, 36–39.

Slovic, P., Fischhoff, B., & Lichtenstein, S. (1980). Facts and fears: Understanding perceived risk. In R. Schwing & W. A. Albers, Jr. (Eds.), *Societal risk assessment: How safe is safe enough?* (pp. 181–214). New York: Plenum Press.

Slovic, P., Fischhoff, B., & Lichtenstein, S. (1984). Behavioral decision theory perspectives on risk and safety. *Acta Psychologica, 56,* 183–203.

Smith, V. K., & Desvousges, W. H. (1986). *Measuring water quality benefits*. Boston: Kluwer-Nijhoff.

Starr, C. (1969). Social benefit versus technological risk. *Science, 165,* 1232–1238.

Starr, C., & Whipple, C. (1980). Risks of risk decisions. *Science, 208,* 114–119.

Stokols, D., & Altman, I. (Eds.). (1987). *Handbook of environmental psychology.* New York: Wiley.

Thaler, R. (1980). Toward a positive theory of consumer choice. *Journal of Economic Behavior and Organization, 1,* 39–60.

Turner, C., & Martin, E. (Eds.). (1985). *Surveying subjective values* (2 vols.). Beverly Hills, CA: Sage.

Tversky, A., & Kahneman, D. (1973). Availability: A heuristic for judging frequency and probability. *Cognitive Psychology, 5,* 207–232.

Tversky, A., & Kahneman, D. (1981). The framing of decisions and the rationality of choice. *Science, 221,* 453–458.

Upton, A. (1982). The biological effects of low level ionizing radiation. *Scientific American, 246*(2), 41–47.

U.S. Nuclear Regulatory Commission. (1982). *Safety goals for nuclear power: A discussion paper* (NUREG-0880). Washington, DC: Author.

Vlek, C., & Stallen, P. J. (1981). Judging risks and benefits in the small and in the large. *Organizational Behavior and Human Performance, 28,* 235–271.

14

HOW TO INFLUENCE
PUBLIC POLICY:
A BLUEPRINT FOR ACTIVISM

PATRICK H. DELEON, ANNE MARIE O'KEEFE,
GARY R. VANDENBOS, and ALAN G. KRAUT

Psychology has a long scientific history, but a short political one. All of psychology's intraprofessional accomplishments will do little to ensure its future if psychologists remain unknown to the general public, the insurance carriers that underwrite health services, the local, state, and federal agencies that administer service delivery and research programs, and the elected officials who make public policy. Today less than 25% of the American public can distinguish a psychologist from a psychiatrist—that is, know that the former has a PhD and the latter an MD (Yankelovich, Skelly & White, 1980). Such is our current state of affairs.

Public interest advocacy and political activism are vital to the guild interests of psychology just as they are essential to the evolution of any discipline that seeks professional recognition outside of the university laboratory. Psychology has claimed many professional rights because of its success in taking the first steps toward professionalism. These steps include the development of a specialized body of knowledge and skills, the recruit-

Reprinted from *American Psychologist, 37,* 476–485. Copyright 1982 by the American Psychological Association.

The authors would like to express their appreciation for the encouragement and continuing support of Joseph Matarazzo, Stephen Weiss, Neal Miller, and Jerome Singer in their roles as presidents of APA Division 38 (Health Psychology). We would also like to express our sincerest appreciation for the volunteer help provided by Hazel Thomas, Patty Camp, and Lisa Jonas, staff of the Association for the Advancement of Psychology.

ment and training of individuals in that knowledge and those skills, and securing legal recognition in the form of licensing/certification laws. Professional rights, however, bring professional responsibilities, and these responsibilities constitute another step in attaining professionalism: providing a "service or collectivity orientation" (Goode, 1960) including visible evidence and public recognition that the profession's efforts, especially its exercise of self-regulation, contribute to the betterment of society.

RECENT POLICY ACTIVITIES

Our general point is to suggest that groups of psychologists outside the structure of the APA Central Office (such as divisions and state associations) must make further efforts to build political support if psychology is to play a larger role in our country's public policy. When such efforts are made at the national level—for example, with Congress and federal agencies—we urge coordination with APA and the Association for the Advancement of Psychology (AAP). We do not want to minimize past accomplishments or ongoing activities, however. Organized psychology is a latecomer to the political arena, but it is not unknown.

In 1974 the Association for the Advancement of Psychology was incorporated as a national lobbying organization to:

> promote human welfare through the advancement of the science and profession of psychology by the promotion of the interest of all psychology; by the representation of psychology before public and governmental bodies, by seeking out and contributing to the passage of important social and psychological issues in current legislation and to advocate to the legislative, judicial and executive branches of government the ethical and scientific views of the American Psychological Community. (Association for the Advancement of Psychology, 1977, p. 1)

Several state psychological associations have also organized committees, divisions, task forces, and communications networks that have been very effective in influencing legislation and administrative policies at the state level. The Virginia Academy of Clinical Psychologists, which eventually secured the landmark antitrust decision against Blue Shield, was organized by 125 psychologists to pursue several mutual goals at the local level. A few individual psychologists, such as California State Senator Paul Carpenter, D.C. City Council member Charlene Drew Jarvis, Maine Board of Education member Lewis Lester, and Ft. Collins (Colorado) Mayor Richard Suinn, have personally brought their professional expertise to the political arena.

Perhaps psychology's most visible contributions to the development of public policy have been through individual participation on various national advisory commissions. For example, over 50 psychologists served on the President's Commission on Mental Health that in 1978 published a four-volume report containing numerous recommendations to guide fiscal, legislative, and administrative policies in mental health. Unfortunately, these experts have not been able to systematically share their experiences with the rest of the profession, and their contributions remain generally unknown even among psychologists who have benefited from the Commission's report. Similarly, there has been relatively little recognition of the long-term contributions made by social policy institutions involved with psychology. The four Bush Policy Centers, directed by Edward Zigler, Norma Feshbach, Harold Stevenson, and James Gallagher, along with Nicholas Hobbs' Institute for Public Policy Studies and William Bevan's Roundtable on Science and Public Affairs, are notable exceptions to this general rule.

The systematic involvement of psychologists in the political arena hinges on the ability of the profession to establish mechanisms that promote mutual understanding between psychologists and policymakers. The recent decision of the Wright State University School of Professional Psychology to establish an Institute of Applied Psychology and Public Policy is a significant step in this regard: This represents the first formal recognition of the importance of political impact among the 25 or so schools of professional psychology. Community psychology programs could provide a logical focal point for training and apprenticeships in the public policy arena if their enrollments are maintained.

THE POTENTIAL OF APA DIVISIONS

Several divisions of the American Psychological Association have histories of sporadic involvement in public policy. At its inception in 1937, one of the prime missions of the Society for the Psychological Study of Social Issues (SPSSI, or Division 9) was to gain entrance to then-current policy debates. At a time when our nation's involvement in World War II seemed increasingly inevitable, SPSSI's organizational emphasis was on psychological research regarding attitudes toward war, communism, and fascism. SPSSI continued its commitment to public involvement by actively promoting the development of initiatives of a "psychological nature" in the Works Projects Administration during the Roosevelt era (Miller, 1981).

A profession cannot, however, meet its public responsibilities by reacting only in crisis situations. It is true that effective organizations must be ready to act with little advance notice, but a political commitment to true social change requires more sustained efforts. Individual members of SPSSI have continued to be active, and the division as a whole has exerted a beneficial influence on the formal APA governance structure. But one might reasonably wonder what continuing role the division per se sees for itself in the development of public policy. There is no current dearth of social policy issues, as demonstrated by the "Judicial Notebook" prepared by SPSSI Courtwatch Committee Chair Michael Saks for regular publication in the *APA Monitor*, but it has been more difficult to trace the organized involvement of Division 9 in these issues.

In general, APA divisions are restrained by several structural and procedural limits. They are run by volunteers, their elected officers change annually, committees often work by telephone or mail, the executive committee may meet only twice a year, and only minimal financial resources are available to support division efforts. Further, of the 52,440 full members of APA, nearly 21,000 do not belong to any division. It is tempting to conclude that the divisions are not especially compatible with political activism. However, certain attributes of this structure belie this pessimistic conclusion.

Division membership is based on topical interests (e.g., aging, rehabilitation, mental retardation, child and youth services) that are national in scope rather than regional. Rotating leadership and the voluntary nature of its work may thwart intradivisional continuity, but a division's basic interests remain constant, as do its ready pools of expertise. In addition, each division represents a broad constituency that benefits from gains made in the specialty embodied in the division.

There are similarities between the characteristics of the divisional structure of APA and the structure of our federal policymaking system. The members and leadership of Congress change somewhat with every election. A fairly stable bureaucracy underlies all branches of the federal system, but even more enduring are the social issues that our political process is designed to address. Political change is typically slow, sometimes almost evolutionary. Any major modification in law or administrative priority takes time, but this is as it should be in a democratic process, for it provides many opportunities for input to the system.

AN IMPORTANT LESSON: KEEP TRYING

The time required for the federal policymaking system to implement change may be the most difficult concept for psychologists to understand and appreciate, particularly those who are inexperienced in the political process. On a theoretical basis, being "politically active" sounds glamorous and intriguing. On a practical level political effectiveness requires considerable time and energy for what often seem like very mundane tasks (cf.

Dörken, 1981). Payoffs are not readily forthcoming, especially on a short-term basis. Participants cannot always perceive personal or even tangible benefits in the outcome of their efforts. At best, the incremental steps that are achieved by these efforts provide only abstract and indirect encouragement for an individual. Perhaps this is as it should be, for social policies must be based on broader views than are represented by personal interests.

A recognition of the efforts required for effective political involvement has been spreading to a number of groups within psychology. The applied divisions represent psychologists who have traditionally identified more with their profession than psychologists with university affiliations. However, as fiscal austerity has eroded federal research and training support, academic and research psychologists have increased their political involvement. For example, the APA Research Support Network has notes on over 7,000 letters sent from academic and research psychologists to congressional representatives over the past year. The Reagan administration and the 97th Congress have already reacted to these groups who vigorously protested disproportionate cuts in the federal research budget and the administration's general reluctance to continue any federal support of the behavioral and social sciences. In fact, in December 1981 the President signed an appropriations bill that increased funding for the social and behavioral sciences at the National Science Foundation by $11 million over the administration's original proposals.

One of the most ambitious recent lobbying efforts occurred during the 95th Congress from January 1977 through October 1978. Under the leadership of Legislative Committee Chair Marvin Metsky, Division 12 (Clinical Psychology) attempted *as a division* to directly influence the passage of federal legislation that would ensure the direct recognition of psychologists under Medicare. Two successive division presidents wrote to each division member to urge direct contact of senators and congressional representatives on behalf of bills pending in both houses of Congress (S. 123 and H.R. 2270, respectively). The Legislative Committee of Division 12 received copies of more than 400 letters from psychologists to their elected representatives on this issue, representing responses from nearly 10% of the division membership. Dr. Metsky then diligently corresponded with all of the psychologist-respondents, thanking them for their action and urging them to continue their efforts. He even suggested possible follow-up letters or continued dialogue with specific legislators (Metsky, 1978).

By January 1978, 32 senators and 117 representatives had signed on to cosponsor the respective Medicare reform bills. In August of that year the Senate Finance Committee had hearings entitled, "Proposals to Expand Coverage of Mental Health Under Medicare/Medicaid." This was the first time in seven years that mental health had been the subject of formal hearings by this committee (DeLeon & VandenBos, 1980), the single most important committee in the Senate for controlling funding to almost all federal programs of importance to clinical and counseling psychologists and their patients. Division 12, in conjunction with AAP, had accomplished its interim goal in highly competent style.

Unfortunately, neither S. 123 nor H.R. 2270 was brought to a vote that year, and so with the opening of the 96th Congress in 1979, psychologists had to reinitiate their advocacy efforts and continue to develop the grass roots support necessary to pass this legislation. More unfortunately, Division 12's enthusiasm and drive simply were not sustained. By the end of the 96th Congress, only 13 senators still cosponsored S. 123. Today, halfway through the 97th Congress, there are fewer than 10 cosponsoring senators. The lesson to be drawn from this experience is that political success takes time, energy, and above all else perseverance. We are not convinced that the APA divisional structure is incompatible with maintaining this type of prolonged effort.

There are many goals that are realistic for division programs. In the past several years the number of special interests represented by divisions has increased, and so has their degree of involvement in shaping the political fortunes of psychology. Much of this activity has been generated by clinical and applied groups, who seem to have a firmer commitment to advocacy and a clearer political platform to advance. For example, APA Division 29 (Psychotherapy) recently established a National Commission on Public Policy and Mental Health (involving Jack Wiggins, Marvin Metsky, Gary VandenBos, Ron Fox, Herbert Freudenberger) to prepare several "white papers" addressing, among other topics, the cost-effectiveness of psychotherapy. In addition, a number of divisions hold corporate membership in AAP. The divisions also continue to represent psychology's prime source of specialized expertise. This is important for providing expert testimony in hearings and information to congressional and agency staffs.

But psychologists must also remember that as voting constituents, they wield tremendous power. AAP and APA staff simply cannot gain entrance to some offices on Capitol Hill without being accompanied by a constituent. The attention a cause receives from political officials is proportional to the size of the voting audience interested in it. The Council of Graduate Departments of Psychology (COGDOP) recently held its annual meeting in Washington, and its members met personally with over 60 senators and 120 members of the House of Representatives, thereby establishing direct contact with their representatives in Congress and making the presence of APA and AAP better known.

A FORUM FOR EXCHANGE

The creation of Division 38 (Health Psychology) in 1978 presented us with an opportunity to form a policy-oriented committee based in Washington, D.C., where physical access to federal resources is almost limitless. This includes access to personnel in all branches of policymaking. This committee consists of Pat DeLeon, Anne Marie O'Keefe, Patricia Bryant, Bruce Copeland, Ed Kelty, Kelly Shaver, Steve Weiss, Al Wellner, and Nancy Wexler. During the fall of the following year, the authors also assumed responsibility for a parallel committee of Division 12 and thereby merged the planning, fiscal, and communications resources of both divisions' committees.

Three broad but ultimately far-reaching principles were adopted at the initial planning session. First, to capitalize on our location, we decided to seek local audiences for discussions with national health policy leaders but to broadly disseminate the information gleaned at these meetings. We hoped to keep the tone of our meetings fairly informal, but we also hoped to invite the best individuals in their fields as our guest speakers. Although it was not a primary goal, we hoped incidentally to provide our speakers with an education about health psychology and professional issues in psychology. Our second major decision was to keep a broad focus on health rather than to limit ourselves to mental health per se. We all felt that establishing this committee within the newly formed Division 38 presented an opportunity to be creative. Accordingly, we avoided limiting ourselves to any particular perspective or committing ourselves to any particular issue. Third, we therefore agreed that at least in our initial stages, we would not become directly involved in the then-pressing controversy surrounding national health insurance. It was also agreed that because our potential membership included many federal employees, we would not attempt to influence the outcome of any specific legislation (as lobbying by federal employees is illegal).

During the initial planning we contacted the presidents of all other divisions to advise them of our ideas and to invite their participation. Twelve divisions responded to our inquiries, and we established formal liaisons with them (and with several boards and committees in the APA structure). We arranged our meetings to coincide with divisional and governance structure meetings, and in that way we were sometimes able to share expenses. We welcomed all suggestions for guest speakers and tried to accommodate as many requests as we could.

The meetings began on a small scale, but we actively recruited attendance. We did not want to limit our exposure or our invitations to psychologists, and so a concerted effort was made to include physicians, representatives of the nursing and social work professions, and especially health practitioners and researchers who were serving as staffers on Congressional or White House fellowships. Our initial meetings drew fewer than 10 participants, but attendance has grown steadily to a current rate of between 35 and 40. We have only been refused by guest speakers who had previous commitments, in which case they always offered to meet with us at a later date. Public officials seem to take their public service commitments very seriously, even in off-duty hours.

We have generally been able to schedule one meeting each month, and we try to provide ample advance notice. APA has allowed us to use the facilities in their Washington building, which we reserve for weeknights beginning at 6:30 p.m. to accomodate parking and work schedules. (We have occasionally scheduled "brown-bag" luncheon meetings instead to accommodate the speaker's schedule or budgetary constraints.) The first half-hour is arranged for an informal gathering with soft drinks, wine, and beer. A buffet dinner follows leaving an hour for the speaker's formal presentation and interaction with the audience. A member volunteers to record the minutes at each session, and these are prepared as a report and sent to our entire mailing list. The full mailing list currently numbers around 400. The cost of these dinner meetings ranges between $250 and $300 for prepared food from a catering service. These costs are charged to our committee budget so there is no charge to attendees. Our support services (including preparations, clean-up, and distribution of minutes) have been graciously provided by AAP and APA staff.

STEPS TOWARD SOCIAL CHANGE: WHAT WE HAVE LEARNED

Over the past three years, these dinner/policy meetings have made some strides toward our original objectives. They have afforded psychologists and others the opportunity for personal, in-depth discussion of important concerns with a number of prominent health policy leaders. These meetings have also fostered a mutual education of both audience and speakers that has been both gratifying and refreshing. In several meetings, especially with representatives from the executive branch of government, it became apparent that the guest speakers had received their first staff briefings on how their agencies affected psychology in preparation for the presentation. Without exception our invited speakers left the meetings with a new appreciation for the complexity of psychology as a multifaceted profession. With few exceptions they also expressed personal receptiveness to increased future contact with organized psychology.

Perhaps more importantly, these meetings have given all of us a deep appreciation both for the truly interdisciplinary nature of health care and the very tenuous nature of psychology's participation in its national planning. In almost every program and major piece of legislation presented by the speakers, psychology was perceived and treated as an incidental. Much of the limited recognition that psychology enjoys in national health planning is based on the breadth and vagueness of the federal legislation that created the health program and on the lack of specific limitations that would exclude psychologists from it. Sometimes regulations created by the agency responsible for program implementation mention the participation of psychologists or the inclusion of psychological services even if the legislation created by Congress did not.

Since we began these meetings in 1978, we have attained enough perspective to appreciate the potential of their long-term importance. This is illustrated by Suzanne Woolsey's address to our group in 1979. Dr. Woolsey is a psychologist who was employed at the time as the Associate Director for Human Resources, Veterans, and Labor of the Office of Management and Budget (OMB). We learned that Dr. Woolsey's administrative purview included nearly every federal program of even indirect concern to psychologists. Few of that meeting's attendees had been at all familiar with OMB's jurisdiction in general, let alone with the specifics of its operation. Most of us have since become much more aware of the powers of OMB.

We also had the opportunity to meet with three institute directors from the Department of Health and Human Services (DHHS, formerly DHEW). Lawrence Scadon, the acting director of the National Institute for Handicapped Research, was one of these, and he expressed considerable personal concern over his agency's lack of support for psychosocial research:

> I was shocked to see how little psychosocial research we are supporting. Technology development constitutes about 25% of our budget now. About 50% is in the medical area—mostly spinal-cord injury work. Right now the psychosocial area comprises only 7 to 8% of our entire budget. I would like to see more psychologists on the research side with medical and engineering personnel. I don't want a bunch of MDs reviewing psychosocial research proposals. (Minutes, Division 38 Policy Meeting, March 26, 1981)

Unfortunately for psychology, Mr. Scadon was replaced by a Reagan appointee the following week.

During the last three years we have invited six congressional staff members who are experts in diverse policy areas, including the elderly, programs for handicapped individuals, workers' compensation law, the Employee Retirement Income Security Act (ERISA) of 1974, health maintenance organizations, and Medicare/Medicaid. Our discussion of the extent and adequacy of coverage for chronic diseases under various national health insurance proposals was especially challenging. Several articulate representatives of the Cystic Fibrosis Foundation and the Epilepsy Foundation of America clearly presented some of the pressing issues related to the care and treatment of chronic health problems.

Perhaps the most engaging discussions surrounded presentations made by speakers who administered service-oriented programs in DHHS, including the Deputy Assistant Secretary for Disease Prevention and Health Promotion, who served as principal author for the first Surgeon General's

Annual Report in that area; Former Secretary Califano's Special Assistant on Hospices; and the Deputy Commissioner of the Administration for Children, Youth and Families, which administers Head Start. The speakers summarized the histories of their programs from perspectives that come only with long-time involvement. Each speaker also offered a prediction of the program's future. None of these federal administrators had been aware of the extent of psychology's current involvement in the program's content area. None had ever been personally contacted by a representative of organized psychology in spite of the obvious overlap with the issues addressed by APA boards, task forces, standing committees, and divisions. Speakers almost always expressed a sincere willingness to continue communications and cooperative efforts, but it was obvious by the enormity of their job responsibilities that the psychologists would be obligated to initiate and sustain these cooperative efforts.

Our speakers addressed national health problems and the federal programs designed to solve them from a much broader perspective than most psychologists are ever exposed to in their jobs or graduate training. For example, we met with a senior consultant to the President's Commission on World Hunger who summarized some startling and depressing discoveries the commission had made. According to our speaker, some villages in third world nations are without a single child under 11 years old. Malnutrition is an underlying cause of dramatic death rates from a variety of diseases, so not even epidemiological data reveal the extent of its toll. In the United States measles are often considered a preschool nuisance, but in third world countries up to 50% of those infected may die or become blind.

Another dinner featured a distinguished international health care expert with a very successful record of implementing primary health care systems throughout Africa, South America, and the Pacific Basin. The implementation program he developed (MEDEX) pyramids health-care expertise, placing a traditional health professional at the top. This individual provides supervision for a corps of villagers, already established as healers or community leaders, who are trained and who then operate as midlevel health workers. These personnel in turn provide technical expertise to a cadre of village outreach workers. MEDEX currently supports nearly all primary health services that are available in each of the areas where it has been implemented. Interchangeable "technical modules" have been developed for teaching village outreach workers specialized skills in areas ranging from maternal/child health care to agricultural/nutritional development. The program has succeeded largely because it enjoys the vocal support of not only the highest-level local leadership, but also the demonstrable enthusiasm of the village people.

Perhaps the most memorable presentation was made by President Carter's Assistant Director for Health and Human Services of the White

House's Domestic Policy Staff, James Mongan. Since 1970 Dr. Mongan had also served as professional staff member of the Health Subcommittee of the Senate Finance Committee and as Special Assistant for National Health Insurance to Secretary Califano. Few other individuals in the entire nation possess as great an appreciation for the complexity of attempts to control health care costs or to expand the health benefits established in 1965 under Medicare/Medicaid. From his tenure in the Senate, Dr. Mongan was also personally familiar with psychology's past legislative efforts, so his presentation had special significance. Dr. Mongan addressed our committee on January 6, 1981, after President Reagan had been elected, but before his administration officially replaced President Carter's.

Mongan offered a thoughtful overview and history of various legislative proposals for national health insurance, and he made a number of pertinent, candid, and sobering predictions for the future. He suggested that the Reagan administration would first seek to resolve our current health cost problems through private-sector approaches designed to encourage competition and therefore, theoretically, to compel lower prices. He also predicted, however, that these attempts would fail. Ultimately, in Mongan's judgment, the Reagan administration would have to give serious consideration to regulatory cost control, as was done under Reagan's governorship in California. Dr. Mongan also predicted, with eerie accuracy, many of the budget cuts that psychology and other social and behavioral sciences are now facing from OMB.

THE FUTURE OF SUCH POLICY ACTIVITIES

These divisional efforts have made important strides toward their original goals. Like elected officials in the Senate and House of Representatives, we have capitalized on our access to the nation's leaders in health policy. Unlike the one-way communication that frequently characterizes congressional hearings, we have also been able to educate our guest speakers in return, to sensitize them to our concerns, and to offer our help in accomplishing our mutual goals. Unfortunately, and also unlike the Congress at its best, we seem to have been frequently without resources, or without the ability to muster and apply our resources toward effective follow-up.

Our frustration with the lack of concrete follow-up is partly a by-product of our planning, especially our initial goals. Since we avoided targeting particular legislation for passage or specific regulations for change, we never presented ourselves, covertly or overtly, as a lobbying group. When we shared new information with our speakers we did perform some of the prime functions of a lobby by informing policymakers, providing feedback on the implementation of legislated programs in the field, and offering constructive recommendations for change. Our major mission, however, was self-educative, and we learned a great deal as a group and as individuals.

Related to our avoidance of targeted lobbying efforts, we have been able to expose our members to very broad issues in health and wide-angled perspectives in planning its future. We have learned that the profession of psychology shares many goals with other professions in health policy-making. The frustration we experienced over lack of follow-up to our meetings was heightened by our increasing awareness of the tremendous need for psychological expertise in the planning and delivery of health services. Our frustration probably has also been increased by impatience, a failure to heed our own warning that social change requires time and persistence.

Democratic policymaking is based largely on power; social change presumes some measure of social control. To the extent that power is related to public recognition, we have succeeded somewhat by introducing national health leaders to psychologists and their work. Although these personal introductions may not have produced immediate and specific changes in national policy, they represent an important first step. Psychology must learn how the system works and must become a known quantity in it. Well-planned efforts to accomplish these ends are steps in the right direction. Perhaps in this sense we have imitated the best work done in institutions like the Bush Centers, the Institute for Public Policy Studies, and the Roundtable on Science and Public Affairs, where psychologists are specifically trained for policymaking roles. To whatever extent this is true, we are especially proud.

During the last three years we have accomplished some of our goals, but there is an important continuing lesson in the lingering frustration over lack of follow-up. Our regular mailing list includes 400 national specialists in health. The information gleaned at our dinner meetings has also been disseminated in division newsletters and reports. Although the efforts have enjoyed enthusiastic support from the divisions at large, very few individuals have taken any specific action as a result of what we have generated. Most psychologists do not seem to appreciate the intricacies of the political process or how much hard work is involved in developing public policy and implementing social change.

A prime example of this lack of appreciation followed the presentation of Linda Miller, who spoke to us as the Special Assistant on Hospices to DHEW Secretary Califano. Ms. Miller is unusually familiar with the profession of psychology because a basic purpose of hospice care is to provide interdisciplinary services to dying individuals and their families. She is also a vocal advocate for the hospice movement and has appeared on several national and local media shows to generate public support. Her message concerned the importance of psychologists' involvement in hospices as service providers, evaluators, and researchers. Ms. Miller emphasized that she had never heard from representatives of psychology, a void she characterized as "a singular failure, when the emphasis of the hospice concept is so heavily on the psychosocial circumstances of the patient and family, rather than on typical medical care."

Before this meeting adjourned, plans were begun to contact psychologists who specialized in the study of death and dying, the department heads of training programs, and individual psychologists in the National Institute of Mental Health to solicit their interest and support for expanding psychology's role in the hospice movement. Preparations were also begun to have psychologists attend a national conference on the care of dying patients, which DHEW hoped to sponsor three months later. Although no one anticipated it then, Secretary Califano resigned from his post in the intervening time, Ms. Miller left soon after, and the conference was never held.

The void in hospice care, research and evaluation, and advocacy for the hospice concept that should be addressed by psychology remains. It would be depressing to conclude that psychologists are not involved because hospices offer little monetary reward for their services. If psychologists think what they have to offer a movement is important, they must be visible in it long before government and commercial underwriters create formal reimbursement structures for it. The hospices' reliance on volunteer help is as basic as their psychosocial approach to care. Hospices represent only one example of an opportunity for psychologists to fulfill their public interest obligations.

GENERALIZING THE APPLICABILITY OF THE PUBLIC POLICY COMMITTEE MODEL

Our multidivisional group has been especially pleased with the support it received from AAP, APA, and the staff of both associations. Staff attendance at our meetings has provided an important liaison between psychology's governance structure and the congressional, departmental, and White House staffs who are intimately involved with creating and administering federal health care programs. APA staff have also assumed increasing responsibility for planning our meetings and producing and distributing our minutes. In fact, a large part of our "capital" consists of being located in Washington, DC, so close to the APA Central Office. Because APA serves as the meeting place for many different divisions, boards, and committees, and because the staff represents similarly broad interests, their participation has been important in maintaining our broad scope. With their aid, the committee has promoted discussions that clearly demonstrate roles for psychologists in national health policymaking. We hope they will continue to assume greater responsibility for this important dialogue and for increasing psychology's participation in the process.

Psychologists must remember that their professional and advocacy associations (and staffs) can represent them but cannot do all of the work for them. Organizations are only as strong as the members that comprise them; the same holds for divisions, boards, and committees. When they function well, these governance structures provide a framework, a clearinghouse, and a source of contact. They can also provide advice, but even in this role they are merely a means to an end for psychologists.

In our opinion, most committees, divisions, and associations of psychologists could benefit by developing programs analogous to these monthly policy dinner meetings. It is not necessary to schedule public policy meetings as frequently as once a month. Meetings should accommodate the goals of the sponsors; topics and invited guests may be more suitably targeted to particular issues, geographical interests, or the expertise represented in the sponsoring organization. It is important to encourage interdisciplinary participation in these meetings, both to maintain a "real-world" focus on the problems addressed and to avoid the inclination of psychologists to speak only to themselves.

We are confident that participants would find public officials and policymakers remarkably willing to address interested audiences and remarkably open to being educated in return. There is no shortage of invitees at any level, especially if issues are approached from an interdisciplinary perspective. For example, the Department of Health and Human Services alone supports ten regional offices. Area graduate students should also be encouraged to participate; if the cost of a dinner proves prohibitive for them, a mechanism for them to offer preparation and clean-up services might prove to be a mutually beneficial alternative.

These meetings would seem to be appropriate mechanisms for state association legislative committees to learn about and become known to their state legislature, agency, and program administrators. An important "power broker" that is frequently overlooked is the local business community. Corporate business currently pays more than 25% of all health care costs; General Motors has recently reported spending more per manufactured automobile to cover the health care costs of GM workers than it spends on the steel contained in the vehicle (Long, 1980).

Psychology has a great deal to contribute to society and social change. If the profession is to survive, it must be more deliberate about realizing these contributions. Psychologists must learn how policy is made and how to affect change. Psychology must make its voice heard by learning to speak the appropriate language. It has been our experience over the last three years that the committee meeting format developed under the auspices of Division 38, expanded by Division 12, and supported by APA and AAP can provide the members of our profession with an opportunity to learn of and respond to society's needs.

REFERENCES

Association for the Advancement of Psychology. (1977). *Bylaws of the American Association for the Advancement of Psychology.* Washington, DC: Author.

DeLeon, P. H., & VandenBos, G. R. (1980). Psychotherapy reimbursement in federal programs: Political factors. In G. R. VandenBos (Ed.), *Psychotherapy: Practice, research, policy.* Beverly Hills, CA: Sage.

Dörken, H. (1981). Coming of age legislatively: In 21 steps. *American Psychologist, 36,* 165–173.

Goode, W. (1960). Encroachment, charlatanism and the emerging professions: Psychology, sociology, and medicine. *American Sociological Review, 25,* 902–914.

Long, J. (1980). Health care: Who really pays? Series of articles written for *Oregon Journal.* (Clippings available from Western Center for Health Planning, 703 Market Street, Suite 535, San Francisco, California 94103.)

Metsky, M. (1978). Getting our feet wet in national politics. *Clinical Psychologist, 31,* 10.

Miller, D. K. (1981). *Acceptance speech.* Speech accepting the Psychologist of the Year Award at the meeting of the New York State Psychological Association.

Yankelovich, Skelly & White, Inc. (1980). *American attitudes toward psychiatrists and psychiatry.* Unpublished study for the American Psychiatric Association Joint Commission on Public Affairs. (Available from American Psychiatric Association, 1700 18th Street, N.W., Washington, DC 20009.)

APPENDIX

Chronology of Division 38 and Division 12 Public Policy Committee Meetings

November 3, 1978. Initial planning meeting.

January 18, 1979. Edward Howard, Counsel for Select Committee on Aging, U.S. House of Representatives: "Psychologists should not assume that the Committee is aware of the range of activities in which they are involved."

March 9, 1979. Robert Hoyer, Staff Assistant, Subcommittee on Health, Finance Committee, United States Senate: [On support of health maintenance organizations] "I think the U.S. government is finally realizing they can't just put money out on a stump and turn their backs without requiring anything in return. If HMOs are a viable competitor in health care delivery, they ought to be made to compete."

March 28, 1979. Linda Miller, Special Assistant on Hospices to Secretary of DHEW: "It is a serious failure for psychologists not to be involved with hospices, but I have never gotten a response from them."

June 15, 1979. Suzanne Woolsey, Associate Director for Human Resources, Veterans and Labor, Office of Management and Budget: "It is useful to have very specific proposals in hand. Do their work for them. Given that OMB operates with such uncertainty so much of the time, we are suckers for data."

July 30, 1979. Rebecca Beauregard, Staff Assistant for Health, Senator Harrison Williams (D-N.J.): "Medicare proves that the structure of a reimbursement system can dramatically affect health care delivery."

October 30, 1979. Terry Rogers, Senior Consultant, President's Commission on World Hunger: "I came onto the Commission as a microbiologist, believing I could contribute to their examination of the quality of nutrition at the cellular level. I discovered that quality had little to do with it. Poor people will always have lower 'quality' food. The real problem is calories. They simply do not take in enough calories to stay alive."

January 8, 1980. Gretchen Kolsrud, Assistant to the Director, Office of Technology Assessment: "OTA is in the process of editing its study of psychotherapy with particular attention to the cost/benefit analyses of psychological treatment. . . . APA could be of assistance to OTA in the identification of specialists who might consult on technological issues."

February 29, 1980. Michael Pollard, Office of Policy Planning, Federal Trade Commission: "Under the present health care system, different levels of care are available to the consumer depending on three factors: the reimbursement system; the individual's knowledge of what is available; and the individual's proximity to the available service."

April 18, 1980. Howard Veit, Director, Office of Health Maintenance Organizations, DHEW: "The change most necessary to improve the standing of psychologists within HMOs is a change in the attitude of physicians toward psychologists."

May 15, 1980. J. Michael McGinnis, Deputy Assistant Secretary for Disease Prevention and Health Promotion, DHHS: "The fate of the nation's health is in the hands of those who understand behavior. . . . The issue of behavior change with respect to health should be made a priority goal of APA."

June 13, 1980. Steve Sacher, General Counsel, Committee on Labor and Human Resources, United States Senate: [On the Employees Retirement Income Security Act of 1974] "While there is no substantive rule in ERISA that prohibits freedom-of-choice, ERISA, by virtue of its preemption of state law, would permit an employer to maintain a health benefit plan that excludes psychologists, even if such a plan is in conflict with state law."

September 26, 1980. Michael Goldberg, Counsel, Committee on Labor and Human Resources, United States Senate: "Nationwide, only 5% of occupation-related disease cases are covered by workers' compensation. Work-related psychological problems are covered in even fewer cases."

October 23, 1980. Patricia Forsythe, Staff Director, Subcommittee on the Handicapped, Committee on Labor and Human Resources, United States Senate: "In time of limited resources and high inflation, people are starting to question the value of training severely retarded persons in independent living skills, as opposed to the more traditional training of mildly handicapped persons. . . . The problems involved will be difficult to solve because the use of cost/benefit ratios is dubious where human values are concerned."

November 19, 1980. Jerry Michael, Dean, University of Hawaii School of Public Health; Michael Gemmell, Staff Director, Association of Schools of Public Health: "Health is a state of complete physical, mental, and social well-being, and not merely the absence of disease. The goals of public health do not differ much from the commitment made by psychologists in their graduate training."

December 17, 1980. Robert Butler, Director, National Institute on Aging: "People grow poor as they grow old at least partly because of the ravaging effects of inflation and medical costs. Our current aged population comprises 11% of our total population, up from only 3% in the 19th century; this trend is continuing and portends a demographic revolution that we must address."

January 6, 1981. James Mongan, Assistant Director for Health and Human Services, White House Domestic Policy Staff (under President Carter): "The history of federal intrusion in health planning peaked with the failure of President Carter's hospital cost containment bill. The bill failed in part because of the complexity required to protect the medical industry from being saddled with undue constraints, and in part because it did not receive strong support from special interest groups."

February 13, 1981. Colin Rorrie, Jr., Director, Bureau of Health Planning: "Greater competition and voluntary planning will characterize the health industry of the future. . . . Health service agencies are projected to be phased out completely by 1983."

March 26, 1981. Larry Scadon, Acting Director, National Institute for Handicapped Research: "I would like to have psychologists identify what they consider serious research issues they would like adressed. We try to have input from various disciplines, but the psychosocial area has not been very well represented. . . . Psychologists in the clinical area must also be more aware. When I taught in the department of psychiatry, new residents were afraid to talk to me because I am a handicapped person."

April 9, 1981. Richard Smith, Professor, John A. Burns School of Medicine and International Health Program, University of Hawaii School of Public Health: "My most basic finding in dealing with rural communities around the world is that people want to take responsibility for their own health care."

May 21, 1981. Normal Kretchmer, Director, National Institute of Child Health and Human Development: "Training is in terrible trouble, particularly predoctoral training. . . . It is absolutely critical for the field to be active in Washington."

July 7, 1981. Pamela Coughlin, Deputy Commissioner, Administration for Children, Youth, and Families: "I have been a bureaucrat all my life, but this is the first administration I have seen canceling contracts. This is not a cost-savings effort, mind you, since the outstanding costs on these contracts must be paid anyway. It is a deliberate halting of research."

July 31, 1981. Edith Grotberg, Director of Research, Demonstration, and Evaluation, Administration for Children, Youth, and Families: "People are not attracted to the federal government for money or for prestige, because there isn't much. The attraction is a desire for power and control. I do not say this in the pejorative sense. But you must know what motivates these people in order to deal with them."

October 23, 1981. H. David Banta, Program Manager, Health and Life Sciences, Office of Technology Assessment: "It is clear that there is no basis for allowing only psychiatrists to do psychotherapy."

October 29, 1981. A. David Lester, Commissioner, Administration for Native Americans: "Traditional medical professionals are not typically equipped to deal with the problems of specific communities particularly in terms of prevention strategies. It is an area where psychologists could provide information and assistance."

November 16, 1981. Al Yuen, President and Chief Operating Officer, Hawaii Medical Services Association: "While we were the first Blue Cross/Blue Shield plan to recognize psychologists, I do not believe providers should look to insurance carriers for a quick fix of their recognition problems. Consumer awareness and legal status are essential."

December 8, 1981. Robert Graham, Acting Administrator, Health Resources Administration: "Psychology should pick its political goals very strategically. It should limit them, focus on these few, and pursue them with persistence and patience."

January 12, 1982. Donald L. Custis, Chief Medical Director, Department of Medicine and Surgery, Veterans Administration: "The VA is the largest health care system in the country. What occurs inside this system is often an indication of what will go on outside of the system for the various health professions, including psychology."

15

HEALTH PSYCHOLOGY IN THE 21ST CENTURY: ACQUIRED IMMUNODEFICIENCY SYNDROME AS A HARBINGER OF THINGS TO COME

MARGARET A. CHESNEY

Of the 295 articles published in *Health Psychology* during the 1980s, 22% were on or related to coronary-prone behavior, reflecting a widespread interest in this topic. Members of Division 38 (Health Psychology) questioned whether this focus was in the best interest of the field, suggesting that health psychology might be better served by more balance among topics (Stone, 1984). In retrospect, this focused attention fostered innovations in behavioral assessment of cardiovascular reactivity; theoretical models examining complex interactions of stressors, cognitive behavior, personality, and physiology; and the recognition of the potential health consequences of hostility. Now, some members again are questioning if researchers are focusing too much attention on one topic—the human immunodeficiency virus (HIV). This article argues that this focus is prudent not only because (a) HIV has had a devastating effect on so many lives in the United States and abroad and (b) HIV challenges health psychology in a way no other problem has to date, but because HIV is introducing researchers to five trends and issues that have broad implications

Reprinted from *Health Psychology*, *12*(4), 259–268. Copyright 1993 by the American Psychological Association.

This work was supported in part by National Institute of Mental Health Grants R01MH46805 and P50MH42459. I wish to thank Susan Folkman for her support and valuable contributions to this article.

for public health in the future: the early identification of people who are at risk for disease, the rising expectations for successful behavior change programs, the growing populations of those who are coping with chronic disease, the increasing shift to include community and public health perspectives, and the emerging need to address health problems on a global scale.

HIV AND HEALTH PSYCHOLOGY

While health psychology was in its early years, a microbiological time bomb was detonated in its midst (Osborn, 1990). In 1981, the initial cases of what was to become an epidemic appeared in 5 gay men who were diagnosed with pneumocystis carinii pneumonia (Centers for Disease Control [CDC], 1981). At the time it was considered a medical anomaly, and in a nationally televised press conference Margaret Heckler announced that a cure and vaccine would be discovered within 5 years. Unfortunately, her prophecy was not fulfilled. The number of those infected with HIV and those who have succumbed to acquired immunodeficiency syndrome (AIDS) has risen. In 1981, 189 cases were reported, 77% of which were in New York and California. Only 3% of the cases involved women, and no children were known to have HIV (CDC, 1991). By October 1992, the dimensions of the HIV epidemic were formidable. The number of AIDS cases in the United States reported to the CDC was 233,907, and the cumulative number of deaths was 158,243. Every state and territory in the United States had reported cases and deaths. There were 25,947 AIDS cases in adolescent and adult women, and 4,051 AIDS cases in children less than 13 years of age (CDC, 1992a). However, these cases represent only the tip of the iceberg. An estimated 1.5 million Americans are infected with HIV. The World Health Organization (WHO) projects that by the year 2000, the number of infected adults and children worldwide will increase to 30–40 million (Mann, 1991).

Although the routes of HIV infection are well known, there is no vaccine to prevent infection. Changing high-risk behavior constitutes the only effective prevention strategy. Once individuals are infected, no current treatment is capable of eliminating the virus, and individuals face an inevitable decline. Given the paucity of pharmacological weapons, health psychology has a preeminent role to play in combating this epidemic by providing behavioral interventions that prevent the transmission of HIV and by providing cognitive–behavioral strategies to assist infected individuals in coping with their chronic disease. Even when vaccines and treatments become available, behavior change will be an essential factor in the prevention and the course of HIV (Coates, 1990). Not only does HIV place a new set of demands on health psychology, it serves as a lens through which we can see the future, a harbinger of things to come.

TREND 1: EARLY IDENTIFICATION OF PEOPLE WHO ARE AT RISK FOR DISEASE

Biologists engaged in deciphering the human genome are discovering the genetic origins of many human diseases (Hood, 1988), including the mutant p-53 oncogene that is associated with increased risk of certain cancers (Arbeit, 1990). These advances, part of what former National Institutes of Health director Bernadine Healy referred to as the "revolution in biology," allow the detection of individuals who are at high risk for disease (Healy, 1992; p. 312). Recent advances have provided diagnostic deoxyribonucleic acid (DNA) probes for Huntington's disease, cystic fibrosis, and a number of hemoglobinopathies (Masys, 1989). In the future, DNA analyses of biopsies heretofore considered benign will be carried out to uncover genetic patterns that indicate an inherited susceptibility to cancer (Arbeit, 1990).

These biotechnological advances will have profound effects on clinical medicine. The impact will first be seen with DNA analysis becoming a mainstay in individual diagnosis. The DNA scanners capable of performing these analyses are nearing development (Masys, 1989). Ultimately, the biotechnological diagnoses will marshal in a new generation of therapies. However, until these therapies are available, many individuals will be confronted with the decision of whether to undergo testing to determine their risk status for developing diseases. Those who choose to be tested will need to assimilate the results into their lives.

HIV Testing and Counseling

Prior to the HIV epidemic, advances in screening and early identification made by the biomedical community received only modest attention from health psychology. The psychological effects of labeling individuals at risk for hypertension (Irvine, Garner, Olmsted, & Logan, 1989) and responses to screening for breast cancer (Lerman, Trock, & Rimer, 1991) had been studied recently and found to be associated with increased negative moods, such as anxiety and worry. These thoughtful studies, however, did not prepare health psychologists for the sequelae associated with HIV testing and notification of a positive serostatus.

With the development of the HIV-antibody test in 1985, the medical community moved quickly to advocate HIV testing to obtain prevalence estimates of the infection and to encourage those who were infected to change behaviors to prevent further transmission of the virus (CDC, 1986, 1987). There was considerable resistance to voluntary testing despite this public health rationale. Indeed, within the high-risk population of homosexual men in San Francisco, a sizable number of the men remained untested as of 1989 (Folkman, 1993). Data from the Coronary Artery Risk Development in Young Adults (CARDIA) Study, which is being conducted in four cities in the United States, indicate that 44% of the gay men had not been tested (Berrios et al., 1992). Prior to the advent of antiretroviral therapies capable of slowing disease progression, learning that one was infected with the virus meant that the future would involve the development of an AIDS-defining condition and, ultimately, premature death. Concern about the effects of notification of positive HIV serostatus on mental health prompted the call that all testing be accompanied by informed consent and counseling (Coates & Lo, 1990). Health psychologists were recruited to conduct behavioral research on the effects of testing, to design programs that would increase voluntary testing among high-risk individuals, and to reduce the practice of high-risk behavior among those tested.

Consequently, research focused on the psychological and behavioral effects of HIV testing and notification of positive HIV serostatus. The findings demonstrated the dynamic relationship between decisions about being tested and perceptions of the potential consequences of knowing one's HIV status. The psychological effects of learning test results have changed over time. Whereas, studies conducted prior to 1988 generally report elevated levels of distress and suicide ideation, studies after 1988 report relatively lower levels of both distress and suicide ideation (Kelly & Murphy, 1992). Early in the epidemic, positive serostatus notification was associated with depression, anxiety, somatic complaints, and suicide ideation (Jacobsen, Perry, & Hirsch, 1990; Moulton, Stempel, Bacchetti, Temoshok, & Moss, 1991; Ostrow et al., 1989; Tross, Hirsch, Rabkin, Berry, & Holland, 1987). In one study conducted prior to 1988, just waiting for test results was associated with considerable distress and lowered immune function both in individuals who were later classified as seronegative and in individuals who were seropositive (Ironson et al., 1990).

Concerns about the psychological impact of HIV were elevated early in the epidemic by a report based on 1985 suicide records suggesting that the relative risk of suicide in men with HIV in New York City was 36 times higher than that of comparably aged men in the general population (Marzuk et al., 1988). The California Department of Health Services (Kizer, Green, Perkins, Doebbert, & Hughes, 1988) reported that the relative risk of suicide of men with HIV in California in 1986 was 17 times that of men without HIV. Although both of these accounts were criticized (Schneider, Taylor, Hammen, Kemeny, & Dudley, 1991) for not using the appropriate comparison group (i.e., men who are homosexual and/or use injection drugs), they alerted the community to the psychological trauma that can accompany HIV infection from the point of notification of serostatus through the progression of disease. The adverse psychological consequences of HIV infection observed early in the epidemic were attributed to the presence of a life-threatening condition, uncertainty about the future, the lack of established treatment options, guilt, social isolation, and discrimination (Dilley, Ochitill, Perl, & Volberding, 1985; Zones et al., 1986).

Research on the psychological effects of notification of positive serostatus conducted in cohorts after 1988 failed to observe a relationship between notification and psychological distress (Coates et al., 1988). For example, studies of suicide ideation published after 1988 indicate (a) an absence of such ideation in gay men who had AIDS for at least 3 years (Rabkin, Remien, & Katoff, 1991) or (b) levels of ideation in relatively asymptomatic HIV+ gay men that are no higher than levels in an HIV− comparison group (Schneider et al., 1991). Some researchers have suggested that the pretest and posttest counseling reduced the distress previously associated with receiving positive results (Perry et al., 1990). In addition to more adequate counseling with testing, Kelly and Murphy (1992) argued that the reduction in distress may be due to an improved public understanding of HIV transmission, a higher concordance between individual's expectancy and actual test results, the distinction drawn between HIV infection and AIDS, and the availability of medical treatments that can slow disease progression. Indeed, now with evidence that antiretroviral therapy can slow the progression of HIV (Volberding et al., 1990), it is important for individuals to be tested so that they can take advantage of the available treatments.

Testing and Primary Prevention of HIV

Primary prevention of HIV transmission provided a further rationale for testing (CDC, 1986, 1987). Specifically, the biomedical community argued that testing would reduce the incidence of high-risk behavior both in those receiving positive results and in those receiving negative results. In 1985, 79,000 HIV tests were performed in publicly funded testing centers. By 1991, the number had increased to 2,090,635 (CDC, 1992b). Despite the increase in testing, the literature does not reveal a consistent impact of testing and counseling on risk behavior, with the exception of heterosexual couples with one HIV-infected partner (Higgins et al., 1991). No effects of awareness of antibody status on protective behavior were observed among homosexual men living in Chicago (Ostrow et al., 1989) and Boston (McCusker, Stoddard, Zapka, Zorn, & Mayer, 1989). The strongest predictor of posttesting sexual practices is sexual practices prior to testing (McCusker et al., 1990). Similar findings were observed among men and women who were tested as part of blood donor screening at the New York Blood Center, an area of high HIV prevalence (Cleary et al., 1991) and those tested at anonymous testing centers in North Carolina, an area of low HIV prevalence (Landis, Earp, & Koch, 1992). In the latter study, 46% of those who tested positive for HIV did not even return for their results, and of those who did return and learn their serostatus, less than 10% notified their previous partners of their risk. The failure to see changes in risk-related behavior following voluntary testing points to an area where additional expertise in behavior change is needed and adds to the argument against mandatory testing as a strategy to stop the spread of HIV (Hein, 1991).

An important issue for health psychology is the effect of negative tests results on individuals who have practiced unsafe behaviors. Negative test results might engender a sense of invulnerability and reduce pretesting levels of perceived threat of HIV, which would be accompanied by high-risk behavior (Sherer, 1988). Research examining this possibility provides an inconsistent picture. In a 5-year follow-up of a sample of gay and bisexual men residing in San Francisco, HIV+ men reported lowering risk behaviors to avoid infecting others and to prevent further exposure to HIV, whereas HIV− men reported continuing to engage in high-risk behavior (Catania et al., 1991). Three other observation studies have reported similar findings (Fife et al., 1988; Fox et al., 1987; McCusker et al., 1988). Conversely, in a study of homosexual men in the Netherlands (van Griensven, de Vroome, & Tielman, 1989) and in a study of a multiethnic sample of patients attending an urban sexually transmitted disease (STD) clinic (Wenger, Linn, Epstein, & Shapiro, 1991), knowledge of one's negative antibody status was associated with lower risk behavior.

Early Identification and Intervention

An important challenge to health psychology and medicine is created by the extended period of time between identification of risk status and the onset of illness. An objective of biomedical advances in early identification is to create a window of opportunity for intervention to reduce or eliminate the risk of illness, often through behavior change. With HIV, this period can be a decade or longer. The challenge here becomes an opportunity to identify psychosocial, behavioral, physiological, and environmental factors that are associated with disease progression. As risk factors are identified, health psychologists are needed to design and evaluate behavioral interventions that may delay or prevent the onset of disease. Early efforts in this direction are represented by the application of cognitive–behavioral stress management interventions to assist HIV+ individuals in coping with their disease (Antoni, 1992; Antoni et al., 1991;

Chesney & Folkman, 1994; Ironson, Antoni, Schneiderman, LaPerriere, & Fletcher, 1992).

The extended period between identification of risk status and illness also provides a window for clinical trials that evaluate pharmacological treatments for HIV. Two central issues in HIV clinical trials require the expertise of health psychologists. The first issue involves moving beyond the traditional trial outcome of disease progression. With HIV, the delay of progression achieved with pharmacological treatment is often accompanied by severe side effects that interfere with daily functioning. Therefore, HIV clinical trials are attempting to evaluate treatment efficacy in terms of quality of life as well as the rate of disease progression. Although health psychologists have measured quality of life with considerable success in other illnesses (Shumaker, Anderson, & Czajkowski, 1990), there is a need for this expertise in clinical trials of potential treatments of HIV. Furthermore, as medical scientists begin to identify treatments that can slow the progression of disease, issues of delay in seeking care, access to care, and adherence become paramount. Problems have been recognized in each of these areas. For example, nonadherence threatens the effectiveness of the AIDS clinical trials. In the landmark studies testing the efficacy of zidovudine in asymptomatic HIV-infected patients, almost 30% of the patients either withdrew from the study or were lost to follow-up (Fischl et al., 1990; Volberding et al., 1990). Testing of new therapies for the secondary prevention of HIV will be compromised unless adherence is increased, a prospect that led clinical trials investigators to seek out health psychologists.

Bolstered by biotechnology, the trend in medicine toward earlier identification of risk has important implications for health psychology. Testing and screening are becoming commonplace in preventive medicine. However, medicine is not well equipped to address behavioral issues that emerge with this technology. HIV brought a new sense of urgency to the need for more behavioral research to develop and test models that focus on issues such as risk perception, decisions to be screened, the psychological and behavioral impact of learning results, treatment seeking, and interventions to increase adherence and to prevent disease progression. It is evident that this research agenda, which reaches far beyond HIV, needs to move forward and parallel the advances in medical technology.

TREND 2: RISING EXPECTATIONS FOR SUCCESSFUL BEHAVIOR CHANGE PROGRAMS

The second trend in medicine involves an increasing demand for programs that foster lasting behavior change. Modifying behavior is a hallmark of clinical health psychology. Over the past decade, health psychologists have identified risk factors such as cigarette smoking and obesity that are causally related to diseases such as coronary heart disease. Health psychologists have designed and tested theoretically based interventions for changing these behaviors. Although health psychologists are able to help individuals who are at risk to change their behavior, they have been far less successful in maintaining behavior change (Brownell, Marlatt, Lichtenstein, & Wilson, 1986; Marlatt & Gordon, 1985). HIV has refocused attention on this recurring issue. In other contexts, when behavior change has been unsuccessful or short-lived, as in the case when weight loss is regained, behavior change strategies can simply be repeated, or alternative interventions, such as pharmacotherapy, can be used. However, behavior change is the only available strategy for stopping the spread of HIV infection. A relapse of behavior can have serious consequences. It is as though behavior change technology is being given a scientific treadmill test, and the limits of this technology are painfully apparent.

Before health psychologists were heavily involved in HIV prevention, public health officials tried and failed to achieve reductions in high-risk behaviors such as unprotected sexual intercourse and needle sharing. The initial public health effort, similar to the antismoking efforts mounted several years ago, focused on providing information and arousing fear of infection. The assumption was that once the public was aroused by fear and provided information, the practice of high-risk behavior would cease. Numerous surveys indicated that the public showed an increase in factual knowledge, although persistent misconceptions about the risk of infection by casual contact remained, perhaps a result of the emphasis on fear arousal (DiClemente, Boyer, & Morales, 1988; Marin, 1989). Despite the change in public knowledge, there was little indication of widespread behavior change. Adolescents, for example, did not delay their age of sexual initiation and continued to show high-risk behavior, including low rates of condom use (DiClemente et al., 1988; Kegeles, Adler, & Irwin, 1989; Rotheram-Borus, Koopman, & Haignere, 1991). This came as little surprise to health psychologists, who found with previous public health campaigns that fear messages increase awareness but do not reliably lead to behavior change (Chesney & Coates, 1990).

Health psychologists working with adolescents, gay populations, or injection drug users were among the first to respond to calls for assistance in designing behavior change programs for populations at high risk for HIV infection (Coates, Temoshok, & Mandel, 1984). Innovative programs were introduced for high-risk individuals. These interventions, based on variations of the health belief model, were designed to increase knowledge about HIV, raise awareness of vulnerability, and teach specific risk-reduction skills. One such intervention was carried out among patients in methadone maintenance programs (Sorenson, Heitzmann, & Guydish, 1990). Following participation in these programs, patients were often more knowledgeable about HIV, realized their vulnerability to infection, and knew how to engage in risk-reduction activities. However, as in the case with the intervention for methadone maintenance patients, high-risk subjects continued to share needles and engage in unprotected sexual intercourse (Sorenson et al., 1990) despite changing their knowledge and attitudes about HIV and learning how to clean needles and how to use condoms.

In contrast to injection drug users and the heterosexual population, gay men in urban communities showed changes in AIDS-related high-risk behavior that far exceeded changes typically observed in response to public health efforts (Coates, 1990). The community of gay men in San Francisco provides an example of the scope of this change. In a probability sample of gay men surveyed in 1985, the prevalence of unprotected anal insertive and anal receptive intercourse was reported by 37.4% and 33.9% of the men, respectively (Stall, McKusick, Wiley, Coates, & Ostrow, 1986). In a follow-up survey in 1988, these behaviors were reported by only 1.7% and 4.2% of the same sample of men (Ekstrand & Coates, 1990). These self-reported changes in behavior were paralleled in a citywide decline in HIV incidence and gonoccal proctitis (Evans, Rutherford, & Amory, 1988). Gay men in other cities, including Denver (Judson, Cohn, & Douglas, 1989), Long Beach, Chicago, and Seattle (O'Reilly et al., 1989), have shown similarly notable changes.

Although the behavior changes made by gay men residing in urban communities represent one of the few positive points in the effort to contain HIV, there is increasing evidence from numerous industrialized nations that many gay men who initiate change do not consistently maintain it. (Ekstrand, 1992; Kelly & Murphy, 1992). The failure to change behavior in some risk groups and to relapse in other groups presents a challenge to health psychology to develop more effective approaches to achieving and maintaining meaningful health behavior change.

In an attempt to identify factors associated with behavior change, studies have compared those who have reduced their risk behavior with those who have not. Among gay men, factors associated with behavior change include self-efficacy for low-risk behavior (McKusick, Horstman, & Coates, 1985), awareness of personal vulnerability (Kelly, St. Lawrence, Brasfield, Lemke et al., 1990; McCusker et al., 1989), less substance use (McCusker et al., 1990; Ostrow et al., 1990; Stall et al., 1986), and perceptions that low-risk behavior is the norm for one's peer group (Joseph et al., 1987; Kelly, St. Lawrence, Brasfield, Lemke et al., 1990; Kelly, St. Lawrence, Brasfield, Stevenson et al., 1990). Research with populations other than gay men confirm that many of these factors are associated with behavior change. For example, in a study of high-risk adolescent women, the strongest predictors of condom use were perceptions of social norms as supporting low-risk behaviors and self-efficacy for the performance of low-risk behaviors (Kegeles, 1991). Retrospective and prospective studies have associated similar variables with a failure to maintain low-risk behaviors. In particular, relapse is related to low self-efficacy (Kegeles, 1991), depression (Kelly, St. Lawrence, & Brasfield, 1991), perceptions that unsafe sex is more pleasurable (Ekstrand & Coates, 1990; Stall, Ekstrand, Pollack, McKusick, & Coates, 1990), alcohol and drug use (Stall et al., 1986), and perceived norms in support of low-risk behavior (Stall et al., 1986).

New interventions that address the dynamic contextual determinants and consequences of risk behaviors are needed. These new interventions should focus on changing social influences that encourage a return to high-risk behavior, including the perception that low-risk behavior is less pleasurable and more difficult to carry out than are high-risk behaviors. Emphasis should be placed on positive features and erotic descriptions of safer sex and on peer education approaches that modify norms and enhance self-efficacy for low-risk behavior (Ekstrand, 1992).

The limited success of early efforts to reduce risk of HIV infection through behavior change highlights the limitations of behavior change technology. Research in HIV recites familiar problems in achieving and maintaining change, and health psychologists can expect pressure from the medical community to improve their record of success. New interventions underscore the importance that the social environment and social reinforcers play in determining behavior and suggest new directions for behavior change in general that incorporate social and normative approaches.

TREND 3: GROWING POPULATIONS OF THOSE WHO ARE COPING WITH CHRONIC DISEASE

The U.S. population that is 65 years of age or older currently numbers 31 million and is expected to increase by another 28 million by the year 2020 (U.S. Department of Health & Human Services, 1984; WHO, 1987). These changing demographics have significant implications for health psychology. Approximately 80% of those 65 years of age and over have at least one chronic condition such as hypertension, heart disease, arthritis, diabetes, depression, and declining cognitive function (U.S. Department of Health & Human Services, 1984). This aging trend, combined with the trend of earlier identification of individuals who are at risk, will result in a substantial proportion of the population that is coping with chronic conditions and disease.

The HIV-infected individuals represent a new, sizable, and growing cohort within the population of individuals who are coping with a chronic condition. Health psychologists working with HIV patients hear infected individuals frequently report a need for psychological counseling and support (Crystal & Jackson, 1989; Donlou, Wolcott, Gottlieb, & Landsverk,

1985). Targets for counseling include anxiety and fear associated with a progressing illness, hopelessness and depression that often accompany increased HIV symptomatology, stresses associated with health maintenance, adherence to prescribed care, and maintenance of hope and quality of life.

Descriptive studies identified processes such as hope, coping, and social support that mediate the effects of living with HIV. For example, in a study of 208 HIV-infected gay men (Rabkin, Williams, Neugebauer, Remien, & Goetz, 1990) hope was positively related to perceived social support and negatively related to depressive symptoms. In a longitudinal study of 425 gay men living in San Francisco (Folkman, Chesney, Pollack, & Coates, 1993) perceived control and coping affected the relationship between stress and depressed mood. Specifically, perceived control over stress predicted lower levels of depression through its influence on three forms of coping: planful problem solving, seeking information, and reappraising the stress in a positive light. Conversely, several types of coping— including keeping one's feelings to oneself, distancing, and cognitive escape–avoidance—were associated with higher levels of stress and depression. Indicative of the level of distress in this and similar populations confronting HIV, the level of depressed mood was observed to be 2.8 standard deviations above the norm for men in the general population.

Interventions focused on enhancing coping skills, and social support among HIV-infected individuals were an inevitable response to the adverse psychological impact of HIV. The first intervention study to attempt to decrease emotional distress, reduce high-risk behavior, and a low disease progression was conducted by Coates, McKusick, Kuno, and Stites (1989). Gay men who participated in the stress-management treatment group reported less depression and lower risk behavior, but no effect was found on immune markers thought to reflect rate of disease progression. More recently, researchers from the University of Miami (Antoni, 1992; Antoni et al., 1991; Ironson et al., 1992) reported reduced distress and immunologic decline following serostatus notification in HIV-infected individuals who participated in a 10-week cognitive–behavioral stress management program. A group-based intervention described as Coping Effectiveness Training (CET), based on a cognitive theory of stress and coping and on principles of cognitive–behavioral approaches to stress management, is being evaluated at the Center for AIDS Prevention Studies at the University of California, San Francisco. In a pilot test with 40 HIV-infected and non-HIV-infected men, CET was found to be effective in improved coping and positive morale as well as in decreasing depression and self-blame among both HIV-infected and non-HIV-infected individuals (Folkman & Chesney, 1995). A full-scale controlled clinical trial is now evaluating the effect of CET on mood, adherence to care, and immunologic variables in HIV-infected homosexual men (Chesney & Folkman, 1994).

The growing number of individuals who are identified as HIV infected represent a new cohort in the growing proportion of the population that is coping with chronic disease. Others in this population include (a) those identified by screening as being in the early stages of illnesses such as cancer and (b) the aging population, which must cope with declining capacity. The number of individuals with chronic disease points to a need for behavioral research to move beyond strategies that emphasize individual, face-to-face treatment and rehabilitation. Recognizing the need for innovative strategies for program delivery, the CET intervention described earlier is designed to be amenable to adaptation to a peer-led format. Biomedical and behavioral scientists need to forge a partnership to design programs for healthy living and management of chronic conditions and to develop new models for program delivery that can take advantage of new technologies and community resources to sustain quality of life.

Significant others, including immediate family members, partners, and friends, are also affected when individuals are confronted with chronic diseases such as HIV infection. One of the most immediate effects is that significant others are called on to provide direct caregiving. Research on caregivers of patients with Alzheimer's disease testifies to the extent to which significant others provide care and to the psychological toll that caregiving can take (Ward, 1990). At the present time, the majority of HIV-infected individuals receive extensive care at home from caregivers. There are estimates that this caregiving saves the public millions of dollars each year (Arno, 1986, 1988). With HIV, the fact that caregivers are often also HIV infected adds to the poignancy of this health care trend. Psychological distress among significant others caring for HIV-infected patients can be as high as that of the HIV-infected patients (Lamping et al., 1991). Research is currently examining the ways in which HIV+ and HIV− partners (Folkman & Chesney, 1992) cope with this challenge. Once factors that facilitate or interfere with adaptive coping are identified, there will be new opportunities for interventions to assist those who are affected by chronic disease.

TREND 4: INCREASING SHIFT TO INCLUDE COMMUNITY AND PUBLIC HEALTH PERSPECTIVES

Traditionally, the focus of health psychology has been on the individual. The trends in medicine noted in this article call for widening the lens through which health psychologists view their mission. The scope of the HIV epidemic has led some researchers to think anew about the integration of health psychology with perspectives from community psychology (Schneider, 1987; Sorenson et al., 1990) and public health (see also Winett, King, & Altman, 1989). As Coates (1990) wrote, "The HIV epidemic issued an important challenge to the public health and behavioral science community: Business could not (and still cannot) be conducted as usual" (p. 59).

A multidisciplinary effort among public health professionals, community psychologists, and health psychologists has been needed to successfully respond to the HIV epidemic. Public health contributes epidemiological approaches to understanding patterns of disease prevalence and routes of transmission at the population-based level of analysis. These approaches are bringing the influence of sociocultural factors on risk behaviors to the foreground and providing persuasive data on the economic consequences of failing to arrest the epidemic. Community psychologists are providing expertise in modifying community norms and evaluating field trials (Sorenson et al., 1990). Health psychologists are contributing theoretical approaches to explaining behavior, methods for obtaining detailed information at the individual level that provide information about factors associated with risk taking and risk reduction, and a set of tested strategies for modifying high-risk behavior. The impact of this multidisciplinary effort is reflected in epidemiological studies that have added questions about motivations for high-risk behaviors and barriers to low-risk behaviors to surveys (Ekstrand & Coates, 1990) or in behavioral interventions studies carried out in community-based settings (Coates, 1990).

This trend has implications that reach beyond the HIV epidemic. Reviewing work in smoking cessation over the last decade, Lichtenstein and Glasgow (1992) called for a "broader perspective and greater respect of the limited role of the individual and even small group interventions" (p. 525) and a need to "shift from a predominantly clinical approach to a public health perspective" (p. 518). Individually applied clinical interventions cannot meet the needs of the numerous individuals who place themselves at risk for disease by their behavior or who are attempting to cope with the illnesses and their sequelae. Although this point was made in the context of cigarette smoking, and it certainly applies to HIV, it is also highly relevant to primary prevention of illness and to most risk behaviors, including obesity and physical inactivity.

Recognition of the sociocultural influences on risk behaviors that range from cigarette smoking to unprotected sexual intercourse underscores the importance of multidisciplinary efforts that span the individual, community, and public health levels. Community-based media campaigns mounted in schools and work sites for smoking cessation were early products of this collaboration. The urgency of working at the community level to change social norms and to stop the transmission of HIV was emphasized by the National Research Council (of the National Academy of Sciences) in its policy recommendations for responding to the HIV epidemic in the 1990s (Turner, Miller, & Moses, 1989). Experience with community-based interventions to prevent HIV transmission illustrated how such programs can provide information and skills for behavior change by using the avenues of communication and influence indigenous to the community and by building and maintaining a social environment conducive and supportive of healthful change (Coates, 1990). To have a significant effect on the prevention and treatment of HIV, heart disease, and cancer, a vision that includes community and public health perspectives and the development of research methods and intervention approaches for use at the community level must be maintained.

TREND 5: EMERGING NEED TO ADDRESS HEALTH PROBLEMS ON A GLOBAL SCALE

Technological advances in communication and travel and developing social and economic alliances among nations have increased our awareness that many issues, from protection of the environment to the spread of infectious diseases, are best addressed as global problems rather than as local, national, or regional problems. AIDS has the distinction of being the first truly global epidemic (Mann, 1992). In 1980, estimates indicate that there were approximately 100,000 HIV-infected individuals (Mann, 1990). By 1990, this number had increased 100-fold to 10 million HIV-infected people throughout the world: 6 million in Africa, 1 million in North America, 1 million in South America, 1 million in Asia, and 500,000 in Europe. For the 1990s, it is projected that there will be 5 million AIDS cases. More than half of these projected cases will occur regardless of how effective prevention efforts are, given that these cases will develop in people infected during the 1980s (Chin & Mann, 1990). Although HIV infection will continue to challenge the western world, the largest growth will be in the developing world. Thailand provides a dramatic demonstration of this growth. In late 1987, less than 1% of IV drug users in Bangkok were HIV infected. By 1990, a survey indicated that 34% of IV drug users were HIV infected (Choopanya et al., 1991).

Because AIDS is a global crisis, it was inevitable that prevention and treatment efforts, and the health psychologists involved in them, would cross national borders. There is every indication that this trend to examine health from an international perspective will continue beyond the HIV epidemic. Jonathan Mann, former director of the World Health Organization's Global Program on AIDS cautioned that the global scale of HIV is not unique:

> HIV spread around the world, silently and unnoticed. . . . There is a great warning and lesson in this silent period of the HIV pandemic. The conditions of the modern world are uniquely favorable to rapid global spread of infectious disease. AIDS demonstrated how swiftly remote or seemingly obscure health events elsewhere can become to-

morrow's health crisis here. . . . A global approach is needed now to detect, as rapidly as possible, the pandemics yet to come. (Mann, 1992, p. 247)

Moreover, chronic illnesses such as heart disease and cancer know no boundaries. Research that unravels complex causal factors in these illnesses, that determines better strategies for sustained health behavior change, and that prevents disease or slows its progression will benefit humankind on a global level. Some years ago health psychology and behavioral medicine began establishing international networks such as the International Society of Behavioral Medicine. Now these networks provide forums for the exchange of ideas. If the response to HIV is an example of future trends, international teams will be formed to address health problems that transcend political borders. Scientists will increasingly work in a global laboratory and select populations for study because they present particular problems or unique research opportunities. For example, an international, multidisciplinary team is studying innovative strategies for primary prevention of HIV transmission in 60 heterosexual couples in which one partner is HIV infected and the other partner is not (Allen et al., 1992). Although this project requires a special population that is available in Rwanda, its results will generalize to prevention efforts in couples worldwide.

The HIV epidemic vividly demonstrates the interdependence of nations, drawing health psychologists into the global health arena. The lessons we learn in responding to the worldwide challenge of HIV and conducting research in the global laboratory will serve us well as we move into the 21st century. Epidemiological and biomedical scientists are proceeding to document the worldwide prevalence and incidence of other diseases and to identify certain risk factors, which, if addressed, offer promise for prevention and treatment. Without the involvement of health psychologists in these efforts, behavioral risk factors that are amenable to intervention are likely to be overlooked. Furthermore, programs to prevent disease through modification of risk factors in most circumstances will center on behavior change. Without the involvement of health psychologists, these programs may repeat the errors of the past, falling short of preventing disease transmission and failing to improve the quality of life for those who are infected. The experience with the HIV epidemic suggests that health psychologists have an important role to play as they look beyond national borders and toward global health and that the participation of health psychologists in the global arena will provide heretofore unseen opportunities to accelerate science.

SUMMARY

The AIDS epidemic presents a major challenge to the health community. It is evident that this epidemic is governed to a large extent by behavioral factors. Therefore, behavioral scientists, particularly health psychologists, are essential members of the multidisciplinary team needed to respond to this challenge. Furthermore, HIV provides a microcosm of five important trends and corresponding challenges for health psychology in the 1990s and into the 21st century.

There are at least 1 million to 1.5 million Americans who are currently HIV infected. Many of these individuals will experience the stresses of being identified as being at risk for disease (Trend 1). Without a vaccine, the only way to stop further spread of this disease is through effective behavior change that is maintained over time (Trend 2). For those who are infected, health psychologists are designing programs to assist them in coping with chronic disease (Trend 3). The scope of the HIV epidemic and the projections for the future require expanding the vision of health psychology beyond the individual level to that of the global community (Trends 4 and 5).

These trends, however, reach far beyond the AIDS crisis. Moreover, health psychology has become a central player on the multidisciplinary health team. Health psychology has been conducting research that is directly relevant to trends revealed by the challenge of HIV. Health psychologists who are not working with AIDS will benefit from the experiences of those who are and thus will be better prepared to respond as these trends unfold beyond HIV.

In the case of HIV, the questions for health psychology include the following: Will our theoretical models, our research designs, our methods, and our commitment to health adequately respond to the challenges presented by this disease? Will we discover effective strategies to prevent further transmission of this virus? Will we make meaningful contributions to address the needs of those who are already infected? Will our experience with HIV help us foresee trends that will shape health psychology and create new challenges for us in years to come?

REFERENCES

Allen, S., Tice, J., Van de Perre, P., Serufilira, A., Hudes, E., Nsengumuremyi, F., Bogaerts, J., Lindan, C., & Hulley, S. (1992). Effect of serotesting with counseling on condom use and seroconversion among HIV discordant couples in Africa. *British Medical Journal, 304,* 1605–1609.

Antoni, M. H. (1992, July). *Behavioral intervention effects on coping strategies, emotional expression and immune measures among individuals dealing with traumatic events: Implications for psycho-oncology?* Paper presented at the Second International Congress of Behavioral Medicine, Hamburg, Germany.

Antoni, M. H., Baggett, L., Ironson, G., August, S., LaPerriere, A., Klimas, N., Schneiderman, N., & Fletcher, M. A. (1991). Cognitive behavioral stress management intervention buffers distress responses and immunologic changes following notification of HIV-1 seropositivity. *Journal of Consulting and Clinical Psychology, 59*, 906–915.

Arbeit, J. M. (1990). Molecules, cancer, and the surgeon. *Annals of Surgery, 212*(1), 3–13.

Arno, P. S. (1986). The non-profit sector's response to the AIDS epidemic: Community-based services in San Francisco. *American Journal of Public Health, 76*, 1325–1330.

Arno, P. S. (1988). The future of voluntarism in the AIDS epidemic. In D. Rogers & E. Ginzberg (Eds.), *The AIDS patient: An action agenda* (pp. 65–70). Boulder, CO: Westview Press.

Berrios, D. C., Hearst, N., Perkins, L., Burke, G. L., Sidney, S., & McCreath, H. E. (1992). HIV antibody testing in young, urban adults: The Populations AIDS Risk Study (PARS). *Archives of Internal Medicine, 152*, 397–402.

Brownell, K. D., Marlatt, G. A., Lichtenstein, E., & Wilson, G. T. (1986). Understanding and preventing relapse. *American Psychologist, 41*, 765–782.

Catania, J. A., Coates, T. J., Stall, R., Bye, L., Kegeles, S., Capell, F., Hene, J., McKusick, L., Morin, S., Turner, H., & Pollack, L. (1991). Changes in condom use among homosexual men in San Francisco. *Health Psychology, 10*, 190–199.

Centers for Disease Control. (1981). Pneumocystis pneumonia—Los Angeles. *Morbidity and Mortality Weekly Report, 30*, 250–252.

Centers for Disease Control. (1986). Additional recommendations to reduce sexual and drug abuse-related transmission of human T-lymphatropic virus type III/lymphadenopathy-associated virus. *Morbidity and Mortality Weekly Report, 35*, 152–155.

Centers for Disease Control. (1987). Public Health Service guidelines for counseling and antibody testing to prevent HIV infection and AIDS. *Morbidity and Mortality Weekly Report, 36*, 509–515.

Centers for Disease Control. (1991). Update: Acquired immunodeficiency syndrome—United States, 1981–1991. *Morbidity and Mortality Weekly Report, 40*, 358–369.

Centers for Disease Control. (1992a, October). HIV/AIDS surveillance report. *HIV/AIDS Surveillance, pp. 5–13.*

Centers for Disease Control. (1992b). Publicly funded HIV counseling and testing—United States, 1991. *Morbidity and Mortality Weekly Report, 41*, 613–617.

Chesney, M. A., & Coates, T. J. (1990). Health promotion and disease prevention: AIDS put the models to the test. In S. Petro, P. Franks, & T. R. Wolfred (Eds.), *Ending the HIV epidemic: Community strategies in disease prevention and health promotion* (pp. 48–62). Santa Cruz, CA: ETR Associates.

Chesney, M. A., & Folkman, S. (1994). Psychological impact of HIV disease and implications for intervention. *Psychiatric Clinics of North America, 17*(1), 163–182.

Chin, J., & Mann, J. M. (1990). HIV infections and AIDS in the 1990's. *Annual Review of Public Health, 11*, 127–142.

Choopanya, K., Vanichseni, S., Plangsringarm, K., Sonchai, W., Carballo, M., & Des Jarlais, D. (1991, June). *Prevalence and risk factors of HIV-infection among injecting drug users in Bangkok.* Paper presented at the Seventh International Conference on AIDS, Florence, Italy.

Cleary, P. D., Van Devanter, N., Rogers, T. F., Singer, E., Shipton-Levy, R., Steilen, M., Stuart, A., Avorn, J., & Pindyck, J. (1991). Behavior changes after notification of HIV infection. *American Journal of Public Health, 81*(12), 1586–1590.

Coates, T. J. (1990). Strategies for modifying sexual behavior for primary and secondary prevention of HIV disease. *Journal of Consulting and Clinical Psychology, 58*, 57–69.

Coates, T. J., & Lo, B. (1990). Counseling patients seropositive for human immunodeficiency virus: An approach for medical practice. *The Western Journal of Medicine, 153*(6), 629–634.

Coates, T. J., McKusick, L., Kuno, R., & Stites, D. P. (1989). Stress reduction training changed number of sexual partners but not immune function in men with HIV. *American Journal of Public Health, 79*, 885–887.

Coates, T. J., Stall, R. D., Kegeles, S. M., Lo, B., Morin, S., & McKusick, L. (1988). AIDS antibody testing: Will it stop the epidemic? Will it help people infected with HIV? *American Psychologist, 43*, 859–864.

Coates, T. J., Temoshok, L., & Mandel, J. (1984). Psychosocial research is essential to understanding and treating AIDS. *American Psychologist, 39*, 1309–1314.

Crystal, S., & Jackson, M. M. (1989). Psychosocial adaption and economic circumstances of persons with AIDS. *Family and Community Health, 1*, 77–88.

DiClemente, R., Boyer, C., & Morales, E. (1988). Minorities and AIDS: Knowledge, attitudes, and misconceptions among Black and Latino adolescents. *American Journal of Public Health, 142*, 82–85.

Dilley, J. W., Ochitill, H. N., Perl, M., & Volberding, P. A. (1985). Findings in psychiatric consultations with patients with acquired immune deficiency syndrome. *American Journal of Psychiatry, 142*, 82–85.

Donlou, J. N., Wolcott, D. L., Gottleib, M. S., & Landsverk, J. (1985). Psychosocial aspects of AIDS and AIDS-related complex. *Journal of Psychosocial Oncology, 3*, 39–54.

Ekstrand, M. L. (1992). Safer sex maintenance among gay men: Are we making any progress? *AIDS, 6*, 875–877.

Ekstrand, M. L., & Coates, T. J. (1990). Maintenance of safer sexual behavior and predictors of risky sex: The San Francisco Men's Health Study. *American Journal of Public Health, 80*, 973–977.

Evans, P. E., Rutherford, G. W., & Amory, J. W. (1988, June). *Does health education work?* Paper presented at the Fourth International Conference on AIDS, Stockholm, Sweden.

Fife, K. H., Jones, R. B., Marrero, D. G., Katz, B. P., Serpe, R. T., & Scott, J. (1988, June). *Behavioral changes among sexually active homosexual men after learning they are negative for HIV antibody.* Paper presented at the Fourth International Conference on AIDS, Stockholm, Sweden.

Fischl, M. A., Parker, C. B., Pettinelli, C., Wulfsohn, M., Hirsch, M. S., Collier, A. C., Antoniskis, D., Ho, M., Richman, D. D., Fuchs, E., Merigan, T. C., Reichman, R. C., Gold, J., Steigbigel, N., Leoung, G. S., Rasheed, S., Tsiatis, A., & the AIDS Clinical Trials Group (1990). A randomized controlled trial of a reduced daily dose of zidovudine in patients with the acquired immunodeficiency syndrome. *The New England Journal of Medicine, 323*(15), 1009–1014.

Folkman, S. (1993). Psychosocial effects of HIV infection. In L. Goldberger & S. Breznitz (Eds.), *Handbook of stress* (Vol 2, pp. 658–681). New York: Free Press.

Folkman, S., & Chesney, M. A. (1995). Coping with HIV infection. In M. Stein & A. Baum (Eds.), *Perspectives on behavioral medicine* (pp. 115–134). Hillsdale, NJ: Erlbaum.

Folkman, S., Chesney, M. A., Pollack, L., & Coates, T. (1993). Stress, control, coping and depressive mood in HIV+ and HIV− gay men in San Francisco. *Journal of Nervous and Mental Diseases, 181*(7), 409–416.

Folkman, S. K., & Chesney, M. A. (1992, August). *Coping with caregiving and bereavement in the context of AIDS.* Paper presented at the 100th Annual Convention of the American Psychological Association, Washington, DC.

Fox, R., Ostrow, D., Valdisseri, R., Van Raden, M., Visscher, B., & Polk, B. F. (1987, June). *Changes in sexual activities among participants in the multi-center cohort study.* Paper presented at the Third International Conference on AIDS, Washington, DC.

Healy, B. (1992). Is this your father's NIH? and other strategic questions. *Science, 257,* 312–313, 414–415.

Hein, K. (1991). Mandatory HIV testing of youth: A lose–lose proposition. *Journal of the American Medical Association, 266*(17), 2430–2431.

Higgins, D. L., Galavotti, C., O'Reilly, K. R., Schnell, D. J., Moore, M., Rugg, D. L., & Johnson, R. (1991). Evidence for the effects of HIV antibody counseling and testing on risk behaviors. *Journal of the American Medical Association, 266*(17), 2419–2429.

Hood, L. (1988). Biotechnology and the medicine of the future. *Journal of the American Medical Association, 259*(12), 1837–1844.

Ironson, G., Antoni, M. H., Schneiderman, N., LaPerriere, A., & Fletcher, M. A. (1992, July). *Stress management interventions and psychological predictors in HIV.* Paper presented at the Second International Congress of Behavioral Medicine, Hamburg, Germany.

Ironson, G., LaPerriere, A., Antoni, M. H., Klimas, N., Schneiderman, N., & Fletcher, M. A. (1990). Changes in immune and psychological measures as a function of anticipation and reaction to news of HIV-1 antibody status. *Psychosomatic Medicine, 52,* 247–270.

Irvine, M. J., Garner, D. M., Olmsted, M. P., & Logan, A. G. (1989). Personality differences between hypertensive and normotensive individuals: Influence of knowledge of hypertension status. *Psychosomatic Medicine, 51*, 537–549.

Jacobsen, P. B., Perry, S. W., & Hirsch, D. A. (1990). Behavioral and psychological responses to HIV antibody testing. *Journal of Consulting and Clinical Psychology, 58*, 31–37.

Joseph, J. B., Montgomery, S. B., Emmons, C. A., Kessler, R. C., Ostrow, D. G., Wortman, C. B., O'Brien, K., Eller, M., & Eshleman, S. (1987). Magnitude and determinants of behavioral risk reduction: Longitudinal analysis of the cohort at risk for AIDS. *Psychology and Health, 1*, 73–96.

Judson, F. N., Cohn, D., & Douglas, J. (1989, June). *Fear of AIDS and incidence of gonorrhea, syphilis, and hepatitis B, 1982–1988.* Paper presented at the Fifth International Conference on AIDS, Montreal, Canada.

Kegeles, S. (1991, August). Adolescent women's AIDS risk behavior. Paper presented at the 99th Annual Conference of the American Psychological Association, San Francisco, CA.

Kegeles, S. M., Adler, N. E., & Irwin, C. E. (1989). Adolescents and condoms. *American Journal of Diseases of Children, 143*, 911–915.

Kelly, J. A., & Murphy, D. A. (1992). Psychological interventions with AIDS and HIV: Prevention and treatment. *Journal of Consulting and Clinical Psychology, 60*, 576–585.

Kelly, J. A., St. Lawrence, J. S., & Brasfield, T. L. (1991). Predictors of vulnerability to AIDS risk behavior relapse. *Journal of Consulting and Clinical Psychology, 59*, 163–166.

Kelly, J. A., St. Lawrence, J. S., Brasfield, T. L., Lemke, A., Amidei, T., Roffman, R. E., Hood, H. V., Smith, J. E., Kilgore, H., & McNeil, C. (1990). Psychological factors that predict AIDS high-risk and AIDS precautionary behavior. *Journal of Consulting and Clinical Psychology, 58*, 117–120.

Kelly, J. A., St. Lawrence, J. S., Brasfield, T. L., Stevenson, L. Y., Diaz, Y. E., & Hauth, A. C. (1990). AIDS risk behavior patterns among gay men in small Southern cities. *American Journal of Public Health, 80*, 416–418.

Kizer, K. W., Green, M., Perkins, C. I., Doebbert, G., & Hughes, M. J. (1988). AIDS and suicide in California [Letter to the editor]. *Journal of the American Medical Association, 260*, p. 1881.

Lamping, D. L., Sewitch, M., Clark, E., Ryan, B., Gilmore, N., Grover, S. A., Williams, J. I., Meister, C., Hamel, M., & Dimeco, P. (1991, June). *HIV-related mental health distress in persons with HIV infection, caregivers, and family members/significant others: Results of a cross-Canada survey.* Paper presented at the Seventh International Conference on AIDS, Florence, Italy.

Landis, S. E., Earp, J. L., & Koch, G. G. (1992). Impact of HIV testing and counseling on subsequent sexual behavior. *AIDS Education and Prevention, 4*(1), 61–70.

Lerman, C., Trock, B., & Rimer, B. K. (1991). Psychological side effects of breast cancer screening. *Health Psychology, 10*, 259–267.

Lichtenstein, E., & Glasgow, R. E. (1992). Smoking cessation: What have we learned over the past decade? *Journal of Consulting and Clinical Psychology, 60*, 518–527.

Mann, J. M. (1990). Global AIDS into the 1990's. *Journal of Acquired Immune Deficiency Syndrome, 3*, 438–442.

Mann, J. M. (1991). Global AIDS: Critical issues for prevention in the 1990's. *International Journal of Health Sciences, 21*(3), 553–559.

Mann, J. M. (1992). AIDS—The second decade: A global perspective. *Journal of Infectious Diseases, 165*, 245–250.

Marin, G. (1989). Prevention among Hispanics: Needs, risk behaviors, and cultural values. *Public Health Reports, 104*, 411–415.

Marlatt, A. G., & Gordon, J. R. (1985). *Relapse prevention: Maintenance strategies in the treatment of addictive behaviors.* New York: Guilford Press.

Marzuk, P. M., Tierney, H., Tardiff, I. K., Gross, E. G., Morgan, E. B., Hsu, M. A., & Mann, J. (1988). Increased risk of suicide in persons with AIDS. *Journal of the American Medical Association, 259*, 1333–1337.

Masys, D. R. (1989). Biotechnology computing: Information science for the era of molecular medicine. *Academic Medicine*, 379–381.

McCusker, J., Stoddard, A., Zapka, J., Zorn, M., & Mayer, K. (1989). Predictors of AIDS preventive behavior among homosexually active men: A longitudinal analysis. *AIDS, 3*, 443–448.

McCusker, J., Stoddard, A. M., Mayer, K. H., Zapka, J., Morrison, C., & Saltzman, S. P. (1988). Effects of HIV antibody test knowledge on subsequent sexual behaviors in a cohort of homosexually active men. *American Journal of Public Health, 78*(4), 462–467.

McCusker, J., Westenhouse, J., Stoddard, A. M., Zapka, J. G., Zorn, M. W., & Mayer, K. H. (1990). Use of drugs and alcohol by homosexually active men in relation to sexual practices. *Journal of Acquired Immune Deficiency Syndromes, 3*, 729–737.

McKusick, L., Horstman, W., & Coates, T. J. (1985). AIDS and sexual behavior reported by gay men in San Francisco. *American Journal of Public Health, 75*, 493–496.

Moulton, J. M., Stempel, R. R., Bacchetti, P., Temoshok, L., & Moss, A. R. (1991). Results of a one year longitudinal study of HIV antibody test notification from the San Francisco General Hospital cohort. *Journal of Acquired Immune Deficiency Syndromes, 4*, 787–794.

O'Reilly, K., Higgins, D. L., Galavottio, C., Sheridan, J., Wood, R., & Cohn, D. (1989, June). *Perceived community norms and risk reduction: Behavior change in a cohort of gay men.* Paper presented at the Fifth International Conference on AIDS, Montreal, Canada.

Osborn, J. E. (1990). AIDS: Politics and science. *Preventive Medicine, 19*, 744–751.

Ostrow, D. G., Joseph, J. G., Kessler, R., Soucy, J., Tal, M., Eller, M., Chmeil, J., & Phair, J. P. (1989). Disclosure of HIV antibody status: Behavioral and mental health correlates. *AIDS Education and Prevention, 1*(1), 1–11.

Ostrow, D. G., Van Raden, M., Fox, R., Kingsley, L., Dudley, J., & Kaslow, R. A. (1990). Recreational drug use and sexual behavior change in a cohort of homosexual men. *AIDS, 4*, 759–765.

Perry, S., Jacobsberg, L. B., Fishman, B., Weiler, P. H., Gold, J. W. M., & Frances, A. J. (1990). Psychological responses to serological testing for HIV. *AIDS, 4*, 145–152.

Rabkin, J. G., Remien, R., & Katoff, L. (1991, May). Suicidality in long-term survivors of AIDS. Paper presented at the Annual Convention of the American Psychiatric Association, New Orleans, LA.

Rabkin, J. G., Williams, J. B. W., Neugebauer, R., Remien, R. H., & Goetz, R. (1990). Maintenance of hope in HIV-spectrum homosexual men. *American Journal of Psychiatry, 147*, 1322–1326.

Rotheram-Borus, M. J., Koopman, C., & Haignere, C. (1991). Reducting HIV sexual risk behaviors among runaway adolescents. *Journal of the American Medical Association, 266*, 1237–1241.

Schneider, S. F. (1987). Community psychology and AIDS. *Community Psychologist, 21*, 7.

Schneider, S. F., Taylor, S. E., Hammen, C., Kemeny, M. E., & Dudley, J. (1991). Factors influencing suicide intent in gay and bisexual suicide ideators: Differing models for men with and without human immunodeficiency virus. *Journal of Personality and Social Psychology, 61*(5), 776–788.

Sherer, R. (1988). Physician use of the HIV antibody test: The need for consent, counseling, confidentiality, and caution. *Journal of the American Medical Association, 259*(2), 264–265.

Shumaker, S., Anderson, R., & Czajkowski, S. (1990). Psychological tests and scales. In B. Spilker (Ed.), *Quality of life assessments in clinical trials* (pp. 95–113). New York: Raven Press.

Sorenson, J. L., Heitzmann, C., & Guydish, J. (1990). Community psychology, drug use and AIDS. *Journal of Community Psychology, 18*, 347–353.

Stall, R., Ekstrand, M., Pollack, L., McKusick, L., & Coates, T. (1990). Relapse from safer sex: The next challenge for AIDS prevention efforts. *Journal of Acquired Immune Deficiency Syndromes, 3*, 1181–1187.

Stall, R., McKusick, L., Wiley, J., Coates, T. J., & Ostrow, D. G.: (1986). Alcohol and drug use during sexual activity and compliance with safe sex guidelines for AIDS. *Health Education Quarterly, 13*, 359–371.

Stone, G. C. (1984). A final word—Editorial. *Health Psychology, 3*, 585–589.

Tross, S., Hirsch, D., Rabkin, J., Berry, C., & Holland, J. C. B. (1987, June). *Determinants of current psychiatric disorders in AIDS spectrum patients.* Paper presented at the Third International Conference on AIDS, Washington, DC.

Turner, C., Miller, H., & Moses, L. (Eds.). (1989). *AIDS, sexual behavior, and intravenous drug use.* Washington, DC: National Academy Press.

U.S. Department of Health and Human Services (1984). *Executive summary: Aging and health promotion: Market research for public education.* Washington, DC: U.S. Government Printing Office.

van Griensven, G. J. P., de Vroome, E. M. M., & Tielman, R. A. P. (1989). Effect of human immunodeficiency virus (HIV) antibody knowledge on high-risk sexual behavior with steady and nonsteady sexual partners among homosexual men. *American Journal of Epidemology, 129*, 596–603.

Volberding, P. A., Lagakos, S. W., Koch, M. A., Peltinelli, C., Meyers, M. W., Booth, D. K., Balfour, H. H., Reichman, R. C., Bartlett, J. A., Hirsch, M. S., Murphy, R. L., Hardy, W. D., Soeiro, R., Fischl, M. A., Bartlett, J. G., Merigan, T. C., Hyslop, N. E., Richman, D. D., Valentine, F. T., Corey, L., & the AIDS Clinical Trials Group (1990). Zidovudine in asymptomatic human immunodeficiency virus infection: A controlled trial in persons with fewer than 500 CD4-positive cells per cubic millimeter. *New England Journal of Medicine, 322*(14), 941–949.

Ward, D. (1990). Gender, time and money in caregiving. *Scholarly Inquiry for Nursing Practice, 4*(3), 223–236.

Wenger, N. S., Linn, L. S., Epstein, M., & Shapiro, M. F. (1991). Reduction of high-risk sexual behavior among heterosexuals undergoing HIV antibody testing: A randomized clinical trial. *American Journal of Public Health, 81*(12), 1580–1585.

Winett, R. A., King, A. C., & Altman, D. G. (1989). *Health psychology and public health: An integrative approach.* Elmsford, NY: Pergamon Press.

World Health Organization (1987, March). *Prevention of cardiovascular diseases among the elderly: Report of a WHO meeting.* Paper presented at Geneva, Switzerland.

Zones, J. S., Beeson, D. R., Echenberg, D. F., Frigo, M. A., O'Malley, P. M., & Rutherford, G. W. (1986, June). *Personal and social consequences of AIDS antibody testing and notification in a cohort of homosexual and bisexual men.* Paper presented at the Second International Conference on AIDS, Paris, France.

16

U.S. MENTAL HEALTH POLICY: PROACTIVE EVOLUTION IN THE MIDST OF HEALTH CARE REFORM

GARY R. VANDENBOS

The United States needs health care reform. In the process of achieving such reform, the United States must explicitly establish a multifaceted national mental health policy that emphasizes prevention, outpatient care, and rehabilitation. In the past 25 years, the percentage of the gross national product (GNP) spent on health care has doubled, without major improvement in the health of Americans. Articles on health care reform by Kerrey and Hofschire (1993), Daschle, Cohen, and Rice (1993), Bingaman, Frank, and Billy (1993), and Durenberger and Foote (1993) serve to provide psychologists with an overview of the concerns and suggestions for health reform before the U.S. Congress as the 102nd Congress concludes and the 103rd Congress (and President Clinton's administration) begins.

Their messages are several, and they are clearly presented. The key points are (a) approximately 35 million Americans, 15% of the United

Reprinted from *American Psychologist*, 48, 283–290. Copyright 1993 by the American Psychological Association.

I gratefully acknowledge the assistance of many individuals in the preparation of this chapter. My associate, Elizabeth Q. Bulatao, provided invaluable research support; other APA staff, Laura E. Dworken, Sandra C. Pisano, and Marion Coates assisted in library searches. I appreciate the substantive comments the following individuals provided in reviewing earlier drafts of this manuscript: Donna Daley, Patrick H. DeLeon, Robert G. Frank, Alan E. Kazdin, Charles A. Kiesler, and Brian L. Wilcox. I also thank Rodolfo A. Bulatao for providing World Bank health and economic projections, and Dorothy P. Rice for sharing material on the economic costs of alcohol, drug abuse, and mental illness.

States population, are not covered by private health insurance or state/federal health care programs, and coverage for this subset of individuals, primarily low-income working families, is vitally needed; (b) the United States, as a nation, is consuming far more health care than it is actually paying for in taxes or insurance premiums, such that, out of the over $800 billion spent on health care in 1992, over $225 billion (or over 28%) was "deficit spending," which contributed directly to the federal deficit; and (c) on a number of health indicators, the United States ranks lower than many other nations that are spending far less per capita on health care than the United States. It is clear that health care reform is needed. The challenge, then, is, how to reform health care.

MAGNITUDE OF FINANCIAL CHALLENGE

The cost of health care, and its increasing negative impact on the budgets of state governments and the federal government, is the primary factor forcing policy attention to health care reform (Dorken & DeLeon, 1986). Although other factors are important, they are secondary in policy discussions. Absolute cost, relative cost (i.e., as a percentage of GNP), and magnitude of annual increases are the central themes. The percentage of GNP devoted to health care continues to expand by a significant amount each year. Many economists and policymakers believe it has reached the limit of what is supportable, and it must be capped in a manner that allows growth in absolute dollars but not as a relative percentage of GNP. However, they also believe that, for multiple reasons, it is essential to extend health care coverage to those who are currently without public or private health care coverage. This adds to the financial challenge.

Congress could decide to simply extend a typical health care package to those who are now without insurance coverage (at the federal government's expense, without payment of an insurance premium or a tax increase). What would this cost? The figure usually quoted on Capitol Hill is $60 billion, although it could be as high as $140 billion, if it was assumed that the newly covered 15% would consume health care services at the identical level as the 85% of Americans currently covered. This would have expanded total 1992 health care spending to between $860 and $940 billion, and it would have increased the magnitude of deficit spending for health care to between $285 and $365 billion—or somewhere in the range of 33.1% to 38.8% of all 1992 health care expenditures. This is unrealistic and unsound, and Congress is unlikely to do this. It is also inconsistent with the prime factor motivating national attention to health care reform—lowering, or at least restraining, health care costs.

What would it take to fully address the congressional concerns about universal coverage and a "balanced health care budget" without spending more on health care? If one wanted to both extend coverage to those currently not covered and eliminate all deficit financing of health care, then the annual dollar value of health care expenditures by every American would need to be reduced by over 45%. The prospects of Congress discovering a reasonable mechanism that would cut every individual's health care consumption in half seems somewhat improbable. Obviously, another way to balance the health care budget would be through a combination of expense reductions and tax increases (or even solely by tax increases and health insurance premium increases); however, this would also further increase the percentage of GNP devoted to health care, something that most policymakers are trying to avoid.

There is yet another perspective on how to cover those individuals not currently covered and at least reduce the magnitude of deficit spending. It is hinted at by various Congressional health reform spokespersons but not necessarily fully articulated as "the source" of the funding. This is by eliminating unnecessary medical services, estimated to account for as much as 30% of current health care costs (Brook, Kamberg, & Mayer-Okaes, 1989), and by eliminating fraud in health care billing, which is estimated at 10% of annual health care expenditures (General Accounting Office [GAO], 1992). It also has been suggested that a "single payer" system of paying for health care could eliminate duplicate administrative costs and reduce annual national health care expenditures by as much as 5%. When the monetary value from these sources and indirect hidden "cost-shifting" are totaled, the sum of identified funds exceeds the 45% of needed funds noted above. If the estimates are valid, then it is theoretically possible to extend coverage and balance the health care budget through these sources. But, is it practically possible?

This is the health care reform challenge before the Clinton administration, and the American public, as the 103rd Congress begins its work. The question of cost (or financing) is the primary policy and political issue. America's appetite for health care services (and mechanisms to pay for it) has grown and grown over the past 25 years. Can the process be restricted or reversed? Should it be stopped? Will consumers, hospitals, and other providers and insurers allow it? Can the ever-expanding demand for services be focused into a more coherent package of services that is reasonable and responsive to the diverse health care needs of the full range of Americans?

A RIGHT TO HEALTH CARE?

The most fundamental health policy issue is whether we, as a nation, believe that access to health care as a fundamental right for all U.S. citizens should be guaranteed by the federal government in the same manner that we strive to guarantee basic physical safety, national defense, access to education, basic economic resources, and so forth. The vast majority of the American public appears to hold this view (Blendon & Edwards, 1991). It would appear that many, perhaps nearly all, of our nation's highest elected officials view this issue as resolved in the positive, as there seems to be consensus that universal access to health care is to be treated as a given that must be achieved in any health care reform. It is less clear how much health care, provided in what form, should be included in that fundamental right.

WHAT MIGHT "MANAGED COMPETITION" LOOK LIKE?

The concept of "managed competition" has been embraced in Washington policy circles the same way that the general concept of "competition" was embraced 12 years ago when President Reagan took office. However, no one seems to agree on what managed competition is (Rovner, 1992), although the concept is linked to the so-called Jackson Hole Group and Alain Enthoven (Cohn, 1992).

Most managed competition plans include a standard minimum benefit package, universal access to this standard minimum benefit plan, and price competition among plans through purchasing cooperative groups. In the simplest terms, the essential mechanisms of influence in managed competition appear to be three: (a) the process for setting the standard health care benefit package, (b) the creation and operation of an intermediary that would act on behalf of health consumers to obtain the lowest price per unit of service for those services in the minimum benefit package, and (c) policies that cause a greater proportion of funds spent on health care (particularly health insurance premiums) to be paid in after-tax dollars—that is, by shifting some of the indirect compensation that is currently not taxed into taxable income, both to generate additional tax revenues and to involve individual Americans in health care cost containment. There also has been the suggestion that a predetermined national cap on health care expenditures be set—either lower than current expenditures, at say 10% of GNP, or slightly above current expenditures, such as 15%.

Most proposed health care reform plans involving managed competition assume that some powerful, semi-autonomous, federally created board will be empowered to establish, on an annual basis, the standard set of benefits to be available through all plans to all Americans. The proposals differ in terms of how much detail is provided about the establishment and operation of such a board, and many details remain to be settled about who would be appointed to this board, how it would operate, what procedures and data it would use, or how the relationship between Congress and this board would be handled. However, it is clear that its primary purpose would be to define annually the services to be included in the standard benefit package for the next year. Some descriptions of these plans imply that this set of benefits should be "comprehensive" whereas others describe it as the "minimum set."

If a comprehensive model is followed, including a full array of psychological services available to consumers through direct access to psychologists, such a national benefit package would have all of the features of comprehensive "mandated mental health services" and national "freedom of choice" legislation. Such an eventuality should be viewed positively by consumers, psychologists, and most of the mental health field. However, this is unlikely.

To the extent that all currently existing "customary and usual" services by all provider groups are included, the definition of a standard package of benefits will have little or no effect on health care delivery practices. To the extent that the package of covered services is either small or selective, it will influence different areas of health care delivery differentially. This should be of concern to the mental health field, which has historically been discriminated against because of the bias of biological-oriented physicians and misconceptions about mental health care among insurance officials.

A minimum benefit package will have a smaller price tag that needs to be covered through governmental funds (for health care programs provided by state and federal governments) and by corporate payments (for private health insurance coverage for employees through commercial health insurance premiums). This would lessen the portion of health care costs paid for by government and business. Only the insurance premium for the minimum benefit package would be deductible by employers as a business expense. Employers could offer additional health insurance coverage to their employees, but both the employer and the employee would have to pay such premiums with after-tax dollars. The net effect for individuals would be to increase the percentage of health care costs covered directly from their personal budgets for health insurance premiums, deductions, copayments, and excluded fee amounts.

Most descriptions of the proposed federal health board mention that it would use evaluation data in determining basic benefits. However, little detail is provided about how it would do this or what data it would use. Some policymakers are primarily worried about overly rapid spread and excessive use of high-cost, high-tech medical technologies before they have been demonstrated to be cost-effective alternatives to existing medical technology. Evaluations such as those done by the Office of Technology Assessment are often the model behind such thinking. This approach is primarily useful in the evaluation of emerging technology and determining whether (or how rapidly, or how selectively) to admit it into the body of clinically acceptable and financially reimbursable procedures.

Other policymakers urge using empirical clinical outcome data in determining reimbursible medical services. This is a good long-term goal (and one to which I will return), but it is mostly impractical today. Only about one third of today's medical interventions have been found by modern scientific methods to be of established benefit, one third are of uncertain benefit, and one third are suspected of not being beneficial at all (Hennen, 1992). It is frequently noted that more than one half of all visits to physicians are made by patients who demonstrate an emotional, rather than an organic, etiology for their physical symptoms (Cummings, 1977). In a similar manner, more than one half of all medical office visits result in no treatment, although there may have been various laboratory tests, other procedures, and follow-up office visits in the process of determining that no medical intervention was needed or was likely to be effective. Most new biological illness is self-limiting, and probably half is never definitively diagnosed (Hennen, 1992). The simple and sole application of such empirical criteria, as such data exists today, would mean that somewhere between 50% and 80% of physician visits and medical diagnostic tests would be excluded from the basic definition of the benefits package. Such an eventuality seems unlikely.

Any federal panel determining covered services should consider empirical data on outcome and cost-effectiveness. In fact, organized psychology has long supported strong evaluation measures and accountability control as an integral part of any national health insurance strategy (cf. Kiesler, 1979; DeLeon, VandenBos, & Cummings, 1983; APA Task Force on Continuing Evaluation in National Health Insurance, 1978). The key will be how cost-benefit data (Yates & Newman, 1980) are handled and utilized. It is essential that mental health services not be required to meet unfairly higher standards than physical health services in order to be included in a standard package of care.

Most proposed health care reform plans would involve the creation of large purchasing cooperatives to secure bids from insurance carriers, networks of health care facilities and/or providers, and making these purchasing options available to all Americans. It is generally assumed that these organizations would be statewide or regional, to cover a large enough population to have substantial purchasing power and avoid adverse selection problems. In some descriptions of these purchasing entities, however, it has been suggested that large employers and other clusters of purchasers might be allowed to form their own health care purchasing cooperatives (which could raise other kinds of problems). The primary purpose of cooperative purchasing entities would be to represent the consumer in front-end negotiations with private insurers and in quality control activities. In general, it is argued that such purchasing cooperatives would exert the presumed purchasing power of the masses, serve as quality control watchdogs for consumers, increase consumer participation, and avoid "divide-and-conquer" strategies by insurance carriers that create opportunities for adverse selection.

The goals of achieving more (and truly effective) competition in the health care marketplace and creating more opportunity for consumers to be meaningfully involved in their own health care are good ones. There is little question that the current health care system offers little meaningful competition, even when opportunities for such competition exist (e.g., nurse midwives vs. obstetrician-gynecologists, optometrists vs. opthalmologists, psychologists vs. psychiatrists). It is unlikely that purchasing cooperatives will do anything to stimulate such reasonable, needed, and appropriate competition among providers and provider groups.

It would be an advance to involve patients meaningfully in their health care and the cost of the health services they use. However, to achieve this, the individual consumer would need to be directly involved in clinical decision making or cost–benefit decision making regarding his or her own health care. This would require truly "informed consumers" (of health care) and a health care financing system that truly involves the individual consumer/patient. In the current health payment system, few of the individuals making the decisions to use or pay for health care ever interact directly with each other or consider all of the issues (VandenBos, 1983). There is, in the present system, a four-party chain of relationships between consumers, providers, insurers, and employers whereby each interacts with the next party in the chain, with different issues being addressed at each link in the chain. All of the parties never come together, and each party has incomplete information on the central issues of the other interacting pairs.

Employees and their families are pressured by the ever-escalating expense of health care (and the catastrophic financial risk that major or chronic illness represents), and they understandably want all aspects of health care to be covered. Employees/patients, however, do not by and large deal directly with physicians about their fees or with insurance companies about premiums. When patients deal with their providers, they are seeking health care services to make them well or to keep them healthy. Physicians are pressured by their patients for more health care and better health care, and physicians are paid by insurance carriers or the government for virtually all services rendered or ordered. Insurers are pressured by providers (and to a lesser extent by consumers) to reimburse for all services deemed by the provider as needed, which they mostly do—setting future premiums on previous year expenditures. Carriers inform employers of the new, higher premiums, which the employers pressure the carriers to hold down, but they eventually settle on a premium amount (which is fully deducted as a business expense). The employers then inform employees of the benefit plan, level and nature of reimbursement, copayment and premium sharing features, and so forth for the next year. It is unclear that health care purchasing cooperatives will do anything to improve such contact and communication—or, in short, to truly involve individual consumers and providers in health care cost containment.

CHALLENGE BEFORE AMERICA'S MENTAL HEALTH PROFESSIONALS

From a cost perspective, reform of financing mechanisms and funding decisions is clearly needed. The challenge before psychology, on behalf of the citizens of the United States, is to ensure the continuation of adequate and timely access to appropriate and needed psychological and behavioral health care. This will be a major challenge, because there has never been a meaningful mental health policy in the United States. In addition, involvement of psychological practice beyond the mental health area is not as fully recognized as its contribution within mental health. It is vital that psychological health and illness be explicitly recognized during the coming health care reform. It is equally vital that mental health policy not be treated as a mere extension of physical health policy.

EVOLUTION OF NATIONAL HEALTH AND MENTAL HEALTH POLICY

Before 1920, health care was a personal financial responsibility, although those without the means to provide for themselves could receive charity health care (VandenBos, Cummings, & DeLeon, 1992). The massive growth in voluntary health insurance began in response to the catastrophic economic depression of the 1930s (Falk, 1964). Later, during World War II, employer-paid health insurance plans expanded rapidly (when such benefits were exempt from wartime antiinflationary restrictions on wage increases). Between 1945 and 1960, the availability of health insurance increased to the point that 69.2% of the U.S. population had some form of health insurance (U.S. Department of Health, Education, & Welfare, 1962). In the 1960s, health policy emphasized expanding access to needed health care, and this period included the passage of Medicare, Medicaid, and other health legislation (VandenBos et al., 1992). Efforts over the past 25 years to increase access to or consumption of health care have worked. In 1990, health care represented over 12.2% of GNP, more than double the percentage of GNP in 1965. In constant dollars, 1990 health care expenditures represent a 400% increase over 1965 (Congressional Budget Office, 1991, p. 61; Levit, Lazenby, Cowan, & Letsch, 1991, p. 29).

Federal mental health policy began to emerge with the establishment of the National Institute for Mental Health in the late 1940s (VandenBos, 1980). It received more systematic attention and articulation when a federal commission, the Joint Commission on Mental Health and Illness, was established in the 1950s. As an outgrowth of the work of the commission, the Community Mental Health Centers Act was passed in 1963 as a means of making mental health care more readily available to all Americans in all areas of the country through community-based clinics (VandenBos et al., 1992). Efforts by citizens' groups, unions, and mental health professionals to convince most private insurance carriers that mental health care was an important and critical health service that should be fully recognized and reimbursed under health insurance plans succeeded during the 1960s and 1970s (Cummings & VandenBos, 1983). Inclusion of psychological care within federal programs lagged behind its acceptance and inclusion under private plans (DeLeon & VandenBos, 1980), although it was included in the initial federal legislation supporting health maintenance organizations (HMOs) in 1973 (DeLeon, VandenBos, & Bulatao, 1991). Mental health policy received major policy attention in 1977–1978 when President Carter established the President's Commission on Mental Health (Kiesler, Cummings, & VandenBos, 1979). Unfortunately, many aspects of the legislation resulting from the Carter Commission were reversed shortly after President Reagan took office.

Critics of mental health care sometimes argue that it is a welfare issue. This is simply untrue. Mental health is a valid and critical component of health care. Although such a "health care as welfare" conceptualization may have been appropriate for all of health care in 1920 (and when those viewed as "crazy" and completely unable to function in normal society were relegated to a county "poor house" or a state mental hospital/farm), the general and well-documented view now is that between 15% and 18% of the U.S. population in any given year manifest significant symptomatology that warrants mental health intervention (Regier et al., 1988). Such psychological and behavioral dysfunctions occur in all segments of the U.S. population, and many individuals who seemingly are functioning well are, in fact, experiencing serious symptoms with severe negative effects on their physical health, interpersonal functioning, and economic productivity. Although some stigma about mental health services still exists, most Americans understand the value and appropriate use of psychotherapy, and over 26% of Americans have utilized mental health care at some point in their lives (Kulka, Veroff, & Douvan, 1979).

RELATION OF HEALTH POLICY TO MENTAL
HEALTH POLICY

Kiesler (1992) has presented a comprehensive description of how health policy fails miserably when mental health policy is treated as a mere extension of physical health policy. He argued that such a mental health policy is inevitably doomed because the U.S. health policy is itself inherently flawed. Kiesler views the essential flaw in U.S. health policy as the overemphasis on acute care, short-term general hospital care, and surgery. He argued that short-term acute acre and hospital practice do not match up well with the nation's health care needs, leaving 40% of the population without critically needed preventive services and leaving chronic health problems of all age segments of the population inadequately met.

Kiesler (1992) convincingly illustrated how current national health policy represents national *general hospital* policy, not health policy. When such policy favoring hospitalization is inappropriately extended into mental health care, the consequences are devastating. It distorts the dollar allocation between inpatient and outpatient mental health care. A large percentage of mental health funds are used to pay for inpatient services to a small percentage of those in need of mental health care, while the benefit of that inpatient care is not greater (and may well be worse) than the same service for the same patients provided less expensively on an outpatient basis. Kiesler (1982a, 1982b; Kiesler & Sibulkin, 1987) concluded that, in mental health, outpatient care works better than inpatient care for similar seriously disturbed patients, but funding for inpatient care continues to increase while outpatient care is difficult to fund—because of the biases in existing hospital-based and acute care health policy.

NATURE OF MENTAL HEALTH NEEDS

Psychological problems are complex and multifaceted. Not all psychological problems are the same. Some mental health patients have very severe problems that are manifested in every aspect of their physical and behavioral functioning. Other patients have more limited or focused problems. All are painful, and they cause psychological dysfunction, behavioral disruption, and somatic difficulties in varying degrees and combinations. Such psychological and behavioral problems must be treated in the most timely and efficient manner, and as early as possible in their development—so that the productivity of our nation's industries is not diminished, the physical health care system does not waste resources treating psychological difficulties masquerading as physical complaints, and educational opportunity is not wasted. The mental health needs of Americans cannot be viewed as a singular type of difficulty, but rather, as an array of psychological care needs.

CONTINUUM OF PSYCHOLOGICAL HEALTH CARE SERVICES

The array of psychological health needs of our citizens must be recognized. They translate into the same array of service needs that exist in relation to physical illness. That is, preventive services, screening, early intervention, assessment, short-term treatment, moderate-term treatment, episodic intervention, long-term treatment, and rehabilitation. Psychological care is not merely one service consisting of one intervention. Likewise, psychological care is not merely "specialty health care"—some psychological services are primary care services (VandenBos, DeLeon, & Belar, 1991).

Psychological care can be, as seen above, divided into four types of services or interventions: (a) preventive care, screening, and assessment; (b) short-term acute care and psychotherapy; (c) rehabilitation and rehabilitative psychotherapy; and (d) long-term chronic care. At present, only acute care psychotherapy even approaches being adequately covered in most insurance plans. Reimbursement for preventive psychological interventions is largely nonexistent. Likewise, rehabilitative services, consisting of psychotherapy and/or other interventions, are often not available to those with long-standing psychological dysfunctions. Periodic care and supportive services for the seriously mentally ill and mentally disabled are limited.

It is vital that, as health care reform is undertaken, congressional policymakers recognize that psychological services are not limited to "specialized service" (in the way that psychiatry is a limited "medical specialty"), but rather are arrayed among prevention, acute, specialized, rehabilitative, and chronic care services. Access to and coverage for each type of psychological service must be assured. It is vital that, in the process of health care policy reform, a bias toward the most expensive and least effective mental health interventions (i.e., hospitalization) does not occur. Priority must be on making interventions as early as possible, before the consequences for the patient become devastating and before the need for intervention is massive and excessively expensive.

PSYCHOLOGICAL CARE BEYOND THE MENTAL HEALTH ARENA

Over the past several decades, basic and applied researchers have expanded the range of psychology's knowledge base, which has in turn led to applications in ever-expanding areas of practice (VandenBos et al., 1991). Research in health psychology and neuropsychology has mushroomed in the past two decades. Health psychology encompasses both psychological aspects of physical illness and treatment and promotion of physical health and prevention of biological illness. Behavior plays a significant role in each of the seven top major health risk factors facing our nation today (tobacco use, diet, alcohol, unintentional injuries, suicidal behavior, violence, and unsafe sex).

Behavioral and psychological treatments are now considered either the treatment of choice or a necessary component of intervention for many psychophysiological disorders. As health professionals, psychologists are involved in a wide variety of services that are *not* dependent on the diagnosis of psychopathology (as would be the case in the mental health area). For example, psychologists are involved in assessment, intervention, and consultation related to management of pain, coping with stressful medical procedures, control of pharmacological side effects, training in physical self-examination and health monitoring, recovery from illness and surgery, neuropsychological functioning, cognitive rehabilitation, behavioral health, adherence to health care regimens, organ transplant decisions, and work site injury prevention and health programs.

As organized psychology works with Congress and the Clinton administration on health care reform during the 103rd Congress, psychology will need to inform and remind policymakers that psychologists, as independent professionals, provide health services in areas of health care beyond mental health. It is critical that they be recognized as eligible providers of such services as the details of health care reform are set in place.

ROLE OF EVALUATION RESEARCH

A system of evaluation research should be a component of national health policy and mental health policy. The *Principles for Mental Health Care in Health Care Reform* (American Academy of Child and Adolescent Psychiatry et al., 1992) recently adopted by 17 national health organizations (with the American Psychiatric Association not supporting them) encourages reviews and evaluations to ensure that all health and mental health services are both cost-efficient and effective. Without a meaningful commitment to outcome evaluation, any national health care monitoring system would be no more useful than the computerized files of Medicare (APA Task Force on Continuing Evaluation in National Health Insurance, 1978).

At least three types of data would be needed for a reasonably useful national evaluation system. At the most fundamental level, there should be a basic set of incident-defining variables, such as patient identification, provider identification, presenting health problem (or preliminary diagnosis), treatment intervention, and fees (and related expenses). This would be needed for accounting, reimbursement, and description of practice patterns and service utilization. However, this merely constitutes an administrative management system: It cannot generate cost-effectiveness data.

A second level of data would be needed that could be fully integrated with the basic data set—that is, clinical outcome data. Having such outcome data is essential if there is a sincere desire for cost-benefit and cost-effectiveness data for use in future years. Some such evaluations could be done as formal research projects, but it would also be critical that, at least periodically, parallel information be collected in everyday clinical practice, so that effectiveness under the less controlled conditions of everyday clinical patterns could be achieved. It is also important to add a cautionary note against the overcollection of information. One should not collect more data per encounter than one actually intends to analyze and use. There is considerable cost involved for providers in collecting such data and preparing it for transmission and use by a central authority, and there are additional costs for the central authority for inputing, storing, and analyzing data. However, if clear attention is given at the inception to a national clinical outcome data collection system, it has the potential of greatly improving health care in the future—and making the delivery of health care both more cost-efficient and more clinically relevant and effective.

Managed care systems today largely ignore issues of quality of care and access to care. They do not address quality and outcome, because they have no incentive to do so. Earlier HMO research appears to have been genuinely motivated by the twin and coequal principles of seeking the lowest cost intervention and the most clinically effective intervention (DeLeon et al., 1991). There is some evidence to suggest that, as managed care has become a popular concept, it has shifted somewhat toward an access-denying and cost-controlling mode (cf. Welch, 1986a, 1986b; Buie, 1987, 1989a, 1989b, 1990; GAO, 1988). There is no reason that it needs to be this way. However, as long as managed care systems do not include clinical outcome data, they will never operate on the basis of true cost-effective care.

There is a third way in which national health policy could (and should) support empirical evaluation of health care service delivery. This is at the individual practitioner level. Kazdin (1993) has begun the process of articulating a "methodology of clinical practice" for mental health practitioners that would encompass the individualized assessment of clinical problems, targeted intervention, and outcome assessment. There is not as yet a fully articulated and disseminable method for evaluating individual cases in day-to-day clinical practice in mental health, but it is a beginning. Likewise, no such methodology exists for analyzing individual clinical interventions in primary care medical practice, although there, too, beginning efforts are emerging (cf. Stewart, Tudiver, Bass, Dunn, & Norton, 1992; Tudiver, Bass, Dunn, Norton, & Stewart, 1992). Such efforts should be stimulated in any national health policy, perhaps by providing practitioners who engage in such practices with a 5% premium in their reimbursement to cover their added costs.

OVERCOMING PREVIOUS POLICY BIASES, ACHIEVING AN APPROPRIATE VOICE

When policymakers think about health care, they think about physical illness (cf. Durenberger & Foote, 1993) and medical interventions provided primarily by physicians (cf. Kerrey & Hofschire, 1993). Psychological and behavioral health care, and the clinical services of psychologists, get addressed in policy decisions as an afterthought, usually through the simplistic extension into areas related to psychological care of the decisions already made related to physical illness. This often results in poor and inappropriate policy (DeLeon, Wedding, Wakefield, & VandenBos, 1992).

As organized psychology works with policymakers and administration officials on health care reform, psychology must ensure that psychological and behavioral health care perspectives are expressed, recognized, and represented. Mental health represents about one tenth of health care. The extension of physical health care policy into the provision of psychological services extends all of the flaws of the physical health system into the psychological care arena—resulting in a mismatch with the actual mental health care needs of our nation. It would be necessary to ensure that a minimum of 10% of the voices on the federal health board represented mental health, and the seats should be distributed in a manner that reflects the distribution of needed mental health services (e.g., emphasizing outpatient care and nonphysician providers). To truly achieve needed change and movement away from previous flaws and biases in policy would require overrepresenting the underrepresented voices. That would mean representation of mental health promotion initiatives, health psychology perspectives, outpatient rehabilitation and continuing care perspectives, and an outpatient psychotherapy view (and probably making a concerted effort to avoid having representation for inpatient psychiatric services, as that perspective would inherently be represented through the fundamental biases in current health policies and the power of the general hospital perspective represented in the physical health care arena).

There are many "shareholders" who have economic and other interests in health care reform, in the composition of and mandates to the federal health commission, and in the development of health care purchasing cooperatives. They will all work to secure their voices in these processes that will have massive impact on the "health care industry" (which represents one seventh of our national economy). If psychology wishes to ensure public access to needed psychological care, and if psychology wants to have psychological services recognized and governed in an appropriate manner, then psychology needs to ensure its presence in the process and ensure that the gatekeepers to psychological care are not once again nonpsychologists biased against psychological services or in active competition with psychologists.

REFERENCES

American Academy of Child and Adolescent Psychiatry, American Association for Marriage and Family Therapy, American Association for Partial Hospitalization, American Association of Pastoral Counselors, American Association of Psychiatric Services for Children, American Association of Private Practice Psychiatrists, American Psychoanalytic Association, American Psychological Association, Anxiety Disorders Association of America, International Association of Psychosocial Rehabilitation Services, Federation of Families for Children's Mental Health, Mental Health Law Project, National Association of Protection and Advocacy Systems, National Association of Social Workers, National Association of State Mental Health Program Directors, National Council of Community Mental Health Centers, & National Mental Health Association. (1992, December 14). *Principles for mental health care in health care reform.* Unpublished working document.

American Psychological Association, Task Force on Continuing Evaluation in National Health Insurance. (1978). Continuing evaluation and accountability controls for a national health insurance program. *American Psychologist, 33,* 305–313.

Bingaman, J., Frank, R. G., & Billy, C. L. (1993). Combining a global health budget with a market-driven delivery system: Can it be done? *American Psychologist, 48,* 270–276.

Blendon, R. J., & Edwards, J. N. (1991, May 15). Caring for the uninsured: Choices for reform (Editorial). *JAMA: Journal of the American Medical Association, 265,* 2563–2565.

Brook, R., Kamberg, C. J., & Mayer-Okaes, A. (1989). *Appropriateness of acute medical care for the elderly: Analysis of the literature* (R3717). Santa Monica, CA: Rand.

Buie, J. (1987, September). Evidence of HMO flaws mounting. *APA Monitor, 18,* p. 45.

Buie, J. (1989a, June). Given lemons, they make lemonade. *APA Monitor, 20,* p. 20.

Buie, J. (1989b, November). Managed care debate covers pros and cons. *APA Monitor, 20,* p. 21.

Buie, J. (1990, March). HMO's quality of care challenged by lawsuits. *APA Monitor, 21*, p. 13.

Cohn, V. (1992, November 3). New deal on health care: Advice from the Jackson Hole gang. *The Washington Post, Health News*, p. 7.

Congressional Budget Office. (1991). *Rising health care costs: Causes, implications, and strategies*. Washington, DC: U.S. Government Printing Office.

Cummings, N. A. (1977). The anatomy of psychotherapy under national health insurance. *American Psychologist, 32*, 711–718.

Cummings, N. A., & VandenBos, G. R. (1983). Relations with other professions. In C. E. Walker (Ed.), *Handbook of clinical psychology: Theory, research, and practice* (Vol. 2, pp. 1301–1327). Homewood, IL: Dow Jones–Irwin.

Daschle, T. A., Cohen, R. J., & Rice, C. L. (1993). Health-care reform: Single-payer models. *American Psychologist, 48*, 265–269.

DeLeon, P. H., & VandenBos, G. R. (1980). Psychotherapy reimbursement in federal programs: Political factors. In G. R. VandenBos (Ed.), *Psychotherapy: Practice, research, policy* (Sage Studies in Community Mental Health 1, pp. 247–285). Beverly Hills, CA: Sage.

DeLeon, P. H., VandenBos, G. R., & Bulatao, E. Q. (1991). Managed mental health care: A history of the federal policy initiative. *Professional Psychology: Research and Practice, 22*, 15–25.

DeLeon, P. H., VandenBos, G. R., & Cummings, N. A. (1983). Psychotherapy—Is it safe, effective, and appropriate? The beginning of an evolutionary dialogue. *American Psychologist, 38*, 907–911.

DeLeon, P. H., Wedding, D., Wakefield, M. K., & VandenBos, G. R. (1992). Medicaid policy: Psychology's overlooked agenda. *Professional Psychology: Research and Practice, 23*, 96–107.

Dorken, H., & DeLeon, P. H. (1986). Cost as the driving force in health care reform. In H. Dorken & Associates (Eds.), *Professional psychology in transition: Meeting today's challenges* (pp. 313–349). San Francisco, CA: Jossey-Bass.

Durenberger, D., & Foote, S. B. (1993). Beyond incrementalism: Designing an infrastructure for reform. *American Psychologist, 48*, 277–282.

Falk, I. S. (1964). Medical care: Its social and organizational aspects. Labor unions and medical care. *The New England Journal of Medicine, 270*, 22–28.

General Accounting Office. (1988). *Medicare physician incentive payments by prepaid health plans could lower quality of care* (GAO/HRD-89-29). Washington, DC: U.S. Government Printing Office.

General Accounting Office. (1992). *Health insurance: Vulnerable payers lose billions to fraud and abuse* (GAO/HRD-92-69). Washington, DC: U.S. Government Printing Office.

Hennen, B. K. (1992). Foreword: Assessing interventions in primary care. In F. Tudiver, M. J. Bass, E. V. Dunn, P. G. Norton, & M. Stewart (Eds.), *Assessing interventions: Traditional and innovative methods* (Research Methods for Primary Care, Vol. 4, ix–xii). Newbury Park, CA: Sage.

Kazdin, A. E. (1993). Evaluation in clinical practice: Clinically sensitive and systematic methods of treatment delivery. *Behavior Therapy, 24*(1), 11–45.

Kerrey, B., & Hofschire, P. J. (1993). Hidden problems in current health-care financing and potential changes. *American Psychologist, 48,* 261–264.

Kiesler, C. A. (1979). Testimony of the American Psychological Association at the National Health Insurance Hearing, October 4, 1977. In C. A. Kiesler, N. A. Cummings, & G. R. VandenBos (Eds.), *Psychology and national health insurance: A sourcebook* (pp. 45–47). Washington, DC: American Psychological Association.

Kiesler, C. A. (1982a). Mental hospitals and alternative care: Noninstitutionalization as potential public policy for mental patients. *American Psychologist, 37,* 349–360.

Kiesler, C. A. (1982b). Public and professional myths about mental hospitalization. *American Psychologist, 37,* 1323–1339.

Kiesler, C. A. (1992). U.S. mental health policy: Doomed to fail. *American Psychologist, 47,* 1077–1082.

Kiesler, C. A., Cummings, N. A., & VandenBos, G. A. (1979). *Psychology and national health insurance: A sourcebook.* Washington, DC: American Psychological Association.

Kiesler, C. A., & Sibulkin, A. E. (1987). *Mental hospitalization: Myths and facts about a national crisis.* Beverly Hills, CA: Sage.

Kulka, R. A., Veroff, J., & Douvan, E. (1979). Social class and the use of professional help for personal problems: 1957 and 1976. *Journal of Health and Social Behavior, 20,* 2–17.

Levit, K. R., Lazenby, H. C., Cowan, C. A., & Letsch, S. W. (1991). National health expenditures, 1990. *Health Care Financing Review, 13,* 29–54.

Regier, D. A., Boyd, J. H., Burke, J. D., Jr., Rae, D. S., Myers, J. K., Kramer, M., Robins, L. N., George, L. K., Karno, M., & Locke, B. Z. (1988). One-month prevalence of mental disorders in the United States. *Archives of General Psychiatry, 45,* 977–986.

Rovner, J. (1992, November 28). Managed competition. *Congressional Quarterly,* 3715.

Stewart, M., Tudiver, F., Bass, M. J., Dunn, E. V., & Norton, P. G. (Eds.). (1992). *Tools for primary care research (Research Methods for Primary Care,* Vol. 2). Newbury Park, CA: Sage.

Tudiver, F., Bass, M. J., Dunn, E. V., Norton, P. G., & Stewart, M. (Eds.). (1992). *Assessing interventions: Traditional and innovative methods (Research Methods for Primary Care,* Vol. 4). Newbury Park, CA: Sage.

U.S. Department of Health, Education, and Welfare. Public Health Service. (1962). *Medical care financing and utilization* (No. 947, Health Economics Series, No. 1). Washington, DC: U.S. Government Printing Office.

VandenBos, G. R. (1980). Introduction. In G. R. VandenBos (Ed.), *Psychotherapy: Practice, research, policy* (Sage Studies in Community Mental Health 1, pp. 9–22). Beverly Hills, CA: Sage.

VandenBos, G. R. (1983). Health financing, service utilization, and national policy: A conversation with Stan Jones. *American Psychologist, 38,* 948–955.

VandenBos, G. R., Cummings, N. A., & DeLeon, P. H. (1992). A century of psychotherapy: Economic and environmental influences. In D. K. Freedheim (Ed.), *History of psychotherapy: A century of change* (pp. 65–102). Washington, DC: American Psychological Association.

VandenBos, G. R., DeLeon, P. H., & Belar, C. D. (1991). How many psychological practitioners are needed? It's too early to know! *Professional Psychology: Research and Practice, 22,* 441–448.

Welch, B. (1986a, October). Professional point. *APA Monitor, 17,* p. 35.

Welch, B. (1986b, December). Professional point. *APA Monitor, 17,* p. 30.

Yates, B. T., & Newman, F. L. (1980). Approaches to cost-effectiveness analysis and cost-benefit analysis of psychotherapy. In G. R. VandenBos (Ed.), *Psychotherapy: Practice, research, policy* (Sage Studies in Community Mental Health 1, pp. 103–162). Beverly Hills, CA: Sage.

IV

POLICYMAKERS: THEIR VIEW

INTRODUCTION

PSYCHOLOGISTS' CONTRIBUTIONS TO THE POLICY PROCESS

HENRY TOMES and ANNETTE U. RICKEL

Policy making is influenced by a complex array of interest groups, such as service providers, researchers, labor unions, and advocacy groups representing poor individuals, aged persons, women, and other disenfranchised groups. Social policy represents what society wants for itself, and it is a crystallization of popular sentiment. However, no policy becomes effective public policy until money is allocated at the local, state, or federal level to implement the policy. Nonetheless, social policy, even in the absence of hard cash, may determine priorities in our society (e.g., the Surgeon General's position on smoking as a health hazard).

Policy development does not occur in a vacuum. It occurs in response to socially perceived public needs, and its specific form and content is shaped by political power as well as data. However, sound public policy also often requires the administrative skills of talented managers at all levels of government to "make it happen."

Some of the previously published articles appearing as chapters in this section provide examples of the personal commitment of policymakers operating within the congressional arena to address needs of citizens and their resultant legislative actions. Other chapters provide examples of how talented and committed psychologists, serving as heads of key federal research agencies, were able to implement socially responsible policy.

The aim in this section is twofold: (a) to demonstrate how various policymakers have advocated for the needs of citizens and as a result have significantly influenced legislation and (b) to learn how the psychological community has played and can continue to play a role in shaping public policy.

In the first chapter in this section, "Children and the Congress" (see chap. 17), former U.S. Representative George Miller discusses his role in creating the Select Committee on Children, Youth and Families in 1982. Although the committee had no legislative responsibility, it did provide a bipartisan forum where attention could be given to the issues affecting children and youth. The committee operated in this capacity for 12 years until, in 1994, it was disbanded along with several other select committees for economic reasons.

It is interesting to note that in 1983 when this chapter appeared in *American Psychologist*, George Miller was deeply concerned about the magnitude of the budget cuts in programs affecting children. He cited several examples of programs being proposed for dismantling by the Reagan administration and Congress, despite their documented achievements (e.g., the Supplemental Feeding Program for Women, Infants, and Children; Title I of the Elementary and Secondary Education Act; and Head Start). Representative Miller called on psychologists to use their knowledge and research experience to aid policymakers in reaching decisions regarding maintaining programs and funding for federal initiatives that had proven to be effective. Due to the efforts of the American Psychological Association (APA) and more than 140 organizations serving children and youth, many of the programs slated for the cutting block were spared.

More than 10 years later, a similar debate has arisen regarding the dismantling of programs by the 104th (1995–1996) Congress. A case in point is the Violent Crime Control and Law Enforcement Act of 1994. The House and Senate proposed revisions in the act that would eliminate important prevention efforts impacting children, youth, and families. The programs cited for elimination include prevention and intervention programs to reduce adolescent pregnancy, child abuse, substance abuse, summer and after-school education, and recreation programs. Funding priorities instead were directed toward prison construction, stricter sentences, and a wider latitude to prosecute juveniles as adults.

Once again, psychologists must make their voices heard regarding the impact of these changes, because even the proposed programs do not begin to serve a majority of the eligible population of children and youth. Support for maintaining these crucial preventive efforts must be built from their expertise and knowledge base.

The last chapter in this section by Senator Joseph R. Biden, Jr. (see chap. 20) deals with violence against women. Written in 1993, it detailed the epidemic proportions of violence against women (i.e., 95% of domestic violence victims are women). In fact, as Senator Biden pointed out, the most common cause of injury treated among female medical patients is battering. It is more common than automobile accidents, rapes, and muggings combined, and it accounts for one third of all women's emergency room visits. Violence against women also negatively impacts children who witness their mother's abuse. Researchers have found that the most violent teens tend to come from low-income homes where there has been interpersonal violence and abuse.

Biden discussed his efforts to address this issue through federal legislation introduced as the Violence Against Women Act. This act would create new laws for crimes of domestic violence, would provide resources to survivors, would educate the criminal justice system, and would be the first legal remedy for women who are victims of violence. The act subsequently became part of the 1994 Crime Bill as Title IV, the Violence Against Women section, and as of this writing, it does not appear to be in danger of being eliminated from the legislation.

As Biden pointed out, the APA has contributed greatly to the public's understanding of violence against women. In 1994, the APA published in book form the results of a Task Force on Male Violence Against Women. The book, coauthored by Mary Koss and five psychologist colleagues, is entitled *No Safe Haven: Male Violence Against Women at Home, at Work, and in the Community.* Psychologists have also testified at congressional hearings to raise awareness about domestic violence and have sought to educate health and mental health providers about the symptoms and treatment.

The efforts of Miller and Biden represent those of elected officials to propose legislation to effect change in the lives of persons in need who could be helped by federal intervention and assistance. The remaining two chapters in this section are by psychologists David Bertsch Gray and Alan Leshner, who were serving as federal officials implementing policies designed to provide federal resources to persons with physical and mental disabilities.

Gray, in his chapter, "Disability and Rehabilitation Research from Policy to Program: A Personal Perspective" (see chap. 18) demonstrates how he was able to effect significant change in a federal research institute. Gray, a quadriplegic, served as director of the National Institute on Disability and Rehabilitation Research (NIDRR) from 1986 to 1987. In this short period of time, he was able to streamline granting mechanisms and at the same time develop programs through flexible use of the agency's budgetary authority.

There is much to learn from Gray's description of his activities, but the overriding message is that competence in understanding and managing a research bureaucracy is necessary but may not be sufficient. Clearly Gray, a disabled person, brought the necessary organizational sophistication along with a commitment to have NIDRR focus its efforts on improving the lives of persons with disabilities. His leadership got persons with disabilities involved in policy and operational matters and empowered them to address desired outcomes important to persons with disabilities and their families. Out of these efforts arose coalitions consisting of disabled persons, their families and advocates, researchers, and service providers, which created an "Institute interdependency" and a consensus regarding needs of disabled persons. The importance of Gray's disabled status on his decisions cannot be overemphasized, but his understanding of federal bureaucratic processes permitted him to effect rapid change by funding new initiatives, such as a new program for persons with traumatic brain injuries and research on neural recovery. Gray's short stint at NIDRR was related to his perception that future changes were not likely to be made at that point in the Reagan presidency. However, in his short stay, he demonstrated that a talented psychologist with a high level of personal commitment was able to move NIDRR "from paternalism to consumerism."

In 1991, psychologist Alan Leshner, acting director of the National Institute of Mental Health (NIMH), described NIMH as a complex research funding and policy environment (see chap. 19). He described the behavioral sciences agenda of NIMH and pointed out that psychologists as primary investigators do very well in a highly competitive funding process. Leshner, like Gray, is highly skilled in the intricacies of mental health research policy development. He understands the facilitating roles played by scientists who accept key administrative and management responsibilities in agencies such as NIMH. He encourages psychologists to look more favorably on filling such key positions themselves.

Leshner wrote during the time when NIMH was the prime mental health research institute in the Alcohol, Drug Abuse and Mental Health Administration (ADAMHA) and before it was moved into the National Institutes of Health (NIH), along with the National Institute of Drug Abuse (NIDA) and the National Institute of Alcohol and Alcohol Abuse (NIAAA). He is now the Director of NIDA. However, his views and policy implementation strategies are applicable in other research and policy environments.

As an administrator with a keen sense of policy and resource development, Leshner shared his insights regarding productive ways to handle conflict in a highly visible research agency. Acknowledging the role of a range of policy development sources (including Congress, the administration, advisory bodies, and NIMH staff), he expressed that public and acrimonious debate as to whether biological or behavioral research should receive the lion's share of resources for example, is shortsighted. He suggested a balanced approach as opposed to one of winner take all, but also recommended encouraging and supporting research efforts on the interface between the two. Such a strategy suggests that psychologists seek equitable funding of psychological research in biological and behavioral areas as well as develop alliances with others to advocate for research support in the area of interaction between behavior and biology. This course of action in these as well as other situations leads to unified efforts and avoids nonproductive polarization and fragmentation in important areas of concern.

17

CHILDREN AND THE CONGRESS: A TIME TO SPEAK OUT

GEORGE MILLER

All children deserve our nation's unqualified commitment. Over the last 50 years, policies that honor this commitment have been forged, put into place, and modified to meet the changing needs of our nation's children and families. But today, the pressures of budget austerity, fueled by the ideology of the "New Right," pose a serious challenge to this commitment.

As a congressperson deeply concerned about the well-being of children, I appreciate this opportunity to discuss the present status of legislation concerning children and youth and to offer my perspective on the roles that others, including psychologists, can play to promote and protect the welfare of children.

Reprinted from *American Psychologist, 38,* 70–76. Copyright 1983 by the American Psychological Association.

The Honorable George Miller (D-California) has long been recognized in the House of Representatives as the outstanding advocate for children and families. Miller was elected chair of the Subcommittee on Labor Standards at the beginning of the 97th Congress.

THE ASSAULT ON CHILDREN

The present Administration is systematically retreating from commitments to services, legal protections, and regulatory safeguards for children that took decades to develop and that have a proven record of success. No program or policy has been exempt. No age group has been spared. With each abandonment of a program or a policy, we will lose children. We will lose them to birth defects and infant malnutrition, to vast foster care institutions, to illiteracy and inadequate job preparation, and ultimately, to unemployment, poverty, and illness.

The magnitude of the budget cuts affecting children's programs is a cause for serious concern. But what I find even more distressing is the arbitrary and indiscriminate manner in which the Administration and the Congress have acted. Programs have been proposed for dismantling or severe cutting without regard to their merit, accomplishments, proven cost effectiveness, or equity considerations, and without any evidence that the programs are ineffective or wasteful. In several instances, studies supported by the federal government have documented the achievements of these programs ("Foster Care Maintenance," 1980; U.S. Department of Agriculture, 1980; U.S. Department of Education, 1982). Indeed, time and again before my committee, high officials of this Administration defended their proposals to cut drastically specific programs in the same breath as they cited the evidence of these programs' successes.

Several examples will serve to demonstrate the comprehensive range of programs that have been affected.

1. The Supplemental Feeding Program for Women, Infants, and Children (WIC) was enacted in 1972 following reports by the March of Dimes that high infant mortality rates, birth defects, and mental retardation resulted from malnutrition among low-income, pregnant, and nursing women. WIC provides nutritional supplements to 2.2 million pregnant, postpartum, and breast-feeding women and their children who are medically certified to be at high nutritional risk. In its first year, the Administration proposed to cut WIC by 30%, and during 1982 attempted to merge WIC with the Maternal and Child Health Block Grant and to reduce funding for this cluster of programs by 35%. In both instances the Congress resoundingly rejected the Administration's proposals.

2. Title XX of the Social Security Act, established in 1975, is the single largest federal social services program. Title XX provides funds to states to finance a wide number of social services such as child care, which has consistently consumed the largest share of this money, including $200 million of earmarked funds until 1981. During the Administration's first year, funds for this program were cut by 19%. In 1982 the Administration sought to cut an additional 17%, but Congress protected Title XX from further cuts.

3. In 1980, the Adoption Assistance and Child Welfare Act, which I authored, passed with resounding bipartisan support. This landmark legislation created procedures and financial incentives for welfare agencies to reunite families whenever possible or to place children in stable adoptive homes, thereby breaking the cycle of foster care placements. The Administration has persistently, but unsuccessfully, attempted to repeal this legislation and to reduce funding for all child welfare services by about one fourth.

4. Title I of the Elementary and Secondary Education Act and Head Start are the exemplars of this country's compensatory education efforts. Established in 1965, these programs offer low-income children the comprehensive preschool and educational opportunities that are essential stepping stones to productive adult years. Although the Reagan administration has repeatedly professed to protect Head Start from budget cuts, sizable reductions in the Child Care Food Program, Title XX, and CETA have drained at least 6,000 classroom staff and $60 million from this program, thereby forcing some Head Start programs to close and others to reduce their enrollments. Title I was slotted for cuts that by 1983 would have amounted to a cumulative 50% reduction in funds from 1980 levels. The Administration was successful in obtaining a 36% cut, although this year Congress restored $139 million to its $3.025 billion budget. The Administration has also succeeded in repealing critical federal requirements for parent participation and for federal and state monitoring of Title I programs.

5. In the face of 23.7% youth unemployment, the Administration has attempted to dismantle all four youth employment programs. The Young Adult Conservation Corps has been completely eliminated. The Youth Employment Demonstrations program was proposed for reduction and inclusion in a state-administered employment program. Finally, the Summer Youth Employment program and Job Corps have both been consolidated into a new, but substantially smaller, job training program.

6. The three major programs that provide basic income assistance, health, and nutritional services to impoverished families—Aid to Families with Dependent Children (AFDC), Medicaid, and Food Stamps—have suffered particularly severe cutbacks. Children comprise 70% of the AFDC population, 48% of those receiving Medicaid, and 55% of Food Stamp recipients. These three programs constitute 5.2% of all federal spending, but accounted for about 10% of the 1982 budget cuts.

These funding reductions have been justified as critical to a balanced budget and the economic health of our nation. However, even a cursory examination of federal spending reveals that we could eliminate every dollar spent on children and this nation would still be faced with the largest federal deficit in history.

If we entirely eliminate the AFDC, Food Stamp, and Medicaid programs—the centerpieces of the antipoverty effort—the projected federal deficit for 1983 will decline from $155 billion to $118 billion. If we also eliminate all spending for compensatory education and social services, we will pare the deficit down by about another $7 billion. To lend perspective to these examples, note that Social Security is expected to cost $158 billion in 1982 and defense spending will reach $183 billion. In fact, the cumulative $1.6 trillion that has been allocated for military spending over the next five years amounts to a *daily* expenditure of $900 million—an amount approaching half of the *annual* budget for the major Title XX social services program.

These figures illustrate that the current efforts to abrogate federal responsibility for social programs are motivated by ideology, not fiscal responsibility. In this ideology, children's programs are identified with social services, public assistance, and other programs for the poor—a common misperception that extends to child care, education for the handicapped, foster care, and other children's programs that serve middle-income, as well as poor, families. This ideology equates programs of public assistance with minority families, who while they are disproportionately represented relative to their total numbers, have never constituted the majority of recipients.

This ideology endorses the abandonment of long-standing federal responsibility for providing children's services in favor of increasing state and private sector initiatives at a time when neither is in a particularly good position to do so.

Moreover, there has been no evidence for the Administration's claim that the charitable and private sectors can or will fully compensate for the loss of federal support. Charities and private industry have traditionally formed a partnership with the federal government to eradicate hunger, disease, and illiteracy as everyday realities for large segments of our population. However, it is unlikely that the private sector can replace what has been lost by massive reductions in federally supported programs.

The Urban Institute, a nonprofit research organization, has documented that between 1982 and 1985, private charitable agencies will receive $35 billion less in federal aid than necessary to sustain services at their 1980 levels (Palmer & Sawhill, 1982). Individual contributions, which account for the overwhelming majority of charitable giving, may decline as a result of reductions in real disposable income and sustained high unemployment. Private giving would need to increase by 22% this year—a jump of over $4 billion—to offset the effects of inflation and reductions in federal aid.

The impact of the lost federal funds will likely be felt disproportionately by social welfare, education, and community development programs. Voluntary organizations active in these areas would have had to expand their activities by as much as 30% in 1982 to fill the gap created by the federal cutbacks.

CHILDREN: THE INVISIBLE CONSTITUENCY

A central factor in the assault on children's services is the low visibility of children within the bargaining rooms of the Congress and the political parties. Children are a politically disenfranchised group. They are neither partisan nor powerful. They do not lobby, do not make campaign contributions, and do not vote. Yet their lives are profoundly affected by social conditions that they did not create and political decisions that are beyond their control.

The future political career of every member of Congress hinges on contributions and votes; good intentions and humanitarian goals, unfortunately, do not guarantee reelection. It is therefore no accident that the programs serving our youngest constituency, and particularly poor and minority children, are the first to feel the harsh impacts of a political climate that favors a shrinking rather than an expanding federal role. Little political price is paid for supporting cuts in children's services, and there are virtually no serious, short-term consequences for ignoring the needs of children. Only recently have organizations begun to hold elected officials accountable for their votes for children. These organizations have also begun to use the sophisticated lobbying and electoral strategies of their more affluent corporate lobbyists and PAC cousins.

Both the structure of the House and the legislative process exacerbate the invisibility and meager political power of children. The elaborate and fragmented committee structure of the Congress militates against comprehensive consideration of children's needs. More than 13 full committees, including Agriculture, Armed Forces, and Ways and Means, and a panoply of subcommittees, share responsibility for the federal programs and policies on children. Jurisdiction over child care programs, for example, is splintered among four committees, including those with primary responsibility for taxation, defense, and education.

Second, the congressional committee system has encouraged a reactive and program-focused stance toward policy issues. The working agenda of most committees leaves limited opportunities for thorough oversight activities or long-range planning. When committees do conduct oversight, existing federal programs or immediate crises usually define the parameters for review—a system that promotes narrow constituencies, intense competition among interest groups, and defensive program analysis. Congressional hearings rarely focus on issues that cut across subcommittee boundaries, examine the broad contexts that impinge on the lives of children, or consider the continuity of programs designed to serve children. As a case in point, the Head Start program was largely protected from direct budget cuts (although the supportive services essential to the effectiveness of Head Start have suffered severe cutbacks). However, the Title I compensatory education program, which serves Head Start graduates when they enter elementary school, was slated to lose 50% of its budget in 1982.

Third, children are easily obscured in the intricate procedures of the federal budget process, yet critical decisions about children's services are decided in budget deliberations. Only the initiated are able to read behind the esoteric language of the budget to note, for example, that the funding ceiling assigned to "function 500" is a barometer for our nation's commitment to meeting children's needs for education, foster care, and adequate health care. Moreover, in recent years, the budget process has been used to force votes or across-the-board budget cuts that protect members of Congress from accountability to particular constituencies.

Finally, thoughtful consideration of issues affecting children is limited by the ideological divisiveness that has permeated discussion of these issues, as illustrated by the emotion-charged controversies that have stymied family planning and child care legislation. Reasoned debate and even-handed approaches to these issues are all-too-often replaced by shrill rhetoric and polarized viewpoints. It is especially frustrating that this polarization has discouraged many moderate members of Congress from speaking out on behalf of children for fear of offending one constituency or another.

THE CREATION OF A SELECT COMMITTEE ON CHILDREN, YOUTH, AND FAMILIES

To overcome these barriers to the thoughtful consideration of issues affecting children, youth, and families, I believe we must establish a bipartisan forum where reasoned debate can flourish and the needs of children and youth can be the primary focus of attention. This forum should be exempt from the pressures facing standing committees, which have the responsibility to move legislation and to protect and defend specific programs.

Accordingly, after many years of active efforts to bring greater visibility to the needs and problems of children, I proposed, and the House of Representatives approved, a special congressional oversight committee solely focused on this constituency. Congress gave the Select Committee on Children, Youth, and Families a broad mandate:
(1) To conduct a continuing comprehensive study and review of the problems of children, youth, and families, including but not limited to income maintenance, health (including medical and child development research), nutrition, education, welfare, employment and recreation;

(2) To study the use of all practical means and methods of encouraging the development of public and private programs and policies which will assist American children and youth in taking a full part in national life and becoming productive citizens; and

(3) To develop policies that would encourage the coordination of both governmental and private programs designed to address the problems of childhood and adolescence.

Colleagues from both parties and of the broadest ideological diversity have joined me in supporting the establishment of this important committee, which has the potential to focus congressional and public attention on our children and youth.

The Select Committee can use its aegis to draw a portrait of children, youth, and the changing social and economic circumstances in which children and families find themselves. Using the tools of hearings, investigations, and studies, the Select Committee will have the opportunity to identify scientific evidence about problems children face and successful approaches to addressing these problems. The Committee will have the flexibility to synthesize and highlight research that has not received sufficient attention and to stimulate research where current evidence is either unavailable or inadequate. Examining the impact of economic conditions, including the costs and benefits of our policies, on the lives of children and their families will also be within the new Committee's purview.

The Select Committee will also be a place where a heterogeneous constituency of professionals, academics, clinicians, and advocates with interests in children, youth, and families can exchange ideas and enhance their collective wisdom concerning children. This multidisciplinary approach to deliberations about children and youth will be an essential trademark of the Committee's operations.

ROLE OF THE PSYCHOLOGICAL COMMUNITY

The political events of the last two years present a discouraging scenario to psychologists and others committed to developing policies that serve the best interests of children and youth. Discouragement is an understandable reaction. The real challenge facing psychologists today is how best to use their knowledge and experience to aid policymakers in making crucial decisions regarding policies, programs, and funding. Clearly, new roles must be forged and new issues must be addressed with the recognition that psychologists will be involved in a political process.

Children are the common concern of psychologists and politicians who are committed to domestic issues. Each group subsumes a healthy diversity of viewpoints about children's needs, about the appropriate goals of research, and about the values and integrity of political action. This diversity has fueled controversy about the relationship between research and policy.

Much of the debate about this relationship has revolved around the desirability of the relationship itself and whether it should be strengthened. Researchers often presume that research and policy are independent endeavors and that there is a choice about whether to join them. I believe that this presumption draws an artificial distinction between the two endeavors and leads to nonproductive debate about the "appropriate" role of research.

Research and policy are intimately and inextricably linked. For example, research that has readily apparent policy applications has been used to point to the detrimental impacts of youth employment on school achievement, family attitudes, and substance abuse. These revelations, made during hearings on the Administration's proposal to relax certain aspects of the child labor laws, captured the attention of the Subcommittee on Labor Standards and the press alike, and led the Administration to extend the period of public comments on its proposal through January 13, 1983.

But far more compelling than my personal accounts and observations are the facts about children's programs that I have already described. Lack of involvement by researchers whose work can contribute to more effective child and family policies is a luxury that we can no longer afford and that cannot be justified on the grounds of objectivity. The knowledge generated by research does not develop in isolation from the needs of the larger society, and their association is strengthened by the extensive public funding of social science research. When consistent conclusions emerge from research, it is incumbent upon researchers to apply their knowledge to addressing social needs.

Accordingly, as the work of the Select Committee on Children, Youth, and Families begins, I foresee an important role for psychologists interested in contributing to the welfare of children and youth to ensure that the information-gathering activities of the Committee are characterized by high standards and that the deliberations are based on the best information available within the time constraints and competing interests that are an integral part of the policy process. Based on their knowledge of current research and different methods of collecting information, and on their professional experience in a variety of service delivery systems, psychologists can be very helpful in affecting the agenda of the Select Committee. Given the broad mandate of the Committee I have described in the previous section, we need to identify the key questions regarding children and youth that can suggest options for the Committee's oversight and investigatory responsibilities. The Committee welcomes assistance in framing these questions so that useful, policy-relevant answers can be found. If the research suggests that certain questions have been neglected or incorrectly framed, we need to know this.

Research can also play a role in defusing the emotion-charged divisiveness that has militated against reasoned debate about crucial issues affecting children. Rhetoric flows far more freely in the absence of factual information. For example, the debate regarding requirements for parental consent prior to issuing prescription contraceptives to teenagers has frequently devolved into accusations of obstructing the rights of parents, on the one hand, and accusations of increasing teenage pregnancy, on the other hand. Research that examines the consequences of imposing such a requirement on teenagers' use of family planning programs and subsequent sexual activity would answer some of the concerns that are now cast solely in inflammatory language. It is precisely because research is not primarily directed toward political action that it can serve as a catalyst for achieving compromise and building coalitions, as was the case in the area of my foster-care legislation.

Through prepared testimony and policy-relevant reports, psychologists can bring research to the attention of the Committee, particularly bodies of evidence that have not been previously known to policymakers. In all of these activities, I would hope psychologists would point out the nature of the available evidence, the methods upon which the research is based, and the limitations and generalizability of the findings, so that policies for children are based on the best, most reliable work available.

As professionals engaged in education and health service systems, psychologists can engage in careful assessments of how policies are actually implemented and their effects. Since psychologists work in both private and public facilities (some in both), their comparative experience would be valuable to the Committee as it considers alternative approaches to serving children and their families. Psychologists' front-line experience with service delivery places them in an appropriate position to comment on how programs can be made more effective and more accessible to those who need them. These contributions of the psychological community will be weighed and sifted with those of other professions and interest groups to achieve a comprehensive overview of how policies for children and families interact and impinge on children's lives.

The oversight and information-gathering activities of the Select Committee will rely heavily on statistics collected by our federal agencies. However, virtually every federal statistical agency that collects and analyzes information pertinent to children and their families has experienced sizable budget cuts and staff reductions. These cuts may seriously impair the quantity, quality, and timeliness of our information about children. The sample size of the annual Current Population Survey, which provides our unemployment, family structure, and child care statistics, has been pared down substantially, thereby reducing its scope and reliability. The Panel Study of

Income Dynamics (PSID), a crucial source of longitudinal data about children and families, is likely to suffer major losses in funding due to reductions in support from the Department of Health and Human Services (DHHS) budget. The survey of recipients of Aid to Families with Dependent Children (AFDC) has also been canceled by DHHS, although it is the only source of state-by-state information about families who rely on this income maintenance program.

Psychologists must become involved in calling attention to the shortsightedness of crippling our federal statistical base. The need for demographic information, for longitudinal data, and for information about the characteristics of service recipients is self-evident to those who seek empirical approaches to problem solving. The serious consequences of inadequate financial support for data collection and analysis suggest another topic that deserves much more serious attention.

The potential loss of information is particularly disturbing because it coincides both with an unprecedented reversal in attitudes about federal responsibility for children and with sweeping changes in the structure, employment patterns, and economic well-being of American families. By the end of this decade there is projected to be a 14% *increase* in the number of children under age 10. Close to half of these children can expect to live with only one parent at some time during their childhood. There is an influx of mothers of infants and toddlers into the labor force. The teenage unemployment rate has soared from 19.7% to 23.7% in the last year, and has reached 44% for minority youths. In 1981, the poverty rate climbed to its highest level since 1967, and the poverty rate for children has jumped from 16% to 20% in the last two years alone.

These statistics have far-reaching implications for the numerous domestic policy decisions that confront members of Congress every day. As the appropriate federal role in the area of domestic policy is being debated, members of Congress may be denied the critical information base that is essential for evaluation and refinement of these policies.

We cannot rely on state data and private research alone. Data collection efforts of national scope are beyond the capabilities of university departments and private firms. Even if states somehow manage to conduct surveys within their own boundaries, the lack of uniformity across states would render opportunities for national-level analyses impossible. Years of lost data are irretrievable.

The detrimental consequences of severely crippling the federal statistical system are readily apparent to the research community. Our policies are only as sound as the data on which they are based. I fear that we will proceed without the statistical and research information that is essential to the formation of policies designed to advance the future health and well-being of our nation's children.

The reductions in support for data gathering and statistical analysis have two important consequences for social policies affecting children. In the absence of information about the effects of major budget cuts on programs serving children, youth, and families, accountability becomes a moot issue. Elimination of efforts to evaluate the impacts of public policies on the status of children are tantamount to shooting the messenger who brings bad news. Without the messenger, few alarms are likely to be sounded and few efforts to rectify harmful situations are likely to be initiated. At the same time, beneficial outcomes of programs are more likely to remain unknown. Knowledge about what works and what needs improvement will simply not be available in the future.

CONCLUDING REMARKS

The assault on children has been pervasive. While the budgetary process has occupied center stage, equally serious erosion of policies designed to protect children has occurred through administrative decisions regarding legal safeguards and threats to deregulate important programs. The irony of the disproportionate burden that children have suffered as a result is that none of the programs of proven effectiveness have ever served even the majority of the eligible population. Head Start serves approximately 20% of the children who can be part of this comprehensive preschool program, while Title I has served only 45% of those eligible. The WIC program, with its clearly demonstrated cost effectiveness in terms of children who do not later impose a fiscal drain through expensive medical care, serves fewer than one out of four eligible women and children. The recent budget cuts only exacerbate the already inadequate coverage and limitations in accessibility to services that continue to characterize the federal commitment to children.

In this climate of fiscal conservatism, arguments for the preservation of children's programs have increasingly relied on demonstrations of cost effectiveness. A program's capacity to demonstrate cost savings on the initial investment of federal dollars is crucial. Politicians are under pressure to demonstrate immediate results from federal expenditures. We must keep our priorities clear, however, and not be blinded by the promise of "instant benefits" from federal spending. Ultimately, children must be cherished for what they offer today, not just for the contributions they eventually can make to society. We must not lose sight of the humanitarian values that have long provided the fundamental impetus for public and private efforts to provide services to children. A renewed case needs to be made that children's claim on social resources arises from their position as important, albeit dependent, human beings to whom adult society has a special responsibility.

The victory of establishing the Select Committee on Children, Youth, and Families was largely due to the coordinated efforts of over 140 diverse organizations serving children and youth. But creating the Committee was probably the easiest of the tasks we face. When specific policies are carefully scrutinized, and when professional turf is sure to be the subject of criticism, we must work to surmount the all-too-familiar fragmentation of this fragile coalition.

I am hopeful that knowing the past history of efforts to create policies on behalf of children, we will learn from our previous mistakes, educate ourselves, and work together to craft policies that, at the very least, do not harm, and most desirably, enable all our children to develop into productive and healthy members of our society.

REFERENCES

Foster care maintenance assistance and adoption assistance (Child Welfare Services, Financial Impact Statement, U.S. Department of Health and Human Services). (December 31, 1980). *Federal Register, 45,* 86812–86852.

Palmer, J. L., & Sawhill, I. V. (Eds.). (1982). *The Reagan experiment.* Washington, D.C.: Urban Institute Press.

U.S. Department of Agriculture. (1980). *The benefits and costs of the WIC program.* Washington, D.C.: U.S. Department of Agriculture, Office of Programming, Planning, and Evaluation, Food and Nutrition Service.

U.S. Department of Education. (1982). *Annual evaluation report on Title I of the Elementary and Secondary Education Act.* Washington, D.C.: Author.

18

DISABILITY AND REHABILITATION RESEARCH FROM POLICY TO PROGRAM: A PERSONAL PERSPECTIVE

DAVID BERTSCH GRAY

The National Institute on Disability and Rehabilitation Research (NIDRR)[1] is a federal agency established to fund rehabilitation research. I served as director from 1986 to 1987. My goal for the agency was to implement a policy of interdependence between the needs of individuals with disabilities and the expertise of researchers and service providers.

PROGRAMS FUNDED BY NIDRR

Created by the Rehabilitation Act of 1973 and implemented in 1978, the NIDRR is a federal agency within the U.S. Department of Education under the Office of Special Education and Rehabilitative Services (OSERS). The NIDRR distributes funds on the basis of projects described in written applications. These applications are reviewed by peers of the

Reprinted from *American Psychologist*, 45, 751–756. Copyright 1990 by the American Psychological Association.

The author became a C5/6 quadriplegic when he fell off a roof in 1976. In 1986 he became the director of the NIDRR. He has since returned to the National Institutes of Health.

The opinions expressed in this article do not represent the U.S. Department of Education or the Department of Health and Human Services.

[1]The name of the National Institute of Handicapped Research (NIHR) was changed in 1986 to the National Institute on Disability and Rehabilitation Research (NIDRR).

applicants, recommended for funding by the Director of NIDRR, and selected for award by the Secretary of Education. Programs funded by the NIDRR are intended to assist individuals with disabilities in improving the quality of their health, education, employment, social adjustment, transportation, housing, and general activities of daily life (National Council on the Handicapped, 1986). Most of the funds (over 75% of $48.5 million in fiscal year 1987) are awarded for research on topics selected by the NIDRR. The major types of NIDRR-directed programs are rehabilitation research and training centers (RRTCs), rehabilitation engineering centers (RECs), research and demonstration projects (RDs), and utilization and dissemination projects (UDs). The NIDRR funds non-institute-directed projects through field-initiated research (FIR), the innovative grant program (IGP), and several career development (CD) programs.

As a director of a national research institute, my aim was to implement public policies related to disability and rehabilitation research through efficient and effective program administration. Two major areas of responsibility for a director are making recommendations for funding applications and developing program plans.

REVIEW OF APPLICATIONS AND FUNDING RECOMMENDATIONS

Through my experiences with peer review systems at the National Institutes of Health (NIH), the National Science Foundation (NSF), and private foundations, I have come to appreciate that the integrity of an agency rests in large part on the perception of a fair, open, timely, and helpful system of review of grant applications and contract proposals made to the agency (U.S. Department of Health, Education, and Welfare, National Institutes of Health, 1976, 1978). No institute director, regardless of how well prepared in research, can be an expert in all the subjects covered by the 600 to 800 applications submitted annually to the NIDRR. Effective management of an institute rests on an application process and peer review system that encourages excellent applications and thoughtful reviews of the grant applications made to the institute.

I spent several months examining how the grant application and review process used by the NIDRR operated. In an apparent attempt to avoid creating an "old boy" network of reviewers that could establish policy and direct programs through control of permanent study sections, the NIDRR had developed a system that used many ad hoc, small, rapidly assembled peer review panels to assess the merit of grant applications. During the spring of 1986, I observed the system in action and witnessed many problems. Subsequently, I met with the staff several times, read over 100 letters containing advice on how to modify the system, and responded to telephone calls from many applicants who expressed their dissatisfaction with the process. Among the criticisms of the process were that (a) having three reviewers per panel was insufficient to cover the diversity of applications being reviewed, (b) the time provided for the reviewers to read, comment on, and score the applications was inadequate for a thorough analysis of the proposed research, (c) feedback from the reviews was not helpful in improving the application, (d) reviewers differed each time the application was reviewed, making modifications in response to reviewer comments meaningless, (e) matches between reviewer expertise and the subject matter of the grant application were poor, (f) use of consumer advocates and federal employees to review applications was controversial, (g) the opportunity to apply once per fiscal year eliminated the possibility of modifying applications, (h) receipt dates for applications were announced at varying times during the year, (i) the data tracking system for identifying potential peer reviewers and locating grant applications was not effective or efficient, (j) uniform scoring criteria did not match the diversity of the research programs announced by the NIDRR, and (k) scores assigned by different peer review panels were not comparable.

MODIFICATIONS TO THE APPLICATION AND REVIEW PROCESS

Making informed funding recommendations on the basis of the information provided by this grant application and review process was difficult. Therefore, I decided to make the process more evaluative, efficient, and effective. As a blueprint for change I used the grant application process and peer review system detailed by the National Council on the Handicapped (1981). The immediate benefit would be to improve reviews for the fiscal year 1987 applications. The intermediate gain would be to develop a cohort of experienced peer reviewers who would not only provide improved feedback to applicants but would also lend stability, creditability, and expertise to the process of awarding NIDRR funds on the basis of excellence and relevance (Fuhrer, 1988). In the long term, such a system would contribute to the improved quality of grant applications sent to the Institute, as it would be used by the best researchers competing for funds to study problems faced by individuals with disabilities.

Over the next year, significant changes were made in the grant application process and peer review system. Late in fiscal year 1986, a plan modifying the time table for grant applications and their review was approved. The plan included standard receipt dates for several competitions that provided increased time for applicants to prepare their applications and for the NIDRR staff to arrange for their review. In addition, two competitions for field-initiated research were announced within one fiscal year.

This provided sufficient time between receipt dates to allow feedback from the panel of peer reviewers to be used by applicants to improve their application for the second receipt date.

A modified peer review system was implemented in 1987. The size of the review panels was increased from three to as many as eight. An attempt was made to balance the panels with experienced and first time reviewers. The number of federal employees serving as reviewers was decreased from over 30% to less than 10% of the total number of reviewers used. Increased numbers of scientists with disabilities were recruited to serve as panel members.

Several NIDRR staff members were assigned to administer the modified application process and peer review system. They managed the larger peer review panels, wrote summary statements of the review, and presented the review groups' results at the Director's review meeting. They attempted to balance the need for reviewers with a strong scientific background with panel members who had experience in service delivery or were themselves disabled. The quality of the panel review was improved through written summary statements that contained descriptions of the work to be supported, strengths and weaknesses of the research design, and a funding recommendation for the proposal.

The development of several computer data bases was an important step in making the new system work. One data base contained information on individuals who could be selected for peer review. The second contained information on grant applications. These data bases allowed the NIDRR staff to match the expertise of the reviewer with the applicant's description of the research. This change helped to decrease the amount of time necessary for the formation of panels and allowed the staff adequate time to mail grant applications to peer reviewers in advance of their meetings. The grant application data base was used to coordinate the feedback to applicants. The data on these files could be categorized by review panel, scientific discipline, disability, and functional problems. These various displays of the data provided a context for the Director's review meeting in which recommendations for funding were made. With these modifications, the quality and quantity of information I received prior to making funding recommendations greatly improved.

PROGRAM DEVELOPMENT

The second broad area of responsibility for a director of the NIDRR is to develop a coherent program plan to meet the primary mission of the Institute—improving the lives of Americans with disabilities. A description of the process involved in beginning several new programs in fiscal year 1987 provides an illustration of some of the complexities involved in implementing policy. A primary factor in making programmatic changes is the budget. The NIDRR budget for fiscal year 1987 contained $14 million in discretionary funds; $8.7 million in "previously committed" funds; $1.5 million in *congressionally designated* funds and $3.8 million in *undesignated* funds (see Figure 1). The *designated discretionary funds* were used to fund three centers that had purposes and geographic locations directed by Congress. The remaining $12.5 million provided the necessary funds to competitively renew some projects, to increase the number of new field-initiated research awards, and to begin programs that had been advocated by individuals with disabilities, researchers, and service providers. The new directions included research, training, demonstration, and information utilization in the areas of supported work, language development in individuals with hearing impairments, information networking to improve independent living, and several projects directed toward the needs of individuals with traumatic brain injury (TBI).

For a period of three years, advocates for increasing rehabilitation research in the area of TBI had been meeting with members of Congress, congressional committees and Department of Education officials. In the spring of 1986 a policy decision was made, and I began to develop programs to meet the needs of individuals with TBI.

Implementing this policy decision was accomplished through the use of a variety of existing programs. The research and demonstration program was used to fund a data base to track treatment outcomes, to support research on community living, and to develop programs using supported work

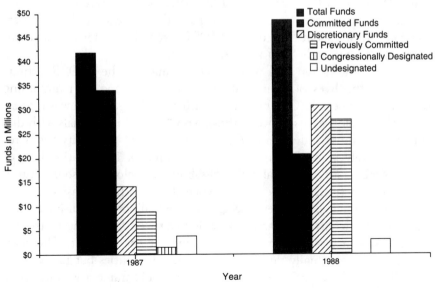

Figure 1. Committed and discretionary NIDRR funds in fiscal years 1987 and 1988.

in the rehabilitation of individuals with TBI. To improve the information network available to parents, affected individuals, service providers, and researchers, one award was made by the NIDRR's dissemination and utilization program. Several field-initiated research awards were made in fiscal year 1987 in the area of cognitive and physiological aspects of rehabilitation, and three awards were made in the area of TBI and supported work. Innovative grant awards were made in fiscal year 1987 that addressed the problems associated with information dissemination and community adjustment.

The importance of this illustration of implementing policy through program development is that a variety of NIDRR resources, both Institute directed and field initiated, were used to meet the needs for improved rehabilitation research and services described by affected individuals, their advocates, the service providers, and the research community—interdependency in action.

DEVELOPMENT OF THE CENTERS PROGRAM FOR FISCAL YEAR 1988

Moving from policy to a specific plan for the Rehabilitation Research and Training Centers and the Rehabilitation Engineering Centers programs was a major challenge. The urgency of developing such a plan was apparent because 40 centers funded in fiscal year 1987 were in the final year of a five-year funding cycle. The history of NIDRR funding illustrates the relative importance of the RRTC and REC programs to the Institute (see Figure 2). If the NIDRR fiscal year 1988–1992 budgets were to be distributed in the future as they had in the past, then funds for these centers would constitute about 50% of the NIDRR expenditures for the next five years, or approximately $125 million (see Figure 1).

I received written and oral advice on making the NIDRR centers relevant to the lives of individuals with disabilities and on maintaining excellence in research. One clear lesson from all the guidance was that an unhealthy tension exists between those who "do for" individuals with disabilities and those individuals with disabilities. The university-based researchers rarely seemed to understand the complex interrelationships of problems facing an individual with a disability. Developing a solution to a single problem (e.g., a stair-climbing wheelchair) without considering the effects of the change on other aspects of individual's life (e.g., using a stair-climbing wheelchair in an adapted vehicle) proved frustrating to the individual with a disability and disappointing for the scientist. The term *relevance* was continually raised by those with disabilities but rarely operationalized to the point at which researchers could frame a well-designed study to shed light on the issue. In an attempt to resolve these differences,

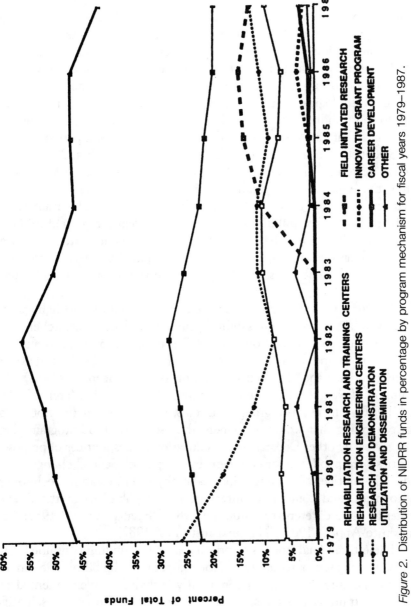

Figure 2. Distribution of NIDRR funds in percentage by program mechanism for fiscal years 1979–1987.

I had many discussions with scientists, parent advocates, and individuals with disabilities. A conference with representatives of research and service providers was convened. These efforts resulted in some guiding principles for planning NIDRR's programs.

Empowerment was central to a long list of needs expressed by the community of disabled individuals and their families (Frieden & Veerkamp, 1984). Empowerment takes the form of having affordable and reliable access to information on equipment and programs that allows individuals with disabilities to maximize their own functional abilities. Empowerment means the opportunity to make informed decisions on the selection of medical, psychological, vocational, recreational, and other community services. In short, individuals with disabilities want problem-oriented research with results that can be applied within a five-year funding period.

Scientists want research excellence rewarded by a fair and open competition for funds. They express the need for an emphasis on systems research, the importance of funding projects that allow them to examine infrequent cases, the necessity for expanding opportunities for training researchers, and the desirability of increasing the number of field-initiated research awards. Studies that assess the efficacy of rehabilitation aimed at particular functions are not only sought but required by service providers, individuals with disabilities, and budgetary constraints on funding for programs.

The fiscal year 1988 priorities were developed not only in light of the input given by persons with disabilities, (university-based) researchers, and advocates but also evolved from a NIDRR staff review of progress made at existing centers and from the long-range plan developed by the NIDRR in conjunction with the National Council on the Handicapped (1984). Beginning in November, 1986 and continuing through early March of 1987 the NIDRR staff met as a group to discuss, write, and edit the notices of priority funding that would implement the fiscal year 1988 program plan. After review by other Department of Education offices, notices of proposed priorities were published for comment by the public. Several changes were made. Final notices of funding priorities in physical restoration, technology development, and community integration were published in the *Federal Register* at three different times during 1987 ("Final Funding," 1987; "Invitation to Apply," 1987; "National Institute," 1987).

These three final notices of priority areas for funding contained general and specific sets of requirements for competition eligibility. The general principles guiding the research community included problem-oriented research and training programs; synergistic programs of research; scientific studies of specific areas; interdisciplinary training for researchers, physicians, and service providers; and information sharing through "state of the science" workshops and consensus conferences as well as publications in textbooks, edited topical books, and professional journals.

Grant priorities were changed to require that centers disseminate information using formats that are accessible by individuals with disabilities. The centers must provide training for individuals with disabilities and their families for the purpose of improving coping, managing, and survival skills. In many centers, an additional requirement was that individuals with disabilities be involved in planning, implementing, and reviewing center programs. In effect, these requirements defined the process of empowerment for individuals with disabilities.

Accountability of the grantees in meeting the funding priorities was addressed in two ways. The recipients of the new awards were required to meet NIDRR staff shortly after initiation of the award to review the applicant's implementation plans. In addition, the priority notices contained required reviews of progress within the first three years of the center operation. These reviews provide the director of the NIDRR with the option to continue funding centers at intervals other than every five years. The importance of these changes is that planning, budgeting, and reviewing approximately 50% of the NIDRR programs could be spread over five years rather than an 18-month period.

The *absolute priorities* for each RRTC or REC provided the potential applicant with specific topics for programs that could be reviewed for funding. Ten areas in the field of physical restoration (medical rehabilitation) were announced. For example, the notices for the spinal cord injury centers were written with absolute priorities that encouraged work in specified domains including the prevention of secondary health problems, the study of neural recovery, and the development of community-oriented health services.

Twelve final priorities were published in the areas of employment, community integration, environmental access, and special populations. The need to provide a national resource for studying how to make buildings accessible was described in the proposed priority on "access to community living environment." This priority was planned in cooperation with the Architectural Transportation Barriers and Compliance Board and was developed in response to the need for such an initiative was described by the National Council on the Handicapped (NCH, 1986).[2] The enactment of the Fair Housing Act of 1988 and its adaptable housing requirements has underscored the importance of this center as a national resource both for individuals with disabilities and for those who are responsible for designing and building adaptable structures. A second new area for the centers program at NIDRR was the examination of special problems faced by minority and economically deprived individuals with disabilities in requesting and receiving rehabilitation services.

---

[2]The name of the National Council on the Handicapped was changed to the National Council on the Disabled in 1986.

The priority notice for 11 Rehabilitation Engineering Centers described competitions in a wide variety of areas. As an example of one initiative, in response to the recommendations of the National Council on the Disabled an effort was made to encourage the examination of a variety of transportation systems that are used by, or potentially can be used by, individuals with disabilities. The efforts of this center may provide some assistance in gaining a better understanding of options available for development should the Americans with Disabilities Act become law (H.R. 2273, 1988; S. 933, 1988).

The process I used to develop the priorities in funding for the NIDRR in fiscal years 1987 and 1988 illustrates the variety of methods available for implementing public policy changes at a research institute. The new directions in programs reflect an attempt to bring individuals with disabilities into all aspects of the planning and conduct of rehabilitation research without alienating the researchers and service providers. Whether the new directions for rehabilitation research I helped to initiate will meet the needs of individuals with disabilities in our society depends, in large part, on the skillful implementation of programs by those researchers who are funded and by individuals with disabilities who become involved in each of the centers.

Although the changes made in the administration and peer review of grant applications[3] improved the quality of research at NIDRR, I felt that further changes were unlikely to be implemented during the remaining days of the Reagan administration (Finn, 1989). Therefore, in October of 1987 I returned to the National Institutes of Health. Having been the director of the NIDRR gives me a significantly different view of where research, disability issues, and personal values fit into the sequence of events that translate public policy into administrative programs. Policy is rarely formulated solely by those in the executive branch. Individuals with disabilities, scientists, service providers, and many other interested parties play significant roles at all points on the complex and convoluted pathway from policy to program.

Active participation of well-trained psychologists in the field of disability and rehabilitation research both in peer review and program development has a significant impact on the policies and programs at the NIDRR. Likewise, talented individuals with disabilities are proving to be an essential link in the formation of policies and implementation of programs. The paradigm may have shifted from paternalism to consumerism, but all are needed in the effort to improve rehabilitation research and the quality of life for individuals with disabilities.

---

[3]The description of the changes made at NIDRR apply only to the period when I was director. The policies, programs, and management of peer review may have changed significantly since September 26, 1987.

REFERENCES

Fair Housing Amendments Act of 1988, Pub. L. No. 100-430, 42 U.S.C. 3601 et seq.

Final funding priorities for fiscal year 1988; National Institute on Disabilities and Rehabilitation Research. 52 Fed. Reg. 35380–35385 (1987, September 18).

Frieden, L., & Veerkamp, E. (1984). A national profile of independent living programs for people with disabilities. Houston, TX: Institute for Rehabilitation Research.

Finn, C. E., Jr. (1989). Policy, interest groups, and the "gang of 237." Education Week, 7(33), 32, 24.

Fuhrer, M. J. (1988). Rehabilitation research in the 1980s. In M. G. Eisenberg (Ed.), Advances in clinical rehabilitation (Vol. 2, pp. 232–256). New York: Springer.

H.R. 2273, 101st cong., 1st Sess. (1988).

Invitation to apply for new awards under the National Institute on Disabilities and Rehabilitation Research (NIDRR) program of rehabilitation, engineering centers. 52 Fed. Reg. 31804 (1987, August 24).

National Council on the Handicapped. (1981). Policies governing the National Institute of Handicapped Research. Washington, DC: Author.

National Council on the Handicapped. (1984). National Institute of Handicapped Research long-range plan: 1981–1983. Washington, DC: Author.

National Council on the Handicapped (1986). Towards independence: An assessment of federal laws and programs affecting persons with disabilities—with legislative recommendations. Washington, DC: U.S. Government Printing Office.

National Institute on Disabilities and Rehabilitation Research: Proposed funding priorities for fiscal year 1988. 52 Fed. Reg. 37574–37583 (1987, October 7).

S. 933, 101st Congress, 1st Sess. (1988).

U.S. Department of Health, Education, and Welfare, National Institutes of Health. (1976). Grants Peer Review Study Team. Grants peer review: Report to the director, Phase I. (Vols. 1–3). Washington, DC: Author.

U.S. Department of Health, Education, and Welfare, National Institutes of Health. (1978). Grants Peer Review Study Team. Grants peer review: Report to the director, Phase II. Washington, DC: Author.

19

PSYCHOLOGY RESEARCH AND NIMH: OPPORTUNITIES AND CHALLENGES

ALAN I. LESHNER

For more than four decades, the National Institute of Mental Health (NIMH) has played a major role in supporting psychology research in the United States, and psychologists have played a major role in NIMH research. Facets of that relationship may have changed over the years, but the essential synergy has not. For example, the Alcohol, Drug Abuse, and Mental Health Administration (ADAMHA), the parent agency of NIMH, is the primary federal funder of basic research in psychology, and within ADAMHA, NIMH is the major psychology research funder.

Psychology is, by any measure, the leading discipline receiving NIMH research support. Both in research dollars received and principal investigators supported, psychologists command the largest proportion of NIMH resources devoted to any disciplinary group—about 35% of NIMH research dollars and about 45% of NIMH-supported researchers. In addition, among those who apply for NIMH research support, behavioral scientists are consistently more successful than the average applicant in obtaining approved and funded grants. During the past 10 years, their success rate has consistently remained a few percentage points ahead of other applicants.

Reprinted from *American Psychologist*, 46, 977–979. Copyright 1991 by the American Psychological Association.

The author, Director of the National Institute of Drug Abuse, prepared these Observations at the request of the journal Editor.

In recent years, NIMH research support to the field has been growing dramatically. The impressive growth of the NIMH extramural research budget—from $128 million in fiscal year (FY) 1980 to $335 million in FY 1990—has permitted the NIMH to increase substantially its support for behavioral and social science research. Within the past five years alone, NIMH research funding of the behavioral and social sciences has more than doubled, from a total of $102.8 million in FY 1985 to $225.8 million in FY 1990. In a nutshell: NIMH and psychology have a long, productive, and mutually supportive history together, and that strong collaboration continues to this day.

And what of the future? Prophecy is an extremely tricky business in times as volatile as ours. No one can now predict how the national economic, political, and social climate will shape the federal biomedical research budget—or more specifically, the NIMH budget—in the next 5 or 10 years. But I expect that, as its scientific achievements and clinical payoffs continue to multiply, mental health research will fare at least as well as other key areas of biomedical research. I am even more certain that, as a critical mental health research discipline, psychology will continue to be a bulwark of NIMH research.

My optimism is based on more than my own chauvinistic belief in psychology. It reflects the inescapable fact that psychologists bring absolutely essential knowledge, skills, and perspective to the mental health research field.

It is by now a truism that mental disorders are complex psychobiological phenomena that have their origins in the interaction of behavioral and biological factors. But having said that, how do we study them? My own view is that there should be studies of behavioral aspects in their own right, of biological aspects in their own right, and of the interface between the two in its own right. Because psychology encompasses all three approaches, we expect that psychologists will continue to make distinguished contributions to all three types of studies, as they have in the past. We are proud of the extraordinary contributions of NIMH-funded psychologists to such diverse areas as the development of effective cognitive and interpersonal therapies for affective and anxiety disorders, the emerging understanding of brain structure and function in mental health and illness, and the increasingly refined delineation of both genetic and environmental influences in animal and human development and behavior. We strongly encourage the continuation of this strong psychology research tradition.

Looking more specifically at NIMH research directions relevant to psychology, it is important to remember that federal research-management philosophies have changed over time and vary across agencies. A given agency's policies may change along several continua, for example, from reactive to proactive and from field-generated ("let a thousand flowers bloom") to more centrally planned ("put a man on the moon"). In times of funding plenty, we have a tendency to accept and support a wider range of research approaches and questions; when budgets are tight, we tend to develop more targeted initiatives.

Funding philosophies also tend to differ by research type; regardless of agency, there is a natural tendency for the basic research portfolio to be relatively wide ranging in focus, whereas the applied research portfolio tends to be much more targeted. Clinical research, which bridges between basic and applied research, usually falls between them in this dimension.

Since its founding in 1948, NIMH has tended historically to favor the relatively laissez faire, reactive, "thousand flowers," field-driven approach to research support. However, it has moved over the years toward more targeted initiatives—chosen, of course, in conjunction with the field. As NIMH's acting director, I am now striving to retain a good balance between agency-planned initiatives and those reflecting the full spectrum of interests of individual investigators and the field.

The sciences relevant to mental health and illness are progressing at such a rapid rate that we are constantly challenged to stay on top of what is happening, especially now that technological developments are driving many of the most exciting new research advances. The NIMH research-support philosophy that we have adopted to respond to these rapidly changing opportunities and challenges was best articulated by ice-hockey star Wayne Gretsky when he said, "I skate to where I think the puck is going to be." For us, skating in the right direction means setting our research priorities and initiatives to anticipate and facilitate the field's most fertile growth areas.

During the past three years, NIMH has developed four important strategic plans or research agendas to help it skate in the right direction: the National Plan for Schizophrenia Research, the Decade of the Brain Plan (for neuroscience research), the National Plan for Research on Child and Adolescent Mental Disorders, and the National Plan for Research to Improve Care for Severe Mental Illness. The first three are already being implemented, and the fourth was recently released.

In each of these plans, NIMH research initiatives have been carefully developed to respond to problems, opportunities, and constraints identified through the extensive participation of diverse consultants. Stimuli for NIMH research initiatives in the behavioral sciences, as in other substantive areas, come from a variety of sources, including the field, formal advisory bodies, NIMH staff, Congressional interests and directives, and Administration policies and priorities. NIMH standing advisory bodies include the National Advisory Mental Health Council, the Extramural Science Advisory Board, the Board of Scientific Counselors, and 18 standing initial review groups. Some of these bodies have contributed recently to important science analyses and reviews of NIMH's behavioral science research program. These reviews include "New Frontiers in Behavioral Sciences and

Mental Health: An Assessment (1987–1989)" and a review completed in 1989 by the NIMH Extramural Science Board and Ad Hoc Consultants.

As a result of these reviews, several areas have been identified as NIMH behavioral science research priorities: cognitive science (including cognitive neuroscience, development of cognition, and fundamental perceptual processes); behavioral genetics; behavioral patterns and physiological systems; and personality, motivation, emotion, and interpersonal processes. NIMH also has major behavioral sciences initiatives in the areas of acquired immunodeficiency syndrome (AIDS) prevention and determinants of high-risk behaviors, as well as in research demonstrations related to the prevention of conduct disorder and youth suicide. NIMH is working with the broad field of psychology to help shape a national psychology research agenda.

Among its responses to problems and constraints in the field of mental health research, NIMH has focused considerable energy and resources on infrastructure support through a variety of mechanisms and approaches. These include researcher recruitment and training, career scientist support, general and specialized centers, multisite studies, specialized facilities, national resources, and targeted programs.

We have also recently reorganized the structure of our extramural basic science program to make it more responsive to current and emerging multidisciplinary approaches to understanding brain, behavior, and their interactions. The former NIMH Division of Basic Sciences previously had three main branches: Behavioral Sciences Research, Neuroscience Research, and Psychobiology (Health and Behavior) Research. The newly renamed and reorganized NIMH Division of Basic Brain and Behavioral Sciences now contains seven research branches—Basic Behavioral and Cognitive Sciences, Basic Prevention and Behavioral Medicine, Cognitive and Behavioral Neuroscience, Molecular and Cellular Neuroscience, Neuroimaging and Applied Neuroscience, Personality and Social Processes, and Psychopharmacology—four of which have a particularly strong psychological orientation.

The reorganization has created a number of new branch chief and program chief openings within the NIMH Division of Basic Brain and Behavioral Sciences. We strongly urge APA members and their colleagues to take advantage of this unusual opportunity to serve the research community and the mental health field by applying for these important federal research positions.

I am optimistic that the long and fruitful collaboration between NIMH and psychology will continue to be extremely rewarding. But given the many uncertainties we face in the near future, appreciable growth in mental health research will undoubtedly require more highly sophisticated and ecumenical advocacy efforts by all concerned parties. To make those of psychology as effective and appropriate as possible, its messages need to be examined and honed periodically. From an NIMH perspective, one area deserving more attention concerns the tendency of some mental health advocates to pit behavior against biology and to disparage research or treatment approaches grounded in the "wrong" orientation. These exercises in polarization give rise to picturesque rhetoric about "mindless brains" versus "brainless minds," but do not benefit the field, knowledge we seek, or clients we serve. Unfortunately, the popular press, eager for controversy, often encourages one-sided discussions of mental disorders or treatments that emphasize either environmental or biological factors but not their interactions.

Advocacy arguments that emphasize one approach at the expense of the other do not reflect today's understanding of mental health, and they are counterproductive. *Biological* and *behavioral* are *not* competing levels of explanation. Rather, they are different and complementary foci of study or levels of analysis. In our advocacy efforts we must avoid *both* spurious reductionism *and* spurious "up-uctionism." In advocating for mental-illness-related research, we need to provide equal encouragement for studies of behavioral aspects, studies of biological aspects, and studies of the interface between them. By adopting a broad-based advocacy strategy predicated on the science of mental illness, our efforts are likely to advance both psychology and the mental health field.

20

VIOLENCE AGAINST WOMEN: THE CONGRESSIONAL RESPONSE

JOSEPH R. BIDEN, JR.

Every day, every hour, indeed every minute, a woman in the United States suffers the pain and violence of a physical attack. Every six minutes, a woman is raped (Federal Bureau of Investigation [FBI], 1989). The former Surgeon General Antonia C. Novello announced in 1992 that domestic violence is the leading cause of injuries to women aged 15–44 (Novello, Rosenberg, Saltzman, & Shosky, 1992). Spouse abuse is more common than automobile accidents, muggings, and cancer deaths combined (U.S. Senate Judiciary Committee, 1992).

Yet, America as a nation has for too long failed to grasp either the scope or the seriousness of violence against women. If the leading news-

Reprinted from *American Psychologist*, 48, 1059–1061. Copyright 1993 by the American Psychological Association.

Joseph R. Biden, Jr., is a Democratic senator from Delaware. He is an active member of the Senate Foreign Relations Committee. A former trial lawyer, he was a principal architect of the major crime bills enacted in 1984 and 1990 and passed by the Senate in 1991, as well as major antidrug legislation enacted in 1986 and 1988. He is particularly interested in family issues and women's rights, especially gender-related abuse and violence. A graduate of University of Delaware and the Syracuse University College of Law, Senator Biden is an adjunct professor at the Widener University School of Law. He commutes to Washington from Wilmington, Delaware, where he lives with his wife and daughter. The Bidens have two sons in law school.

This chapter appeared as part of an invited series by public officials designed to inform psychologists about policy issues of concern to psychology and the public at large. The views expressed are those of the author and do not necessarily reflect the views of the American Psychological Association or its officers.

papers were to announce tomorrow a new disease that, over the past year, had afflicted from 3 to 4 million citizens, few would fail to appreciate the seriousness of the illness. Yet, when it comes to the 3 to 4 million women who are victimized by violence each year, the alarms ring softly. We live in a nation that has three times as many animal shelters as battered women's shelters (McCarthy, 1991). We live in a nation where crimes against women are still perceived as anything but crime—as a family problem, as a private matter, as "sexual miscommunication."

Since 1990, I have conducted a series of hearings in the Senate Judiciary Committee on violence against women, exploring the causes and effects of this violence. Prominent psychologists and psychiatrists have helped me, my colleagues, and the American public to understand this issue better. We have learned, for example, that public authorities have underestimated rape rates by as much as 10–15 times the actual rate (Koss, Dinero, Seibel, & Cox, 1988). We have learned that family violence is far from a trivial push or shove: One third of all such incidents, if reported, would be classified as felony rape, robbery, or aggravated assault; the remaining two thirds involve bodily injury at least as serious as the injury inflicted in 90% of all robberies and aggravated assaults (National Institute of Justice, 1990). Indeed, we now know that family violence accounts for a significant number of murders in this country; in 1990, one third of all female homicide victims died at the hands of a husband or boyfriend (FBI, 1990).

Through the hearings, we have come to understand the cost of violence against women. From survivors we have heard tragic accounts of the personal cost—necks broken and faces scarred, careers abandoned and college educations interrupted, suicides attempted and marriages broken (U.S. Senate Judiciary Committee, 1990). We have heard testimony about the societal cost: the billions of dollars lost to the economy, the lives left unfulfilled because of the fear of violence (U.S. Senate Judiciary Committee, 1990, 1991), and the children who must live with the terrifying memories of their mothers' battering.

Violence against women is far from the private matter those who minimize its importance would have us believe. It is a public tragedy of several dimensions. It is a serious public health problem: More than one million women a year seek medical assistance for injuries caused by violence at the hands of a male partner (Stark & Flitcraft, 1982). It is a serious education problem: Approximately a half million high school girls will be raped before they graduate (Warshaw, 1988). And it is a serious criminal justice problem: In some jurisdictions, prosecutors refuse to bring acquaintance rape cases to court because convictions are virtually impossible to obtain (Colorado Supreme Court Task Force on Gender Bias in the Courts, 1990; U.S. Senate Judiciary Committee, 1991).

I believe that one of the major reasons we have underestimated the scope and intensity of violence against women is that we have underestimated the staying power of subtle prejudices that blunt society's outrage. Such stereotypical expressions as "She asked for it," "No harm was done," and "She made it up" are frighteningly common. These stereotypes perpetuate a regime of silence, denial, and neglect—a regime in which survivors assume they will not be believed and outsiders continue to disbelieve. We cannot hope to respond effectively to violence against women unless we confront and condemn the attitudes that nurture the violence.

Although legislation cannot hope to change these attitudes directly, the legislative process can help to alert the public. For this reason I introduced the Violence Against Women Act in 1990 and have held hearings on this issue. The legislation's overarching aim is to telescope our vision, highlighting past obstacles, flushing out improper stereotypes, and recognizing the problem for what it is: a national tragedy played out every day in the lives of millions of American women at home, in the workplace, and on the street.

Over the past two decades, important legislation has addressed specific problems relating to violence against women. In the 1970s, Congress reformed federal rape laws to focus on the defendant's conduct, not the victim's past sexual history (Privacy Protection for Rape Victims Act of 1978). In the mid-1980s, Congress began to encourage and fund battered women's shelters (Family Violence Prevention and Services Act of 1984). It also created a special fund to compensate crime victims out of the fines paid by criminals, granting priority compensation to rape and domestic violence survivors (Victims of Crime Act of 1984).

These much-needed legislative efforts are each important in their own right, but none have sought to address the problem of violence against women as a whole. When I introduced the Violence Against Women Act, I aimed to address a more general problem shared by women victimized by violent behaviors—whether it be a beating in the home, a rape by a neighbor, or an assault on the street. I wanted to call this violence by a common name so that we could begin to understand that, although the particular acts may differ, the violence is a shared problem, shared by all women in America.

The Violence Against Women Act takes aim at the problem from four different perspectives: rectifying imbalances, helping survivors, providing education, and requiring equal treatment. First, the act provides leadership at the national level by strengthening and creating new laws for crimes—such as rape and domestic violence—that have traditionally received second-class status in state criminal justice systems. Second, it authorizes funds for service providers to give survivors the resources they need, giving priority funding for rape crisis centers and battered women's shelters. Third, it provides resources and training for education—education for participants in the criminal justice system, such as judges, police, prosecutors, and victim advocates, as well as education in our schools. Finally, it creates the first legal remedy for victims of violence motivated by gender discrimination, sending a powerful message that violence based on gender—like violence based on race or religion—assaults an ideal of equality shared by the entire nation.

On May 27, 1993, the Violence Against Women Act was reported favorably out of committee, clearing it to be voted on by the full Senate. The House companion bill, H.R. 1133, introduced by Representative Patricia Schroeder, remains in committee.

Members of the American Psychological Association have already contributed greatly to the public's understanding of this issue and have provided unparalleled assistance in understanding both the scope and the causes of violence against women. I commend them on their efforts and urge them to continue to help us gain a greater and deeper understanding of this problem.

REFERENCES

Colorado Supreme Court Task Force on Gender Bias in the Courts. (1990). *Gender justice in the Colorado courts*. (Available from Office of the State Court Administrator, 1301 Pennsylvania St., No. 300, Denver, CO 80203)

Family Violence Prevention and Services Act, Pub. L. No. 98-457 (1984, October 9).

Federal Bureau of Investigation. (1989). *Uniform crime reports*. Washington, DC: U.S. Department of Justice.

Federal Bureau of Investigation. (1990). *Uniform crime reports*. Washington, DC: U.S. Department of Justice.

Koss, M. P., Dinero, T. E., Siebel, C., & Cox, S. (1988). Stranger, acquaintance, and date rape: Is there a difference in the victim's experience? *Psychology of Women Quarterly, 12*, 1–24.

McCarthy, C. (1991, July 23). Countering violence at home. *Washington Post*, p. D13.

National Institute of Justice. (1990). *Civil protection orders: Legislation, current court practice, and enforcement*. Washington, DC: Author.

Novello, A., Rosenberg, M., Saltzman, L., & Shosky, J. (1992). From the Surgeon General, U.S. Public Health Service. *The Journal of the American Medical Association, 267*(23), 3132.

Privacy Protection for Rape Victims Act of 1978, 92 Stat. 2046 (1978, October 28).

Stark, E., & Flitcraft, A. (1982, Summer/Fall). Medical therapy as repression: The case of battered women. *Health and Medicine*, 29–32.

U.S. Senate Judiciary Committee. (1990, October 19). *Report No. 101–545 accompanying S.2754 (The Violence Against Women Act of 1990)*. Washington, DC: Author.

U.S. Senate Judiciary Committee. (1991, October 29). *Report No. 102–197 accompanying S.15 (The Violence Against Women Act)*. Washington, DC: Author.

U.S. Senate Judiciary Committee. (1992, October). *Violence against women: A week in the life of America* (prepared by the majority staff of the Senate Judiciary Committee). (Available from Hart Office Building, Room B04, Washington, DC 20510).

Victims of Crime Act, Pub. L. No. 98–473 (1984, October 12).

Warshaw, R. (1988). *I never called it rape*. New York: Harper & Row.

V

THOUGHTS FROM
THE PUBLIC POLICY
FRONT LINE

21

MOVING PSYCHOLOGY TOWARD (SELF) RECOGNITION AS A PUBLIC RESOURCE: THE VIEWS OF A CONGRESSMAN PSYCHOLOGIST

TED STRICKLAND

On January 5, 1993 I found myself in a rather humbling situation. On that day I was sworn in as a member of the U.S. House of Representatives from rural southern Ohio's 6th congressional district. I was the first psychologist to have been elected to the U.S. Congress. As I stood in the historic House chamber and contemplated the challenges that lay ahead of me, I was aware that I brought to the office a professional point of view as well as personal convictions. I was proud to be a psychologist in Congress and strongly believed that psychology had something important to bring to public policy.

How did I get to Congress? What was my experience there, and how did my psychology background influence me? Why do I believe that psychologists must be involved in public policy? That is the subject of this chapter.

GETTING THERE: THE FIRST THREE DECADES

I did not get to Congress by accident—or overnight. It was a long process, starting with my developing an intense interest in politics while a doctoral student in the early 1970s and culminating in my election in

1992. However, due to the strong influence of my family, it is likely that the roots of my political career were planted during my childhood.

I was born in 1941 and reared in a working-class family where being a Democrat and supporting organized labor were family values. My dad, a steelworker who experienced the trauma of the Depression, taught me two things while I was very young: (a) Franklin Delano Roosevelt had saved America from social and economic collapse, and (b) the Steelworkers Union of America had enabled him to earn a decent living and keep our family out of poverty.

Ours was not a formally educated family, but we had a keen intuitive sense of the world around us. If Maslow's hierarchy of needs were used to chart our energies in those days, it would show that most were concentrated on the bottom rung of the ladder: food, shelter, and clothing. Like many Appalachian parents of their era, my parents were bright, but neither had progressed past the eighth grade. Dropping out of school to work was also the norm for my brothers and sisters.

As the eighth child, I had more opportunities than my older siblings. I was the only one to attend college, and, in a way, I felt as if I were going to college for all of them. My family seemed to have high expectations for me in spite of the fact that I had a significant stuttering problem.

Looking back, I can see that my decision to attend college was not based primarily on an educational motive but was most significantly influenced by my religious beliefs at the time. I had become interested in the religious life during my senior year of high school and wanted to attend a conservative Christian college. As a result of that decision, I spent my undergraduate days attending a small liberal arts college where chapel was required three times each week and every class began with prayer.

I knew I wanted to enter the ministry, so following college, I attended theological seminary for 3 years and received a degree in divinity. After seminary, I pastored a Methodist church in Ohio for 1 year. The bishop then appointed me to work in a Methodist Children's Home in Kentucky. While there, I saw the complexity of problems affecting children who came to us. I remember a little girl threatened with expulsion from kindergarten for destructive behavior who had been sexually abused by her stepfather, three young brothers who had been traumatized by an emotionally disturbed mother, and many teenagers who were involved in drug abuse. We had one social worker and no other mental health staff. It did not take me long to realize that these children needed a level of help and expertise beyond my Thursday night chapel service.

So, I entered the PhD program in counseling psychology at the University of Kentucky. I continued to embrace a fundamentalistic theological perspective and an extreme social conservatism, which I tried to communicate to others with evangelistic zeal. The extent of my commitment to put my beliefs into action included spending a summer working with an evangelical missionary group in Graz, Austria. I spent part of that summer going door-to-door distributing religious literature and telling people that God loved them and had a wonderful plan for their lives. (I can still say those phrases in German.)

With this background it is reasonable to ask, What happened? How did a socially and theologically conservative Methodist minister become a psychologist and a Congressman with a decidedly left-of-center political philosophy? This question has come from my liberal friends who are pleased about my conversion to a progressive worldview, and from my conservative Christian friends who are concerned that I have "backslidden" and lost my faith. It is a question that I have asked myself, because on the surface, it seems that my decision to run for Congress was made without sufficient prior thought—an impulsive act that defied reason.

In retrospect, I believe that decision was my personal response to the prevailing zeitgeist—the chaotic social and political climate of the 1960s and 1970s. The civil rights movement, the deaths of the Kennedy brothers, the Vietnam War, and the unfolding of the Watergate fiasco had shaken my confidence in much that I had been taught to believe. So many societal changes in such a brief historical period had prompted me to examine my social and spiritual values and to question my life goals. In addition to the unfolding historical events and the influence of my graduate studies, it was during this time that I met certain individuals, including my future wife, who had a profound effect upon my personal growth.

In short, my rigid values were exposed to new models of behavior. One such model came in the form of a young conscientious objector who came to work at the Methodist Children's Home as an alternative service to the Vietnam War. He was a great addition to our staff, and we soon became good friends. His deep spirituality, unconditional acceptance of others, and relaxed attitude of indifference toward conventional expressions of personal piety simultaneously intrigued and troubled me.

During that period of my life, I had rigid ideas about what constituted moral behavior. For example, I would never have used "curse" words or drunk alcoholic beverages. My friend, on the other hand, would listen to music from *Hair*, with its sexually explicit lyrics—and yet sing soulful hymns with beauty and conviction! "Hear Oh Lord, the sound of my voice, Hear Oh Lord and answer."

This created cognitive dissonance as I came to feel that my conscientious objector friend had a more mature and ethical view of religion, politics, and social responsibility than I possessed. In addition, my graduate training was expanding my understanding of human behavior, deepening my appreciation for diversity, and leading me to clarify my own values. I was an evolving person being both challenged and changed by historical events, intellectual stimulation, and good friends. As a result, I came to believe that John Kennedy was right when he said, "On this earth, God's work must truly be our own" (Inaugural Address, January 20, 1961).

Growing out of these circumstances came a decision that appeared to others, and even to myself at the time, as impulsive and disconnected to my previous goals. I now understand that it was neither of these. Rather, it was the culmination of a process—a "Eureka experience," if you will—that propelled me into the world of politics and public service.

The linkages between philosophy, theology, and psychology are generally accepted, so my movement from minister to psychologist is not difficult to understand. The bridge that connected these two careers was my acceptance of the principles of humanism. For example, the theories of Carl Rogers and Abraham Maslow provided the therapeutic foundation I could relate to in my work at the children's home, and, at the same time, they were consistent with my evolving theological leanings. Although the most accepting of my conservative friends conceded that humanism may be a helpful philosophy in trying to overcome the problem of "man's inhumanity to man," most were critical of my acceptance of a humanistic worldview. They considered humanism, especially humanistic psychology, to be antithetical to orthodox Christian theology.

I was growing weary of esoteric philosophical and theological debate and becoming more comfortable with ambiguities. I accepted the fact that it may be impossible to find definitive answers to all of life's existential questions. There was one thing, however, that I knew for certain. I wanted to do something to help alleviate the human suffering I saw—so I moved deeper into my psychology training. Interestingly, I now see that it was this desire to help others and my commitment to humanistic principles that served as the bridge for my transition also from psychology to political involvement—except that in politics, humanism is labeled *liberalism*.

The First Three Campaigns

It was 1975 and I was in the midst of my doctoral dissertation work when I made a sudden decision to lay aside my research, return to my hometown in Ohio, and challenge William Harsha, a powerful incumbent Republican representing the 6th congressional district. Although my opponent was the ranking minority member of the Public Works and Transportation Committee, I did not believe that he had used his power to help the people in our poor Appalachian district. I knew I could do better.

I convinced a friend, who would become my wife 12 years later, to go with me to Ohio and help with the campaign. Frances Smith had been working on a PhD in educational psychology as I worked on my degree.

We had shared coursework and an office, and we found that we shared an idealism about political action. So we optimistically launched my campaign. To say that we were naive is a gross understatement. We did not know all the difficulties that lay ahead, nor did we know that in the next 6 years, I would run three times for Congress.

Obviously, I was most naive as I started that first campaign in 1976. I didn't know the district boundaries, didn't know a single prominent political person, and didn't know how to run for office. Frances and I started by visiting the Democratic chairs in each of the 12 counties of the district to solicit their help. Without exception, they wished me well but said there was no way to win. But we worked hard, raised $14,000, and focused on issues of economic opportunity, education, and honesty. When the votes were counted, the chairs were right, but we had made a decent showing (36%) against a popular, established incumbent.

After the loss, I returned to Kentucky to teach and work on my graduate degree, but I was back in campaign mode again for the 1978 election. This time, the experience was more negative. Because of my respectable showing in the previous campaign, Harsha took the campaign seriously and the race took on a more hostile tone. This time, we spent about $40,000 raised from a grassroots effort that included yard sales, bake sales, and auctions. The results were about the same, but I was left with a bitter taste after two defeats.

I returned to Kentucky, worked as a teaching assistant at the University of Kentucky, and focused on finishing my dissertation. On the morning that I was defending my dissertation, a reporter from the *Dayton Daily News* called to tell me that Congressman Harsha had announced that he would retire. This meant an opportunity to run for an open seat and a much better chance to win.

I came back to Ohio and started to organize my third campaign. My friend Frances again offered to help, as campaign manager. This time, though, we were better known and had more success raising money.

The issues of taxes and spending priorities dominated the campaign. My opponent, Bob McEwen, agreed with presidential candidate Ronald Reagan that we could cut taxes, significantly increase military spending, and balance the budget. I disagreed, saying that priority spending coupled with tax cuts would explode the deficit. I received most of the newspaper endorsements, and by August, the race was a dead heat. By election time however, we had been outspent, $190,000 to $85,000. Even with the Reagan landslide though, we still received 46% of the vote.

After the election, I wrote to a friend, "I'm going to take W. C. Fields' advice: 'If at first you don't succeed [1976], try [1978], try again [1980]. After that, give up, because there's no sense being a damn fool about it.'"

Return to Psychology

I set aside my political aspirations, left southern Ohio, and went to Columbus, where I could complete my postdoctoral internship and become licensed to practice. There, I worked for the next 7 years as a psychologist in a variety of settings. As a staff member at a community mental health center, I evaluated people who were mentally ill to determine if they should be hospitalized involuntarily. I also worked as ward psychologist at the Central Ohio Psychiatric Hospital.

The Columbus, Ohio community mental health system is one of the best in the nation. Still, I was disturbed by what I saw: seriously mentally ill people being discharged to open shelters, mentally ill people being incarcerated in prisons, and the treatment of mentally ill people being driven by political and economic considerations.

By the mid 1980s, I also began psychological consulting in the maximum security prison at Lucasville. At that time, more than 300 severely disordered inmates were on the psychiatric caseload. Some who come to mind include a young man who had more than 20 abdominal operations after repeated self-mutilations; a young man who pulled out all of his hair because of auditory and tactile hallucinations; and another who covered his head with feces because the "voices" were calling him a "shithead."

At the prison, as in community mental health, I was disturbed by the conditions around me. Here again, I saw needless human suffering as a result of public policies that were divorced from knowledge derived from social science research.

In 1987, Frances Smith and I were married. We moved to Lucasville, where I continued psychological consulting at the prison and taught at Shawnee State University. Frances pursued her career as an educational psychologist. We remained politically and socially active in our community but had no plans to run for political office again. We had watched during the 1980s as a Democratic Congress caved in to the Reagan agenda, resulting in a quadrupling of our national debt. During the Bush years, however, we were even more disheartened over societal attitudes that became increasingly harsh and more punitive toward the poor, the incarcerated, and the mentally ill.

The Fourth Campaign

Before the 1992 election, Ohio lost one congressional seat because of population growth in the south and west. In redrawing the boundaries, my district, which had formerly been primarily Republican, became more evenly balanced between the parties. Also, two Republican incumbents were to be pitted against each other, Congressman Clarence Miller and Congressman Bob McEwen, whom I had run against in 1980. Both had strongly conservative voting records. Neither had used his Republican influence to deal with major economic and poverty issues of the district. So, I said, "The hell with W.C. Fields, I'm going to run again."

Frances once more put aside her work to become my campaign manager and chief strategist. This time, however, I did not have the automatic blessing of the county chairpersons. Some reminded me that I was a "three-time loser." Also, a successful Democratic mayor opposed me in the primary. However, there was a surprising amount of support left over from my earlier campaigns, and I carried 13 of 14 counties to easily win the nomination. I came out of the primary in a strong position to wage an effective general election campaign.

My Republican opponent did not fare as well. A bitter feud between the McEwen and Miller campaigns left a weakened McEwen as victor. McEwen was hurt also by the House of Representatives check writing scandal, had missed many House votes, and traveled frequently on foreign junkets. In spite of these problems, he was a popular Congressman who received substantial support from religious conservatives for his positions in favor of school prayer and in opposition to abortion.

After winning the nomination, I still had to convince contributors that I was a viable candidate worthy of their support. Here, psychologist colleagues played an early, pivotal role by contributing dollars from nearly every state in the nation. This early funding from psychologists kept our campaign going until we were able to show sufficient strength to attract contributions from other sources.

The issues in the 1992 campaign continued themes from the 1970s: education, jobs, children, and the new concern of health care. This time, our campaign was well planned and organized. Both Frances and I had learned a great deal from the three earlier races. We identified our natural supporters (organized labor, pro-choice voters, educators, and human-service workers) and incorporated them into our Democratic party base. In addition to the campaign organization, we developed a strategy that involved challenging McEwen to a series of public debates. He accepted, and more than 350 people showed up for each of these events. The debates were also widely disseminated by the electronic media. This time, the voters heard our message, and I won with 50.7% of the vote. After years of trying, Frances and I were finally on our way to Washington to work on the critical policy issues of health care, children, education, and the economy.

BEING THERE: KEEPING PROMISES, GETTING RESULTS

From the moment I realized that I had won, I felt a heavy responsibility for my supporters and my district. Of Ohio's 19 congressional districts, mine is first in its percentage of children who live in poverty. In addition, we have high levels of unemployment, low educational achievement, and the lowest per capita income in the state. Some 37,000 people in the district have no health insurance, and many of these are children from working poor families.

The concerns that drove my campaign guided my work as a member of the 103rd Congress. After all, I had pursued the office over a 16-year period of time, and now the opportunity had finally come my way. I was determined not to waste it.

Getting started as a freshman is overwhelming. Within days after the election, Frances and I were receiving requests for assistance from our new constituents. Hundreds of letters and files piled up in our living room, waiting for attention weeks before I had an office or staff or was sworn in. Frances had a routine of walking to our local post office each day to get the mail. The onslaught of correspondence was so great that she had to wear her backpack in order to carry it home. NBC News showed up on my doorstep within a week of the election to begin a series of stories about my transition from a prison psychologist to a member of Congress. I needed to find an apartment in Washington, hire a staff, develop a plan for district offices, and become oriented to the technical requirements of being a Congressman.

Having never served in any elected office or legislative body, I knew that there were certain background experiences possessed by many of my freshman colleagues that I totally lacked. On the other hand, I knew that as a result of my educational and professional experiences, I possessed unique knowledge and skills—abilities that I hoped would enable me to make a distinctive contribution to the decision-making process in Washington.

In order to demonstrate my commitment to all of my constituents, I decided to take the oath of office in each of the 14 counties of the district prior to the official swearing-in ceremony in Washington, DC. It was a good decision, as scores of citizens, Democrat and Republican alike, showed up at the local county courthouses for these events. More than 700 people came to the event in my home county, held in my old high school. An atmosphere of optimism and goodwill seemed present throughout the district, and the stage was set for a successful first term.

On my first full day in office, I was talking to a reporter when I suddenly experienced a severe pain in my chest. I was rushed to a local hospital and spent the next several days recuperating from gallbladder surgery. It was not the most desirable way to begin a freshman term in Congress, but with the help of Frances, my staff, and colleagues, I did not fall behind in my duties.

Because my district is so poor and my predecessor was perceived as having abused the privileges of office, I felt that I should try to lead by example. I wanted to run a low-cost yet effective and responsive congressional office. Consequently, I kept my staff to below the maximum number allowable, Frances and I paid for our own health insurance, I did not use the congressional franking privilege for mass mailings, I paid for all of my travel in my congressional district, and I returned the cost-of-living increase that I received after the election. As a result, it cost less to operate my office than any of Ohio's other 18 congressional offices.

I also understood that in order to be reelected, it was important to stay in close touch with my constituents. So I returned home every weekend but two during my term in office. Usually, I would leave Washington on Thursday evening and return on Tuesday morning. The rest of my time was spent traveling throughout my sprawling rural district.

After a short time in office, I recognized that I had a serious staff problem. My chief of staff was not a good fit with my legislative agenda or management style. With great reluctance I made the decision to replace him. At that point, Frances agreed to once again lay aside her work as an educational psychologist and become my unpaid chief of staff. I will be forever grateful for her willingness to do that for me.

As I put together a staff of 16 full-time employees, I looked for people who were primarily motivated by a commitment to public service and a desire to serve others. I was successful in that effort, and with Frances as the manager of that wonderfully talented and dedicated team, I always felt confident that my constituents and the country were being well served.

I learned two things during my first year in office. First, being a congressman was much easier than I had expected. Second, being a congressman was more difficult than I had imagined. These may seem to be contradictory messages, but they are not if one understands how Congress works and what constituents expect. It is my opinion that any socially competent individual, with average intellectual and conceptual abilities and a high level of motivation can serve effectively as a member of Congress.

On the other hand, constituent demands and expectations can be almost overpowering. I am not referring to political criticism or policy disagreements; I am talking about the personal side of being a member of Congress. Many constituents seem to feel "ownership" so that any personal identity apart from being "the Congressman" is taken away. A member is expected to be always available, always willing to express an opinion on a wide variety of issues, always positive, and always public. I remember a distraught veteran calling me at 3:00 a.m. When I asked why he had not waited until morning to call, he replied, "I heard you say you were going to work day and night for us." After a 45-minute conversation, he felt better and I returned to bed.

It is the public part that can be so troublesome to members of Congress with young families. Frances and I had only ourselves to think about when schedules and travel plans were made. In that regard we were fortunate. However, I observed many of my colleagues struggle to make themselves available to their constituents without neglecting their own families. They often shared the conflict that they felt when congressional responsibilities prevented them from being the kind of spouse or parent that they wanted to be.

Perhaps the most reasonable way to deal with such dilemmas would be simply to cut back on activities. This is easier said than done—especially if one wants to be reelected. Except for the most secure members of Congress, if one wants to remain in office, unrelenting efforts must be focused on the next election. This means taking every opportunity to interact with constituents. It also means raising campaign funds on a continuous basis.

Why do it? Why would anyone disrupt a career, voluntarily relinquish their privacy, spend time shuttling between Washington and the home district, give up time with family and friends, work 12- to 14-hour days, campaign on most holidays, engage in constant fundraising, endure increasingly negative campaign attacks, and take a chance of being defeated every 2 years? The answer, based on my personal experience and observations of congressional colleagues, has to do with achieving "power and influence"—terms I do not use pejoratively. The truth is that only by being in office can one directly translate one's values and beliefs into law. Because most members of Congress care deeply about the issues facing the country and want to influence public policy, they accept the price they have to pay to be in office.

One of the reasons I wanted to be in Congress was to have the chance to reform health care. I was convinced, and still believe, that the need to reform our health care system is the most significant domestic problem facing the country. The failure to pass a comprehensive health care reform package during the 103rd Congress was my greatest disappointment.

I was totally committed to achieving universal coverage for every citizen, and I spent a large part of my term in office working to get it done. In Washington, I was asked to serve on Hillary Clinton's health care task force. My efforts were directed toward rural health care needs and mental health issues. Back home in Ohio, I conducted a public health care forum in each of my district's 14 counties and brought Mrs. Clinton to the district for a health care town meeting.

In addition, I worked closely with representatives of the American Psychological Association (APA) to see that the administration's reform plan would not discriminate against psychology. My work with the APA also focused on the expansion of outpatient services and the inclusion of psychologists in federally funded training programs. The administration and congressional committees were receptive to our suggestions. Had the administration's reform bill passed, I am confident that it would have reflected changes helpful to psychology because of our efforts. When the President's Health Security Act was introduced in November 1993, there was an atmosphere of optimism that masked the depth of opposition to the plan and the degree to which powerful interests would go to keep reform from happening. Most of my congressional colleagues of both political parties initially voiced support for some degree of reform. I remember having breakfast with Senator Jay Rockefeller (D–WV) and hearing him say, "We have finally reached the point where we no longer have to ask if health care reform will happen. It will! The only question now is when will it happen and in what form?"

It seemed that every significant constituent group had climbed aboard the reform bandwagon. Hospitals, physicians, business groups, and consumers acknowledged the problems in our current system and called for change. But the devil turned out to be in the details; and as opposition grew, widespread public support for reform gradually faded, making political gridlock inevitable.

What caused reform to fail? I think there were two major reasons. The insurance industry joined with other business groups and spent millions of dollars to convince the American people that the Clinton plan would put government in charge of our health care system and lead to the rationing of care. In addition, the issue became hopelessly politicized. The Republicans recognized, correctly in my judgment, that President Clinton and the Democrats in Congress would be politically strengthened if health care reform were accomplished. Senator Phil Gramm (R–Texas) responded by saying, "The Clinton Health Care Plan will pass over my cold, dead, political body."

In a story headlined, "Policy Is Politics to Haley Barbour," the *Logan Daily News* reported, "During the health care debate, when many Republicans were inclined to strike a compromise with President Clinton, Barbour (Chairman of the Republican National Committee) helped talk them off the slippery slope."

As I watched the disintegration of the reform effort, I reached a conclusion about the American political system. In short, I concluded that power and influence can be used for destructive purposes as well as for positive ones.

Taking the Tough Votes

The most frequently asked question was, "Congressman, are you going to vote the way you feel about an issue or the way your constituents want you to vote?" The questioner usually showed no recognition of the fact that my constituents were diverse in their opinions about nearly every issue which came before the Congress. Nevertheless, I always considered it an important question and the true answer for me was, "If I can determine the wishes of my constituents and they differ from my opinion, then it will depend on the issue." In other words, not every issue can be or needs to be decided on the basis of some moral principle or clear rational argument. Most issues, in fact, call for a judgment to be made between competing arguments that have merit. Those were the easy decisions to make. I simply tried to do what I thought was best for my constituents, especially those who were the most vulnerable. Hubert Humphrey was on target when he said, "The moral test of government is how it treats those who are in the dawn of life, the children; those in the twilight of life, the aged; and those who are in shadows of life, the sick, the needy, and the handicapped" (An excerpt from the last speech of Hubert Humphrey, Washington, DC, November 1, 1977). In short, I tried to look out for the "little guy."

My vote for the 1993 Clinton budget, which raised taxes, cut spending, and resulted in a declining deficit was probably the most significant vote I cast. Although it was politically risky, it was the right thing to do, and I have never regretted doing it.

The tough votes were the "set-up" ones—votes designed to get me and other members "on record" regarding polarizing and emotionally inflammatory issues. The first of these resulted from President Clinton's effort to prevent discrimination against gay men and lesbians serving in the military. I will never forget walking up the steps of the Capitol on my way to vote on the issue and passing a young man who was lobbying in behalf of the gay and lesbian community. As I walked by, he said, "Congressman, I hope you will stand with us on this vote." Entering the chamber, I thought to myself, "Ted, you're a psychologist. If you don't take a stand against discrimination, how can any member of this body be expected to do it?" I cast my vote, knowing it would damage me politically, but also knowing that my personal values and my identity as a psychologist prevented me from doing otherwise.

There were other votes that tested my humanistic principles. Opposing the Hyde Amendment, which prohibits federal funds from being used to fund abortions for poor women; supporting the National Endowment for the Arts; and supporting Pell Grants for prisoners were three such votes. Did the Christian Coalition and my election opponent criticize me for them? Absolutely! Am I convinced, even after losing my reelection bid, that I did the right thing? Absolutely!

The 1994 Election

As the November 1994 election approached, it looked as if I were going to win. I held a commanding lead in the polls throughout the summer and fall. Fundraising was going better than expected. Psychologists from around the nation continued to be very generous with their contributions.

Six of seven newspapers gave me strong endorsements, and my opponent made numerous gaffes. He was widely ridiculed for saying the Greeks and Romans were homosexuals and perhaps died off because of an AIDS-related disease. He also refused to affirm, in response to a reporter's question, that private citizens should not be allowed to possess nuclear weapons. However, when the votes were counted, I came up short. Frank Cremeans had reclaimed the Republican party's long-standing hold on the 6th congressional district seat.

Looking back, I see that I may have contributed to my loss by reacting in a confrontational manner to certain interest groups. For example, as the vote approached on the 1993 stimulus package, I received a fax message from a conservative interest group, Citizens for a Sound Economy. They urged me to vote "No" and threatened to run critical radio spots in my district if I supported the bill. I knew that the group was financed by oil interests, and I responded on the House floor by saying, "It is time for the Congress to tell the big oil lobbyists to go straight to hell." It was a strong statement against those I perceived to be using tactics of fear and intimidation to influence my vote. As a result, I became a target of conservative business interests.

A second episode pitted me against a powerful element of religious conservatives. Soon after I voted for the 1993 budget, the Christian Coalition began a telephone attack campaign against me. Specifically, the Coalition called senior citizens in my district, most of whom had modest incomes, and told them that I had voted to increase taxes on their Social Security. I remember a distraught 85-year-old woman calling my office to ask why I would do such a thing. When I tried to assure her that neither I nor the President had taken any action that would increase her taxes, she responded, "I watch Pat Robertson nearly every day. I don't believe he would lie to me." I was furious that such tactics would be directed toward older people. Once again, I went to the floor of the House, identified the Christian Coalition by name, and severely criticized them for manipulating and frightening senior citizens in order to further their conservative political agenda.

Was I unwise to respond to the Citizens for a Sound Economy and the Christian Coalition as I did? Perhaps. But I felt it was important to confront these special-interest "bullies" in a direct and clear manner. I only wish more of my colleagues had been willing to respond as I did.

It is probably not possible to determine exactly why I lost the election. A light voter turnout obviously hurt me. Additionally, a weak slate of statewide Democratic candidates and the Republican governor's winning margin of 74% had a spillover effect on the congressional race. My opponent spent over $1 million—half of which he borrowed from a local bank. Also, the Christian Coalition retaliated. They circulated a "nonpartisan" candidate "scorecard" in numerous churches that accused me of voting for "homosexual marriages" and "obscene art." It was difficult to overcome this last-minute distortion of my record, because as Mark Twain said, "A lie gets halfway around the world before the truth puts on its boots."

The final blow to my reelection bid came from my own lips. In a debate 7 days before the election, I was asked if we could achieve universal health care coverage without raising taxes. Part of my response was, "We may have to raise some taxes." I went on to say that I did not favor a tax increase and I felt that we could reach universal coverage by reforming our delivery system and spending our health care dollars more efficiently. However, I had uttered the kind of quote that makes political pols whoop or wince, depending on which side they are on. Tuesday night's sound bite became Thursday night's TV commercial. "We may have to raise some taxes," said the sound bite. "Excuse me?" said the announcer. "We may have to raise some taxes," repeated the debate snippet. I had given my opponent a silver bullet and could only wait for the inevitable. The results: Strickland 49.1%, Cremeans 50.9%.

I took some comfort from a postelection analysis of my loss made by one of my district's newspapers. Their conclusion? I lost because I was too honest with the voters. Not a bad political epitaph, but I'm not ready for burial. I look forward to challenging Cremeans in 1996, and I will continue to advocate for health care, education, economic opportunity, and social justice. It is imperative that we sort out our nation's priorities and set our course for the next century. As a citizen, psychologist, former and—I hope—future member of Congress, I intend to be a participant in that process.

WHY PSYCHOLOGISTS MUST BE INVOLVED IN PUBLIC POLICY

The fact that I believe that psychologists must be convinced to become involved as public policy advocates is telling in itself. The question, "Why do many psychologists shrink from the political process?" may need to be answered before the importance of participation is stressed.

After serving a single term in the U.S. House of Representatives and observing the legislative process "up close and personal," I can say with absolute certainty that the input of professionals like psychologists is greatly appreciated by members of Congress. It is true that each member has his or her own priorities, and the specific concerns of psychology may be toward the bottom for some. However, for those who are heavily involved in issues such as health care reform, the knowledge that psychologists can provide is welcomed.

The problem in Congress is the vast array of issues and the need to learn the pros and cons in order to make an informed decision, all within a relatively compressed period of time. Professionals and professional associations who work intimately with problems on a daily basis can quickly distill all of the claims and counterclaims down to the essence of an issue. This provides an invaluable service to members seeking to understand not only the anticipated direct results of legislation but its potential unintended consequences as well. Managed care is a good case in point. In a theoretical sense, managed care offers positive benefits in terms of reduced costs and efficiency. However, psychologists whose clients face restricted access and limited benefits due to some managed care arrangements can bring balance and realism to the debate about managed care. This is but one example of how psychologists can enrich legislative debate based on their actual experiences as well as on hard data generated by the profession. Although organized psychology's potential to make significant contributions to public policy is great, that potential has been for the most part unrealized. However, other professional groups have become involved at all levels of the legislative process, and they are tenacious in their efforts to win friends and influence legislation.

I am convinced that organized psychology must bring its behavioral science expertise to bear on the process of public policy development. This is essential if psychologists are to fulfill the mandates of our ethical principles, protect patients' access to needed psychological care, support vital research, and secure psychology's right to be a full participant in the provision of mental health services to the nation's citizens.

Psychologists embrace a unique epistemology that sets them apart from many other groups working to influence legislation in Washington and in state capitals throughout the nation. Because a majority in Congress have legal or business backgrounds, it is widely believed they have a constricted perspective and approach to problem solving. This attitude is reflected in the frequent criticism that "too many politicians are lawyers." That may be a debatable conclusion, but the fact is that psychologists have much to contribute to the legislative process and should be involved. They can broaden the debate, identify relevant scientific findings, and provide expertise about individual and group behavior vis-à-vis the adoption and implementation of legislation.

What are the elements of an approach to public policy that should be promoted by organized psychology? In my judgment, they must include: (a) an emphasis on reasoned judgment, (b) a strong reliance on data, (c) an understanding that different data have different values, (d) an awareness of the need for cautious interpretation when basing conclusions on group data, and (e) a recognition of the limitations of anecdotal information.

I think it is accurate to say that, when dealing with complex social issues, organized psychology often has a perspective that is among the most informed and properly focused. This is because the science of psychology helps make clear that no law can be divorced from the social context in which it is passed and implemented. For example, reasonable goals of health care legislation could be to reduce costs and increase benefits for society, increase personal satisfaction, or improve public lifestyles in terms of health. Legitimate outcomes may be quite diverse, depending on the values and goals of those engaged in legislating.

Because the development of public policy is a dynamic and value-laden process, it is critical for psychology to be a participant—both to protect the interests of all aspects of psychology and to protect the needs of those who depend on psychology for service and knowledge. Unfortunately, there is an anti-intellectual approach to governing today that minimizes, and even rejects, scientific findings—and that holds the social sciences in disdain. The body of knowledge that we call "behavioral science" is often ignored by legislators. The efforts of organized psychology are essential for changing that reality.

The Knowledge Problem of Congress

Policies advocated by some of my colleagues in Congress often had no logical connection to the results of scientific research that was readily available to them. The criminal justice legislation passed by the 103rd Congress is a poignant example of this tendency to ignore science and embrace simplistic answers to many of the country's most complex problems. The crime bill emphasized more prisons and longer sentences; its provisions for the rehabilitation and treatment of offenders were grossly inadequate. Legislators who tried to point out the benefits of prison-based education and other rehabilitative programs were accused of favoring the criminal over the victim. In short, the crime bill debate was driven by emotional reactions and personal biases rather than by a commitment to scientific inquiry and rational problem solving.

In spite of these criticisms, I believe that most members of Congress are sincerely motivated to do what is best for the country. How then can they reach such widely divergent conclusions on matters of public policy, especially when they are looking at the same set of historical facts, competing priorities, and empirical data? In my experience, there is no single answer to this question.

Some lawmakers avoid exposure to new or clarifying information and refuse to engage in empirical inquiry. Rather, because of political considerations or personality characteristics, they seek out information that merely confirms preexisting political philosophies or value-laden mental schemas. Deeply held political beliefs and emotionally charged mental schemas are difficult to modify under the most conducive of circumstances. However, today's political climate is characterized by circumstances far from conducive to thoughtful introspection and decision making. It is an atmosphere loaded with angry and polarizing debate. With the advent of

10-second sound bites, ever-present cameras, C-Span coverage, and turgid partisan pressures, it is increasingly unlikely that political thinking will be subject to alteration through a deliberative, rational process. That is the nature of modern-day politics.

In addition, some lawmakers use an approach to legislating that can be characterized as an "as if" mode of thinking. In other words, legislative decisions are often made "as if" a given set of facts is accurate. Unfortunately, that set of facts is sometimes incomplete. There can be an inadequate reliance upon, and in some cases an outright rejection of, empirical data and scientific hypothesis testing. An example of this occurred on February 2, 1995 during a committee hearing on welfare reform. Representative Jim Nussle (R–IA) said: "Regardless of the studies, and facts, and information that is out there . . . we still have all of these problems . . . ." His comment clearly indicated a willingness, apparently growing out of frustration, to discount the importance of studies, facts, and information.

In fairness, it must be pointed out that many lawmakers work hard to get a comprehensive array of information considered during the legislative process. It also must be acknowledged that they are confronted with a great deal of complex, and at times conflicting, information. There is a tendency for narrowly focused special-interest groups to make information available to legislators in a selective manner, which is not surprising. Although it is understandable that the emphasis would be on their particular goals, it is also true that a biased presentation of information may result in other lawmakers' looking askance at all information channeled their way from that particular source.

In my office, Frances was particularly concerned that I would "go out on a limb" based on faulty information. Once she learned that some group or other was slanting the evidence in dishonest ways, she was finished with them. I remember her asking on numerous occasions, "Where do we go for the truth?" She would have reams of paper on her desk or in her hands. She certainly did not need more information. Rather, her question revealed a desire for credible, objective, and valid truth. Often, especially during the health care reform debate, we would turn to the APA for help. I will always have deep respect for the APA staff, because their information held up under scrutiny. In fact, I think many members of Congress value the information and testimony coming from the APA as among the most balanced, reasoned, and empirically based. This reflects well on psychology.

Being a Psychologist: An Orientation

I think most psychologists recognize that the practice of psychology is both a science and an art. Historically, they have valued each of these integral aspects of their professional skills. Nevertheless, some in the profession see the dichotomy of art and science as an uncomfortable forced-choice option. They struggle with a perceived conflict between the dual roles of scientist and practitioner. This conflict is heightened when the additional role of political advocate is encouraged by the professional association. It is especially true for those who see politics as a "dirty business," not worthy of their involvement, or for those who feel it is somehow "unprofessional" to stake out positions on matters of public policy, fearing their actions will be viewed as divisive or self-serving. I believe that psychologists must move beyond such abstruse considerations and embrace the multiple professional obligations of scientist, practitioner, and political advocate.

Many years ago, Carl Rogers spoke about the conflict that can result from having to fill multiple professional roles. He sought to reduce the dissonance experienced by practitioners trying to reconcile the role of scientist-practitioner by pointing out that the scientific method is an effective way of preventing self-deception in regard to our subjective hunches. Rogers also stressed, however, that to whatever extent the scientist tries to prove something to someone else, there is a danger of using science to bolster his or her own biases. Contending that science cannot be separated from its application by people, Rogers argued that "science [is] something which exists only in the subjective experiences of persons, so also is its utilization. [Therefore], 'science' will never depersonalize, or manipulate, or control individuals. It is only persons who can and will do that" (Rogers, 1961, p. 221). If Rogers is correct, and I think he is, psychologists should not be hesitant to use their science in pursuit of the public good; neither should they shrink from political advocacy, so long as their motive is to benefit society.

Broadening the Discussion of Public Policy

Political advocacy is a tool that may be used to promote understanding, enhance freedom, and enrich the human experience. Alternatively, it may be used to control, manipulate, even destroy. The choice depends on the values embraced and methods used by the advocate. Accepting this premise as accurate, one can say that political advocacy—using the science and ethics of psychology—can further the public good and benefit the profession at the same time.

Perhaps one of the special contributions that organized psychology can play in lawmaking is to present information in an objective, multidimensional manner. Unlike many advocacy groups, psychology is a broad-based profession. Its interests are grounded in humanistic concerns for men, women, and children. The profession has a strong research orientation. Its ethical principles are consistent with the highest standards of professionalism.

Psychologists can help legislators avoid a common pitfall—a tendency to view the merits of legislation solely from a cost–benefit perspective. For example, there are at least three separate goals that may merit support, regardless of the specific legislative initiative under consideration. Each would be of interest to organized psychology as well as to society at large. Certainly one goal should be a positive cost–benefit outcome. This can be determined through an analytic process designed to identify the various positive and negative tradeoffs involved in any particular public policy initiative. Such an analysis is not easily accomplished when dealing with social policy, due to the fact that the very definitions of "cost" and "benefit" are value laden and subject to interpretation. However, in spite of the difficulty of such research, it needs to be done, and psychologists have the unique research skills necessary to do it.

A second goal could focus on the level of personal satisfaction of all citizens to be realized from a legislative initiative. This involves a recognition that most laws have personal impact as well as social consequences. For the psychologist, a concern regarding the consequences of legislation upon individuals is consistent with the profession's ethical principles.

A third goal could be enhanced, healthy lifestyles—and a generally positive impact on the welfare of all citizens. This consideration goes beyond the benefits of legislation as perceived or experienced by individuals in terms of feelings of personal well-being. It involves judgments regarding whether a particular policy contributes to the development of a healthier lifestyle and sense of safety and well-being, both for the individual and the community.

Achieving Psychology's Potential

Political advocacy is especially important for psychologists because the issues currently under consideration by Congress and the state legislatures will have a direct bearing on the future practice of psychology. As far as I am concerned, one choice is clear, and in spite of obvious risks, I believe that psychologists must be activists and they must encourage their colleagues to be psychologists-advocates. This conclusion comes not only from a belief in the usefulness of psychology as a foundation for lawmaking but from a concern that psychology, as psychologists experience the profession, may not survive into the future without such political advocacy. The loss for the nation would be enormous.

Political decisions will be made in the next year, and the next decade, affecting public welfare, health care, education, research, and various social policies—all of which are of particular interest to psychology and psychologists. Legislation that will, in very specific ways, affect the right of psychologists to practice and define the scope of their ability to practice will continue to surface in the years to come. Such policy decisions will have major impact on those served by psychologists. In a practical sense, the opportunity for psychologists to participate as valuable and essential service providers, as reflected in reimbursement rules and procedures, will be determined by legislators at multiple levels of government—often by individuals who may have little or no understanding of the science and utility of psychology.

I believe that the primary issue facing psychology can be summed up in two choices. Psychologists will either stand passively on the sidelines and merely watch the unfolding legislative battles, convinced that psychology cannot or should not proactively use its science and ethical principles to serve the process of public policy development, or they will act on their social principles, which state in part, "Psychologists are aware of their professional and scientific responsibilities to the community and the society in which they work and live. They apply and make public their knowledge of psychology in order to contribute to human welfare. Psychologists are concerned about and work to mitigate the causes of human suffering." (APA, 1992, p. 160).

I conclude my appeal for political advocacy by sharing a parable from the Book of Judges:

> "The trees went forth on a time to anoint a king over them; and they said unto the olive tree, 'Reign thou over us.' But the olive tree said unto them, 'Should I leave my fatness, wherewith by me they honour God and man, and go to be promoted over the trees?' And the trees said to the fig tree, 'Come thou, and reign over us.' But the fig tree said unto them, 'Should I forsake my sweetness, and my good fruit, and go to be promoted over the trees?' Then said the trees unto the vine, 'Come thou, and reign over us.' And the vine said unto them, 'Should I leave my wine, which cheereth God and man, and go to be promoted over the trees?' Then said all the trees unto the thornbush, 'Come thou, and reign over us.' And the thornbush said unto the trees, 'If in truth ye anoint me king over you, then come and put your trust in my shadow: and if not, let fire come out of the thornbush, and devour the cedars of Lebanon.' " (Judges 9:8–15)

The relevancy of this parable is obvious. The trees, seeking political leadership, went to the most competent and productive among them. However, the olive tree, fig tree, and grapevine refused to participate, saying they had more important functions to fulfill. They apparently considered political involvement beneath them. The thornbush, however, eagerly responded, stepped into the gap, and assumed political leadership over the trees—at great cost to the prized cedars of Lebanon.

Psychologists must not allow the thornbushes to usurp their responsibilities. Rather, they must step forward and advocate policies that are good for the profession and good for those who need their professional services. If they do, psychology, the clients, and the country will have a brighter future.

REFERENCES

American Psychological Association. (1992). Ethical principles of psychologists and code of conduct. *American Psychologist, 47*, 1597–1611.

Rogers, Carl R. (1961). *On becoming a person.* Boston: Houghton Mifflin.

APPENDIX

APA Congressional Fellows, 1974–1995

Fellowship year & name of Fellow	Fellowship assignment	Present position
1974–1975 Pamela Ebert Flattau, PhD	Senate Subcommittee on Children & Youth (Labor & Human Resources)	Director, Studies & Surveys Unit, Scientific & Engineering Personnel, National Research Council, Washington, DC
1975–1976 Lawrence Froman, PhD	Senate Committee on Labor & Human Resources	Associate Professor/ Consulting Psychologist, Department of Psychology, Towson State University, Towson, MD
1976–1977 Sara C. Schurr, EdD	Rep. David Obey	*Address unknown*
1977–1978 Ralph E. Cooper, PhD	Rep. Doug Walgren	Consultant, American Institute of Hazardous Waste Management, San Antonio, TX

continues

Fellowship year & name of Fellow	Fellowship assignment	Present position
1978–1979		
Daniel M. Koretz, PhD	Congressional Budget Office	Resident Scholar, RAND Corporation, Washington, DC
1979–1980		
Nancy Morency Curran, PhD	Rep. Robert Drinan	Consultant, Demarest, NJ
1980–1981		
Robinsue Frohboese, PhD, JD	Sen. Edward M. Kennedy	Senior Trial Attorney, Special Litigation Section, Civil Rights, U.S. Dept. of Justice, Washington, DC
1981–1982		
Lyn G. Aubrecht, PhD	Rep. Austin J. Murphy	Professor, Department of Psychology, Meredith College, Raleigh, NC
1982–1983		
Judith C. Meyers, PhD	Rep. David Obey	Consultant, Geneva, NY
David M. Stonner, PhD	Rep. Claudine Schneider	Senior Legislative Policy Analyst, Office of Legislative & Public Affairs, National Science Foundation, Arlington, VA
1983–1984		
Diana M. Zuckerman, PhD	Rep. Pat Williams	Science Adviser, White House Office of Science & Technology Policy, Washington, DC
James F. Brennan, PhD	Rep. Edward J. Markey	Professor and Chair, Department of Psychology, University of Massachusetts–Harbor Campus, Boston, MA
1984–1985		
Victor Indrisano, PhD	Rep. Edward R. Roybal	*Deceased*
Bohne G. Silber, PhD	Sen. Albert Gore, Jr.	President, Silber and Associates, Clarksville, MD
1985–1986		
Elaine Anderson, PhD	Sen. Paul Simon	Associate Professor, Department of Family Studies, University of Maryland–College Park, College Park, MD
Ruth Ann Parvin, PhD, JD	Sen. Ted Stevens, Sen. Paula Hawkins	Director of Counseling, A Place to Talk, Portland, OR

Fellowship year & name of Fellow	Fellowship assignment	Present position
1986–1987		
J. Thomas Puglisi, PhD	House Select Committee on Aging	Chief, Compliance Oversight Branch, Division of Human Subject Protections Office for Protection from Risks, National Institutes of Health, Bethesda, MD
Trudy Vincent, PhD	Sen. Bill Bradley	Legislative Director, Office of Sen. Bill Bradley, U.S. Senate, Washington, DC
1987–1988		
Andrea L. Solarz, PhD	Sen. Tom Harkin	Senior Program Officer, Division of Biobehavioral Sciences & Mental Disorders, Institute of Medicine, Washington, DC
Krista J. Stewart, PhD	Senate Committee on Labor & Human Resources	Social Science Analyst, U.S. Agency for International Development, Washington, DC
1988–1989		
Wendy Pachter, PhD, JD	Sen. Bill Bradley	Health law consultant, Washington, DC
May Kennedy, PhD	Senate Committee on Labor & Human Resources	Postdoctoral Fellow, Centers for Disease Control at Emory University School of Public Health, Atlanta, GA
1989–1990		
Denis Nissim-Sabat, PhD	Sen. Paul Simon	Professor, Psychology Department, Mary Washington College, Fredericksburg, VA
Mitchell M. Handelsman, PhD	Rep. Sander M. Levin	Professor, Psychology Department, University of Colorado–Denver, Denver, CO
1990–1991		
Jo Ann Lee, PhD	Senate Subcommittee on Aging (Labor & Human Resources)	Associate Professor, Department of Psychology, University of North Carolina, Charlotte, NC
Katherine Nordal, PhD	Rep. Mike Espy	Psychologist, The Nordal Clinic, Vicksburg, MI
Danny Wedding, PhD	House Committee on Government Operations	Director, University of Missouri–Columbia, Missouri Institute of Mental Health, St. Louis, MO

continues

Fellowship year & name of Fellow	Fellowship assignment	Present position
1991–1992		
Allison A. Rosenberg, PhD	Senate Appropriations Subcommittee on Labor, Health & Human Services, Education & Related Agencies	Senior Program Officer, Government/University/ Industry Research Roundtable, National Academy of Sciences, Washington, DC
Joseph G. Baum, PhD	Sen. Albert Gore, Jr.	Clinical Psychologist, American Biodyne, Inc., Medco Behavioral Health Care, Tampa, FL
Melanie-Anne Taylor, PhD	Senate Committee on Labor & Human Resources	*Address unknown*
1992–1993		
Evelyn Becker-Lausen, PhD	Senate Labor & Human Resources Committee, Subcommittee on Children, Family, Drugs & Alcoholism	Assistant Professor, Department of Psychology, University of Connecticut, Storrs, CT
Karen Anderson, PhD	Rep. Jolene Unsoeld	Director of Policy Research, National School Boards Association, Alexandria, VA
Ernest Lenz, PhD	Rep. Patsy Mink, Rep. Bob Inglis	Colonel & Chief, Department of Psychology, Tripler Army Medical Center, U.S. Army Honolulu, HI
Debra Lina Dunivin, PhD (also 1993–1994)	Sen. Daniel K. Inouye	Major, U.S. Army/Department of Defense Pharmacology Fellow, Washington, DC
Annette U. Rickel, PhD	Sen. Donald W. Riegle, Jr.	Director, Mental Health & Development, National Committee for Quality Assurance, Washington, DC
1993–1994		
Charles Barone, PhD	Sen. Paul Simon	Legislative Assistant, Subcomm. on Employment & Productivity, Senate Committee on Labor & Human Resources, U.S. Senate, Washington, DC
Debra Lina Dunivin, PhD (also 1992–1993)	Sen. Daniel K. Inouye	Major, U.S. Army/Department of Defense Pharmacology Fellow, Washington, DC

Fellowship year & name of Fellow	Fellowship assignment	Present position
1993–1994 *(continued)*		
Karen E. Kovacs, PhD	Rep. Ed Markey	APA Science Policy Fellow, White House Office of Science & Technology Policy, Washington, DC
Brian Smedley, PhD	Rep. Robert Scott	Acting Assistant Director for Public Interest Policy, Public Policy Office, American Psychological Association, Washington, DC
Elliot A. Weiner, PhD	Sen. Paul Wellstone, Sen. Barbara Boxer, Sen. Max Baucus	Lead Recruiter for Microsoft, Microsoft, Inc., Redmond, WA
1994–1995		
Douglas J. Peddicord, PhD	Rep. Ben Cardin	Health Policy Analyst, University of Maryland School of Medicine, Baltimore, MD
Elizabeth Street, PhD	Senate Comm. on Labor & Human Resources, Office of Sen. Edward M. Kennedy	Professor, Department of Psychology, Central Washington University, Ellensburg, WA
Janice Gail Williams, PhD	Senate Committee on Veterans' Affairs	Associate Professor, Department of Psychology, Clemson University, Clemson, SC

AUTHOR INDEX

Numbers in italics refer to listings in reference sections.

Ryan, W., 132, 142, *144*

Saks, M. J., 82, 84, 85, 88, 91, 96
Saltzman, L., 361, *364*
Sameroff, A. J., 234, *246*
Sampson, E. E., 6, 7, 8, 10, *19*, 103, *112*
Samuels, R. M., 49, 50, *53, 54*
Sander, F. E. A., 96, 97
Sarason, S. B., 9, 11, 15, *19*, 25, 31, 33, 35, *39*, 103, *113*
Sawhill, I. V., 334, *342*
Scarr, S., 221, *246*
Scheff, T. J., 138, *144*
Scherl, D. J., 68, *77*
Schneider, S. F., 4, 9, 12, 13, *19*, 284, 285, 292, *302*
Schneiderman, N., 286, 287, 299
Schroeder, C. S., 50, *54*
Schroeder, S. R., 50, *54*
Schulze, W. D., 257, 259
Schwartz, B., 103, *112*
Schweinhart, L. J., 222, 226, 229, 232, 234, *243, 246, 247*
Scott, R. A., 166, *181*
Seabury, P., 145, *163*
Seitz, V., 231, *247*
Shaffer, L. S., 165, *181*
Shapiro, M. F., 286, *303*
Shapiro, S. M., 209, *218*
Sharfstein, S. S., 68, 73, *77, 78*
Sharpe, L. J., 240, *247*
Shasky, J., 361, *364*
Shemo, J. P., 72, *78*
Sherer, R., 286, *302*
Shore, A., 166, *181*
Short, E. T., 223, *246*
Short, T., 58, *78*
Shumaker, S., 287, *302*
Sibulkin, A. E., 71, 73, *78*, 107, *112*, 314, *321*
Siebel, C., 362, *364*
Simons, S. E., 68, *79*
Simpkins, C. G., 68, *78*
Singer, J. E., 249, *259*
Skeels, H. M., 223, *247*
Skinner, B. F., 8, *19*
Skodak, M., 223, *247*
Slovic, P., 175, *181*, 252, 253, 254, 255, 256, 258, *259, 260, 261*
Smith, B. J., 223, *247*
Smith, B. L. R., 153, *163*
Smith, M. B., 108, 110, *112*

Smith, V. K., 250, 257, *262*
Snipper, A. S., 222, *243, 245*
Snow, C. P., 92, 96
Snyder, S. W., 223, *243*
Sorenson, J. L., 288, 289, 292, 293, *302*
Spieker, S. J., 48, *54*
Spitz, R. A., 223, *247*
Springer, J. R., 210, 216, *219*
St. Lawrence, J. S., 289, 290, *300*
Stagner, R., 30, *39*
Stall, R., 289, 290, *302*
Stallen, P. J., 255, 256, *262*
Stallings, J., 187, *191*
Stambaugh, R. J., 166, *180*
Stark, E., 362, 365
Starr, C., 252, 253, 256, *262*
Starr, P., 212, *219*
Steiner, A. Y., 183, *191*
Stempel, R. R., 284, *301*
Stern, P., 193, *200*
Stern, R. L., 209, *219*
Stevenson, L. Y., 289, *300*
Stewart, M., 318, *321*
Stier, S., 165, *181*
Stipek, D. J., 230, *246*
Stites, D. P., 291, *298*
Stoddard, A., 285, *301*
Stokols, D., 249, *259, 262*
Stone, G. C., 281, *302*
Strain, P. S., 223, *247*
Sullivan, M. J., 23, 25, 28
Sullivan, W. M., 103, *112*
Sutton, L. P., 88, 96
Sweinhart, L. J., 224, *246*
Swidler, A., 103, *112*

Takanishi, R., 207, *219*, 221, *247*
Talbott, E., 250, *261*
Talbott, J. A., 73, *78*
Taube, C. A., 68, 73, *77*
Taylor, R. B., 108, *112*
Taylor, S. E., 284, *302*
Temoshok, L., 284, 288, *298, 301*
Teska, J. A., 229, *245*
Test, M. A., 68, *78*
Thaler, R., 258, *262*
Thibaut, J., 93, 96
Thienhaus, D. J., 68, *79*
Thier, S. O., 70, *79*
Tielman, R. A. P., 286, *303*
Tipton, S. M., 103, *112*
Tizard, J., 224, *247*

SUBJECT INDEX

Canada, 64
Capitation, 60
Caregiving, 292
Causality
    attribution bias in psychology
        research, 128–135, 139–140
    person-blame model of social
        science, 135–139, 140–143
    problem definition in psychology
        research, 125–128
Children. *See also* Early childhood
        education
    adolescent employment, 186–187
    adoption and foster care, 187
    application of research findings,
        185–187
    current policy issues, 184–185
    data for policy making, 339–341
    divorce and custody issues, 186
    legislative trends, 331–335, 341–342
    organized psychology as political
        advocates for, 337–341
    policy trends, 326
    policy-making timetable, 189–190
    political advocacy for, 335–342
    political atmosphere of policy
        making, 184
Chronic disease, 290, 292, 296
Chrysler Corporation, 62, 65, 67
*City of Akron v. Akron Center for
        Reproductive Health*, 212
Civil rights movement, 100–101
Commonwealth v. Golston, 82
Community
    education and, 31–32
    effects of early childhood
        intervention, 234
    individual health behavior and,
        292–294
    organized psychology and, 15–16
    practice in, 29–30
    program for social change, 35–37
    public interest concept, 104–107
Community Progress Inc., 35–37
Comprehensive Crime Control Act of
        1984, 88
Conditions of participation, 47
Confidentiality, 212–213
Congress
    future prospects for organized
        psychology, 273–275
    health care reform options, 306–307

legislation affecting children,
        331–335
    organized psychology's relations with,
        267–273
    presence of organized psychology,
        41–42
    psychologist/congressman's
        experiences in, 44, 375–380
    psychology-related legislation,
        46–48, 267–268
    science establishment and, 151–152
Conservative thought, 105–106
Consortium for Developmental
        Continuity, 222
Consortium for Longitudinal Studies, 222
Consumer interests
    health care system reform, 66
    liability damages, 85–86
Contributions of organized psychology,
        356
    AIDS/HIV intervention/research,
        283–290
    characteristics of useful research,
        171–177
    to federal legislative process, 42–43
    in filing *amicus curiae* briefs,
        211–216
    in health care reform, 270–273,
        318–319
    inappropriate comparisons, 11
    in judicial decision making, 204
    misapplication of research, 119–120
    opportunities in policy making,
        41–42, 249, 326–329,
        382–384
    opportunities in public interest,
        17–18, 71–76, 386–389
    organized psychology's perception of,
        10–13
    policymakers' perceptions of, 1–3,
        213–214
    in policy making, 14–15, 117–120,
        264–265
    political context of, 119, 249–252
    professional issues, 109–110, 111,
        140–143
    in public interest, 100–101,
        107–109
    public perception of, 3, 6, 263
    public policy involvement, 117–118,
        264–265
Coping Effectiveness Training, 291–292

researcher/scientist understanding of,
159–162, 266–268
risk assessment, 252–259
social science research and, 151,
165, 171–173
special interest group politics in, 151
stance of organized psychology,
14–15
status of organized psychology, 318
subject–matter expertise of Congress,
41–42
tax-exempt status and participation
in, 209
Politics
accommodation, 7–10
APA divisional activities, 265–270
blame displacement, 137–138,
141–143
child advocacy, 184, 335–342
congressional campaigns, 369–375,
380–382
congressional representative,
experiences of, 375–380
current research environment and,
1–2
in designing early childhood
interventions, 224–227,
240–242
future prospects for organized
psychology, 273–275
government–academic relations,
156–158
local activities, 16, 264, 267
monthly meetings with
policymakers, 276
within organized psychology,
99–100, 107–109
organized psychology as special
interest group in, 5–10
organized psychology's participation
in, 264–265, 385–386
organized psychology's understanding
of, 266–268
public recognition and, 274
regional psychology organizations in,
264, 276
research and, 183
science and, 119, 150
single-issue, 151–152
Power relations
accommodation of dominant group,
7–10

collective movements, 7
in democratic change, 274
in health care system, 66
organized psychology in policy
making, 14–15
single issue politics and, 151–152
Preferred provider organizations, 61
Preventive interventions, AIDS/HIV,
285–290
Privacy Protection for Rape Victims Act
of 1978, 363
Pro bono service, 110–111
Professional ethics, 109–110
policy making and, 119–120, 388
Prospective payment system, 60, 68
Psychiatry
amicus curiae briefs, 213
prescription privileges for
psychologists, 50–51, 213
psychology's comparison to, 11
Psycho-Educational Clinic, 31–32, 36
Psychological Abstracts, 133 n4
Psychology education and training. *See
also* Graduate education
demographic trends, 153
economic trends, 152–153
faculty tenure, 153
history of, 10–11
pharmacotherapy, 51–52
recent trends, 2
Psychology practice
as advice giving, 37–38
community-health, 15–16, 292–294
in educational settings, 15
emergent service settings, 71–73
health care system reform and,
25–27, 44–48, 57, 66–69
judicial interventions, 208
outcome studies, 317–318
political activity and, 4, 385–386
prescription privileges, 49–52
pro bono tradition, 110–111
process of organizational change, 38
professional identity, 9
professional issues as public interest,
109–110, 111, 120–121
public policy goals, 70–71
relationship with nursing profession,
48–49
restrictions on autonomy, 46–48
social context, 29–30, 36–37
statistical trends, 67

Psychology practice (*Continued*)
    vertical integration, 68–69
Public interest/welfare
    APA contributions, 100–101
    challenges for organized psychology,
        124
    conceptualizations of, 27, 102,
        104–107, 111
    disagreement within organized
        psychology, 101–102, 107
    individualism and, 102–104
    opportunities for organized
        psychology to contribute,
        17–18, 71–76, 99
    pro bono psychology, 110–111
    professional issues within psychology,
        109–110, 111, 120–121
    psychology's professional identity
        and, 43–44
Public interest/welfare
    responsibility of organized
        psychology, 13–14
    social science research and,
        123–124, 158–159
    violence against women and, 32
Public perception/understanding
    AIDS/HIV, 288
    democratic process and, 274
    of early childhood programs, 225,
        226–227
    organized psychology's policy-making
        influence and, 16, 250
    organized psychology's understanding
        of, 3–5
    political manipulation of, 381–382
    of psychology's role, 3, 6, 263
    of risk, 252–259
Public policy. *See also* Policy-making
        process; Politics
    changes in research mission,
        356–357
    children as focus of, 184–190,
        234–243, 326
    domains, 23
    environmental issues, 252–259
    failures of, explanations for, 137–138
    health care issues, 23–27, 58, 69–71
    mental health care, 70–71
    opportunities for organized
        psychology to contribute,
        26–27, 41–42, 249–250,
        326–329, 382–384, 386–389

organized psychology as focus of,
        205, 206, 267–268
    participation of organized
        psychology, 45–46, 117–118,
        203, 264–266, 382–384
    perception of psychology's
        contribution to, 1–3, 213–214
    perception of researchers by
        policymakers, 178–180, 183
    program evaluation, 187
    public service and, 43–44
    responsibility of organized
        psychology, 13–14, 120–121,
        387–389
    restrictions on psychologist
        autonomy, 46–48

Quality of care issues, 24, 48

Regional psychology associations, 276
Rehabilitative care, 315, 327–328
    research funding, 343–352
    substance abuse, 73
Reimbursement systems, 45, 46
    cost containment strategies, 59–60
    federal, 46, 47
    health outcomes and, 59
    managed competition plan, 308–312
Research. *See also* Outcome studies
    academic environment, 153–154
    AIDS/HIV, 281–282
    in *amicus curiae* briefs, 209–210
    application and funding process,
        344–346
    Baconian approach, 148
    basis for insanity defense, 83–84
    biological vs. behavioral, 328–329,
        356–359
    Cartesian approach, 146–148
    changes in policy goals, 356–357
    contribution of social science, 165
    cost–benefit analyses, 387
    cumulative nature of, policy making
        and, 187–189
    current political environment and,
        1–2
    on early childhood education,
        222–223, 227–229
    economic environment, 152–153
    on effects of legal interventions,
        91–94
    funding process, 328

Special interest groups
  effects on policy making, 151–152
  in health care reform, 379
  judicial advocacy, 209
  models, 6–7
  organized psychology as, 5–10
  scientists as, 158
Suicide/suicidal behavior
  among AIDS/HIV-infected persons,
    284–285
Supplemental Feeding Program for
    Women, Infants, and
    Children, 332
Supreme Court Rule 36.1, 209

*Tarasoff v. Regents of the University of
    California*, 216
Tax-exempt status, 209
Technology
  medical, 63, 283, 309–310
  for science research, 153–154
Theory development
  schools as social systems, 32

social change processes, 38–39
social organization, 30–31
*Thornburgh v. American College of
    Obstetricians and Gynecologists*,
    215
Tort reform, 85–86

Underserved populations, 71
  health trends, 73
Utilization review, 65

Vertical integration, 25, 61–62, 68–69
Victim blaming, 132 n3
Victims of Crime Act, 363
Violence against women, 326–327,
    361–364

Women, violence against, 326–327,
    361–364
Workplace issues
  adolescent employment, 186–187
  early childhood education, 226
  health insurance under managed
    competition, 311–312

ABOUT THE EDITORS

Raymond P. Lorion received his PhD in clinical psychology at the University of Rochester in 1973. He has held academic positions at the University of Rochester, Temple University, the University of Tennessee, and the University of Maryland at College Park, where he is Professor of Psychology and director of the doctoral program in Clinical/Community Psychology. Between 1982 and 1984, Lorion served as Visiting Scientist to the Center for Prevention Research of the National Institute of Mental Health (NIMH) and as the Acting Associate Administrator for Prevention at the Alcohol, Drug Abuse and Mental Health Administration. Since 1989, he has served as Editor of the *Journal of Community Psychology*. Lorion has been actively involved with the Council of Community Psychology Program Directors, and he was Chair of the Council of University Directors of Clinical Psychology between 1989 and 1992. He has been a member of the March of Dimes Social and Behavioral Sciences Review Panel and the NIMH Child and Adolescent Prevention Research Panel. Lorion has authored or edited more than 12 books and 70 scientific papers, many on theoretical and methodological issues in preventive intervention research and policy.

Ira Iscoe is Ashbel Smith Professor of Psychology at The University of Texas (UT) at Austin. He received his PhD in child clinical psychology from the University of California, Los Angeles in 1951 and started as an Assistant Professor at UT–Austin the same year. Recognizing the need for psychology to leave the university laboratory for the wider, more challenging laboratory of the community, he set up the first free-standing community psychology training program in the United States within the Psychology Department at UT, which was the first in the Southwest to be awarded APA accreditation. In 1960 he was a Fellow at the Harvard School of Public Health in the Community Mental Health Research Program directed by Gerald Caplan. He has been President of the Texas Psychological Association and the Southwest Psychological Association. He was President of the Division of Community Psychology in 1970 and received the award for Distinguished Service to Community Psychology in 1976. In 1978 he was appointed a Distinguished Visiting Scientist at NIMH. In 1980 he became the Director of The Institute of Human Development and Family Studies at UT. Iscoe has served on numerous state and national committees and is heavily involved wit the role of psychology in the public domain. His recent efforts have focused on the Public Academic Liaison (PAL), bringing together state agencies and university departments on issues and problems of common concern. He is focused especially on the role of psychology in dealing more effectively and humanely with problems of severely emotionally disturbed persons, homelessness, and juvenile violence within community settings. He also maintains an active interest in primary prevention of human dysfunctioning.

Patrick H. DeLeon received his PhD in psychology from Purdue University and his JD from Catholic University. He is administrative assistant to U.S. Senator Daniel K. Inouye; member of the National Advisory Committee of the Institute for Public Policy Studies, Venderbilt University; recording secretary for the Board of Directors of the American Psychological Association (APA); and former chair of the APA Board of Professional Affairs. His major professional interests are in public service and the interface between psychology and the law. He has written extensively on the reciprocal impact between the profession of psychology and public policy, including "Evolution of Professional Issues in Psychology: Training Standards, Legislative Recognition, and Boundaries of Practice" (with R. J. Resnick and G. R. VandenBos) in *Beginning Skills and Professional Issues in Clinical Psychology*, J. R. Matthews and C. E. Walker, editors (in press); "Health Psychology and Public Policy: The Political Process" (with R. G. Frank and D. Wedding) in *Health Psychology* (1995); and "Federal Government Initiatives in Managed Health Care'" (with E. Q. Bulatao and G. R. VandenBos) in *Managed Behavioral Health Care: An Industry Perspective*, edited by S. A. Shueman, S. L. Mayhugh, and B. S. Gould (1994). He is the Editor of *Professional Psychology: Research and Practice* and a section editor for the *American Psychologist*. He received the APA Board of Scientific Affairs Distinguished Contributions Award to Psychological Science Policy in 1994 and the 1991 Ruth Knee/Milton Wittman Award for Outstanding Achievement in Health/Mental Health Policy from the National Association of Social Workers.

Gary R. VandenBos received his PhD in clinical psychology from the University of Detroit. He served as research coordinator for the Michigan State University Psychotherapy Research Project with Schizophrenics; as Director of the Howell-Area Community Health Center in Howell, Michigan; as APA staff liaison to the President's Commission on Mental Health during the Carter Administration; and as the first director of the APA Office of National Policy Studies. He was a visiting professor of clinical psychology at the University of Bergen, Norway from 1982 to 1984. He is currently the Executive Director of the Office of Publications and Communications of the APA. He has coauthored and edited numerous publications, including *Psychology and National Health Insurance: A Sourcebook* (with Charles Kiesler and Nicolas Cummings) and *Psychotherapy of Schizophrenia: The Treatment of Choice* (with Bertram Karon). He is an Associate Editor of the *American Psychologist*, the Managing Editor of *Professional Psychology*, and a columnist for *Psychiatric Services*. He is a Diplomate of the American Board of Forensic Psychology and a practicing clinical psychologist. He received the Early Career Award for Contribution to Psychotherapy from Division 29.